INDECOROUS THINKING

Indecorous Thinking

FIGURES OF SPEECH IN EARLY MODERN POETICS

COLLEEN RUTH ROSENFELD

FORDHAM UNIVERSITY PRESS
New York 2018

This book's publication was supported by a subvention from Pomona College.

Copyright © 2018 Fordham University Press

All rights reserved. No part of this publication may be reproduced, stored in a retrieval system, or transmitted in any form or by any means—electronic, mechanical, photocopy, recording, or any other—except for brief quotations in printed reviews, without the prior permission of the publisher.

Fordham University Press has no responsibility for the persistence or accuracy of URLs for external or third-party Internet websites referred to in this publication and does not guarantee that any content on such websites is, or will remain, accurate or appropriate.

Fordham University Press also publishes its books in a variety of electronic formats. Some content that appears in print may not be available in electronic books.

Visit us online at www.fordhampress.com.

Library of Congress Cataloging-in-Publication Data available online at https://catalog.loc.gov.

Printed in the United States of America
20 19 18 5   4 3 2 1
First edition

for Tyson

CONTENTS

Introduction. The Spectacle of Care: From Figure to Form   1

Part I

1. Inventing Figures of Speech   23
2. Figure Pointing in the Humanist Schoolroom   48
3. Queenly Fig Trees: Figures of Speech and *Decorum*   73

Part II

4. "Such as might best be": *Simile* in Edmund Spenser's *Faerie Queene*   95
5. Fighting Words: *Antithesis* in Philip Sidney's *Arcadia*   120
6. Withholding Words: *Periphrasis* in Mary Wroth's *Urania*   141

Coda. *Indecorous* Forms   165

Acknowledgments   179
Notes   183
Bibliography   273
Index   295

Indecorous Thinking

INTRODUCTION

The Spectacle of Care: From Figure to Form

A dead butterfly, impaled upon a spider's pincer and trapped in his perilous web—this is "the spectacle of care" with which Edmund Spenser closes his poem *Muiopotmos: or The Fate of the Butterflie*. Envious of the artistic ease with which he associates all butterflies, Spenser's spider lies in wait until Clarion, flitting from flower to flower, wends his way into the finely spun net. And then, the spider kills him:

> Under the left wing stroke his weapon slie
> Into his heart, that his deepe groning spright
> In bloodie streames foorth fled into the aire,
> His bodie left the spectacle of care.[1]

Trading in the apparently carefree poetics of *sprezzatura*, "the spectacle of care" combines the exquisite wings of the butterfly—"Painted with thousand colours, passing farre / All Painters skill"—with the spider's "weapon slie."[2] Clarion's careless wings meet the studied labor of the arachnid's industry.[3] As what is "left" at the end of the poem, Clarion's spiritless carcass is a remainder of the spider's revenge narrative, but "the spectacle" of these wings is also an artistic production, a highly wrought display that exerts a centripetal, interpretive pull on the poem that it closes and that provides a reflection of the poet's own "care" in making that poem. As an emblem of the vexed alliance between art and labor, Spenser's "spectacle of care" raises these questions: What remains of the butterfly after he has expired? What is the value of belabored ornament?

As he stabs the butterfly, Spenser's spider pins down effortless artifice and turns it into something that we can look at and study, though the price of this knowledge is the butterfly's life. *Muiopotmos* revels in *indecorum*: the asymmetry between its stylistic ambition and its subject matter. Featuring more colors than Iris's rainbow, more variety than a peacock's tail, and "distinguished with manie a twinckling starre," Clarion's wings offer a visual distillation of the figures of speech with which Spenser elevates his trifling insect to the status of epic.[4] With the butterfly's final expiration, Spenser's poem doubles down on its commitment to the *indecorous*: in the end we are left with nothing but pretty wings. But "the spectacle of care" also suggests an alternative to ease, nonchalance, spontaneity, and the aesthetics of *celare artem* because its wings remain as beautiful as ever. What is more, if (as the narrator suggests) it is the greatest desire of court ladies to transform Clarion's wings into handheld fans, those wings have never been more available for such ornamental repurposing.[5]

This is a book about artifice at its most conspicuous: poetry that rings out with the bells and whistles of ornamentation and lays bare the time and effort of poetic labor.[6] I argue that early modern poetic making, or *poiēsis*, offers us a model of fiction according to which the conditions of possibility within a poetic world are largely determined by how that world is made.[7] When a poem points to the *poesie* out of which it is made, it writes a history of composition that structures its imaginative domain. In *Timber: Or, Discoveries* (1640), Ben Jonson describes this orientation toward *poiēsis* as the difference between "the doing" and "the thing done":

> A *Poeme*, as I have told you, is the worke of the Poet; the end, and fruit of his labour, and studye. *Poesy* is his skill, or Crafte of making; the very Fiction it selfe, the reason, or forme of the worke. And these three voices differ, as the thing done, the doing, and the doer; the thing fain'd, the faining, and the fainer; so the *Poeme*, the *Poesy*, and the *Poet*.[8]

In what follows, I take up the register or, in Jonson's capacious grammar, the "voice" of "the doing" in order to consider the relation of "Crafte of making" to "the very Fiction it selfe." "Poesy" is "the doing" because it is a quality of action that shapes how a poem is made and transforms that poem into a model for other makings. My organizing hypothesis states that what is possible within a fiction is fixed by how that world came into being. A poem's answer to the question of 'how' may operate according to a logic of reference and truth-value that is distinct from that belonging to the historian who, as Philip Sidney suggested in his *Defence of Poesy* (c.1580), is bound to the indicative: "the bare 'was.'"[9] Reading for *poesie* or "the doing" permits us to tell a history of composition from the perspective of what Jonson called the "forme of the worke."

Figures of speech are the focus of this book because they offered early modern writers a set of forms distinguished by their peculiar concentration of art and study. In the sixteenth century, humanist instruction in the art of rhetoric and the canon of *elocutio*, or style, prized a student's ability to recognize figures of speech and call them out by name—*zeugma, epanalepsis, polyptoton*.[10] This act of figure pointing rendered a piece of artifice, at once eccentric and typical, reproducible: it treated a figure of speech as an instrument of making. The very conspicuousness of figure that guided this pedagogy, however, also threatened to violate the widely circulating imperative that art disguise the artifice out of which it is made. In *A Treatise of Schemes and Tropes* (1550), Richard Sherry lambasts "common scholemasters" who cultivate conspicuous artifice when they "saye unto their scholers: *Hic est figura*: and sometime to axe them, *Per quam figuram*" but "go no further." "Nothyng," he concludes, "is more folyshe than to affecte or fondly to laboure to speake darkelye for the nonce."[11] Anthony Grafton and Lisa Jardine's field-defining critique of humanist pedagogy in *From Humanism to the Humanities* (1986) was anticipated by early modern educators themselves: What had figure pointing to do with the fashioning of good subjects, let alone moral citizens?[12] *Indecorous Thinking* shows how early modern poetic practices activated figures of speech in their capacity to produce a certain kind of knowledge that is not reducible to logical arguments, affirmations, or propositions. This knowledge is, instead, poetic.

At least since Aristotle, the art of rhetoric advised its practitioners to be wary of obvious art: conspicuous figures of speech might give the lie to the rhetorical production of probability.[13] Forensic oratory taught the orator that his version of events would be most persuasive if it appeared to be the mere representation of what actually happened. Where the orator speaks with obvious art, he exposes the inauthenticity of his emotions and the unnatural construction of the whole thing.[14] Poets learned from rhetoric to align the boundaries of plausibility with the invisibility of their artifice. In the *Defence*, Sidney describes the field of possibility that underwrites both the reading and writing of poetry as the "imaginative ground-plot of a profitable invention," thereby locating its authority in the rhetorical canon of *inventio*: the set of procedures and protocols for determining the logical relations among things and assisting the orator in his construction of a likely version of events.[15] According to this paradigm, a fictional world is at its most plausible when it conforms to what the rhetorical tradition thinks the public thinks is most probable.

In what follows, by contrast, I argue that conspicuous figures of speech are significant to a history of early modern poetics because they were instrumental to determining the parameters of possibility within a fictional world. Drawing on a wide range of archival material from the history of rhetoric, poetics, and dialectic in the sixteenth and early seventeenth centuries—from grammar-school exercises to university lectures, from manuscript marginalia and commonplace books to printed textbooks popular in the schoolroom and vernacular handbooks looking to popularize these arts—I show how the very tradition that warned against conspicuous artifice also encouraged practitioners to experiment with the inventive capacities of figure. For early modern poets—especially for Edmund Spenser, Philip Sidney, and Mary Wroth—the conspicuousness of figure became not a measure of the degree to which a fiction failed to create its world but, rather, an operating condition of that world.[16] Their *poesie* reveals that figures of speech, ostentatious and unavoidable, index the organization of poetic worlds and the poet's privileged claim, as Sidney described it, to knowledge of "what may be."[17] What follows is thus a thought experiment in the ontology of poetry according to which technique determines the modality of poetry's existence. In a revision of Jonson's definite article, *poesie* is "a doing" that is always also capable of doing otherwise.

This book tells the story of figure's secret capture of poetic invention.[18] I argue that early modern *poesie* developed a model of the mind in which figures of speech drive thinking and act as the constitutive engines of poetry's imaginative worlds. From exercises in double translation and *metaphrasis* to the study of Cicero's orations and the memorization of Ovid's exile elegies, early modern humanists routinely described figures of speech as a central focus of the schoolroom.[19] Figures of speech constituted a way into and out of exemplary texts. Both activities in *analysis*, or what the schoolmaster John Brinsley called in his *Ludus Litterarius* (1612) the "unmaking" of a text, and activities in *genesis*, or "the making it againe," turned on figures of speech.[20] The canon of *elocutio* therefore provided a body of forms into which a text could be "unmade" even as the enumeration of those forms articulated something like a skeletal structure. These same figures of speech also supplied readers with a set of *formulas* for composition: they could make the exemplary text, as Brinsley would say, "againe," and as Roger Ascham feared, anew.[21]

It was figure's capacity to be abstracted from the exemplary text and transformed into an engine of composition that challenged humanist accounts of reason. Early modern debates over the arts of rhetoric and dialectic cohere around a set of questions: Were figures of speech instrumental to thinking? Did they therefore act as constitutive structures of the mind? Or were figures of speech ornamental to thinking as such? In the final decades of the sixteenth century, the pedagogical reforms proposed by Peter Ramus offered one answer to these questions by redistributing the canons belonging to the arts of rhetoric and dialectic and by inscribing the relative value of *elocutio* to *inventio* into a paradigmatic account of the compositional process. Responding to an apparent redundancy in the material belonging to rhetoric and dialectic, the Ramist reforms reduced rhetoric to style (*elocutio*) and delivery (*pronuntiatio*) while reserving the discovery of arguments (*inventio*) and the judgment of their validity (*dispositio*) for the art of dialectic. This seemingly simple redistribution carried a polemic. Stripped of its engagement with *res*, or things, limited only to the adornment of *verba* or words, rhetoric became the lesser handmaiden to dialectic.[22] According to this paradigm of composition, figures of speech provided, as the Ramist Dudley Fenner put it in *The Artes of Logike and Rhetorike* (1584), the "garnishing of speeche . . . whereby the speach it selfe is beautified and made fine."[23] In the chapters that follow, I examine how early modern *poesie* challenged humanism's increasingly dogmatic subordination of *elocutio* to *inventio* by treating figures of speech as generative forms of thinking.

Indecorous Thinking enters into a vibrant field of scholarship invested in the value of what Sean Keilin has called "vulgar eloquence": the curious manner in which the rich capacities of English poetry in the sixteenth century announce themselves as the virtuosic expression of extreme incapacities.[24] Building off of the work of Paula Blank and Margaret Ferguson, recent books by Carla Mazzio, Jenny C. Mann, and Catherine Nicholson have taught us to value vicious, affected, and eccentric language for its role in the formation of the early modern English subject and nation even as the kinds of speech this language made possible—mumbling, halting, unruly, outlaw, outlandish, vagrant, strange, exotic, alienated and alienating—has widened the range of what we recognize as a subject or what constitutes the English nation.[25] As Nicholson writes, "Eloquence thus finds a place within the vernacular that is as extravagant as it is English."[26] *Indecorous Thinking* extends these studies by turning from problems of subject and nation formation to problems of epistemology.[27] I am therefore interested in what Mazzio calls "the inarticulate utterance" for its capacity to "make space for alternative temporalities and directions of thought otherwise eclipsed by the flow of verbal fluency."[28] Figures of speech were central to early modern debates about thinking and the style of thought's "fluency"—how it happens and what it looks like—as well as the distinctive knowledge claims of the arts of dialectic, rhetoric, and poetics. I offer here a defense of ornament not as the sign of the aesthetic but as the source of a particular kind of thinking closely aligned in the early modern period with the emergent field of vernacular *poesie*.[29]

I call this thinking *indecorous*. A translation of the Greek *propon* (or "appropriateness") and regularly aligned with English synonyms including apt, decent, seemly, and comely, *decorum* described that aspect of art and composition which even the most systematic of humanists understood as fundamentally unteachable.[30] As Ellen MacKay has so succinctly put it, *decorum* described "an aesthetic judgment that retrospectively affixes its formal justification onto a supposedly intrinsic but in fact unspecified and unspecifiable trait."[31] This is why Michael Leff (drawing on Ricoeur) has described *decorum* as the art of rhetoric's "substance": it is the principle according to which one "orders the elements of a discourse and rounds them out into a coherent product relative to the occasion."[32] If "at the global level, decorum is pure process," Leff nonetheless maintains that it helps rhetoric achieve "ontological density" because *decorum* continues to reside within the particular artifact as "the way such processes congeal."[33] Among the peculiarities of early modern humanism, however, is the persistent sense that *decorum* might govern not only the orator's composition or the schoolboy's letter to his parents but just about everything. In *Arguments in Rhetoric against Quintilian* (1549), Ramus wrote that "decorum covers such a wide field that it is clearly ridiculous to assign it to rhetoric as if it were its property alone."[34] For Ramus, "there will never be any separate and distinct precept concerning decorum . . . because decorum is that harmonious perfection which the arts by their precepts, and human reason and wisdom by themselves, reveal."[35] *Decorum* was thus the judgment of "what is truly fitting and what is not": "from grammar, decorum in purity and elegance of speech is understood; from rhetoric, decorum in style and delivery," but also "from arithmetic, geometry, music, and astrology, decorum in calculation of numbers, in division of great quantities, in harmonies and sounds in the movement of the stars," and "from natural science, decorum in roots, plants, and animals."[36] For Ramus, *decorum* did not belong to the art of rhetoric alone because the judgment of *decorum* distributed all knowledge among the various arts by determining what lies within and what lies without their respective domains.

Early modern poetic theory therefore treated *decorum* as the guarantee of plausibility: *decorum* was the abstraction of reigning ideological commitments into a principle of design. *Indecorum*, by contrast, provided poetry with a means of distinguishing itself from the world and its dominant ideologies: rather than mediation, *indecorum* performed the work of disarticulation.[37] By reversing the traditional priority of *inventio* over *elocutio*, *indecorous* thinking locates the origin of composition in the figures of speech and therefore permits poetry to define itself in distinction from the world to which both the principle of *decorum* and the places of *inventio* would have it bound. It may be, as Demetrius suggested in his treatise *On Style*, that using figures of speech to describe a wobbling teacup produces an *indecorous* alignment of words to things, but *indecorous* thinking also distinguishes imaginative realms and their alternative constructions of possibility through innovative acts of evaluation and the distinctive channels of relation that figures afford.[38] In spite of the prefix at its start, the work of *indecorum* does not amount to a simple inversion or undoing of *decorum*'s regulation. The *indecorous* describes, instead, an alternative method of "the doing": rather than subordinating figures of speech to a determination of likelihood formed by the places of *inventio*, an *indecorous poesie* displays the avenues of thinking opened up by the figures themselves. As this book progresses, I map out a constellation of terms that inform early modern theories of *indecorum* and allow us to approach its operations from a series of distinct perspectives: those terms include deformity or disformity; vices, vanities, and *vanus* (vain or empty speech); and affectation. Through readings of Spenser, Sidney, and Wroth, I show how figures of speech organize imaginary worlds along peculiar axes of relation that amount to the physical laws of their universes.[39] These axes of relation and the *heterocosms* that they produce are precisely the kind of thinking that figure performs.

From Figure to Form

From the shape of the human body to a set of converging geometrical lines, from the image or representation of something that is otherwise immaterial to the modeling of the plastic arts, the diagram, the written symbol (a letter in the alphabet), *figure* encompasses a broad range of forms dedicated to artifice, both as an achievement or a product (*the figure*) and as an act or a process (*to figure*).[40] A translation of the Greek *schēma*, the early Latin *figura* described form in its outward appearance. Unlike *forma*, which was persistently associated with Platonic and Aristotelian conceptions of *morphē* and *eidos*, the term *figura* migrated toward material artistic practices ("statue," "image," "portrait").[41] As a result, *figura* treated outward form, as Erich Auerbach suggested, both in its relation to an inside (an inside that might be empty) and in its orientation toward a process (a process to which it was instrumental). Auerbach's gloss for *figura* as a process is "dynamic form": this "plastic" *figura* was a favorite with Ovid (who was interested in a way of thinking about form in its capacity to change).[42] It is the peculiar dynamic of *figura*—a shape that allows you to see something in its capacity to be empty and a shape that allows you to see something in its capacity to be otherwise than it is—that informs the vexed and vibrant history of the uses, abuses, and potentials of the most technical of all of the definitions of figure: the figures of speech.

In recent years, early modern studies—as well as literary studies more broadly—has proclaimed a rededication to "form." Variously conceived of in terms of Plato's "idea," Aristotle's "formal cause," in relation to content or in relation to matter, and in opposition to (or as an elaboration of) romanticism's "organic form" and its bequest to the New Criticism, these acts of rededication—or of "reading for form," as Susan Wolfson has described it—offer valuable insights into the relation of form to politics and into the history of particular forms while the practice of formalism is at once, as Heather Dubrow has put it, "variously and simultaneously an unwelcome and an honored guest."[43] Studies of early modern rhetoric plot a unique terrain in this critical field. Building off of the significant insights of Patricia Parker, the recent surge of scholarship on figures of speech, including the important work of Gavin Alexander, the essays collected in *Renaissance Figures of Speech* (2007), and Mann's *Outlaw Rhetoric* (2012), has increased the range of cultural and political practices we understand figures to engage.[44] These illuminating discussions of rhetorical style, however, tend to deal in the vocabulary of trope, scheme, and figure while generally leaving the category of "form" alone.[45] Yet early modern discussions of the canon of *elocutio* are poised to provide precisely that "prehistory of form" called for by Ben Burton and Elizabeth Scott-Baumann in *The Work of Form* (2014).[46]

I argue that figures of speech allow us to approach the problem of form from an oblique but productive angle. At least as early as Plato's *Gorgias*, figures of speech were a prime target in philosophy's denigration of rhetoric as an empty art, one parasitic on knowledge to which it could claim no right and irresponsible in its promotion of persuasion over the advancement of truth.[47] The powdered sugar on rhetoric's puff pastry, figures of speech were (at best) useful in the manipulation of the passions and (at worst) windy verbiage. In response to such attacks, rhetoric tended to defend itself on philosophy's terms: figures of speech worked in the service of persuasion and, therefore, founded and maintained civilizations.[48] It is from such defenses that Brian Vickers, for example, developed his widely accepted account of "the expressive function" of figures of speech, an account that highlights figure's ability to represent the affect of a speaker and to remake his audience in the image of that affect (an account that has been useful to elaborations of the social dimension of rhetoric, work on the history of affect, and a recent resurgence of interest in dramatic character and its formations).[49] Such a defense, however, pits itself against the uses of figures, which it calls abuses, that stray from the *telos* of persuasion. According to this defense, the practitioner of such ostentatious eloquence suffers from affectation, fails at the art of rhetoric, and produces bad art.

A historically nuanced account of figures of speech need not, however, reduce them to the affective instruments of ideology. *Indecorous Thinking* reads artifice at its most conspicuous as an index to the time and labor of poetic production.[50] Figures of speech offer us a theory of form finely calibrated to early modern *poesie*: figure turns form from teleology to process.[51] Early modern *poesie* suggests that form is a noun that is always acting like a verb because it is inseparable from the process in which it is involved.[52] Form is the thing with which one text is assembled, and form is the thing by virtue of which another text takes shape (but multiplied ad infinitum). In the *Defence of Rhyme* (1603), Samuel Daniel goes some distance toward outlining the significance of this claim. Rhyme was regularly characterized as the vernacular counterpart to the figures of speech known as *homoioptoton* and *homoioteleuton* (or, *similiter cadens* and *similiter desinens*). Because figures of speech ought to be used, as Thomas Campion writes in *Observations in the Art of English Poesie* (1602), "sparingly," rhyme as such was therefore described as an excessive or *indecorous* use of those figures.[53] By this account, the interminable iterations or "tedious affectation" of rhyme threatened to drive invention off course.[54] In response to this kind of criticism, Daniel replies:

> All excellencies being sold us at the hard price of labour, it follows, where we bestow most thereof we buy the best success; and rhyme, being far more laborious than loose measures (whatsoever is objected), must needs, meeting with wit and industry, breed greater and worthier effects in our language. So that if our labours have wrought out a

manumission from bondage and that we go at liberty, notwithstanding these ties, we are no longer the slaves of rhyme, but we make it a most excellent instrument to serve us.[55]

Against the social and aesthetic imperatives of *sprezzatura* and *celare artem*, Daniel argues that it is precisely the "labor" of rhyme that increases the value of the poetic product. Poetic labor or *poesie* becomes both a measure of the poet's freedom and the currency in a transaction between poet and poem. The sign of mastery is not nonchalance but a poetic form distinguished by its visibility—the stylistic excess by virtue of which a figure of speech transforms into rhyme. From a certain perspective, poetry (routinely described as rhetoric's licentious counterpart) comes into being as an *indecorous* elaboration of *elocutio*. Diverging from the *telos* of persuasion, figures of speech point to a particular way of knowing that does not rely on the invisibility of style. And, rather than promoting civilizations through the reproduction of ideology, figures of speech can instead cultivate and gratify desires that diverge from ideals of social harmony.

Unabashed about its labor, *indecorous* thinking also suggests that figures of speech are precisely the point at which form meets history: figures provide a kaleidoscopic perspective on the literary text and its constitutive pieces such that the text itself opens up as a history of its own composition. Like Simon Jarvis, I want to suggest that poetry is capable of thinking thoughts that are particular to its techniques and that cannot be thought elsewhere and by other means. This book is therefore an exercise in what Jarvis calls "philosophical poetics," which is "historical insofar as it takes technique to be at once the way in which art thinks and the way in which the work of art most intimately registers historical experience."[56] In his 1953 entry on "form" for the *Dictionary of World Literature*, Craig La Drière defined form by opposing it to "style." He wrote:

> The concept of style cannot in practise be dissociated from that of some *process*. This is sufficient to distinguish it from the concept of form, since as we have seen form is a concept relevant only to objects as such, to things and not to processes. But what is a formal element in an object from the point of view of analysis of the constitution of that object may be an element of style from the point of view of analysis of a process in which the object is involved. Some formal elements in things are indeed simply suggestions of process. These may be, like the brushwork in a painting, themselves vestiges of the process that produced the thing.... In short, what is form in the object conceived as such is style in the process in which the object is conceived as being involved.[57]

Introduction 11

For La Drière, a concept of "style" accounts for an object's history of production and a concept of "form" identifies the element of that history that remains available to empirical observation and might be more or less significant to the interpretation of that object. From the perspective of the painting as a made thing, the brushstroke is a formal element, but from the perspective of the painting as a process of making, the brushstroke is a stylistic element. La Drière goes on to suggest that what is interesting about style in particular is that in order for us to perceive an object as being made in this particular way, we have to be able to imagine that it could have been made in some other way:

> To find a style in a literary work is impossible unless we conceive that something is being done in the work or with it, that it is not just an object but an element in or embodiment of a process; and is impossible unless we conceive that the thing done might be done or have been done otherwise.[58]

While La Drière's intention may have been to pull form and style apart, I want instead to suggest that his discussion defines the dynamic intersection between form and style that is also the work of early modern figures of speech:

1. The point where product meets process: Like the brushstrokes of La Drière's exemplary painting, figures of speech function both as formal elements of an object and as vestiges of a process that offer an explanation of how that object came to be. The language of "vestige" suggests that process is a kind of remnant or remainder, with the implication that an ideal product effaces its style. Early modern practices encourage us, however, to consider figures of speech as conspicuous instruments of poetic production.
2. As conspicuous instruments of poetic production, figures of speech render the labor of *poesie* visible and encode a temporality into the poem that I call its history of composition. This history is not reducible to more familiar organizations of historical time (the period, the life of the author); this history is also not reducible to the temporal organizations of fiction (most notably, plot or narrative).[59] It is, however, informed by and interacts with both: the history of composition is the way in which a text tells its own story of becoming.
3. The peculiar temporality encoded by figure—its history of composition—entails the idea that things could have been done

otherwise. Figure is perpetually conceived of as the deviation from another way of speaking (Puttenham, in the *Art of English Poesy*, calls the other way "the ordinary and accustomed").[60] Where figures are instruments in histories of composition, they therefore permit us to read form in a way that highlights neither its necessity nor its inevitability (the sign of aesthetic value is therefore not that the text could not have been done in any other way) but instead its dynamism. From the perspective of figure, we are able to free form from the teleology of the poetic product and understand it, instead, as an index of poetic process and an instrument of poetic labor. Where figure is at its most conspicuous, it suggests that form can index the defining modality of poetry: what may be.

In what follows, my history, theory, and interpretation of figures of speech will rotate around these three axes of interpretation. I will suggest that figure is where form and history meet: as a set of techniques, figures open up to specific histories of reading and writing; figures designate a set of linguistic forms, but figures also treat those forms as already historical. As a closed or finite set of forms that are determined, described, and taxonomized within the art of rhetoric, figures are an object of knowledge (Are you trained in the canon of *elocutio*? Recite to me its ornaments including brief, illustrative examples). Figures are also, however, the engines of knowledge: formally homologous with the places of *inventio*, figures might double as logical arguments, with the result that their thinking looks a lot like humanist accounts of reason. But the kind of knowledge produced by figures also looks exactly like what humanist accounts of reason were looking to expel—sophistry and fallacies. Finally, figures might produce a particular kind of knowledge that would be increasingly aligned with a distinctively poetic mode. As with the mechanical arts, where making and knowing are intimately intertwined, the method of thinking characteristic of *poesie* deals in contingencies rather than necessities, models rather than explanations, and concretizations rather than abstractions. Thinking with figures of speech, that is, produced the imaginative worlds of early modern literature.

By detailing the world-making activity of figure, I am also asking that we extend to figures of speech a privilege we have largely, though not exclusively, reserved for tropes. A legacy of philosophy's charge against the emptiness of rhetorical ornament has been the defense of the trope in distinction to and at the expense of figure.[61] The difficulty the art of rhetoric has in maintaining this division between trope and figure is an index of its conceptual inadequacy to the dynamic forms it treats. I also want to suggest, however, that literary criticism's focus on what Kenneth Burke called the "master tropes" is a symptom of the extent to which we have tended to defend style on philosophy's terms, with the result that we have internalized philosophy's critique of style to the detriment of our theories of poetic form.[62] In what follows, I consider what it meant to think with style in early modern England. As figures of speech capture poetic invention, they also inform a method of thinking, and this method of thinking requires us to expand our sense of what was "thinkable" in the period by redefining what counts as thinking as such. *Indecorous Thinking* is thus an attempt to excavate the vexed place of figure within English humanism so as to understand how figures of speech established the imaginative domains of early modern poetry and to consider how the modality of these domains—what may be—guides a modern criticism that seeks to describe its operations.[63]

Overview

I have organized the book into two parts, each of which contains three chapters. Part One draws on the overlapping histories of rhetoric, dialectic, poetics, and pedagogy in order to articulate a set of approaches to figures of speech that emphasize their instrumentality to the practices of reading and writing in early modern England. Each of the first three chapters approaches the problem of *indecorous* thinking from a distinct perspective from within the archive: Chapter 1 draws on the history of the Ramist reforms; Chapter 2, the history of the humanist schoolroom; and Chapter 3, the history of poetics. Part Two, by contrast, focuses on a single figure of speech in each of the romances that it reads—Spenser's *Faerie Queene*, Sidney's *Arcadia*, and Wroth's *Urania*—and considers the *indecorous* thinking afforded by each figure. The governing organization of this book's argument is therefore not linear but recursive. Later chapters return to the arguments and insights of the earlier ones so as to push them in new directions. The result is, I hope, an anatomy of *indecorous* thinking.

Chapter 1 argues that debates over the canons of *inventio* and *elocutio*, their signature places and figures, informed early modern models of the mind and its thinking—where thinking happens, what it looks like, and what counts as thinking. These specialized debates over the question of the relation of figure to thought provide us with a particular entry point into the problem of fiction: How do style and its constitutive figures of speech set and determine the parameters of possibility for the imaginative worlds of early modern literature? Chapter 2 turns to English grammar schools and the earliest instruction in figures of speech to consider how these figures became *formulas* for composition and the generative mechanisms of these worlds. What these practices reveal is a cultivation of and interest in pleasure—not, as we might expect (following Horace), an accommodation to the pleasure of the audience but instead an activation of the pleasure that a maker might take in his own poetic productions.[64] Chapter 3 examines how artifice at its most conspicuous assigns an original set of values to the things of imaginative worlds. Taking up Aristotle's sense that one should not call a fig tree "queenly," I argue that figures of speech invent alternative hierarchies of evaluation. In this way, Part One of the book unfolds its theory of figures of speech across three distinct registers: a model of the mind that assigns primacy of place to the canon of *elocutio*, the translation of this model of the mind into quotidian habits of reading and writing, and, finally, the kind of poetry these habits produced.

In Part Two, I turn to a set of case studies—attending to the work of *simile*, *antithesis*, and *periphrasis* in the romances of Spenser, Sidney, and Wroth, respectively. *Simile*, *antithesis*, and *periphrasis* occupied a particularly vivid position in the contested intersection between style and invention because of the perceived formal homology between these figures of *elocutio* and the places of *inventio* known as comparison, contraries, and definition. It is on account of this formal homology, for example, that Ramus excluded these three figures from the art of rhetoric.[65] *Simile*, *antithesis*, and *periphrasis* therefore bring problems of classification—place or figure?—into a special kind of focus. Chapter 4 argues that *simile* was instrumental to Spenser's signature construction of "such as might best be" in *The Faerie Queene*; Chapter 5 argues that *antithesis* and its relentless commitment to the coexistence of contraries constitutes a first principle in the world of Sidney's *Arcadia*; and Chapter 6 argues that *periphrasis*—a figure that permits a speaker to take hold of precisely that which she does not name—becomes the governing logic of the world of Wroth's *Urania*.

While *simile*, *antithesis*, and *periphrasis* offer especially powerful examples of the generative tension between the canons of *inventio* and *elocutio*, the set of anxieties that motivated the Ramist reforms were pervasive to humanist instruction at large, where figures of speech are regularly reined in with the same sort of cautions, caveats, and prohibitions that script fairytale adventures (don't look here, don't go there, ask anything but that). The questions of epistemology that underwrite Ramism's redistribution of the canons—where does thinking begin? And, how does the origin of thought determine its veracity?—are frequently treated elsewhere as if they are answerable to a basic arithmetic. The problem of classification becomes a problem of quantity: too many figures of speech crowded into a single passage, or a single figure of speech used too often and extended for too long, threaten to take over a text.[66] In his *Garden of Eloquence* (1593), for example, Henry Peacham offers this final "Caution" for *epanalepsis* (the figure of speech that describes the repetition of a word or clause at the beginning and end of a line or sentence). Peacham warns that the intervening space between a word and its iteration should not be too long, "whereby it looseth the grace and sweetnesse of a repetition," but likewise he warns that the word "ought not to be repeated too soone, lest it returne barraine and emptie."[67] You could almost miss the strangeness of this claim: if a word is "repeated too soone," it comes back as something other than what it was. In the time between articulation and iteration, a word that was fertile and full becomes sterile and void. What is more, this transformation is precipitated not, as we might expect, by a lengthy duration or extension of time but by the very awareness of time's brevity that the figure itself compels. Figure's capacity to transform the language that it shapes is a problem for both the kind of knowledge poetry can be said to produce and the way that knowledge carves out a space for itself in the world.[68]

In short, the problem of stabilizing a system of classification so that it can steadily distinguish between *inventio* and *elocutio*, place and figure, reverberates throughout the art of rhetoric at different levels and scales (is this form a trope or a figure? A figure or a scheme? A figure of thought or a figure of speech?). What is important to these organizations, as is true for the various divisions explored throughout this book, is not whether they are right or wrong but what they tell us about the thinking that motivates them.[69] In *The Art of English Poesy*, Puttenham categorizes *epanalepsis* as a "figure sententious," meaning that it caters to both the "ear" and the "mind": "the ear is no less ravished with their current tune than the mind is with their sententiousness." "The well-tuning of your words and clauses to the delight of the ear," Puttenham explains, "maketh your information no less plausible to the mind than to the ear."[70] By regulating the distance between a word's articulation and its iteration, early modern treatises standardize the acceptable range of shapes that the figure of *epanalepsis* can assume. They also implicitly but crucially align these standards of aesthetic design with the judgment of truth-value: what "delights" is "plausible," and what is "plausible" "delights." That which fails to delight its audience produces the "barraine," the "emptie," the *indecorous*, and the implausible.

Romance is significant to this story because it is the genre within which my exemplary poets send the period's affection for figures of speech into a kind of hyperdrive. Throughout my readings, I propose that the spectacle of *indecorous* thinking compels us to rethink romance and its signature commitment to digression, dilation, and deferral as a problem of style rather than narrative.[71] It is important to note, however, that the kind of thinking that figure makes possible is not exclusive to the genre of romance.[72] It is, instead, that romance provides an especially productive concentration of the artifice and the labor that marked figures of speech as the instruments of poetic making. Philip Sidney's *Arcadia* and Edmund Spenser's *Faerie Queene* were first introduced into print as exhibitions of style in Abraham Fraunce's *Arcadian Rhetorike* (1588), and several of my readings in this book turn on passages selected by Fraunce or John Hoskins's for *Directions for Speech and Style* (c. 1601).[73] By finding *exempla* in Sidney's *Arcadia* or Spenser's *Faerie Queene*, vernacular manuals of rhetoric realize a reading practice that these texts—and Mary Wroth's *Urania* after them—set in motion: reading for style. The revised *Arcadia* offers a proleptic parody of this practice when Zelmane (Pyrocles's Amazonian persona) kisses her beloved Philoclea's hand before setting out to deliver a speech "(as if it should stand there like a hand in the margin of a book to note some saying worthy to be marked)."[74] Whatever words Zelmane would speak, we do not hear them; her discourse is cut off by a lion and a bear. What this means is that Philoclea's hand actually points not to a "saying" but to the figure of speech known as *aposiopesis* (the figure of interruption).[75] If it initially looked like Philoclea's manicule was going to index the kind of passage an early reader might have transcribed into his or her commonplace book, that hand instead points to *poesie*, to a figure of speech made conspicuous by denying us the passage itself.

Jonson's provocative distinction between *poesie* and poem, "the doing" and "the thing done," is one that I return to throughout this book because it defines my object of analysis in terms of the processes in which it is involved and from which it cannot be abstracted. It also encourages me to recalibrate my methodology accordingly: What are the protocols of evidence and explanation for a literary criticism that shifts its focus from poem to *poesie*, from "the thing done" to "the doing"? A central gambit of this book is that attention to the history of *elocutio* not only deepens our reading of early modern literature both historically and aesthetically but also opens up new readings that have been obscured by modern methods for evaluating evidence and assessing the legitimacy of an argument, methods that are themselves indebted to the emergence of empiricism and the exclusion of figure from disciplined thinking in the seventeenth century.[76] This book takes seriously the question not only of how knowledge is produced but also of how knowledge is believed to be produced: the standards

Introduction

of evidence and explanation characteristic of a given discipline or school of thinking as it articulates those standards to itself. In short, what counts as knowledge. *Indecorous Thinking* thus shares a set of interests with scholars of early modern science in that it reads figures of speech as an object of what Lorraine Daston has called "historical epistemology," which she describes as not only "the preconditions that make thinking this or that idea possible" but also the historical determination of the "conceptual categories of argument, explanation, and rationality."[77] In *Rhetorical Figures in Science* (1999), Jeanne Fahnestock defines figure as "a verbal summary that epitomizes a line of reasoning."[78] Where Fahnestock's analysis tends to suggest that any given figure of *elocutio* is reducible to the place of *inventio* of which it is an epitome, *Indecorous Thinking* seeks to release figure from the teleology of the places so as to consider how poets called on figures of speech to do the *work* of invention. My study of the relation of figure to thought thus neither climaxes nor concludes with the emergence of empiricism and advocacy of "the plain style." *Indecorous Thinking* describes a lost legacy of humanism, but it does so in order to suggest the centrality of figures of speech to early modern fiction making.

Throughout, my approach to figure emphasizes the temporality of form as an instrument of making. From Hayden White, I have learned to think of figures of speech as forms that "prefigure" the field of possibility within which fictions and their worlds take shape.[79] My emphasis on "the doing," however, suggests that the text is not fixed but in flux within this field. *Poesie* therefore assumes a shape that is at once precise, definite, and identifiable from within a specific domain of knowledge but also, precisely because it is definite and identifiable from within that domain, always capable of being something other than what it is. In his famous exercise in *On Copia of Words and Ideas*, Erasmus likened this flux to Proteus: the "disaster" of stylistic monotony might "easily be avoided by someone who has it at his fingertips to turn one idea into more shapes than Proteus himself is supposed to have turned into."[80] In the coda, I return to Jonson in order to consider the work of figures of speech in *Every Man Out of His Humour*. I argue there that the conspicuous figures of speech to which the play's characters repeatedly point are not reducible to the targets of a "comical satire" that takes aim at Elizabethan romance and its dubious form of eloquence. Those moments of figure pointing offer, instead, experiments in world making in a play that tests the limits of theatrical viability. It will be the final argument of this book to suggest that one character's *similes*—variously described as transformative, adulterate, and confounding—arrange the capacities of form along a critical spectrum. In *Every Man Out of His Humour*, the emblematic image that organizes this spectrum is not Proteus but the lifeless carcass of a poisoned dog.

At the moment in which *Muiopotmos* holds Clarion's wings up as "the spectacle of care"—as an emblem of belabored artifice—it also returns those wings to their origin. This poem's etiology of the butterfly translates the biblical promise of *ashes to ashes, dust to dust* into the poetic promise of *flowers to flowers*. The very first butterfly began her life as a nymph who was too good at her job: she collected more flowers for Venus than any of her companions. The nymph's jealous competitors insist that she benefits from Cupid's assistance, with the result that Venus transforms the master flower gatherer into a "winged Butterflie":

> And all those flowres, with which so plenteouslie
> Her lap she filled had, that bred her spight,
> She placed in her wings, for memorie
> Of her pretended crime, though crime none were:
> Since which that flie them in her wings doth beare.[81]

By this account, the butterfly's wings stand as witness to that which never was: a "pretended crime, though crime none were." The butterfly becomes the sign of ornament's cruel fiction: its wings speak what is a beautiful lie. When Spenser's spider sees Clarion's wings and weaves the web of his revenge, however, this is not the origin story that he is thinking of. Spenser's spider is instead thinking of his own etiology, where (according to Spenser's revision of Ovid) the arachnid emerges from Arachne's defeat in a competition of artistic skills.[82] When Arachne beholds Minerva's butterfly woven "With excellent device and wondrous slight . . . That seem'd to live, so like it was in sight," she is silenced by the *verisimilitude* of this butterfly's wings (their likeness to the living butterfly, which is itself a sign of what never was—a "pretended crime, though crime none were").[83] The butterfly is an etiological crux: the insect's conspicuous wings point at once to the emptiness at its origin and to its status as a litmus test for plausibility.

Hanging among the flowers of the garden, Clarion's wings trace the history of their own composition by returning his spiritless carcass to the flowers out of which it was originally made.[84] As Heather James has suggested, you could almost mistake Clarion for a humanist schoolboy if it weren't that he "reads wholly for pleasure."[85] We might, then, think of Clarion as an unruly schoolboy who reads for pleasure at the expense of his profit: the flowers on his wings would therefore act like trefoils pointing to the flowers of the garden.[86] When faced with a flower, you can admire it from a distance. You can dissect that flower, or you can pluck it for your dinner table. At the opening of *A Treatise of Schemes and Tropes*, Sherry suggests that you ought to learn that flower's name: this knowledge affords the reader "muche more pleasure, and profit" because it permits him to "useth arte and judgement."[87] *Indecorous Thinking* examines how in early modern England a curious object of knowledge—the canon of *elocutio* and its signature figures of speech—became a method of thinking, and it suggests that this method of thinking established the parameters of possibility for poetry's imaginative worlds. When the spider's pincer transforms Clarion's wings into "the spectacle of care," it also paints them with "bloodie streames," the conspicuous counterpart to the otherwise invisible departure of the butterfly's spirit. In the chapters that follow, I consider the value of conspicuous figures of speech to both early modern literature and its criticism: How might figures serve as a site of access to the historical conditions of poetic production? What kinds of knowledge did figures generate in the early modern period? What happens to that knowledge when figures are distinguished from authoritative models of disciplined thinking? How do the assumptions that underwrite these distinctions get institutionalized? And, how have these assumptions helped shape modern methods for evaluating evidence and judging the legitimacy of an argument, thereby limiting the range of activities we regularly ascribe to figure and to form?

PART I

CHAPTER I

Inventing Figures of Speech

In the *Defence of Poesy* (c. 1580), Philip Sidney famously distinguished the work of imaginative poetry from the work belonging to all other disciplines. Historian and musician, mathematician and natural philosopher—each of these takes "the works of nature for his principal object."[1] "Only the poet," Sidney continues, "disdaining to be tied to any such subjection, lifted up with the vigour of his own invention, doth grow in effect another nature": the poet trades in "what is, hath been, or shall be" for "what may be and should be."[2] This is why Sidney's poet "goeth hand in hand with nature, not enclosed within the narrow warrants of her gifts, but freely ranging only within the zodiac of his own wit."[3] Sidney's account of the imaginative world of poetry has proved a touchstone for scholars of early modern literature and has provided a kind of priority for the work of both poetry and its criticism.[4] Between the "bare 'was'" of history and the sterile imperatives of philosophy, poetry is here defined by its peculiar capacity to build worlds that expand our sense of possibility.[5] Sidney's formulation neither climaxes nor concludes with possibility. As he pivots back from poetry's "golden" world to nature's "brazen," his emphasis falls on the moralizing "should." At its most successful, what poetry actually delivers is a hauntingly homogenous fantasy in which everyone turns into Cyrus.[6]

But at the outset of this study, I want to hold onto Sidney's interest in the language of contingency, the modality of the subjunctive or the potential mood, and the alterative set of coordinates that map "the zodiac of his own wit," in order to examine both a condition of this fantasy and its putative origin in the compositional process.[7] For poetry to remake the "brazen" world in the image of a "golden," its readers must ask not only "why" the poet made Cyrus but also "how that maker made him."[8] As Elizabeth Spiller has suggested, "the poem," for Sidney, "is a 'small world' whose artificiality enables it to create knowledge."[9] I want to suggest that it is in our study of poetry's "artificiality"—the figures of speech that are also a technology of production—that we are best able to articulate the method of thinking that a poem models and the *heterocosm* that such thinking produces.[10] By attributing the poet's unique ascent to "the vigour of his own invention," Sidney points us toward an account of poetic composition that is indebted to humanist pedagogy in the art of rhetoric. By the second half of the sixteenth century, the word "invention" had already begun to tilt toward its more modern sense of the making of something that did not previously exist, but Sidney's use of "invention" in the *Defence* also retains the ancient sense of the rhetorical canon of *inventio*.[11] The expanse of possibility that characterizes Sidney's sense of poetic domain constitutes a temporal field within which the "bare 'was'" of history is but one configuration among many. The rhetorical canon of *inventio* and its signature places (cause and effect, subject and adjunct, etc.) constituted one way of determining the parameters of possibility for that temporal field.[12] In *The Art of Rhetoric* (1560), Thomas Wilson described the places of *inventio* as mechanisms for establishing the likelihood of phenomena: "The finding out of apt matter, called otherwise invention, is a searching out of things true or things likely, the which may reasonably set forth a matter and make it appear probable."[13] According to this formulation, *inventio* establishes the probability of a given set of phenomena because its places constitute a shared source of knowledge about the world, how it is believed to operate, and how we describe those operations to ourselves.[14]

Where the places of *inventio* provided a set of procedures for establishing the probability of "what may be," the rhetorical canon of *elocutio* and its figures of speech posed a special problem for likelihood. As the putatively final step in the compositional process, figures of speech were understood to contribute to plausibility insofar as they represented a speaker's emotions and impressed those emotions upon an audience. This mimetic theory of figures describes *elocutio* as a transcription of speech formulations that are said to occur naturally under a given set of circumstances. Overwhelmed by grief, a person's speech breaks off midsentence: "I never—"; the canon of *elocutio* calls this *aposiopesis*. The orator's text is a study of rhetoric's transcript—desiring to demonstrate grief, he uses *aposiopesis*—and this figure, in turn, produces grief in his audience. To be effective, figures of speech therefore had to appear as if they were spontaneous and natural—something other than artifice.[15] As Quintilian writes in his *Institutes of Oratory*: "Who will endure the orator who expresses his anger, his sorrow or his entreaties in neat antitheses, balanced cadences and exact correspondences? Too much care for our words under such circumstances weakens the impression of emotional sincerity, and wherever the orator displays his art unveiled, the hearer says, 'The truth is not in him.'"[16] According to this paradigm of composition, conspicuous figures of speech alert an audience to the artificial mechanisms at work and give the lie to the seemingly natural arrangement of phenomena. At their most conspicuous, figures of speech threaten the rhetorical invention of plausibility with their own open artifice.

In this chapter, I will argue that the overlapping histories of the arts of rhetoric and dialectic suggest a contrasting theory of figures of speech according to which conspicuous artifice is instrumental to the generation of poetry's "what may be" rather than an immediate threat to its viability. Attending to the pedagogical reforms of Peter Ramus and his English proponents—especially those associated with the Sidney Circle—this chapter will show that as the Ramist reforms redefined the arts of rhetoric and dialectic, they sought to divorce figures of speech from the operations of reason.[17] Drawing on and critiquing classical models of rhetoric in Cicero's *Orator* and Quintilian's *Institutes*, the Ramist reforms promoted an account of reason predicated on excluding figures of speech from official descriptions of disciplined thinking.[18] As a movement, Ramism responds to a potentiality of figure that it also helps produce: figure's capacity to organize the world along axes of relation distinct from those articulated within the canon of *inventio*. Ultimately, this chapter will argue that artifice at its most conspicuous may have played Malvolio to the operations of right reason but that it also provided poets with the tools to rethink and remap the field of possibility that underwrote humanist accounts of reason. Ramism therefore helps us articulate a theory of conspicuous artifice in which figures of speech act as the constitutive engines of poetry's imaginative worlds.

At stake in Ramism is the question of the relation of figure to thought and therefore, also, the relation of figure to what counts as thinking as such. By examining one pedagogical movement's systematic efforts to subordinate figures of speech to the disciplined operations of reason, we are also witnessing a single iteration of a much older and broader dynamic between rhetoric and philosophy. At least since Plato's *Gorgias*, rhetoric had to defend itself against philosophy's charge that it is all style and no matter.[19] Under the pressure of the Ramist reforms, this charge is addressed at the local level of process and composition: Are figures instrumental to the production of knowledge? Or, are figures ornamental to that knowledge? In the *Defence*, Sidney responded to Plato's charge by suggesting that figurative language produces a unique kind of knowledge that is not subject to philosophy's evaluation because it does not deal in affirmations. Because poetry is "not labouring to tell you what is or is not," its speech cannot be subject to the judgments of true and false (or to the charges of liar, cheat, and juggler). It "nothing affirms." One cannot "give the lie," Sidney concludes, "to things not affirmatively but allegorically and figuratively written."[20] As Jeffrey Walker has suggested in *Rhetoric and Poetics in Antiquity* (2000), it is in moments like these that Sidney walks right up to a theory of poetry that he never fully articulates or acknowledges. Walker calls this theory or mode the "tropological fantasia": "an unsystematic system of poetical invention."[21] Where figures drive thought, they also craft a kind of knowledge and a method of thinking that is not reducible to logic's proposition or philosophy's affirmation. This kind of thinking—the model of the mind it implies and the imaginative *heterocosm* it produces—is the subject of this chapter. I call it *indecorous*.

Rhetoric and Dialectic

It is somewhat shocking to witness the speed with which Abraham Fraunce —a Ramist and an affiliate of the Sidney Circle—revises Sidney's famous formulation at the start of his treatise on dialectic, *The Lawiers Logike* (1588). Fraunce dismisses the very distinction by which Sidney sought to make poetry special: "Whatsoeuer it bée," he begins before correcting himself, "nay whatsoeuer thou canst imagine to bée, although it bée not, neuer was, nor neuer shall bée, yet by reason it is inuented, taught, ordered, confirmed."[22] Invested in defining the art of dialectic as the single intellectual process capable of producing all knowledge, Fraunce here denies what Sidney maintained in the *Defence*: that there is a kind of thinking peculiar to poetry and that this kind of thinking is what allows us to imagine that the world can be otherwise than it is.

Fraunce is not taking direct aim at Sidney or even at poetry. He is instead elaborating on the pedagogical reforms of the French philosopher Peter Ramus (of whose *Dialecticae Libri Duo* Fraunce's own *Lawiers Logike* is a close adaptation, and his *Arcadian Rhetorike* (1588) is based on the Ramistic *Rhetoricae Libri Duo*). Responding to a perceived overlap between the arts of rhetoric and dialectic, Ramus reserved the traditional first two canons—*inventio* (or invention) and *dispositio* (or judgment)—for the art of dialectic and restricted rhetoric to the canons of *elocutio* (or style) and *pronuntiatio* (or delivery).[23] This redistribution carried a polemic: stripped of its engagement with *res*, or things, and restricted to the adornment of *verba*, or words, figures of speech became what another Ramist, Dudley Fenner, described in *The Artes of Logike and Rhethorike* (1584) as the "garnishing of speeche ... whereby the speach it selfe is beautified and made fine."[24] When Fraunce writes that "whatsoeuer thou canst imagine to bée" is the product of reason's operations, his aim is to reproduce this Ramist polemic and argue for the art of dialectic's exclusive claim to the processes and places of *inventio*. When Fraunce restricts the origins of "whatsoeuer thou canst imagine to bée" to dialectic's places of *inventio*, he is also denying the epistemological work of the figures of *elocutio*. Though Fraunce takes aim, then, at an art of rhetoric that would claim *inventio* as its own, the effect of his revision is to deny to poetry the kind of thinking that it learned from and shared with rhetoric: a model of the mind in which *elocutio* and its signature tropes and figures act as the engines of thought.

Fraunce was likely introduced to Ramism while a student at Cambridge University, where he overlapped with Gabriel Harvey's stint as praelector in rhetoric. During that time, Harvey delivered a series of lectures that he would subsequently publish as *Ciceronianus* (1577) and *Rhetor* (1577).[25] In these lectures, Harvey recounts his own conversion from the elaborate eloquence of Ciceroniansim to the utilitarian approach characteristic of Ramism, and he states his intention to persuade those who value "words more than content, language more than thought" of the error of their ways.[26] This reversal of values was a central critique of the Ramist reforms—not of the Ciceronian apes alone but of classical instruction in rhetoric more broadly. In the classical division of the arts, demonstrative logic produced certain knowledge, dialectic dealt in probable knowledge, and rhetoric was concerned with persuasive knowledge. The distinction between dialectic and logic had effectively collapsed within the medieval Scholastic tradition, such that Peter of Spain's *Summulae Logicales* treats probable reasoning as if it is capable of producing certainty.[27] In his *De Inventione Dialectica* (1479), Rudolph Agricola renders this conflation an imperative by declaring the art of dialectic capable of producing all knowledge, whether that knowledge is necessary, contingent, or merely persuasive.[28] As Fraunce explains in *The Lawiers Logike*, "although among things conceaued and knowne, some bee necessary and vnfallible, some doubtfull and contingent, yet the Arte of Knowing and Reasoning is only one and the same, . . . as the sight of the eye in perceyuing all colours, bee they chaungeable or not chaungeable."[29] Where dialectic provides a single intellectual process capable of producing all knowledge, rhetoric becomes mere ornamentation. Of the five classical canons belonging to rhetoric, Agricola reduces the art to *elocutio* and *pronuntiatio* while reserving *inventio* and *dispositio* for dialectic.[30] It is the Agricolan reform that Ramus will pursue, describing dialectic as the art that "thinks over and carefully weighs everything" and rhetoric as the art that "deliver[s] with elegant purity the matter that has been examined."[31] The Ramist reforms reduce rhetoric to ornamentation while casting dialectic as the art capable of producing all knowledge.[32]

At its most ambitious, Ramism suggests that redrafting the disciplinary borders of the humanist curriculum involves creating a more accurate representation of the mind itself—an image of how it works.[33] By insisting that the reformed curriculum was a representation of the mind and of natural reason, this curriculum also staked a claim to a kind of mental mimesis.[34] Such reason is "natural" because dialectic's arguments are simply the relations of the natural world reproduced within an art.[35] The mind properly trained in a trivium governed by dialectic will therefore be a reflection of both the arts and the natural world that grounds the relations of those arts—whether such relations manifest as a single argument produced by *inventio* or as the hierarchical organization of the arts themselves.[36] This is why dialectic is the "Art of Arts."[37] As Ramism redrafts the boundaries between rhetoric and dialectic, it creates a model of the mind in which the necessary separation of the arts functions like a geometric law: two disciplinary "field[s]" or planes cannot occupy the same space in time (what Walter J. Ong called Ramism's "cartography of the mind").[38] In *Questions of Brutus* (1548), for example, Ramus justified his protection of disciplinary boundaries in an appeal to "Solon's Law" (the Athenian decree requiring that anyone constructing a wall or a house, digging a grave or a well, or planting an olive or fig tree leave a proportional amount of space before his neighbor's property). "The boundaries and precepts of all the arts," Ramus writes, "should be kept separate." "My field," he continues, "should not run into yours, and yours should not cut into mine." Ramus insists that "their application should be joined," but this commercial transaction between separate fields—"through the sale, purchase and exchange of our materials"—is difficult to map onto the compositional process itself.[39]

The redrafting of disciplinary borders therefore offered a corrective to the conventional, post-Aristotelian distribution of the arts—what was really an image of how the mind ought not to work. In *Rhetor*, Harvey ventriloquizes *Eloquentia* as she marks the boundaries of her rhetorical estate and returns to dialectic the land that has been most inconveniently bestowed upon her by Cicero and his followers:

> Why do you enrich me with the stores and treasures of my sisters, when I am content with my own ornaments and decorations? Why do you force upon me against my will the possessions that belong to others? Why do you make me stray beyond the fixed boundaries and limits of my estate? Why do you take it upon yourself to extend my domain, which I always wanted to be charming and beautiful, with lovely dwellings, rather than vast and spacious? . . . Why do you make me the mistress of all things—sea and land, air and sky—when I am satisfied with my own realm, which is not large to be sure, but bright and flourishing? Why do you place under my power and sway those whom I ought and wish to serve? . . . Is this an act of kindness, is this the role of a sister, to force her eldest sisters, distinguished by the highest excellence, from their own lands and estates?[40]

Harvey reframes the distribution of the canons of *inventio* and *dispositio* as a land grab. Against her will, *Eloquentia* has been forced to take on the work of invention and judgment even though she was "content with my ornaments and decorations." *Eloquentia* mourns the dissolution of her boundaries, and this monstrous "estate" doubles as a kind of body to her voice. The dissolution of perimeters becomes a figure for uncontrollable speech that rules where it ought to serve: it digresses, dilates, and amplifies beyond intelligible parameters.[41] When all is subject to her "power," *Eloquentia* becomes a version of the *hic mulier* (she is enormous in size, wide across the chest, broad in the shoulders).[42] Given too much land, *Eloquentia* grows manly. Where *Eloquentia* takes over the property of *inventio* and *dispositio*, she becomes a kind of chimera (a disciplinary version of the opening image of Horace's *Art of Poetry*): "The head of Eloquence, like a bust of Venus, has been attached to the ill-defined limbs of another body."[43] *Eloquentia* does not simply renounce her "power" but offers herself up as political subject to the art of dialectic.

Harvey's *prosopopoeia* is a fantasy of subjection whereby *Eloquentia* and the canon of *elocutio* desire to be ruled by the art of dialectic. This fantasy of subjection produces a hierarchy of relative value that then informs how the arts of dialectic and rhetoric are combined in practice. Ramus distinguished rhetoric from dialectic according to whether speech is a necessary property of that art:

> Reason and speech are the two universal gifts of the gods granted to men, and the source of almost all the others. Dialectic is the theory of reason. Therefore whatever is the property of reason and mental ability and can be handled and practised without speech, attribute this by right to the art of dialectic.[44]

Ramus pulls thinking and speaking apart: "Since the mind is more distinguished than the tongue, so invention and arrangement, the concern of the mind, are more excellent than style."[45] Whereas *inventio* and *dispositio* are "the concerns of the mind," *elocutio* belongs to the decidedly less important "tongue." Elsewhere Ramus suggests that "Human nature has one senate, one advisory body, namely reason. Its explication and theory Dialectic claims as its own." He describes rhetoric as one of two heralds (the other being grammar) located in the "vestibule of the senate house." As herald, rhetoric's job is to "publish and make known the decrees of the senate" through the "adornment of speech."[46] Rhetoric belongs to a "vestibule" that is a kind of gateway between the mind and the world. It is a place through which "decrees" pass after they have been conceived, debated, and issued. Ornaments, *Eloquentia*'s "decorations," are applied after the fact.

Whether in *Eloquentia*'s desire to reduce her holdings or in the office of the herald, Ramism regularly articulates the relative value of rhetoric to dialectic according to subject positions in the social world. In the voice of Brutus, Ramus scolds Cicero for treating rhetoric as the "mistress" of "wisdom" rather than as its "servant and handmaiden."[47] In this sense, hierarchies of the social world serve to illustrate, even as they consolidate, the subordination of rhetoric to dialectic (and *elocutio* to *inventio*). The separation of the disciplines is, for Ramus, a basic structuring principle of the social world: "In a republic founded on excellent laws and customs, the farms and possessions of individual citizens are governed, limited, and circumscribed by definite boundaries." He therefore likens the classical distribution of the canons to property theft: "When you build a rhetorical wall by the farm of a stranger, the art of dialectic, will you seize and snatch away the middle part of the farm without leaving an intervening foot?"[48] At its worst, the misplanted "rhetorical olive tree" is not just close to dialectic but "covers the whole region of philosophy" with its "roots," thereby justifying Ramus's appeal to the courts of law.[49] The social world within which servant acts as mistress and *Eloquentia* rules takes on the threat of political tyranny. In an elaboration of Solon's law, the respective "fields" become distinct social spheres (first distinguished by Cicero himself): dialectic belongs to "the grounds of the academy" and rhetoric to "the sweatshops."[50]

As Ramism polices the boundaries between rhetoric and dialectic, it also drives a wedge between the activities of thinking and speaking. Even the "disputation" of dialectic that we tend to associate with speech can, for Ramus, "be formed in the mind and practiced without any trafficking of language or speech."[51] While Ramus defines dialectic as "the art of discoursing well," his account of "discourse" emphasizes thought.[52] We might follow Lisa Jardine in considering "discourse" to be "the field of operation" for Ramus's dialectic and "natural reason" to be the "origin" of that field.[53] But because Ramism idealizes origins, advertising its reforms as a kind of apostolic return, its account of dialectic witnesses an ambition to define reason as an operation independent of its own discursive field. In *The Lawiers Logike*, Fraunce's definition of dialectic turns from Ramus's "discoursing well" to "Reasoning": "Logike is an Art of Reasoning."[54] His annotation to this definition attempts to define reason as an operation distinct from speech. Acknowledging that some scholars understand *logos* to "betokeneth spéech or talke," Fraunce is less sure:

> Yet for that the whole force and vertue of Logike consisteth in reasoning, not in talking: and because reasoning may be without talking, as in solitary meditations and deliberations with a mans selfe, some holde the first deriuation as most significant.[55]

Fraunce will subsequently distinguish logic from dialectic along the lines of "form" (taken here as essence) and "manner": logic is "the internall forme, essence, and nature" of the art "consisting in reason," and dialectic is "the externall maner and order of woorking, which is commonly doone by speache and talke."[56] While Fraunce does not insist on a distinction that would forge a division between two arts that Ramus declared to be one, *The Lawiers Logike* betrays a desire to pry reason from the grips of speech by casting speech as incidental or "common" to the expression of reason (which is capable of operating in other modes). Reason, here, becomes proper to the silent, meditative mind.[57]

What would such thinking even look like for an individual trained within the humanist trivium? In its more commonplace iteration, this silent mind, as Ramus describes it in *Arguments in Rhetoric Against Quintilian* (1549), belongs to "numerous dumb persons and many people who live without any outward speech." Such cases evidence that *inventio* and *dispositio* "belong completely to the mind and can be practiced inwardly without any help from language or oration."[58] Take, for example, Fraunce's account of the work of verbs and conjunctions within the art of dialectic:

> It is to be understoode, that I meane not the naked woords: (for that were Grammaticall, and belonging onely to speech; not Logiciall, and perteyning to reason:) but the verbe and coniunction of the minde, wit, and reason: which indeede is commonly, although not alwaies, expressed by some such Grammaticall Uerbe and Coniunction.[59]

The verbs and conjunctions with which an individual constructs arguments and arranges those arguments into syllogisms are not words per se, though they are "commonly . . . expressed" by words that we also call verbs and conjunctions. They are, instead, "the verbe and coniunction of the minde." At its most extreme, what Ong called the "corpuscular" model of the mind suggests that the art of dialectic does not deal in language at all, if we take language first and foremost to be a referential structure.[60] Without a formal account of the concept (derived from sensory experience and to which language conventionally refers), Fraunce here seems to introduce a mental structure that is a nonreferential intellectual process: it is analogous to language but is not language.[61] The disappearance of a theory of predication as well as the necessity of enunciation from the reformed dialectic goes some distance toward explaining this model. For Aristotle, the act of uttering a proposition was the essential endpoint to the production of that knowledge; such a requirement drops out entirely from Fraunce's account.[62] The "coupling" of a conjunction stands in for the act of enunciation, but the reformed dialectic erases the legibility of this substitution. Language becomes not referential but the stuff of the mind.[63]

This is the model of the mind that informs William Temple's Ramist *Analysis* (c. 1585) of Sidney's *Defence of Poesy*. Like Fraunce in *The Lawiers Logike*, Temple insists that the art of dialectic and its canon of *inventio* provide the single intellectual process that governs all thinking. Where Sidney distinguished poetry from all other disciplines by suggesting that only the poet "lifted up with the vigour of his own invention, doth grow in effect another nature," Temple argues that there is no "invention" proper to the poet or to poetry.[64] "You want the essential nature of poetry to be understood as a certain kind of fiction-making," Temple writes, "but can it be that such a making is anything but the invention of something that has never existed?"[65] Consistent with the Ramist claim that dialectic governs the production of all knowledge, "whatsoeuer thou canst imagine to bée, although it bée not, neuer was, nor neuer shall bée" (to quote Fraunce again), Temple understands both what is and what is not (but may be) to be the product of the same operations of reason:

> Anyone who makes fictions, creates what are logical arguments—namely causes, effects, subjects, adjuncts, contraries, comparisons, or the rest of those things which originate from these. In this way Ovid, feigning the realm of the sun, feigned an efficient cause by which it was constructed, matter out of which it was put together, and adjuncts by which it was decorated. But feigning causes, effects, subjects, adjuncts and all other arguments, is nothing other than inventing causes, effects, subjects, adjuncts. Therefore, fiction-making will be the same as the invention of something that does not yet exist.[66]

Pointing to Sidney's source, Temple continues to explain: "When Aristotle, therefore, defines poetry as a fiction-making, he puts poetry, as it were, in the house of logical invention, mixing these two disciplines. And just as often as poets feign, they do so not by some gift peculiar to poetry, but by the faculty of the art of dialectic."[67] According to Temple, when a poem offers you something that does not otherwise exist, it is acting in its capacity as dialectic. What Sidney called "the zodiac of his own wit" is, for a Ramist, charted by "logical arguments" such that the places of *inventio* draw the sole set of coordinates for "what may be." For a Ramist like Temple or Fraunce, the truth-value of a poem lies not in the referential power of its words but the referential power of its reasoning process. The places of *inventio* guarantee that the universals by which poetry stakes its claim to truth have been properly conceived.[68] Temple calls the operations of such reason "the action of either inborn or artificial thought in inventing."[69] The "action" of "inventing" effectively collapses Sidney's distinction between *gnosis* and *praxis* because invention is itself an "action" in the world, a kind of doing. Fiction making neither represents nature nor does such making "grow in effect another nature" (as Sidney would have it); instead, *fictio* intervenes in "nature" through the "action" of *inventio*.[70]

Embedded within Temple's critique of Sidney is an account of the social value of poetry that is not (as it was with Harvey's *Eloquentia* or Ramus's "handmaiden") about the reproduction or consolidation of ideology. If thought is not a linguistic representation of the world but an action in the world—if thought acts on matter in a shared ontology of both what is and what has never been—then faulty thinking can trouble the world.[71] As John Hoskins writes in *Directions for Speech and Style* (c. 1601), "The order of God's creatures" is itself "eloquent"; as a result, "disordered speech is not so much injury to the lips which give it forth or the thoughts which put it forth as to the right proportion and coherence of things in themselves, so wrongfully expressed."[72] It is not simply that fallacious arguments are false representations of the world, where what is significant about those representations is that they are not true. Rather, as an "action" in the mind, faulty thinking has the capacity to alter the world. In order to make the claim that dialectical invention is the single intellectual process capable of producing all knowledge, Temple posits an order of existence that includes and is thus responsive to what has never been.[73]

Elocutio and *Inventio*

In his *Analysis* of Sidney's *Defence*, Temple charts out the Ramist response to the idea that poetry has the peculiar power to speak of "what may be." "I grant you," Temple concedes, "that poets set before our eyes a noble image of virtue and vice. But the essential features of this image, and all the colors by which it is varied and differentiated, are the arguments of logical invention, dressed in rhetorical ornaments."[74] There is no separate faculty, no device unique to the poet that generates knowledge of what does not exist. Dialectic and, especially, its canon of *inventio* produce knowledge of everything ranging from what exists to that which does not yet and may never exist (and rhetoric provides such knowledge with clothing).[75] The relations by which the poet forges his image of Cyrus belong to the canon of *inventio*: "Anyone who makes fictions," Temple writes, "creates what are logical arguments."[76] According to a Ramist like Temple, the places of *inventio* provide the sole set of coordinates for determining a poetic world's field of possibility.

A broader question about thinking structures the Ramist reforms and its claim that the art of dialectic is responsible for the production of all knowledge: How does the site of generation—how does the specialized location of thought's origins in the places of *inventio*—determine the field of possible knowledge? In the previous section of this chapter, I examined how the Ramist mapping of the mind subordinated rhetoric to the operations of dialectic by redrafting the boundaries of disciplinary estates. In this section, I turn to a set of homologous forms that proved troubling to this new set of boundaries: forms that doubled as both dialectic's places of *inventio* and rhetoric's figures of *elocutio*. At stake in the Ramist specification of homologous forms is the question of how our account of the origin of thought—most starkly, whether thinking begins with dialectic's places of *inventio* or rhetoric's figures of *elocutio*—determines what counts as thinking as such. As Ian Hacking has argued, a "style of reasoning" determines not whether a proposition is true or false but instead whether a proposition is "up for grabs as a candidate for being true-or-false."[77] It is in its determination of the very candidacy of a proposition that an art like dialectic establishes the parameters of possibility for thought itself: "whatsoeuer thou canst imagine to bée."[78] When Temple and Fraunce argue that "whatsoeuer thou canst imagine to bée" is set and determined by the canon of *inventio*, they are also suggesting that the places of *inventio* determine what is thinkable insofar as any discourse can stake a claim to thinking. And so, when Ramism works to separate the canon of *inventio* and its signature places from the canon of *elocutio* and its tropes and figures, it also narrows the scope of what counts as thinking and what constitutes the realm of possibility. To think with figure—to invite figure in from the "vestibule" and give it a seat in "the senate house"—is to draw a new set of coordinates for imaginative possibility. Figures of speech issue different "decrees" for the worlds that they govern.

The classical configuration of the canons taught that *inventio* dealt in *res*—in matter or in things—and that *elocutio* dealt in *verba*, or words. "Every speech is composed of matter and words," Quintilian explains, "and that as regards matter we must study invention, as regards words, style."[79] This division governs the distribution of material within Quintilian's *Institutes of Oratory* as it does Erasmus's *On Copia of Words and Ideas*. The polemic that will motivate the Ramist reforms is present within classical and humanist treatments of the art of rhetoric, but it is both more diffuse and more generous toward *elocutio*.[80] Ramism, however, turns the conceptual distinctions of classical rhetoric into categorical separations it then proceeds to reinforce by redrafting disciplinary boundaries. As Ramus insists in *Questions of Brutus*, the "invention of subject matter should not be mixed in" with "rhetorical style," and because "style is the shaping of speech by means, for instance, of the trope in single words and the figure in combination of words . . . we should not mix in arguments."[81] Ramism, therefore, regularly turned its attention to anything that it perceived as overlap between *inventio* and *elocutio*. For example, Quintilian describes *emphasis* as a "virtue" of *elocutio* that "succeeds in revealing a deeper meaning than is actually expressed by the words."[82] In *Arguments in Rhetoric against Quintilian*, Ramus insists that the activity Quintilian attributes to *emphasis* is actually "part of the process of reasoning and of reaching a conclusion; it has nothing to do with a figure. For it does not involve a new form of speech, but rather a careful, keen power of thought."[83] Quintilian understands the "deeper meaning" to be a product of *emphasis*, such that when Virgil describes Cyclops's napping body as extended "throughout the cave," he "by taking the room occupied as the standard of measure, gives an impression of the giant's immense bulk."[84] Ramus, by contrast, argues that what Quintilian attributes to *emphasis* belongs, in fact, to logic, a "keen power of thought" that preexists and determines the style of its expression. It is for the same reason that Ramus dismisses Quintilian's account of *amplificatio* and *sententiae* entirely, "for in these chapters Quintilian has no grasp of any art at all." "These classes of amplification and aphorisms [*sententiae*] result not from the style of words," he explains, "but from the invention of material," and Ramus proceeds to refer his reader to the place of *inventio* or logical argument known as "comparison."[85]

Emphasis and *amplificatio* are examples of forms that were traditionally treated within the art of rhetoric but that Ramus understood as operations of reason and therefore removed from the art of rhetoric. *Commoratio* ("the act of dwelling on or returning to one's strongest argument"), *extenuatio* (or *litotes*, "deliberate understatement"), and *illusio* (or *irony*) are also denied the status of "figures of thought" because lingering over a theme, trivialization, and mockery, "all these can exist without any figure."[86] Ramus will similarly declare that *simile* is not a figure but an argument from the place of *inventio* known as "comparison,"[87] *antithesis* is not a figure but "an argument from unlikes" (the place of *inventio* devoted to "contraries"),[88] and *periphrasis* is not a trope but an argument from the place known as "definition."[89] Chapters 4, 5, and 6 of this book consider the contested status of *simile*, *antithesis*, and *periphrasis* respectively. For now, I wish only to point out that the Ramist separation of *elocutio* from *inventio* also entailed a reduction of the canons themselves. There is no treatment of *simile*, *antithesis*, or *periphrasis* in Fraunce's *Arcadian Rhetorike* (or in any Ramist treatment of rhetoric more broadly). Ramus, likewise, reduced the places of *inventio* to cause, effect, subject, adjunct, opposites, names, divisions, definitions, and witnesses.[90] Ramus claimed that the reduction of the arts made them both more manageable and more teachable, but this reduction is also the result of relegating homologous forms to either the art of dialectic or the art of rhetoric (but never to both).

Ramism's specification of homologous forms calls into question the relation of figure to thought. In its strict separation of the places of *inventio* from the figures of *elocutio*, Ramism effectively removes figures of speech from the methods and protocols of disciplined thinking. As a result, Ramism routinely associates figures of speech with the crafting of beauty, but this beauty is always operating in the service of a *telos* discovered and determined by the places of *inventio*. In one final example, two English Ramists go even further than Ramus himself. As we just saw, Ramus's reduction of the canon of *inventio* retained the place devoted to "names," which included two kinds of arguments classically understood as places in their own right: "notation," or argument from etymology, and "conjugation," or argument from "ofspringes."[91] Perceiving an overlap between these arguments and the figures of *elocutio* known as *paronomasia* and *polyptoton*, Abraham Fraunce and Dudley Fenner follow Ramism through to its logical conclusion by reducing the places of *inventio* even further and doing away with notation and conjugation entirely.[92]

As logical arguments, both notation and conjugation assume a direct correspondence between words and things: the relation that inheres among names also inheres among the things of the natural world to which those names refer. They presuppose that, as Thomas Granger clarifies in his Ramist *Divine Logike* (1620), "the things themselves signified by such words or names be ioyned together by a naturall, and inseperable, bond, link, and consequence."[93] The central questions for a Ramist therefore become: Do these places merely describe a relationship between words? Or do they describe a relationship inhering in things themselves? If the relation belongs only to words, then this activity is proper to the art of grammar; if they facilitate the invention of arguments about things in themselves, they belong to the art of dialectic.[94]

Fraunce and Fenner proceed to dismiss notation and conjugation from the art of dialectic on two grounds. First, they argue that any account of the relations forged among words belongs to grammar.[95] Second, they argue that where these relations are forged among things, they constitute a logical argument that is redundant of the place of *inventio* known as "cause."[96] Both Fraunce and Fenner maintain, however, that a causal relation does not describe everything belonging to notation and conjugation. "But is there nothing els?" Fenner asks, and he answers, "yes."[97] We ask, what is this something else? A Ramist asks, to which art does this something else belong? Both Fraunce and Fenner determine that this something "els" belongs to the art of rhetoric. What is left unexplained in notation by either grammar's dictionary or dialectic's cause is what Fraunce calls "the pretty and conceipted chaunge of the woord" and what Fenner calls "an elegancie of the Trope called *Paranomasia*."[98] Likewise, the work of conjugation belongs, according to Fenner, "to the figure of Rethorike, called *Poliptoton*"; Fraunce writes that where justice, just, and justly "doo fitly allude in the ende and falling," that fitness "commeth from a Rhetoricall figure, called Polyptoton, which concerneth the elegancie that is in the diuers fallinges and terminations of woords."⁹⁹ Both Fraunce and Fenner suggest that the something else unique to these forms defines each as a figure of *elocutio* rather than a place of *inventio*.¹⁰⁰

As they strip notation and conjugation from the canon of *inventio*, Fraunce and Fenner suggest that the something else left over after you have pulled out any causal relation between things is a form that contributes to the beauty of your composition—"the pretty and conceipted chaunge of the woord" and "the elegancie that is in the diuers fallings and terminations of woords"—but with which you should not think. *Paronomasia* and *polyptoton* might hold an aesthetic value—they are "pretty" and bear "elegancie"—but they hold no epistemological value. The reduction of these forms to an aesthetic identifiable only as that which is superfluous to reason paradoxically points to and renders imminent the sort of mind that might think with the very something implied by Fenner's question—"But is there nothing els?" This kind of thinking might generate an entirely different set of coordinates for possible knowledge. Even as the aesthetic is denied epistemological value, the manner of that denial specifies the very forms by which this thinking takes place: the figures of *elocutio*. Fraunce and Fenner's specificity signals a compulsion to ignore the greater potentiality of figure. Thinking again of Solon's Law, this potentiality is figure's possession of and rights to a world that the art of dialectic does not recognize but is epistemologically rich all the same. At his most explicit, Fraunce calls the forms that structure this kind of thinking *fallacies*, and he describes their art as sophistry.¹⁰¹ He thereby reduces the potentiality of figure to *pseudo* or mock reason. They are "the abuse of Logike," by which a speaker pretends to knowledge by "deceiuing the simple with a glorious shew of counterfeit reasons."¹⁰² In this sense, to think with *paronomasia* looks a lot like reasoning from the fallacy of homonyms. Collectively, these fallacies constitute an art of "counterfeit reasons."¹⁰³

The conceptual category of the fallacy, however, is only the most explicit of efforts to identify, contain, and banish the operations characteristic of thinking with figure. Ramism offers the distillation of a tendency pervasive to humanist instruction in rhetoric at large where warnings about the uses and abuses of the figures of *elocutio* read as cautions and caveats. In *The Garden of Eloquence* (1593), for example, Henry Peacham warns that because of its "light and illuding forme," *paronomasia* "ought to be sparingly vsed, and especially in graue and weightie causes." "As the use ought to be rare," Peacham continues, "so the allusion ought not to be tumbled out at adventure."¹⁰⁴ In *Directions for Speech and Style*, Hoskins suggests that the figure is "pretty to play with among gentlewomen" but "otherwise it will best become the tuftaffeta orators to skip up and down the neighborhood of these words that differ more in sense than in sound, tending nearer to meter than to matter." This figure is not "true rhetoric," though preferred by the masses. Its popularity is, in fact, a sign of its unthinking: "And of a truth, if the times gives itself too much to any one flourish, it makes it a toy and bars a learned man's writings from it, lest it seem to come more of the general humor than the private judgment."[105] Neither Peacham nor Hoskins was a Ramist as Fraunce and Fenner were. Yet in their denigration of *paronomasia* as "light" and inappropriate for "weightie causes," in their resistance to the incidental causality of "adventure," in their opposition between "sence" and "sound," "meter" and "matter," we hear the same polemic around which the Ramists rallied. *Elocutio* has the capacity to direct the mind by subjecting thought to the method of its figures.

In the subsequent chapters of this book, I will widen the scope of my archive as I pursue the question of the relation of figure to thought, though I will continue to return to Ramism for the prismatic perspective it affords on early modern theories and methods of poetic composition.[106] In Part Two, I argue that Spenser's *Faerie Queene*, Sidney's *Arcadia*, and Mary Wroth's *Urania* locate the authority of their imaginative worlds in the figures of *elocutio*. In Chapter 4, *simile* becomes the primary instrument with which Spenser negotiates poetry's place between philosophy and history, producing his own variation on the Sidneian ideal, "such as might best be"; in Chapter 5, *antithesis* and its characteristic ability to maintain opposing entities in relation to one another (not unlike the force felt between reversed magnets) becomes both the defining physical law of the *Arcadia*'s world and that world's proof for the existence of the *poein*, or Poet-Maker; in Chapter 6, *periphrasis*, with its signature ability to speak of precisely that which it does not name, becomes a form of possession in the world of Wroth's *Urania*.

Before moving on to these case studies, however, the remainder of Part One seeks to understand how the theories and practices of humanist pedagogy cultivated attention to and affection for the very figures of *elocutio* that Ramism sought to marginalize. In theory, the canon of *inventio* was meant to govern the canon of *elocutio* (to rein in both style and its constitutive figures by subordinating them to the *telos* of its places). Humanist paradigms of composition therefore frequently proceed from a clear division between *inventio* and *elocutio*, and this division permits those paradigms to inscribe the logical priority of *inventio* across a temporal sequence of composition. The complex and dispersed practices of humanist pedagogy, however, encouraged students instead to conceive of figures of speech as *formulas* for composition. As both an index to the labor of poetic production and as the generative engines of composition, figures of speech achieved a peculiar imaginative and epistemological value. As *formulas* for composition, figures of speech establish the organizing logic of the poetic *heterocosms* that they also generate.

Epanodos in *The Faerie Queene*

But what, then, of the art of poetry? If the Ramists insisted that poetry did not permit for a unique kind of knowledge or a unique way of thinking, of what did they think the art of poetry consisted? The answer: meter. Where Sidney maintained in the *Defence* that verse was "but an ornament and no cause to poetry," arguing that "it is not rhyming and versing that maketh a poet," Temple offered this corrective in his *Analysis*: "if poetry is not defined as a fiction," then "the essential nature of poetry is comprised by meter."[107] In classical configurations, rhetoric and poetry intersect precisely at the canon of *elocutio*, where poetry is routinely treated as rhetoric's licentious companion. What is permitted to the orator only in small doses is granted to the poet in greater quantity, more often, and to a greater degree. From the perspective of the art of rhetoric, the poet might get away with a more elaborate artifice, one that would be *indecorous* for an orator. Where, however, poetry understands its Horatian end as to teach and delight, it both shares in the orator's constraints and takes on rhetoric's defensive posture toward philosophy. Moreover, both oration and poem become subject to the demands of a broader understanding of *decorum* that turns not only on the proper alignment of person, time, and place but also on an aesthetic ideal that establishes uniformity of proportion and design as the measure of plausibility.[108] The Ramist reduction of poetry to meter bypasses this classical negotiation: where poetry deals in the figures of *elocutio*, it is acting in its capacity as the art of rhetoric.

Neither Ramus nor his followers wrote a treatise on the art of poetry, but early in his discussion of *elocutio* in *The Arcadian Rhetorike*, Fraunce smuggles in a chapter on "verse and rime." Though he admits that the "dimension and measuring of sounds or words" is "belonging to Poets," he also suggests that it is nonetheless "vsed of Orators" when they deploy figures of speech that "doo sweetlie and fitlie sound among themselues," including *epizeuxis, anadiplosis, climax, anaphora, epistrophe, symploce, epanalepsis, epanados*, and *paronomasia*.[109] After treating these figures individually, Fraunce returns to the question of verse, but he does not justify his return on the same earlier grounds. "Before I leaue of to talk of these figures of woords," he writes, "I will heere confusedlie insert a number of conceited verses, sith all their grace & delicacie proceedeth from the figures aforenamed."[110] While Fraunce first suggests that poetry is a formal resource for figures of speech, he then reverses that priority by suggesting that poetry owes all of its "grace & delicacie" to the figures of *elocutio*.

Fraunce includes one stanza from Edmund Spenser's *Faerie Queene* among his examples of "conceited verses." The first three books of *The Faerie Queene* were not published until 1590. This selected stanza was therefore the poem's earliest entry into print: as the illustration of *poesie* that showcases the figures of *elocutio*. In *The Arcadian Rhetorike*, the following stanza is a lesson to a student setting out to learn the art of rhetoric and its figures of speech:

> Wrath, iealousie, griefe, loue, doo thus expell:
> > Wrath is a fire, and iealousie a weede,
> > Griefe is a floud, and loue a monster fell:
> > The fire of sparkes, the weede of little seede,
> > The floud of drops, the monster filth did breed:
> > But sparkes, seede, drops, and filth doo thus delay,
> > The sparks soon quench, the springing seed outweed,
> > The drops drie vp, and filth wipe cleane away.
> So shall wrath, iealousie, griefe, loue, die and decay.[111]

Of which figure or set of figures is this *poesie* an example? Fraunce does not specify, as he does with his subsequent example, where he argues that the *serpentina carmina*, so called "because they turne and winde themselues *in orbem* like a snake," is nothing but—"their only grace proceedeth from"— the figure of *epanalepsis*.[112] Oddly, this stanza from *The Faerie Queene* seems to make conspicuous use of a set of figures that Ramism does not include in its art of rhetoric or the canon of *elocutio*: the parallel clauses characteristic of *isocolon*, or the figure of *zeugma* (where the verb stated in one clause is understood in the other—"Wrath is a fire, and iealousie a weede, / Griefe is a floud, and loue a monster fell"). Perhaps even more strangely, this stanza is an excellent example of the figure of *epanodos*, which Fraunce does include in his treatise, but it is not an example of *epanodos* as Fraunce defines it. In the classical tradition, *epanodos* describes an orator as he "reiterates things that have already been said, and draws distinctions between them."[113] It is an instrument of amplification designed to partition copious discourse. The Ramist tradition, however, treats this figure's technique of reiteration only in its formal capacity as repetition. For the Ramist, *epanodos* describes the return of sound but without asserting that return's organizing function in discourse.[114] From the perspective of Ramism, this stanza from Spenser's *Faerie Queene* is an illustration of *epanodos* not insofar as it repeats words that bear sense but rather sounds that contribute to a "delicacie of speech."

Given the Ramist separation of figure from thought, it is interesting to find that in book 2 of *The Faerie Queene* the Palmer speaks this stanza. In Spenser's *allegory*, the Palmer seems to combine the virtue of Reason with the person of the schoolmaster. His name by *metonymy* suggests that the schoolmaster's relation to Reason is best represented by his instrument of discipline (the palmer, so called because, by way of another *metonymy*, it is a stick used to slap a student's palms).[115] At this moment in book 2, Phaon has just recounted his story of betrayal and bad judgment to Guyon and the Palmer. Guyon responds with the beginning of what promises to be an optimistic, motivational speech complete with a prescribed schedule of recovery—"all your hurts may soone through temperance be easd."[116] Except that the Palmer interrupts him:

> Then gan the Palmer thus, Most wretched man,
> That to affections does the bridle lend;
> In their beginning they are weake and wan,
> But soone through suff'rance growe to fearfull end;
> Whiles they are weake betimes with them contend:
> For when they once to perfect strength do grow,
> Strong warres they make, and cruell battry bend
> Gainst fort of Reason, it to ouerthrow:
> Wrath, gelosy, griefe, loue this Squyre haue laide thus low.
>
> Wrath, gealosie, griefe, loue do thus expell
> Wrath is a fire, and gealosie a weede,
> Griefe is a flood, and loue a monster fell;
> The fire of sparkes, the weede of little seede,
> The flood of drops, the Monster filth did breede:
> But sparks, seed, drops, and filth do thus delay;
> The sparks soone quench, the springing seed outweed,
> The drops dry up, and filth wipe cleane away:
> So shall wrath, gealosy, griefe, loue die and decay.[117]

If Guyon thinks Phaon might still have recourse to recovery through temperance, the Palmer knows that he is already a lost cause. The possibility that he might "expel" his "affections" before they do "cruell battery bend / Gainst fort of Reason" has already been foreclosed upon. If the Palmer's first imperative command—"do thus expel"—would seem to hold out on the possibility of recovery, his verse nonetheless gives equal assertion to the idea that what follows is an account of how passions expel reason, "thus," or in this way (you can get rid of the passions by dealing with them in their originating forms—as "sparkes," "seedes," and "drops"—but these forms are also an account of how those passions get into you in the first place, insinuating themselves by flying under your radar). The Palmer's second imperative command, "do thus delay," might seem to return to the possibility of action, but a phrase like "drops dry up" recasts that command onto the indicative, where the action belongs to the "drops" themselves. If this lesson is for Guyon, a corrective to the misplaced confidence with which he sought to assure Phaon, it is not entirely clear what Guyon is meant to learn.[118]

This is not the most elegant of Spenserian stanzas. It hardly seems typical of Spenser, though it is ripe for plucking from *The Faerie Queene* precisely because it is atypical, and it is easy to imagine why Fraunce selected it as an example of a stanza that owes its debt of "grace & delicacie" to figures of speech.[119] The form of *epanodos* becomes a spectacle of artificial construction where each of the passions—wrath, jealousy, grief, love—are held in apposition, as if standing side by side in an allegorical lineup where everyone is guilty: "Wrath, gealosie, griefe, loue do thus expel / Wrath is a fire, and gealosie a weede, / Griefe is a flood, and loue a monster fell." The second set of clauses—"The fire of sparkes, the weede of little seede, / The flood of drops, the Monster filth did breede"—culminates in a long-delayed verb that retroactively asks sparks, seeds, and drops to bear more figuration, or a different kind of figuration, than seems quite right. As Harry Berger Jr. has suggested, that final verb casts a gynophobia over the natural world and transforms love's climactic monster into the insidious cause of all: the Palmer's "rhetorical cure" is actually "a conspicuous allegorical whitewash."[120] And this is precisely the point: the conspicuous artifice of *epanodos* seems here to cast the Palmer's lesson as sophistry rather than reason, as if *epanodos* is itself the form by which the passions take over reason.

This is why, according to George Puttenham in the *Art of English Poesy* (1589), the "grave judges Areopagites . . . forbid all manner of figurative speeches" from their courtroom. Declaring figures to be "illusions to the mind and wresters of upright judgment," they conclude that "to allow such manner of foreign and colored talk to make the judges affectioned were all one as if the carpenter, before he began to square his timber, would make his square crooked."[121] It is worth pointing out, however, that the crooked square is not only an emblem of bad justice; it is also an instrument in the carpenter's toolbox. It is with the crooked square, for example, that a carpenter or stonemason is able to make archways.[122] Spenser deploys *epanodos* in the conspicuous manner of the Palmer's lesson only one other time in book 2 of *The Faerie Queene*:[123]

> Eftsoones they heard a most melodious sound,
> Of all that might delight a daintie eare,
> Such as attonce mote not on liuing ground,
> Saue in this Paradise, be heard elsewhere:
> Right hard it was, for wight, which did it heare,
> To read, what manner musicke that mote bee:
> For all that pleasing is to liuing eare,
> Was there consorted in one harmonee,
> Birdes, voices, instruments, windes, waters, all agree.
>
> The ioyous birdes shrouded in chearefull shade,
> Their notes vnto the voice attempred sweet;
> Th'Angelicall soft trembling voyces made
> To th'instruments diuine respondence meet:
> The siluer sounding instruments did meet
> With the base murmure of the waters fall:
> The waters fall with difference discreet,
> Now soft, now loud, vnto the wind did call:
> The gentle warbling wind low answered to all.[124]

The Bower of Bliss. The "melodious sound" designed to please "a daintie eare" defines the bower as a distinct *heterocosm* where "all that pleasing is to liuing eare, / was there consorted in one harmonee." The poem establishes the "harmonee" of the bower's world with *epanodos*: this is the figure that transforms the poet's claim—"Birdes, voices, instruments, windes, waters, all agree"—into the formal condition of this world's composition. If the bower is a kind of aesthetic bio-dome, *epanodos* defines the border that permits its peculiar environment to exist. *Epanodos*, however, does not contain so much as it coordinates: it draws relations among the entities that it treats by way of return and reiteration. Spenser's stanza itself registers the pressure of *epanodos* in its medial couplet: Does the reiterative form of *epanodos* introduce the perfection or the dissolution of the Spenserian stanza? Is that medial couplet an emblem of "harmonee" in the gentle gathering that it twice describes, or is its repetition of "meet" a sign of sterility? Spenser's rhyme doubles down on the logic of *epanodos*, where the variety of elements that compose this world—"Birdes, voices, instruments, windes, waters"—

contributes to "one harmonee" but only by way of iteration. The effect is that of a world defined by an increasingly finite lexicon and a narrowing range of reference. *Epanodos* threatens the poem with redundancy or even tautology.

In the bower, the thinking performed by figure supplies something like the physical laws of its imaginative world. This world is defined—not by boundaries (what lies within and what without)—but by the peculiar axes of relation that figure affords.[125] It is not that figures of *elocutio* are less restrictive than the places of *inventio*, though the sheer number of figures in manuals like Peacham's *Garden of Eloquence* suggests that they offer a wider array of options and configurations relative to the comparatively restricted number of places. Both the places and the figures constitute a set of generative constraints, but the articulation of the constraint as well as the relation it generates are different: *epanodos* instead of cause and effect. From the perspective of figure, the world is organized according to a distinct set of relations, and the distinctiveness of this set entails a shift in the parameters of possibility. In the bower, this shift looks like an occasion for impossible music, what John Hollander described as the bower's signature blend of various kinds of music that were in reality kept separate: "It is almost as if," he writes, "orders of type were coming together as they should, and in actuality could, never do."[126] Where modern critics have been inclined to read the moralizing force of Hollander's *should never* as Spenser's disavowal of the bower's poetics of excess, Hollander also admits for an alternative celebration of the bower's aesthetic resources. Beginning with Spenser's immediate imitators and through the nineteenth century, Spenser's sonic bower became "a triumph of total environmental contrivance."[127] The "contrivance" of figure permits for something in the bower that is impossible in "actuality." These moments of open artifice may seem stylistically atypical, but *The Faerie Queene* has to sound like the conspicuous version of itself in order to access what amounts to the physical laws of its universe. In these stanzas, *The Faerie Queene* turns itself inside out so as to examine its own joints or seams.[128] The poem looks inside, and what it sees is figure.

While we tend to think, following Aristotle, that conspicuous artifice is a violation of plausibility and therefore constitutes a failure of world making, Spenser's use of *epanodos* here supplies a distinct set of coordinates for the world of the bower.[129] If we consider that the bower bears within its *epanodos* a memory of the Palmer's lesson to Guyon, then it may be that the bower is offering its own moment of instruction: This is how poetry thinks.[130] Poetry makes use of forms from the arts of rhetoric and dialectic but not in order to reproduce logic within its domain.[131] This is not, as Temple or Fraunce might maintain, poetry acting in its capacity to double as the art of dialectic. Instead, the kind of thinking that *epanodos* performs returns us to Sidney's definition of poetry: *epanodos* sets the parameters of possibility for the bower by determining "what may be." This is the inventive capacity of figure that alchemy will take up in what Katherine Eggert has described as "the new old rhetoric."[132] For Eggert, poetry's conversion of the "brazen" world into the "golden" is alchemical because its species of *disknowledge* permits literature "to designate a new place for itself in the seventeenth century" where "fiction existing in a world of its own" is "not answerable to the requirements of the *civitas*."[133] Literature thus finds in alchemy its ability to surrender truth for pleasure.[134] But the standard of "what *might* be" is only slack if you take truth in whatever temporality (what was, what is, or what will be) to be the target at which poetry takes aim.[135] An alternative might be that poetic language speaks what is decidedly not true so as to make it possible to believe that things can be otherwise than they are.

Throughout this chapter, I have described the work of invention in its most technical (and restricted) sense, according to which the activity of invention takes place in the canon of *inventio* and is reducible to the places that constitute that canon. Yet as the figures of *elocutio* take over the work of the places of *inventio*, they also tilt invention toward its more modern sense of creation: the sense in which, as Roland Greene has put it, "Instead of answering to a reality principle such as matter, invention is . . . its own reality principle."[136] When George Gascoigne in *Certayne Notes of Instruction* (1575) advises the young man setting out to write a poem "to grounde it upon some fine inuention," the place of *inventio* that he specifies is already orienting away from the natural world: "some supernaturall cause whereby my penne might walke in the superlatiue degree."[137] Yet even in Gascoigne the relation of figure to invention is vexed. Gascoigne begins his treatise by distinguishing invention from *paroemion* (or alliteration), saying "it is not inough to roll in pleasant woordes, nor yet to thunder in *Rym, Ram, Ruff* by letter," and he subsequently warns: "Your Inuention being once deuised, take heede that neither pleasure of rime nor varietie of deuise do carie you from it."[138] By Gascoigne's account, invention is vulnerable to the vagrant drive of figure.

Thus begins our story of figure's secret capture of poetic invention.[139] By usurping the role traditionally reserved for the places of *inventio*, the figures of *elocutio* allowed poets to assert a distinction to (if not the autonomy of) their poetic worlds. Our accounts of early modern poetry and world making have tended to emphasize the plausibility of plot and narrative sequence where *verisimilitude* has to do with the determination of action and likelihood is established by the places of *inventio*.[140] By this account, figures of speech can only violate *verisimilitude* by drawing a reader's attention to the artificiality of the putatively natural temporal sequence on display. Or, we have read poetry's imperial ambitions alongside travel narratives with attention to the wonders that distinguish poetry's worlds from the reader's. By this account, figures of speech function in the way of the curiosity: they constitute a foreign or strange manner of talk imported back home (only to reveal that they've been there all along).[141] By attending to figures of speech as they take over the role of invention, we are able to say something about the field of possibility that underwrites both the construction of narrative and its display of curiosities. Instead of being the anomaly that threatens the plausibility of fiction, figures of speech might generate new parameters for possibility and establish an alternative set of coordinates for the imaginative worlds of early modern literature.

CHAPTER 2

Figure Pointing in the Humanist Schoolroom

This chapter is about an act that I call figure pointing: when one person takes up a poem made by another person and points at its artifice, as if with his finger. In the dedicatory letter to *Epitome of Tropes and Schemes* (1562), Johannes Susenbrotus says that figure pointing is something that he did a lot with his students: "I, indeed . . . have in the course of the reading pointed out clearly as though by my finger, to you and to other former students of mine, the ornaments of this sort of utterance."[1] This gesture might seem to give us humanism at its worst—the reduction of Cicero to form without substance and the cultivation of his iconic apes (bad practitioners who are also the sign of humanism's failure). Figure pointing suggests, however, something that is not true of figures of speech but is a compelling early modern fantasy about them. The act of figure pointing suggests that you can touch figures: that figures of speech, routinely likened to the tools of the mechanical arts (the carpenter's square or his line and level), are material instruments that a student can use to make another text.[2] The act of figure pointing is significant to humanist pedagogy as a moment of abstraction: it renders the particular reproducible. The schoolmaster holds up one peculiar sentence as the example of a form that can make another peculiar sentence or a whole schoolroom of sentences (all of them peculiar).

Figure pointing is among a set of pedagogical practices and techniques whereby humanists promoted their strange but defining claim: By recognizing the artifice out of which your poem is made, I can make a poem of my own. The materialist fantasy at the heart of figure pointing is that if you can touch a figure, then you can turn one text into the tools for composing another. Touch, here, is not tactile but discursive. You point at a figure as though with your finger when you recognize a distinct piece of artifice and name its distinction. That name—*paronomasia*, *polyptoton*, *epanodos*—treats the distinct piece of artifice as one of a kind and therefore as reproducible. It is precisely in the fantasy of their materiality that figures of speech become productive forms or what Susenbrotus called "*formulas*" for composition.[3] From the perspective of the student, the fantasy of figure pointing is the fantasy that I can transform the artifice of your poem into an instrument of my *poesie*. I can transfer your art into my own hands.

In the previous chapter, I argued that a lost legacy of humanism includes figure's secret capture of the places and protocols of the rhetorical canon of *inventio*. By guiding the act of invention, figures of speech become instruments of thinking and substitute their formal operations for the logical arguments characteristic of *inventio*. Figures of speech supply, that is, an alternative set of techniques for establishing the relations among things within a poetic world and for articulating the field of possibility within which those relations inhere: a world of "what may be."[4] Whereas Chapter 1 considered the work of figures of speech in humanist models of the mind and its disciplinary operations, this chapter will turn to the practices of humanist composition, especially those promoted by Elizabethan grammar schools as they translated these models of mind into quotidian habits of reading and writing. Early modern debates over the vexed relation between the arts of rhetoric and dialectic raised the specter of a mind that thinks with the figures of *elocutio* rather than the places of *inventio*, a mind that thinks with style rather than reason. In this chapter, I take a closer look at *indecorous* thinking by considering how figures of speech became *formulas* for composition.

My proposal that we think about figures as *formulas* cuts against the dominant way of defending figure against its reduction to mere flourish (garnish or garment). The traditional defense recovers figures by claiming that they are primarily significant for their capacity to represent a speaker's emotions and to reproduce those emotions in an audience.[5] The fiction of this transaction is that the speaker's emotion is not an effect of his speech act but its cause.[6] According to this defense, figures of speech had a paradoxical referential function: a figure of speech was said to make the passion to which it referred and against which its truth-value might be measured. A figure of speech was thus "true" to the extent that it was an accurate representation of the emotion it was said to produce. A figure of speech was "false" if it gave the lie to this transaction—if its artifice was so conspicuous that it did not appear to emerge out of a natural emotional state and thereby failed to produce that emotion in the listener. Instead of turning the audience into a like-feeling double for the speaker, conspicuous figures of speech alert the audience to the artificial mechanisms at work. They alert the audience, that is, to the labor of production.

In the following pages, I will take up a scene of figure pointing from Philip Sidney's *Old Arcadia* in order to sketch the contours of an art of eloquence dedicated to sheer or mere style. I will argue that Dorus's song to Pamela's empty glove provides the emblem of an art of affectation.[7] According to this art, the poet wields figures of speech not with the aim of delighting his audience or arousing their emotions but in the service of his own pleasure. I then turn to the grammar-school practices that cultivated this curious pleasure in figure by promoting a "preposterous" method of composition.[8] Where figures of speech take over the work of invention, they become *formulas* for composition and produce poems that their critics describe as a *poesie* dedicated to nothing at all. In the final section of this chapter, I return to Dorus's empty glove in order to consider how figures of speech chart the coordinates of an improbable world. *Indecorous* thinking trades in the parameters of plausibility characteristic of the category of fiction for those that generate the kind of speech that Donatus called "*vanus*": empty and implausible.[9] If the pleasure of conspicuous artifice alienates its audience, it is because *indecorous* thinking aligns the pleasure of the poet with the production of an imaginative world no sooner made than destroyed. Dorus's world is not built to last because it is not for an audience. What Dorus's audience calls "nothing" is the pleasure of a *poesie* that breaks from both profit and the community that would benefit from that profit. Dorus's *poesie* nonetheless extends an invitation to its audience: its conspicuous artifice gives the listener all that she needs to experience the pleasure of making for herself.

A World of One

In Sidney's *Old Arcadia*, the young prince Musidorus is dressed as a shepherd named Dorus, and he sits with his childhood friend Pyrocles, who is himself going around as an Amazonian princess named Cleophila. Under the sign of an ideal friendship, each prince communicates openly with the other because each is guaranteed that he will find himself replicated in his friend.[10] The speech of one prince transforms the other prince into a mirror: "a well-grounded object, from whence he shall be sure to receive a sweet reflection of the same joy, and (as in a clear mirror of sincere goodwill) see a lively picture of his own gladness."[11] In this way, the narrator sets us up for a scene of affective doubling according to which the sign of successful communication is the poet's ability to transform his auditor into an image of himself.[12] Things get a bit dicey, however, when Dorus whips out a single, empty glove (pilfered from his beloved Pamela). This glove disrupts the logic of the mirror in what amounts to the *Arcadia*'s version of the child's taunt, *I have something you don't have*: "But see whether you can show me," Dorus challenges his friend, "so fair spoils of your victory."[13] And with that, Dorus displays the glove he has been hiding in his bosom and sings the following song:

> Sweet glove, the witness of my secret bliss
> (Which hiding didst preserve that beauty's light
> That, opened forth, my seal of comfort is),
> Be thou my star in this my darkest night,
> Now that mine eyes their cheerful sun doth miss
> Which dazzling still, doth still maintain my sight;
>   Be thou, sweet glove, the anchor of my mind,
>   Till my frail bark his hav'n again do find.
>
> Sweet glove, the sweet despoils of sweetest hand,
> Fair hand, the fairest pledge of fairer heart,
> True heart, whose truth doth yield to truest band,
> Chief band, I say, which ties my chiefest part,
> My chiefest part, wherein do chiefly stand
> Those secret joys, which heav'n to me impart,
>   Unite in one, my state thus still to save;
>   You have my thanks, let me your comfort have.[14]

Cleophila does not find herself included in the "joys" of this poem. Its style does not invite her sympathetic participation with the poet. Instead, Cleophila sighs "Alas" after an extended pause and speaks the following reprimand: "Can you not joy sufficiently in your joys, but you must use your joys as if you would vauntingly march over your friend's miseries?"[15] The poem leaves Cleophila to feel only her "miseries" because its style is not generous with its "joy." This poem is invested in the pleasure of one.

Cleophila may not experience Dorus's emotions as if they are her own, but she does recognize the artifice that he wields. She recognizes, that is, both the fact of her exclusion and the mechanism by which Dorus hoards all of the "joy" for himself. With her phrase "vauntingly march over," Cleophila points to the figure of speech that organizes the second stanza of Dorus's song: *gradatio* or *climax* (a figure that was routinely associated with the ladder from which both the Greek and Latin names derive).[16] For example, George Puttenham describes *gradatio* in his *Art of English Poesy* (1589) as:

> Ye have a figure which, as well by his Greek and Latin originals, and also by allusion to the manner of a man's gait or going, may be called the Marching Figure, for after the first step all the rest proceed by double the space, and so in our speech one word proceeds double to the first that was spoken, and goeth as it were by strides or paces, it may as well be called the Climbing Figure, for *climax* is as much to say as a ladder.[17]

With the phrase "vauntingly march over," Cleophila sticks her finger in Dorus's poem.[18] She suggests that *gradatio* is the instrument with which the poet violates the very ideal he ought to maintain. Instead of affective doubling, *gradatio* permits Dorus to climb over his audience (or trample that audience beneath his prosodic feet). In this moment, figures of speech are not redeemable on traditional grounds: they do not build communities and they do not arouse pleasure in the service of profit.[19] The pleasure of this poem belongs to its maker rather than to his audience, and this pleasure serves to alienate that maker from rather than reinforce the logic of his immediate community.[20]

The narrator of the *Old Arcadia* invokes the familiar model of the art of rhetoric and the figures of *elocutio*—their ability to transform the listener into a "mirror" or a "lively picture" or an affective double for the speaker—only to dramatize Dorus's flagrant departure from this model. This asymmetrical departure stems from Dorus's claim to possess something that his listener does not possess—that empty glove. Dorus's *gradatio* calls on "hand," "heart," "band," "part," and, finally, "Those secret joys" to "Unite in one": the five degrees of his *climax* correspond to the five fingers of his empty glove. During his extensive discussion of figures of speech, Quintilian warned, "it is as ridiculous to hunt for figures without reference to the matter as it is to discuss dress and gesture without reference to the body."²¹ By conflating the material glove with the figure of *gradatio*, Sidney creates a formal emblem of style without matter even as he lends figures of speech the physical tangibility of a glove. Sidney literalizes the *metaphor* of style as garment, but he also absents from the scene of production the body that authorizes this *metaphor*. The absence of the beloved that characterizes the Petrarchan love lyric (a tradition rife with single, sweet gloves) turns into an experiment in stylistic copia.²² *Gradatio* becomes not a figure subordinate to matter or the body of reason but instead a peculiar object, both empty and tangible. When released from its subordinate position to matter (there is no hand in this glove) as well as the teleology of affective persuasion (this figure alienates the listener), what is it that *gradatio* does?

One answer to this question is a reorientation of *poesie* toward the pleasure of the poet. Part of Cleophila's point in her critique is that Dorus wields figure in the service of his own delight. Following upon the taunt— "But see whether you can show me so fair spoils of your victory"—Dorus "drew out a glove of Pamela done with murrey silk and gold lace, and (not without tender tears kissing it) he put it again in his bosom."²³ As "spoils," the glove is *metonymy* to a "victory" that the narrative does not otherwise describe. This would suggest that the glove is significant as a kind of evidence or a form of proof (Dorus's song will proceed to describe the glove as the "witness of my secret bliss," thereby attributing to the material object something like testimony). The brief space of that *parenthesis*, however, holds open the possibility that the glove is most significant as a *synecdoche* for Pamela herself.²⁴ As Dorus kisses the glove, or as his tears are kissing the glove (the physics of contact is left unclear), the glove becomes a kind of fetish, and Dorus trades in the glove's status as evidence of something else for its capacity to act as an immediate source of pleasure for himself. *Synecdoche* animates the glove in a bizarre moment of prosthesis for Pamela's genitalia.²⁵ By the time we ascend the final steps of Dorus's *gradatio*, we are dealing in autoeroticism:

> Sweet glove, the sweet despoils of sweetest hand,
> Fair hand, the fairest pledge of fairer heart,
> True heart, whose truth doth yield to truest band,
> Chief band, I say, which ties my chiefest part,
> My chiefest part, wherein do chiefly stand
> Those secret joys, which heav'n to me impart,
>   Unite in one, my state thus still to save;
>   You have my thanks, let me your comfort have.²⁶

The first two "degrees" of Dorus's *gradatio* raise the expectation of a blazon as we move from Pamela's "hand" to her "heart." Dorus's verse, however, pivots away from Pamela's body and toward his own by way of a "band" (decidedly abstract in comparison to the "hand" and "heart" that precede it). There is almost a kind of fumbling here, as if Dorus struggles to fill out the form to which the shape of Pamela's five-fingered glove has committed him. The next step in his rise rings of recovery with its exact repetition, "my chiefest part / My chiefest part, wherein do chiefly stand," and if the enjambment permits us to read Dorus's "stand" against the syntax of his preposition, the conclusion of Dorus's *gradatio* turns away from sexual climax and turns toward the form of the glove, a form that proleptically guarantees the fulfillment of Dorus's imperative command: "Unite in one." The redundancy of this command ("in one" simply repeats what "Unite" has already spoken) suggests something of the vulnerability of Dorus's poem. *Gradatio* is instrumental to the onanistic pleasure of a poet who forgets his audience and speaks directly to his own artifice.[27]

Early modern pedagogues routinely deployed a comparison, originally attributed to Zeno and most frequently cited from Cicero's *Orator*, to distinguish between the arts of rhetoric and dialectic: dialectic is like the clenched fist because it is the art with which you sock your listener in the face; rhetoric, by contrast, is like the open palm because it is the art with which you gently caress your listener.[28] While rhetoric's "hand set at large" was regularly praised because, as Richard Rainolde describes it in *The Foundacion of Rhetorike* (1563), "euery part and ioint is manifeste," Patricia Parker has shown how rhetoric's open palm easily slid into a figure for discursive promiscuity and grotesque female sexuality.[29] Dorus's empty glove offers us a variation on this commonplace. Separated from the human hand to which it belongs, Dorus's empty glove allows Sidney to imagine an art of affectation that abandons the naked body of *inventio*'s reason and practices *indecorous* thinking.

When figures of speech take over the procedures and protocols of invention, they permit the poet to establish axes of relation that are not reducible to the places of *inventio*. Compare, for example, Dorus's *gradatio* in *Astrophil and Stella* 1, where Astrophil's use of the same figure of speech names the place of *inventio* from which it takes its cue: "Pleasure might cause her read, reading might make her know; / Knowledge might pity win, and pity grace obtain."[30] Astrophil's *gradatio* takes advantage of the figure's formal homology with dialectic's *sorites* in order to provide something like an epitome of narrative.[31] In Sonnet 1, the degrees of *gradatio* express a chain of causation—"Pleasure might cause her read." At its most extreme, such a use of figure confirms Kenneth Burke's sense that the artifice of *elocutio* can command assent because the form reinforces the plausibility of the causal logic that both authorizes its artifice and reduces its visibility.[32] Dorus's *poesie*, however, does not construct plausibility or command assent on these same terms. The degrees of his *gradatio* are not expressions of logical relations generated by the places of *inventio*. Dorus's art does not instrumentalize the listener's "pleasure" with the aim of enfolding that listener into its narrative. Dorus's song—clumsy, awkward, wearing its artifice on its sleeve—is an alternate version of Astrophil's experiment and therefore requires us to expand our sense of Sidneian poetics and the ethical demands it places on its readers. This art is invested in the pleasure of its maker because its world is a world of one. Trading in affect for affectation, Dorus's song treats *gradatio* as both an engine of composition and a source of the poet's pleasure.[33]

Formulas *for Composition*

To hear Thomas Wilson tell it in *The Art of Rhetoric* (1560), the proper coordination of the canons of *inventio*, *dispositio*, and *elocutio* ought to follow as simple a chronology as getting dressed in the morning: "Whereas invention helpeth to find matter, and disposition serveth to place arguments, elocution getteth words to set forth invention and with such beauty commendeth the matter that reason seemeth to be clad in purple, walking afore both bare and naked."[34] That figures of speech come after *inventio* is here a given: the "bare and naked" body of reason preexists the "purple" garment that *elocutio* provides. Wilson's purpose is to praise *elocutio* and its figures in the face of detractors, but this morning routine transcribes the logical priority that I examined in Chapter 1 onto a temporal sequence that structures the compositional process. You derive your arguments or generate your ideas, and then you dress them up in figures of speech.

But surviving early modern curricula as well as treatises on grammar-school education record the widespread practice of teaching students to work with the figures of *elocutio* before introducing them to the places of *inventio*.[35] The influential humanist John Sturm, for example, advised that "*elocutio* ought to precede the method of *inventing*, because the individual ornaments of speech are easier to be learned: besides, *inventio* is more easily used in the beginning by boys naturally while writing than it can be understood by them from teaching."[36] In spite of the traditional paradigm of composition, a student might thus first study the figures of *elocutio* as a distinct language for artifice and style; by contrast, his initial engagement with the places of *inventio* might not simultaneously be theorized as such. If a student later learns to distinguish an argument as deriving from this or that place of *inventio*, his earliest encounter with the argument might be as a kind of byproduct or even as the occasion for his lesson in *elocutio*. That "if" is genuine: given the attrition rate at early modern grammar schools, a student's education was far more likely to stop short of a formal introduction to *inventio* than it was to extend beyond it.[37] The temporality of the grammar-school curriculum therefore cut against the logical priority that underwrote the traditional paradigm of composition. Schoolroom practices threatened to subordinate *inventio* to *elocutio*. The specter is one of empty, animated clothing.

While theories of composition insisted that students subordinate the figures of *elocutio* to the places of *inventio*, exercises dedicated to the practice of composition taught students to value the figures of *elocutio* independently from the places of *inventio*. A student's earliest formal introduction to figures of speech would probably have been in Lily's *Grammar*, which defines *figura* as "a kinde of speaking on som new fashion" and presents the student with a small subset of figures, including the six species of *metaplasm* and "figures of construction" such as *prolepsis* and *asyndeton*.[38] Knowledge of this subset of figures—sometimes called grammatical schemes—was necessary to perform the advanced stages of grammatical analysis. Confronted with a sentence out of Cicero's *De Senectute*, a prompted student might answer (and ideally learn to ask himself) a series of questions about his translation:

> *Scipio ô* Scipio, *et* and, *Læli ô* Lelius, *artes* arts, *exercitationesque* and exercises, *virtutum* of vertues, *sunt* are, *omnino* altogether, *arma aptissima* the fittest weapons, *senectutis* of old age [the sentence goes on but this fragment is illustrative of the process].[39]

According to John Brinsley's *Ludus Literarius* (1612), a student ought to give the reason for every word, and his account of the main verb *sunt* should sound something like: "*Sunt* is next, agreeing with the Nominative case *artes exercitationesque*; by *Verbum personale cohæret cum Nominatiuo &c.* It is expressed to the one Nominatiue case, and vnderstood to the other, by the figure *Zeugma*."[40] The figure of speech known as *zeugma* explains the reason why "arts" and "exercises" can share the verb "are": "It is expressed to the one . . . and understood to the other." *Zeugma* is the name of the figure that acts as a rule. This rule both permits for and renders reproducible the form of Cicero's sentence.

The figures of speech in Lily's *Grammar* functioned like a curricular pivot between the art of grammar and the art of rhetoric, where they would reappear as one subset among many within the canon of *elocutio*.[41] After an afternoon studying lessons out of Cicero or Virgil "by construing and other grammaticall waies, examining all the rhetorical figures," students at Westminster School would return from a one-hour recess to repeat "a leafe or two out of some booke of Rhetorical figures or choice proverbs and sentences collected by the M^r for that use."[42] Brinsley advised schoolmasters to make their students "perfect in Talaeus Rhetorick," which means to have them memorize the definition of each trope and figure as well as one or two short illustrative examples "so that they can giue the word or words, wherein the force of the rule is."[43] The student should then "be careful to keepe a short Catalogue in his minde, of the names of the Tropes and also Figures (and those both of Grammar and Rhetoricke)" so that "hee shall with practice of examination and obseruation be able to tell any of them, but repeating the heads in his minde."[44] In *On Education* (1531), Juan Luis Vives advises schoolmasters to take the "table of figures of speech" provided in Mosellanus's *Table of Schemes and Tropes* and hang it "on the wall so that it will catch the attention of the pupil as he walks past it, and force itself upon his eyes."[45]

At more advanced forms, the schoolroom practice of *analysis* gave way to annotations attending only to "those which haue most difficulty; as Notations, Deriuations, figuratiue Constructions, Tropes, Figures, and the like." "What they feare they cannot remember by a marke," Brinsley continues, "cause them to write those in the Margent in a fine hand, or in some little booke."[46] Once a student advances to the very highest forms, he ought "to obserue onely for breuity sake the difficulties of Grammar or Rhetorick, speciall phrases, or the like," while the schoolmaster might limit his instruction in parsing to "the like speeches: *Hae sunt difficultates Grammatica. Hae elegentiae Rhetorices*" or, when speaking of poetry, "*Phrases hae: Epitheta ista*."[47] While early stages of *analysis* assumed a flat model of significance (where every word is a word in need of explanation), the more advanced stages of *analysis* and its companion exercises honed in on a small group of persistent "difficulties" that included figures of speech. Figures of speech were thus a foundation of reading and composition from which a student never quite moved on. He circled back to the figures, pulled by the centripetal force of the schoolmaster's pointing finger.

The practice of analysis taught students to identify figures of speech as productive forms or *formulas* for composition. A figure of speech lent a name to both the particular form of the sentence at hand and to the principle of that form's abstraction and reproducibility. Where a figure like *gradatio* supplies a name to a rule of composition, it also specifies the form by which a student might make a new sentence of his own. In short, a figure like *gradatio* becomes a *formula* when it acts as an instrument by which one particular sentence might become many different sentences. The *formula* transforms the figure of speech into a generative constraint. When a reader names a figure in the margin, that reader treats art as a set of practices that can be both the object of *analysis* and an engine of what the pedagogical tradition called "*genesis*." Gabriel Harvey thought about the move from *analysis* to *genesis* by analogy to clothing: "When we inspect it to see whether it was skillfully made, and how well-fitting or attractive or costly it is, or even tear the stitching of the garment to examine within, this is a kind of Analysis. But when we ourselves . . . make clothing, it is Genesis."[48] The "vnmaking" is the permitting condition for a "making" that is always a "making" again.[49] While a student's final product ought, as Roger Ascham wrote in *The Schoolmaster* (1570), to resemble the exemplary by exhibiting "the like shape of eloquence," the priority of figures as both an object of *analysis* and an engine of *genesis* threatened, as Jeff Dolven has put it, "to inevitably obscure wholes by a multiplication of bright parts."[50] Where figures of speech become *formulas* for composition, they prioritize process over product—in Ben Jonson's words, "the doing" over "the thing done"—and promote an aesthetic of conspicuous artifice and maximum labor.[51]

Where figures become *formulas*, they require us to rethink some of the ways in which we account for humanism's signature investment in the move from reading to writing. Scholarship in book history and the history of reading has taught us to recognize what Anthony Grafton and Lisa Jardine call "goal-orientated reading," but archival evidence also suggests that figures of speech might act as formal fulcrums between the activities of reading and writing.[52] These moments encourage us to think of the collection of *sententiae* not only as the gathering of sayings but also as the activation of *formulas*.[53] In the third volume of a copy of *Cicero's Orations* (1532), an early reader names occasional key words as well as a series of figures and tropes at work in the popular *Pro P. Sestio*: including *articulus*, *repetitio*, and *occupatio*.[54] The right margin of one of the more marked pages reads (descending along the page): *ironia*, *metaphora*, *allegoria*, *nobilitas*, *memoria*, *similiter desinentes*, *articulus* (see Figure 1). The notation "*nobilitas*" is the kind of heading we might expect to find in the commonplace

PRO P. SESTIO.

tanq̃ Atlante cęlum niti videretur. Erat deniq̃ hic
omnium sermo:est tamē Reipu.magnum firmūq̃ *ironia*
subsidiũ, habeo quē opponā labi illi, atq̃ cœno.vul
tu mediussidius collegę sui libidinē leuitatēq̃ fran
get.habebit Senatus in hũc annũ quē sequatur.nõ
deerit author & dux bonis. mihi deniq̃ homines
pręcipue gratulabantur, quòd habiturus essem cõ-
tra Tribunũ ple.furiosum,& audacem,cũ amicum
& affinem, tum etiã forte & graue consulem. Atq̃
eorũ alter fefellit neminē.quis enim clauũ tāti im- *metaphora*
perij tenere, & gubernacula Reip.tractare in maxi
mo cursu ac fluctibus posse arbitraretur hominem
emersum subito ex diuturnis tenebris lustrorũ ac
stuprorũ,vino,ganeis,lenocinijs,adulterijsq̃ confe
ctum?cũ is præter spem in altissimo gradu alienis
opibus positus esset, qui non modo tempestatē in- *allegoria*
tueri impendentē temulentus, sed ne lucē quidem
insolitam aspicere posset. Alter multos planè in o-
mnes partes fefellit.erat enim hominum opinioni
nobilitate ipsa blāda cōciliatricula cōmēdatus.O-
mnes boni semper nobilitati fauemus, & quia vti- *nobilitas.*
le est Reip.nobiles homines esse dignos maiorib⁹
suis, & quia valet apud nos clarorũ hominũ senex *memoria.*
de Repu.meritorũ memoria, etiã mortuorũ.quia
eum tristem semper, quia taciturnũ, quia subhorri-
dum atq̃ incultũ videbāt, & q̃ erat eo nomine, vt *similiter de f...*
ingenerata familiæ frugalitas videretur, fauebant, *...tes.*
gaudebant,& ad integritatē maiorum spe sua ho
minem vocabant, materni generis obliti.Ego autē
vere hoc dicā Iud.tantũ esse in homine sceleris, au- *artificium.*
daciæ, crudelitatis, quātum ipse cum Repu.sensi,
nunq̃ putaui. Nequā esse hominē & leuem,& falsa opinione, errore hominũ ab adolescentia com-

bbb j

Figure 1. *M.T. Ciceronis Orationum* (Pariis: Apud Simonem Colinaeum, 1532), 3b₁r. Photo Courtesy of The Newberry Library Chicago. Call # Wing ZP 539 C674.

THE COVNTESSE OF PEMBROKES
ARCADIA, VVRITTEN BY
SIR PHILIP SIDNEI.

The firſt Booke.

T was in the time that the earth begins to put on her new apparell againſt the approch of her louer, and that the Sun running a moſt euen courſe, becomes an indifferent arbiter betweene the night and the day; when the hopeleſſe ſhepheard *Strephon* was come to the ſands, which lie againſt the Iſland of Cithera;where viewing the place with a heauy kind of delight, and ſometimes caſting his eyes to the Iſleward, he called his friendly riuall, the paſtor *Claius* vnto him, and ſetting firſt downe in his darkened countenance a dolefull copie of what he would ſpeake: O my *Claius*, ſaide he, hither we are now come to pay the rent, for which we are ſo called vnto by ouer-buſie Remembrance, Remembrance, reſtleſſe Remembrance, which claymes not only this dutie of vs, but for it will haue vs forget our ſelues. I pray you when we were amid our flocke, and that of other ſhepheards ſome were running after their ſheepe ſtraied beyond their bounds, ſome delighting their eyes with ſeeing them nibble vpon the ſhort & ſweet graſſe, ſome medicining their ſicke ewes, ſome ſetting a bell for an enſigne of a ſheepiſh ſquadron, ſome with more leaſure inuenting new games of exerciſing their bodies and ſporting their wits: did Remembrance graunt vs any holiday, either for paſtime or deuotion, nay either for neceſſary foode or naturall reſt? but that ſtill it forced our thoughts to worke vpon this place, where we laſt (alas that the word laſt ſhould ſo long laſt) did graze our eyes vpon her euer floriſhing beautie: did it not ſtill crie within vs? Ah you baſe minded wretches, are your thoughts ſo deeply bemired in the trade of ordinary worldlings, as for reſpect of gaine ſome paultry wooll may yeeld you, to let ſo much time paſſe without knowing perfectly her eſtate, eſpecially in ſo troubleſome a ſeaſon? to leaue that ſhore vnſaluted, from whence you may ſee to the Iſland where ſhe dwelleth? to leaue thoſe ſteps vnkiſſed wherein *Vrania* printed the farewell of all beautie? Wel then, Remembrance commaunded, we obeyd, & here we find, that as our remembrance came euer cloathed vnto vs in the forme of this place, ſo this place giues new heate to the feauer of our languiſhing remembrance. Yonder my *Claius*, *Vrania* lighted, the verie horſe (me thought) bewayled to be ſo disburdned: and as for thee, poore *Claius*, when thou wentſt to help her downe, I ſaw reuerence and deſire ſo deuide thee, that thou didſt at one inſtant both bluſh and quake, and in ſtead of bearing her, weart readie to fall

A

Figure 2. Philip Sidney, *The Countess of Pembroke's Arcadia* (1598), Ar. Photo Courtesy of The Newberry Library Chicago. Call # Case Y 1565. S556.

down thy selfe. There she sate, vouchsafing my cloake (then most gorgeous) vnder her: at yonder rising of the ground shee turned her selfe, looking backe toward her woonted abode, and because of her parting, bearing much sorrow in her eyes, the lightsomnesse whereof had yet so naturall a cherefulnesse, as it made euen sorrow seeme to smile; at that turning shee spake to vs all, opening the cherrie of her lips, and Lord how greedily mine eares did feed vpon the sweete words she vttered? And here she laide her hand ouer thine eyes, when shee saw the teares springing in them, as if shee would conceale them from other, and yet her selfe feele some of thy sorrow: But woe is me, yonder, yonder, did shee put her foote into the boate, at that instant, as it were diuiding her heauenly beautie, betweene the Earth and the Sea. But when she was imbarked, did you not marke how the windes whistled, and the seas daunst for ioy, how the sailes did swell with pride, & all because they had *Vrania*? O *Vrania*, blessed be thou *Vrania*, the sweetest fairnesse and fairest sweetnesse: with that word his voice brake so with sobbing, that he could say no further; and *Claius* thus answered; Alas my *Strephon* (said he) what needes this skore to recken vp onely our losses? What doubt is there, but that the sight of this place doth call our thoughts to appeare at the court of affection, held by that racking steward, Remembrance? Aswell may sheepe forget to feare when they spie woolues, as we can misse such fancies, when we see any place made happie by her treading. Who can choose that saw her but thinke where she stayed, where she walkt, where she turned, where she spoke? But what is all this? truely no more, but as this place serued vs to thinke of those things, so those things serue as places to call to memorie more excellent matters. No, no, let vs thinke with consideration, and consider with acknowledging, & acknowledge with admiration, & admire with loue, and loue with ioy in the midst of all woes: let vs in such sort thinke, I say, that our poore eyes were so inriched as to behold, & our lowe hearts so exalted as to loue a maide, who is such, that as the greatest thing the world can shewe, is her beautie, so the least thing that may be praised in her, is her beautie. Certainly as her eye-lids are more pleasant to behold, then two white kiddes climbing vp a faire tree, and browsing on his tendrest branches, and yet are nothing, compared to the day-shining starres contained in them; and as her breath is more sweete then a gentle South-west wind, which comes creeping ouer flowrie fieldes and shadowed waters in the extreame heate of sommer, and yet is nothing, compared to the hony flowing speach that breath doth carrie: no more all that our eyes can see of her (though when they haue seene her, what else they shall euer see is but drie stubble after clouers grasse) is to be matched with the flocke of vnspeakeable vertues, laid vp delightfully in that best builded fold. But in deed as we can better consider the sunnes beautie, by marking how he guildes these waters and mountaines, then by looking vpon his owne face, too glorious for our weake eyes: so it may be our conceits (not able to beare her sun-stayning excellencie) will better way it by her workes vpon some meaner subiect employed. And alas, who can better witnesse that then we, whose experience is grounded vpon feeling? hath not the onely loue of her made vs (being silly ignorant shepheards) raise vp our thoughts aboue the ordinary leuell of the world, so as great clearks doe not disdaine our conference? hath not the desire to seeme worthie in her eyes, made vs when others were sleeping, to sit viewing the curse of heauens? when others were running at base, to runne ouer learned writings, when other marke their sheepe, we to marke our selues? hath not she throwne reason vpon our desires, and, as it were giuen eyes vnto *Cupid*? hath in any, but in her, loue-fellowship maintained friendship

Figure 3. Philip Sidney, *The Countess of Pembroke's Arcadia* (1598), Av. Photo Courtesy of The Newberry Library Chicago. Call # Case Y 1565. S556.

book described by Erasmus in *On Copia*.⁵⁵ The word "*nobilitas*" shifts the reader from *analysis* to *genesis* by suggesting that what is significant about Cicero's sentence is its capacity to supply subject matter (the reasons why "all virtuous men naturally look with favor on noble birth"). Notations like "*similiter desinentes*," by contrast, are not quite so teleological. Routinely likened to rhyme in early modern poetics, *similiter desinentes* describes the repetition of case endings in Cicero's sentence.⁵⁶ This notation also acts as a pivot between *analysis* and *genesis*, but what it designates as significant about Cicero's sentence does not belong to the schematic organization of knowledge characteristic of Erasmus's commonplace book. This notation distinguishes the part from the whole in order to render that part a *formula*, to instrumentalize it as an engine of composition. "*Similiter desinentes*" holds Cicero's text up to a different light. From the perspective of the *formula*, Cicero's sentence is significant because it is an empty scheme.

While figure pointing in grammar schools attended to Latin texts like Cicero's orations, the early reception history of Sidney's revised *Arcadia* suggests that it was read, along with Edmund Spenser's *Faerie Queene*, as a handbook of style (and Sidney, as a vernacular Tully).⁵⁷ The early pages of a 1598 edition of Sidney's revised *Arcadia* are filled with the manuscript notations of tropes and figures, ranging from *epanodos* to *prosopopoeia* to *antimetabole* (see Figure 2).⁵⁸ In these early pages of the romance, two shepherds grieve over the departure of their beloved Urania; in the margin alongside a sentence in which Claius checks Strephon's grief, this reader identifies an instance of *gradatio* with reference to its Greek synonym, "Climax with a touche of Anad[iplosis]" (see Figure 3):

> No, no, let vs thinke with consideration, and consider with acknowledging, & acknowledge with admiration, & admire with loue, and loue with ioy in the midst of all woes.⁵⁹

"Climax with a touche of Anad[iplosis]": this is the language of a recipe or receipt. It is reminiscent of imagery that casts figures of speech as a "garnish" or a "spice"—what Susenbrotus calls "some added condiment."⁶⁰ Its ambition is to break style down into its component figures: "climax with a touche"—with a dash, with a pinch—of *anadiplosis*. Where the language of the condiment would seem to maintain the traditional model of composition, I want to suggest that this notation nonetheless holds open the possibility of a meal made entirely from sugar and spice.⁶¹

In a notebook dedicated to the selection of *sententiae* from sixteenth-century prose romances, we encounter another reader who responded to

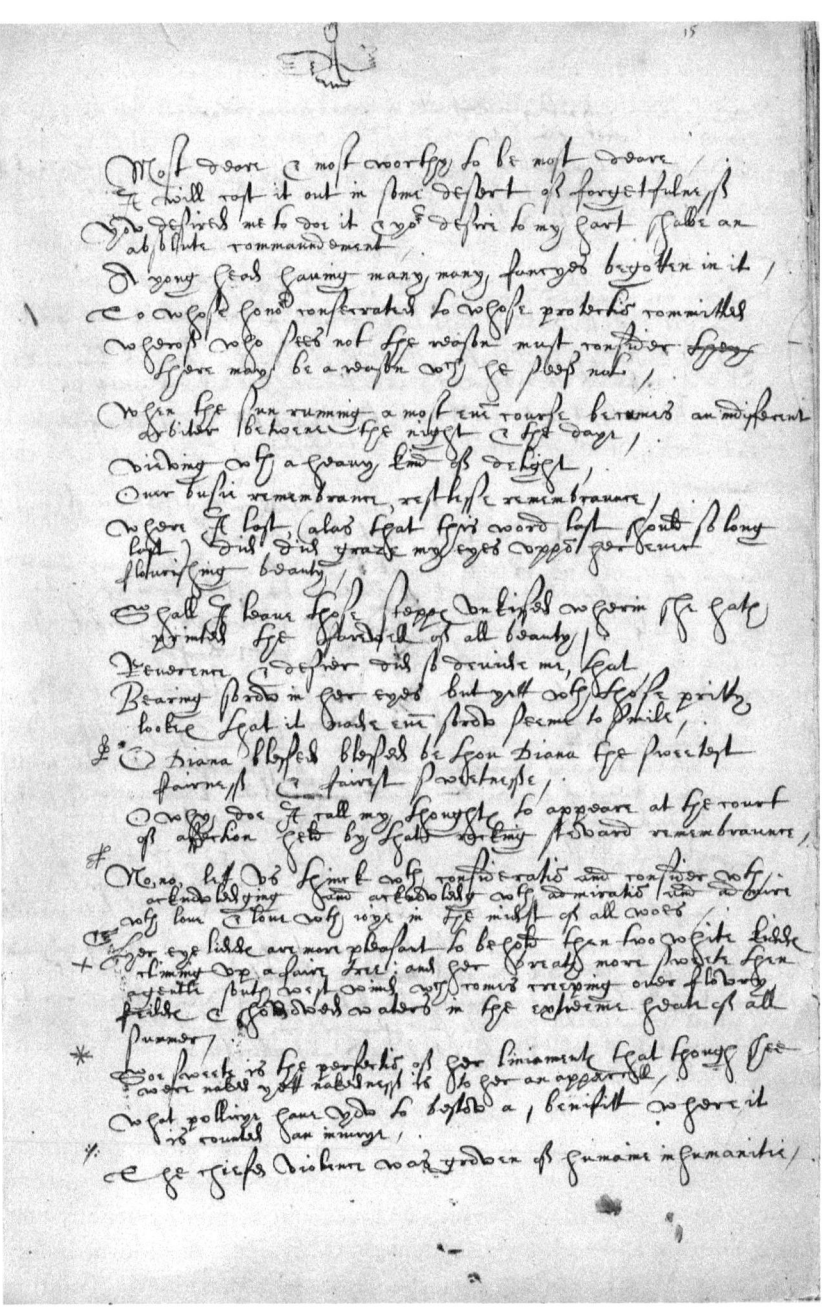

Figure 4. Selections from Philip Sidney's *The Countess of Pembroke's Arcadia*, in a prose miscellany (c. 1610), fol. 15r. Folger Shakespeare Library Shelfmark: Folger V.b.83. Used by Permission of the Folger Shakespeare Library.

largely the same set of tropes and figures in the early pages of Sidney's revised *Arcadia*.[62] This reader selected sentences from a series of romances that he then systematically decontextualized by turning dependent clauses independent or by stripping passages of their Arcadian specificity.[63] This compiler did not, as the Newberry reader did, name the figures that shape Sidney's prose, but, as Heidi Brayman has observed, he is especially attentive to "rhetorical extravagances."[64] For example, he faithfully transcribes the sentence alongside which our previous reader wrote "Climax with a touche of anad[iplosis]" (see Figure 3). The close correlation between the figures that one reader chose to name and another reader chose to transcribe is striking, but I am especially interested in a fleeting moment of transcription error. In the 1598 edition, the manuscript note alongside the following sentence reads "Antimetabole" (related to the more familiar *chiasmus*): "O *Vrania*, blessed be thou *Vrania*, the sweetest fairnesse and the fairest sweetnesse" (see Figure 4). "Antimetabole" here points to the chiastic structure that would have Urania's fairness exhibit superlative sweetness and her sweetness exhibit superlative fairness. When the notebook compiler transcribed this sentence, he transformed "Urania" into "Diana" (in keeping with his impulse to make the particular more generic), but he also doubles the chiastic structure: "O Diana blessed blessed be thou Diana the sweetest fairness & fairest sweetness." With the repetition of "blessed," this compiler makes two *antimetabole* where before there was one. As Brayman suggests, this reader had a particular appreciation for "chiasmuses and sentences with other nifty reverses."[65] This reader transforms Sidney's prose, making more of the original by redoubling on the original (while also turning a blessing into a tautology).

The reader of the Newberry copy names Sidney's tropes and figures; the commonplace book compiler transcribes examples of those tropes and figures. In one final example, those same tropes and figures are fully activated as *formulas* for composition. Garvis Markham opens *The English Arcadia* (1607) by taking up Sidney's *Arcadia* as his stylistic model.[66] The two shepherds who open Markham's text, Carino and Credulo, are curiously conscious of the fact that their laments sound like the laments of others: "Haue not we succeeded both in our loues and admirations, the truely louing *Strephon* and *Claius* whose induring constancies, & forlorne indurances, heaued their *Vrania* beyond the degree of superlatiue?"[67] Pointing to the "love" and "admiration" of their predecessors, Carino and Credulo proceed to shape their speech with the same figure of speech. It is as if the following sentence says what a contemporary reader might write in the margin, *climax, with a touch of anadiplosis*:

> no, no my *Credulo*, it was Vertue that brought foorth wonder, wonder knowledge, knowledge loue, and loue the eternitie of our neuer to be slaine affection.[68]

Markham turns Sidney's sentence the seamy side out and generates a new sentence. He treats Sidney's *gradatio*, that is, as a *formula* for composition.

Reading figures as *formulas* takes seriously philosophy's charge that rhetoric deals in empty ornaments. As it circulates in early modern England, this charge routinely compares *indecorous poesie* to shadows, echoes, and bladders full of wind.[69] William Scott provides an unlikely emblem for this art of affection in *The Model of Poesy* (c. 1599) when he compares excessive love for rhetorical ornaments to the nightingale's song: "For their poems, a man may afford them all the commendaitons a Lacedaemonian gave the nightingale when, having heard her sweet voice and seen her little body, he cried out, 'A voice and nought else': so are their works bare sounds without any proportion of substance in them."[70] "A voice and nought else" is the flip side of "the voice of the shuttle": the achievement of silence is reduced to a lack of meaning.[71] Yet even as they seem to dismiss the products of *indecorous* thinking, such images concede this one point: the "nothing" of which these images speak is a production.[72]

The word that Cleophila uses to describe Dorus's conspicuous artifice is the *vaunt*: "Can you not joy sufficiently in your joys but you must use your joys as if you would vauntingly march over your friend's miseries?"[73] With this adverb, Cleophila locates Dorus's curious joys in discourse: to "vaunt" is "to boast or brag; to use boastful, bragging, or vainglorious language." It derives from the Latin *vanus*, which means something like "vain."[74] More literally, the word's etymology posits a peculiar ontology to the vaunt. The vaunt is a language that "contains nothing." It is "empty, void, vacant."[75] As Quintilian explains in his discussion of *enargeia* (or vividness), "with things which are false and incredible by nature there are but two alternatives: either they will move our hearers with exceptional force because they are beyond the truth, or they will be regarded as empty nothings [*vanis*] because they are not the truth."[76] Cleophila's rebuke ties Pamela's pilfered glove to Dorus's figure of speech by pointing out that they are both—glove and *gradatio*—empty. Their forms lend a shape to something other than the truth. Another way to think about this emptiness might be to say that Dorus's style—"vauntingly"—and the figure of speech with which he generates that style—*gradatio*—clear out space for (make room in the romance for) nothing. If we think about the action of vaulting to which Cleophila's choice of words alludes, then the emptiness of Dorus's style is also a species of motion: "vauntingly march over."

The stakes of this claim come into focus if we think about the "vain" as a category of speech alongside the more familiar categories of fiction and falsehood. In his *Commentary* on Terence's *Eunuchus*, Donatus developed three categories of speech that would carry into the English schoolroom through Landino's commentary on Horace's *Art of Poetry* and Nicholas Udall's *Floures for Latine* (1533): *fictum, falsum,* and *vanum*.[77] *Fictum* or fictional speech describes what did not take place but might take place (fictional speech is not true but is plausible or like the truth). *Falsum* or false speech shares fiction's quality of being *verisimilar*, except that it is a lie (false speech asserts to have taken place what did not in fact take place). In contrast to both the *fictum* and the *falsum*, *vanum* is the word Donatus reserves for speech that names neither what is plausible nor even what is possible (*nec possibile nec verisimile*). *Vanum* or "vain" speech—speech that is "empty, void, vacant"—describes what could not even be made to happen.[78] We "delight" in the *fictum*. We are "deceived" by the *falsum*. We "despise"—where "*contemnimus*" means that we treat our object as "unimportant or of small value"—the *vanum*, which is *stultifictum* ("foolish, senseless, and without reason").[79] In his *Commentary* on the opening sequence of Horace's *Art of Poetry*, Landino distinguishes the "vain" (*vanae*) or "empty" from what is "feigned" (*finguntur*): where "feigned" compositions "did not occur, but could have done," "empty" compositions feature "things which cannot occur."[80] Vain poetry and the conspicuous artifice of its figures of speech deal in what is decidedly *improbable*.

Nothing But

In the dialogue following Dorus's song, Cleophila offers a second rebuke of Dorus's *poesie*, this time from a modified angle. Cleophila questions the idea that the glove evidences Pamela's hand and, therefore, Dorus's "victory." Cleophila "would fain know what assurance you have of the changing favour of fortune." She clarifies: "I have heard of them that dreamed much of holding great treasures, and when they waked found nothing in their hands but a bedstaff."[81] From Cleophila's perspective, what is significant about the glove is not what it once contained but that it is now empty. Dorus's dream is "nothing . . . but" the trifle that lends it a shape. Yet Cleophila's comparison of the glove to the "bedstaff" grants that glove a peculiar power because it is instrumental to the generation of his dream. When Cleophila tells Dorus that he has "nothing" in his "hands but a bedstaff," she sticks a pin in Dorus's balloon. What his dream calls "great treasures" she calls "nothing." Her subsequent qualification, however, identifies the very form that Dorus's dream shares with Cleophila's reality. The empty glove and the figures of speech for which it stands are both the material remainder to and the permitting condition for Dorus's imaginative world.

The art of affectation for which the empty glove acts as an emblem begins not with the places of *inventio* but with the figures of *elocutio* and produces what we might call, in an adaptation of Jeffrey Walker, the *figural fantasia*.[82] Within this preposterous model of composition, figures of speech chart a unique poetic domain or dominion. In the *Defence of Poesy* (c. 1580), Sidney called this unique domain—the product of a mode that "nothing affirms"—a "golden world"; in the *Old Arcadia*, Cleophila calls it an erotic dream.[83] As Dorus pays tribute to Pamela's pilfered glove, his song produces a version of Horace's chimera: "a book, whose idle fancies (*vanae*) shall be shaped like a sick man's dreams, so that neither head nor foot can be assigned to a single shape."[84] Dorus's third hand (which is also a prosthetic for Pamela's genitalia) departs from the unity of form that underwrites Horatian aesthetics and its measure of *decorum*.

In Chapter 3, I will take up the problem of conspicuous artifice in relation to Renaissance theories of *decorum* and the unity of form that they demand, but for the remainder of this chapter, I want to follow through on the logic—which is to say, the figure—of Dorus's dream. From Cleophila's perspective, Dorus's dream is empty—it consists of "nothing"—yet the "bedstaff" that follows her adversative turn pinpoints the very mechanism by which he produces "nothing." *Gradatio* is the instrument of *poesie* that both facilitates Dorus's pleasure and organizes his dream. Dorus's five-fingered glove permits him to speak precisely of impossibilities: a world of what cannot be. *Gradatio* is the figure of speech that marks out the boundaries and asserts the existence of this implausible world.

Because of the repetition that organizes its form, classical and early modern theorists describe *gradatio* as if it is always pushing past the boundaries of plausibility by drawing attention to its own artifice. Quintilian wrote that *gradatio* "necessitates a more obvious and less natural application of art and should therefore be more sparingly employed."[85] John Hoskins similarly warned in *Directions for Speech and Style* (c. 1601) that "in penned speech" *gradatio* "is too academical," though he adds that "in discourse" it is "more passable and plausible."[86] Humanists responded to the problem of *gradatio*'s implausible art by issuing two kinds of caveats: the first asserts a limit to the length of *gradatio* (how high it might climb); the second insists that the figure's sequence represent a hierarchy of values grounded in the organization of the world. With the first caveat, early modern theorists treated the conspicuous artifice of *gradatio* as if it could be measured by counting the rungs on its ladder.[87] In *The Garden of Eloquence* (1593), for example, Henry Peacham advises that in "using the figure we ought to obserue a meane, that there be not too many degrees" (and he further specifies that three or four degrees are acceptable).[88] What is interesting, then, about Dorus's *gradatio* is that its excessive artifice is made to seem natural. The shape of the human hand dictates that the figure be neither longer nor shorter. With the second caveat, early modern theorists treated the conspicuous artifice of *gradatio* as a representation of hierarchies of value as they structure the social world.[89] The sequencing of a *gradatio* (glove and then hand, hand and then heart, etc.) could assert a hierarchy predicated on the natural order of things in the world, or this sequencing could assert a set of causal relations that inhered first among those things in the world.[90] What is interesting here about Dorus's *gradatio* is the comparatively higher value it attributes to the poet's "chiefest part": the central location of those "secret joys" that *gradatio* features on its highest rung and values above all else.

The *indecorous* thinking of Dorus's *gradatio* paradoxically combines a unique hierarchy of values with the spectacle of its open art. Combining figure with argument, Dorus's *gradatio* suggests that artifice at its most conspicuous doubles for what Philip Melanchthon called the "sinews" of reason.[91] The axes of relation that this figure establishes and that distinguish the world of the "dream" are here relations of value. When theorists warned practitioners away from the conspicuous art of *gradatio*, it was because the form of *gradatio* exceeded the boundaries of plausibility. Dorus's song, by contrast, imagines how a figure like *gradatio* might measure a different boundary by disarticulating the world of the poem from the world that would value both the words that it speaks and the things of which it speaks differently.

This chapter has followed Cleophila's finger and singled out *gradatio*, but we might have considered Dorus's curious use of *polyptoton* instead: "sweet" and "sweetest," "fair" and "fairest" and "fairer," "true," "truth," and "truest," etc. (Cleophila herself seems to be thinking with *polyptoton* in her rebuke as "joy" shifts across a series of syntactical registers: "can you not joy sufficiently in your joys but you must use your joys . . .").[92] Aristotle understood *polyptoton* as the place of *inventio* dedicated to establishing what he called "co-ordinates": for example, "'just actions' and 'just man' which are co-ordinate with 'justice.'"[93] As a place of *inventio*, this form suggests that what is most significant about a line like "Fair hand, the fairest pledge of fairer heart" is that it establishes the "co-ordinates" for something like *Fairness* as such so that a speaker might make a series of plausible inferences about what is fair and what is not.[94] As a figure of *elocutio*, *polyptoton* was described as an instrument dedicated to variation (Puttenham called it the "Tranlacer" because it allowed you to "turn and tranlace a word into many sundry shapes, as the tailor doth his garment").[95] In Dorus's song, *polyptoton* seems to combine these two functions by permitting the poet to revise grammar's comparative spectrum of relative values: fair, fairer, fairest. What exactly is that heart "fairer" than? The "fair hand" or the "fairest pledge"? The moment at which Pamela's "hand" becomes a "pledge" is precisely the moment when her hand transforms into the glove (the "hand" relinquishes the glove as if shedding a layer of skin). We might expect the comparative "fairer heart" to settle down somewhere between the "fair hand" and the "fairest pledge"; instead, it exceeds the superlative degree: the "heart" is "fairer" than everything. Figure here attempts to sketch a syntax of ornament by rearranging the syntax of grammar. *Polyptoton* constructs a world in which it is possible to talk about the "truest": that which is truer than true.

The poem doubles down on its attempt to move beyond a boundary that its grammar posits when *gradatio* and *polyptoton* converge to insist on the value of Dorus's "chiefest part." The axes of relation that *gradatio* asserted through sequence and order are here recast through *polyptoton*'s varying of words. By attributing a superlative degree to a word that already demands exclusive rights to significance (that which is "chiefest" is something like *the mostest*), Dorus's *poesie* propels beyond the very syntactical measure that it previously reinforced through the containment of its lines (for example, "True heart, whose truth doth yield to truest band"). The repetition of "chiefest part" disrupts the integrity of the line by extending beyond it: "my chiefest part / My chiefest part wherein do chiefly stand / Those secret joys." The effect is simultaneously to reserve those "secret joys" as the exclusive property of Dorus's "chiefest part" and to disperse them across the degrees of the *gradatio*: Do those "joys" stand "chiefly" as if they are at the head, as if they are in command of his "chiefest part"? Or do those "joys" stand "chiefly," as if they are mostly, predominantly (but not exclusively), in that "part"? The implication would then be that his "joys" are also everywhere else.

It might be useful to think of figures like *gradatio* and *polyptoton* as the tools for making or measuring the form of *hyperbole*, a trope that deals in impossibility and is frequently described as breaking with the possible by exceeding its boundaries and measure (or by rising above it).[96] "Sometimes," Hoskins writes of *hyperbole*, "it expresseth a thing in the highest degree of possibility, beyond the truth, that in descending thence may find the truth; sometimes in flat impossibility, that rather you may conceive the unspeakableness than the untruth of the relation."[97] Early modern texts describe both *gradatio* and *hyperbole* as a challenge to common methods of measurement: they both go beyond—or almost go beyond—a line that they draw only in surpassing it or threatening to surpass it.[98] Peacham defines *hyperbole* as "when a saying doth surmounte and reach aboue the truth."[99] *Hyperbole* and *gradatio* measure out the boundaries of a poetic *heterocosm* by charting what lies beyond the superlative degree. From the perspective of figure, the improbable is simply "aboue the truth." If the matter of *hyperbole* is itself unspeakable (it lies outside of "rule" and "measure"), the excessive iterations of *gradatio*—its open, curious, affected art—limn the form of *hyperbole*. *Gradatio* is an instrument for artificially constructing the "rule" and "measure" of a different world (the world that Cleophila calls a "dream").[100]

By considering how *gradatio* acts as the "bedstaff" that permits and structures Dorus's "dream," we can begin to see how figures of speech set alternative coordinates for possibility in the imaginative worlds of early modern literature. Doubling as both artifice at its most trifling and as the "sinews" of reason itself, a figure like *gradatio* can become a *formula* for composition and a constitutive form of that composition. By describing figures of speech as instruments of poetic production, I do not mean to assert the necessary "logicality" of figure. To do so would be to naturalize the operations of reason and to redeem rhetoric on philosophy's terms.[101] This is why Jonathan Crewe in his study of Thomas Nashe insisted on a "demonic rhetoric," which he describes as "a world of negative energy, of perpetually inverted or subverted order, uninformed by any redeeming principle." "To conceive of an antiworld," he continues, is "to conceive of a world in which an interminable undoing or disruption of good order becomes at once the condition of existence and the source of power."[102] Crewe, however, tends to replace the organizing force of "logicality" with that of the "subject": ultimately, what style inevitably points to is Nashe himself. In this book, by contrast, I aim to suggest how the very instrumentality of figures of speech—at once empty and tangible, particular and reproducible—allows us to glimpse the provisional parameters they drew for imaginary worlds. As Christopher Warley has suggested, this may be how literary criticism can claim access to the "possibility of the impossible": "through strict adherence to form, to a constant respect for and return to the lucidity, organization, and structure of dreams."[103] Cleophila isn't buying Dorus's fiction. What his dream values as "great treasures," she values at "nothing," but her subsequent admission, "nothing ... but," identifies the form that Dorus's dream shares with Cleophila's reality. Dorus's dream is shaped by the very figure of speech that remains accessible to Cleophila as a material object in her world. The glove, the bedstaff, the figure: these permit for the modality of fiction because they organize its irreality, but it is as if Cleophila can only operate in the indicative. She flattens the world by explaining fiction away.

When Sidney revised his *Arcadia*, he cut Dorus's song. A single glove does appear in the revised *Arcadia*, but there it becomes an instrument of narrative digression and dilation rather than stylistic abuse. This glove belongs to Philoclea, and it ends up in the mouth of a dog. While singing a blazon of Philoclea's bathing body, Zelmane watches a "water-spaniell" "come and fetch away one of *Philocleas* gloues; whose fine proportion, shewed well what a daintie guest was wont there to be lodged." Zelmane is initially pleased by the attention paid to Philoclea's glove: "It was a delight to *Zelmane*, to see that the dogge was therewith delighted."[104] But she chases him down when he returns for Philoclea's papers. This chase introduces the central plot twist of the revised *Arcadia* when the dog leads Zelmane to Amphialus (the dog stole only a single glove and some papers; Amphialus's mother will steal both of the sisters). In the *Old Arcadia*, Dorus conflates the form of the glove with a conspicuous figure of speech and creates an *indecorous* lyric. As I will show when I turn to the figure of *antithesis* in Chapter 5, Sidney's revised *Arcadia* translates *indecorous* lyrical proportion into endless narrative. In the mouth of the revised *Arcadia*'s thieving dog, the single, sweet glove acts as stylistic engine of narrative dilation.

Prior to its publication in the twentieth century, there was only one place where you might find Dorus's song in print (and there, you would only find one of the pair of stanzas). In Abraham Fraunce's *Arcadian Rhetorike* (1588), the second stanza of Dorus's song appears as an example of the very figure of speech to which Cleophila points when she accuses her friend of wanting to "vauntingly march over" her own "miseries." It appears just below the more famous example from the opening sonnet of *Astrophil and Stella*:

> *Sir Philip Sydeny 1. Song*
> Louing in truth, and faine in verse my loue to show,
> That the deare she might take some pleasure of my pain,
> Pleasure might cause her read, reading might make her know,
> Knowledge might pity win, & pity grace obtain.
>   I sough fit words, &c.
>   *3. Dorus.*
> Sweete gloue the sweete despoile of sweetest hand,
> Faire hand the fairest pledge of fairer hart,
> True heart whose truth doth yeeld to truest band,
> Chiefe band, I say, which ties my chiefest part,
> My chiefest part, wherein doo chiefly stand
> Those secrete ioyes, which heauens to me impart:
>   Vnite in one, my state thus still to saue,
>   You haue my thankes, let me your comfort haue.[105]

In the *Old Arcadia*, the conspicuousness of *gradatio* acts as a measure of Dorus's affectation and draws the superlative coordinates for an imaginative world that permits for the pleasure of one. It is precisely this same quality of conspicuousness that lends Dorus's stanza a pedagogical value in Fraunce's *Arcadian Rhetorike*. The conspicuousness of Dorus's device enables the exemplarity of the second stanza of his song. The example is the rhetorical manual's attempt to shape textual *genesis*: it offers an ideal image of what a new text ought to resemble. In the end, while Cleophila recognizes the mechanism that excludes her from Dorus's fantasy world, she fails to recognize that this mechanism of exclusion is also a gift. Dorus's *indecorous* thinking offers Cleophila a figure of speech so that she might experience the pleasure of the poet-maker.

CHAPTER 3

Queenly Fig Trees: Figures of Speech and *Decorum*

In the opening verse of his *Art of Poetry*, Horace drew a line in the sand. When a poet (like a painter) attaches "a human head to the neck of a horse," when he fixes "feathers of many a hue" to the body below that neck, and when he selects the limbs for that body from among several different species, the poet steps across Horace's line. Faced with such a chimera, Horace asks, *could you keep yourself from laughter?*[1] The unfortunate image that Horace depicts combines a set of discrete parts into something other than a whole—a mixture of pieces that depart from the mimetic *telos* and come apart from one another at their ill-conceived joints. No matter how hard we might try to contain ourselves, Horace insists that we will laugh at such a dramatic departure from verisimilitude. I would like to suggest that the laughter Horace invokes at the sight of such a hodgepodge production indexes the very distinction that he also looks to naturalize. Horace's line distinguishes the *decorous* from the *indecorous* composition, where *decorum* describes that judgment of art that stakes a claim to origin in and allegiance to the natural world.[2] Laughter here is an involuntary reaction to the violation of plausibility.[3] Laughter is not, for Horace, simply a response to the *indecorous* composition; it is an act of judgment and evaluation legitimized by its claim to physical compulsion.[4]

I open with this image from Horace's *Art of Poetry* because it offers us a versatile emblem for the two-part problem of *decorum* in classical and early modern rhetoric and poetics.[5] According to the definition with which we are most familiar, *decorum* describes the proper alignment of person, time, and place in a given composition.[6] It is in this sense, for example, that George Turbeville invokes Horace's chimera to justify his use of "suche common and ordinarie phrase of speach as Countreymen do vse" in his translation of Battista Mantuan's *Eclogues* (1567): "He that shall translate a shephierd's tale, and vse the talke and stile of an Heroicall personage, expressing the siellie mans meaning with loftie thundering words: in my simple judgement ioynes (as *Horace* sayth) a Horses necke and a mans hed togither."[7] This is a qualitative account of *decorum*: the symmetrical body toward which the rule of *decorum* works is the body social, and *decorum*'s ideological work thus entails disciplining the subject (in the manner of the sumptuary laws to which it is frequently compared). Emphasizing the speaker (or what the rhetorical tradition calls *ethos*), this account of *decorum* has dovetailed nicely with widespread critical interest in the history of subjectivity and affect; most recently, an emphasis on *decorum* and the integrity of the speaker has contributed to renewed interest in dramatic character.[8]

Decorum also, however, describes an ideal of design that emphasizes harmony, proportion, measure, and rule.[9] In *The Model of Poesy* (c. 1599), for example, William Scott invokes Horace's chimera while describing the violation of "that symmetry or conformity of parts proportioned *armonicamente* that pleaseth the eye and mind of the beholder; so is it that suitable correspondency in the parts of our poems that yields a sweet harmony to our ears and a beauty to our eyes." The image, here, is that of "one body of fitly-composed members that have a proportionable greatness and dependency one with and upon another"—what Horace means when he says "your work must be 'unum' and 'simplex,'" or, as Scott paraphrases, "it must not be an hermaphrodite or mongrel."[10] The body toward which this quantitative account of *decorum* works is an aesthetic ideal: *decorum*'s ideological work thus entails the discipline of style so that each constitutive part operates according to the logic of the whole, a logic that locates its authority in the construction of the natural world.[11]

I aim to recover the aesthetic dimension of *decorum* in order to argue for the social and epistemological significance of *indecorous* thinking to both early modern poetry and to literary studies more broadly, where a renewed dedication to the concept of "form" has tended to proceed as if questions of poetic unity are particular to the New Criticism and its reworking of romanticism's conception of the organic whole (and are therefore anachronistic to a study of early modern literature).[12] I want to propose that attention to the *decorous* ideal that George Puttenham called in *The Art of English Poesy* (1589) "multiformity uniform" provides us with an opportunity to rethink the work of form in early modern *poesie*: it allows us to take another turn at Samuel Taylor Coleridge's "unity in multeïty" as if through a kaleidoscope.[13] Horace's distinction between the *decorous* and the *indecorous* composition projects a formal *telos* for each poetic production. We might transform Horace's line into a spectrum. At one end of this spectrum, the formal *telos* of the *decorous* composition posits a continuous shape with matching members, symmetrical and of a single species. This is the corporeal representation of what a poetic composition ought to resemble. The emphasis is on a unity of form, and in his conduct book *Galateo* (1576), Della Casa's old man calls this "Bewtie," "Where iointly & seuerally, euery parte & the whole hath his due proportion and measure."[14] At the other end of our spectrum, we get an idea of what a poetic composition ought not to resemble. This is an *indecorous* form, with mismatched members weak at their impossible joints. Here, the combination of parts resists the sound body and produces, instead, deformity. If "*Bewtie*," Della Casa's old man insisted, "would consist but of one, at the most," then "*Deformitie* contrarywise, measured her selfe by *Many*." Thus, if you see a woman big in the eyes but with a little nose, with "blubbe cheekes" but "flat" at the mouth, "you thinke straite that that face is not one womans alone: but is moulded of many faces, and made of many peeces."[15] Both Horace's chimera and Della Casa's composite woman suggest that departure from *decorum* and deferral from the mimetic *telos* is a matter of multiplicity. In this quantitative sense, deformity means not only "misshapen" (Lt. *de-forma*) but also "difformity," from the medieval Latin *dis-forma*, meaning "of diverse forms."[16]

Indecorous thinking does not simply bend form out of shape. It prioritizes the member over the corpus, the part over the whole. As Cicero's Crassus maintains, the *decorous* style is not reducible to a single limb; it is, instead, the property of the body as a whole.[17] Likening the figures of *elocutio* to man's "eyesight," Thomas Wilson writes in *The Art of Rhetoric* (1560), quoting Quintilian, "I would not have all the body to be full of eyes, or nothing but eyes, for then the other parts should want their due place and proportion."[18] When it comes to figures of speech, *Ne quid nimis* becomes the common refrain: nothing to excess.[19] The problem with an *indecorous poesie*—its tendency toward multiplicity and disformity—is the manufacture of a superfluity that results in artifice at its most conspicuous. Against the social and aesthetic imperatives of *sprezzatura* or *celare artem*, figures of speech align the worth of a composition with the visible labor of its production.[20]

In this chapter, I turn to the poetic practices of a character in Mary Wroth's *Urania*, and I suggest that these practices constitute an experiment in the very *indecorous poesie* at which Horace thought one couldn't help but laugh; ever modest, the characters of the *Urania* simply "all smiled to heere" the "strange relation" of Antissia's discursive extravagancies.[21] Following on Antissia's series of unfortunate misadventures throughout *The First Part*, *The Second Part* of the *Urania* opens with a description of what other characters repeatedly describe as her "madness." Having taken up with a private tutor well versed in the erotic stylings of Ovidian poetry, Antissia dedicates herself to the production of rhetorical exercises and these exercises are treated as a diagnostic tool. Antissius explains to the romance's central heroine, Pamphilia: "My Aunts raging, raving, extravagent discoursive language is most aparantly and understandingly discernd flatt madnes."[22] The problem with Antissia's style in *The Second Part* is that it revels in an ornamental excess from which Antissia, like Dorus in Sidney's *Old Arcadia*, derives pleasure; her immediate auditors do not. Deferring from the aesthetic ideal that underwrites the quantitative approach to *decorum*, Antissia's figures of speech serve as a source of pleasure for the poet-maker. These figures produce a hybrid form—distinguishable as neither prose nor verse—that other characters label "vanities." As we saw in Chapter 2, the category of vain speech is not only significant as a judgment of Antissia, though this may be what her critics intend. Antissia's speech is "vain" because its artifice drafts an alternative set of coordinates for the parameters of possibility in the *Urania* at large.

Characters like Antissius seek to reduce Antissia's style to diagnostics by making "vanity" the problem of an unsound mind (and modern criticism has followed suit).[23] Wroth's *Urania*, however, indicates a different conception of style, one in which the discursive composition is not reducible to the symptom. Antissia's compositions and the figures of speech by which she assembles them—ornaments such as *epanorthosis* (or *correctio*) and the *epithet*—are not so much tokens of madness (what is aberrant and abhorrent in the world of the *Urania*) as they are poetic demonstrations of the constitutive forms of the world of the *Urania*. As we began to see in Chapter 2, one way in which figures of speech become constitutive of imaginary worlds is by assigning value to the things of which they speak:

whether through the scaling of *gradatio*'s ladder or the "co-ordinates" that *polyptoton* maps among the words that it varies, figures of speech distinguish fictional worlds by valuing things differently. My argument in this chapter falls into three parts. First, I will argue that *indecorous* thinking produces a misalignment between words and things, between ornament and subject matter, and that this misalignment constitutes an innovative act of evaluation. Second, I will show how figures of speech act as the technology for this artificial production of value. Finally, I will argue that insofar as *indecorous* thinking assigns an original set of values to the things of which figures speak, it also describes the central, generative mechanism for the construction of imaginative worlds: the assignment of value is one kind of relation that figures might draw. In Mary Wroth's *Urania*, the *indecorous* style is the worthiest style.

On Ornament

In classical poetics, the Greek word *kosmos* referred to both an individual ornament and the harmonious, ordered universe of which that individual ornament is a signifying part.[24] The word *kosmos* therefore ranged in meaning, as Anne Carson puts it in her translations of Sappho, "from the arrangement of planets in the sky at night to the style with which an individual wears her hat."[25] Frequent examples of the *kosmos* or ornament include jewelry, fabric—all of those things that, as Angus Fletcher wrote, serve as "sartorial emblems of position."[26] Rhetorical ornaments performed a similar function when the worth they attributed to the matter at hand conformed to the generally accepted value of that matter.[27] As Demetrius explains in his treatise *On Style*, you would not describe a wobbling teacup in ornate language: to do so would disrupt the ornament's metonymic transaction between quotidian object and large-scale order.[28] Where rhetorical ornament, however, operates in excess of its subject matter, it can disrupt and even revise such a transaction by assigning an original set of values to the things of this world.[29]

In the *Poetics*, Aristotle used the word *kosmos* to refer to both ornamental diction and the harmonious, ordered universe to which that ornamental diction ought to point. Though Aristotle lists the "ornamental word" among his eight types of diction, including ordinary, strange, metaphorical, coined, lengthened, curtailed, and altered, "ornamental" is the one type for which he does not provide an explanation (modern editions of the *Poetics* offer the punctuation of an *ellipsis* in lieu of this explanation, marking out the space where the ornamental word would have been explained or should have been explained).³⁰ When Aristotle raises the *kosmos* in his *Rhetoric*, it is as that which threatens "appropriateness" (Gk. *propon*), or what the Roman and early modern rhetorical traditions call *decorum* (also employing *aptum*) and for which early modern vernacular theorists provide such English synonyms as apt, decent, seemly, and comely.³¹ In the *Rhetoric*, Aristotle sets two conditions for this standard of *decorum* or "appropriateness." A composition is "appropriate," first, "if it expresses emotion and character." Taking the speaker or *ethos* as its primary organizing principle, this is the qualitative approach to *decorum*: the condition that organizes person, time, and place (the fine tuning of *kairos*). Aristotle's second condition for "appropriateness" is related to the first, frequently discussed alongside the conditions of person, time, and place, but gives rise to the distinct set of theoretical problems posed by the quantitative approach to *decorum*:

> Your language will be appropriate if it expresses emotion and character, and if it corresponds to its subject. "Correspondence to subject" means that we must neither speak casually about weighty matters, nor solemnly about trivial ones; nor must we add ornamental epithets to commonplace nouns, or the effect will be comic, as in the works of Cleophon, who can use phrases as absurd as "O queenly fig-tree."³²

When you call a fig tree "queenly," you apply linguistic varnish to an average, everyday word (one that requires neither a glossy finish nor a preservative). Describing a fig tree in ornate language stylistically treats that word and the thing that it names as if both are more valuable than they are.³³ The inappropriate or the *indecorous* therefore describes figures of speech — in Aristotle's example, the "ornamental epithet" — that disrupt the very *kosmic* hierarchy they are meant simply to signify by assigning an original set of values to the things of this world. Calling a fig tree "queenly" is an aberrant act of evaluation. Calling a fig tree "queenly" is also an innovative act of evaluation.

Aristotle's condition of correspondence becomes a basic imperative throughout the history of rhetoric: it mandates that one ought to calibrate figures of speech to the normative value of the *res* or subject matter under consideration.³⁴ Correspondence therefore also served as the art of rhetoric's response to one of its most ancient but persistent critiques — that it is all style and no matter (that, because rhetoric has no subject matter to claim as its own, its practitioners know only how to persuade the ignorant of what they cannot actually claim to understand).³⁵ At the opening of *On the Orator*, Cicero anticipates and responds to this attack by suggesting that, far from knowing nothing, the orator must actually know just about everything: without "a knowledge of very many matters," rhetoric "is but an empty and ridiculous swirl of verbiage."[36] While the good orator is recognizable by "a style that is harmonious, graceful, and marked by a certain artistry and polish," if that same speaker has not "mastered" the "underlying subject-matter," he will be the object of "universal derision." "For what so effectually proclaims the madman," Cicero's Crassus will ask, "as the hollow thundering of words—be they never so choice and resplendent—which have no thought or knowledge behind them?"[37] In moments such as these, the art of rhetoric internalizes philosophy's critique by defending itself on philosophy's terms. Rhetoric only deflects the challenge that its stylized language is devoid of epistemological value by displacing that same challenge onto an ornamentation that does not work in the service of things.[38] The *indecorous* alignment of ornament to matter looks like highly stylized wind.[39]

As a response to this threat, classical theorists developed a subcategory of the canon of *elocutio* known as the "vices of style": a taxonomy dedicated to identifying and naming the various ways in which ornament might deviate from the standard of *decorum*.[40] The vices of style are the art of rhetoric's categorical recognition of an ornamental language that puts on display what philosophy calls a lack of knowledge and what rhetoric itself calls the unpersuasive or the implausible. The vices of style are not simply a separate category of language; they are a state of language into which any otherwise acceptable figure of speech might slip. "Style," Quintilian warned, can "be corrupted in precisely the same number of ways that it may be adorned."[41] Abundance becomes excess when a single figure of speech is used too often or for too long, or when many different figures of speech are used all at once.[42] The *indecorous* style that results from the overuse of ornaments is therefore a threat latent within the canon of *elocutio* at large (a threat for which the category of vices is both a distillation and an attempted purge), such that an otherwise acceptable figure of speech will go under a new name when it slides into superfluity. Puttenham writes of *paroemion* (alliteration), for example: "It is a figure much used by our common rhymers, and doth well if it be not too much used, for then it falleth into the vice . . . called *tautologia*."[43] *Paroemion* becomes *tautologia* "when our maker takes too much delight to fill his verse with words beginning all with a letter." "Many of our English makers use it too much," Puttenham concedes before claiming, "yet we confess it doth not ill but prettily becomes the meter, if ye pass not two or three words in one verse, and use it not very much."[44] Puttenham treats the difference between *paroemion* and *tautologia*—figure of speech and vice of style—as if it is reducible to a basic arithmetic. *Paroemion* is *decorous* "if ye pass not two or three words in one verse." Puttenham also identifies a cause of the *indecorous*: *paroemion* becomes *indecorous* when the poet-maker "takes too much delight" in using it. A surplus of ornamentation becomes the gauge of the maker's immediate pleasure in the act of composition.

What I have outlined here are two distinct but related dimensions of the *indecorous*. Where "O queenly fig-tree" exemplifies a misalignment between ornament and matter, it suggests that the problem with the *indecorous* is its innovative act of evaluation: "Queenly" assigns a value to the fig tree that the art of rhetoric calls implausible. *Never could there be such a fig tree!* Early modern poetic theory also, however, translates this innovative act of evaluation—and the alternative hierarchy of values that it implies—into the language of aesthetic design, where the problem of a misalignment between ornament and matter becomes the violation of or departure from an ideal of harmony, proportion, measure, and rule.[45] Thus, Puttenham not only advises (like Aristotle) that an *epithet* "must be apt and proper for the thing he is added unto"; he also warns that appropriate alignment is in itself an insufficient condition for the *epithet*: "Some of our vulgar writers take great pleasure in giving epithets and do it almost to every word which may receive them, and should not be so, yea though they were never so proper and apt, for sometimes words suffered to go single do give greater sense and grace than words qualified by attribution do."[46] No matter how proper that ornament might be—instead of "queenly," try "fragrant" or "flowering"—you should exercise restraint and favor a stylistic moderation that is a universal norm and in tune with the natural world.[47] This *decorous* ideal of proportion, measure, and rule picks up on an Aristotelian conception of temperance and carefully calibrates a "mean," a "just and reasonable measure," and the "apt joining" of parts into an integral whole.[48] Classical and early modern theorists regularly look to the human body as the iconic illustration of this stylistic ideal.[49] Complaining of the overuse of *sententia*, for example, John Hoskins writes in *Directions for Speech and Style* (1601): "It is like an eye in the body; but is it not monstrous to be all eyes? I take Cyclops to be as handsome a man as Argus. And if a sentence were as like to be a hand in the text as it is commonly noted with a hand in the margent, yet I should rather like the text that had no more hands than Hercules than that which had as many as Briareus."[50] In deferring from the *decorous* ideal, by prioritizing the member over the corpus, the part over the whole, the *indecorous* style produces an Argus-eyed chimera, a hundred-handed assailant.

Indecorous thinking affirms neither traditional hierarchies of value nor the dominant ideological paradigms of the ruling class. In both its innovative act of evaluation—"O queenly fig-tree"—and in the translation of this act into a style that manufactures surplus and excess—bestowing *epithets*, as Puttenham said, upon "almost . . . every word which may receive them"—the ornament disrupts both *doxa* or common sense and the hierarchical universe to which such common sense quietly conforms. Cicero described the judgment of proportion as a "subconscious instinct" endowed to everybody; within early modern pedagogy, the innate judgment of *decorum* became the province of the aristocracy.[51] I want to suggest that "queenly" fig trees build, *epithet* by *epithet*, ornament by ornament, an alternative hierarchy of values. The *indecorous* composition dealing in redundancy and surplus is significant as the stylistic expression of this alternative hierarchy. Like "O queenly fig-tree," artifice becomes conspicuous when that artifice exceeds what its matter is thought to require. By inflating the value of a commonplace noun or by speaking in excess of the matter at hand, *indecorous* thinking departs from the standard shared by rhetoric and poetics alike: the standard of plausibility.[52] *Indecorous* thinking deals, instead, in what the rhetorical tradition called implausible and what philosophy called empty on the inside.

Departing from received hierarchies of value by inflating the value of commonplace nouns and manufacturing stylistic surplus, an *indecorous poesie* produces artifice at its most conspicuous and, therefore, at its least plausible. Figures of speech invert the aims of the places of *inventio*, which, as I argued in Chapter 1, articulate only that knowledge which is already accepted and acceptable. Thinking with figure, by contrast, turns away from the compositional imperative of plausibility (and the putatively natural world from which this imperative derives its authority) and turns toward conspicuous artifice. The designated cause of the *indecorous* is the idea (as with *paroemion* and the *epithet*) that the figures of *elocutio* are an inappropriate source of pleasure for makers. The alternative hierarchy of value produced by the figures of *elocutio* is thus something like a side effect or the byproduct of the maker's own delight in figures of speech and a *poesie* that orients around the pleasure of one.

Sweet Babbling

Sent early in her life as a foster child to the parents of her betrothed, there to be raised by the family into which she would eventually marry, Wroth's

Antissia is an example of the aristocratic gift-child that Patricia Fumerton describes in *Cultural Aesthetics* (1991).[53] What Fumerton calls "living trivialities," aristocratic children occupied a paradoxical position in early modern culture: expendable and dispensable, at the moment at which these children were exchanged, at the very moment when their superfluity was enacted, these same children became the constitutive elements of an aristocratic social network.[54] "Children were trifles," she explains, "whose circulation 'finished' them in the way an artwork is finished."[55] Waylaid by kidnappers, pirates, and would-be rapists, however, Antissia never makes it to her new family (and she does not return to her old). Throughout *The First Part*, she is an aristocratic gift-child gone astray. A glitch in the early modern romance machine, Antissia's narrative *telos* is not so much delayed or deferred as it has simply moved on without her.[56] If, as Fumerton suggests, children were the constitutive ornaments of an aristocratic social *kosmos*, then Antissia is an ornament that remains superfluous to that *kosmos*. Antissia circulates outside of its structuring networks and therefore fails to express or point back to its totalizing vision of culture. Her *poesie* serves as both a critique of the *kosmos* to which she might have referred and the constitutive engine of an alternative *kosmos*.

In an early episode of *The Second Part*, the central cast of characters, including Pamphilia, Amphilanthus, Urania, Steriamuus, and Rosindy (among others), begin to reminisce about an episode in *The First Part* in which Antissia discovered Pamphilia in secret conversation with Rosindy (whom she believed to be her beloved Amphilanthus). Rosindy declares that this moment of mistaken recognition left Antissia with "sum craks still of her braine-sick fury unstopt, though whited over a little with seeming Judgment."[57] Antissia operates according to a "seeming Judgment": that which appears to be (but is not) reason. According to her nephew, Antissius, Antissia has since cultivated her "seeming Judgment" in collaboration with a private tutor well versed in Ovidian poetry. On the isolated island of Negroponte, where she "fell to studdy and gott a tuter," Antissia's style combines the marginalized position of the exiled poet with the erotic license of the very verse that got him exiled in the first place.[58] Antissius declares it "a dangerous thing att any time for a weake woeman to studdy higher matters then their cappasitie can reach to."[59] Emphasizing a misalignment between "higher matters" and Antissia's "cappasitie," Antissius suggests that "seeming Judgment" is something like bad learning or partial learning. Rosindy defines Antissia's style as an "effect," collecting her scattered lines together as an *allegory* of the thing by virtue of which those lines are said to have meaning: jealousy or bad schooling. On account of unruly affect and unruly pedagogy, Antissia's style is rendered decidedly pathological. Later, Rosindy will describe the origin of Antissia's compositions as "her owne brainsick skoole."[60]

The evidence for Antissia's failure to learn that toward which her "cappasitie" extends is her style of composition, including her dress, gesture, and speech.[61] Rosindy first sees Antissia as his boat comes ashore, just barely escaping shipwreck from a perilous storm. "Poore overJoy'd lady," Rosindy exclaims to his assembled audience, "in what a posture did I finde her in":

> I protest next to that phantisy they call poeticall furies, she was upon the sand, neither waulking, running, norr standing still, yett partly exercising all. She neither sange, nor spake, nor cried, nor laughed, butt a strange mixture of all thes together, so discomposed as if pieces of all throwne into a hatt and shouke together to bee drawne out, like Valentines to bee worne by severall persones, noe one to have them all, yett all thes peeces hunge about her att that time.[62]

As Rosindy continues, he describes a sartorial composite to match—Antissia attaches a veil to a straw hat, with a ruff where one would expect lace and a petticoat longer than her skirt—until the language of "strange mixture" settles into the language of *paradox*: "neither drest, nor undrest."[63] As Rosindy's description progresses, his prose reproduces the *paradox* he describes. His clauses pile up on one another—"neither waulking, running, norr standing still . . . neither sange, nor spake, nor cried, nor laughed"—until their accumulation reverses the course of his apparent assertion. An anatomy of everything that Antissia is not doing turns out to be an account of everything that Antissia is doing (only simultaneously). For a moment Rosindy's prose threatens to leave his putative object behind as we get not just a *simile*—"soe discomposed as if pieces of all throwne into a hatt"—but a *simile* of that *simile*: "like Valentines to bee worne by severall persones." Rosindy only recovers the object he has almost left behind by defining Antissia as the composite collection of everybody else's gifts, a collector of ornaments—"yett all thes peeces hunge about her att that time."

Given Antissia's status as a gift gone astray, a trifle that veers outside of its intended social transaction, the image of Antissia hoarding everybody's Valentine's Day favors is an interesting one: one derailed gift, recalcitrantly superfluous to the aristocratic culture to which it refuses to allude, becomes something like a supermagnet, attracting all gifts in the vicinity and wearing them like baubles (thereby disrupting the social transactions *they* were meant to facilitate). As the language of "discomposed" suggests, Rosindy's description of Antissia's demeanor serves as a visual illustration of the speech she delivers once he has made it onto the beach: "She was (when my bote putt a shore hard by wher she was), just then beeginning to say somthing, butt whether prose or verse," Rosindy concludes, "I can not tell." The linguistic counterpart to Antissia "neither drest, nor undrest," Rosindy's subsequent rehearsal of Antissia's speech suggests that the engines of this *paradox*—the *formulas* of composition that challenge the distinction between prose and verse—are figures of speech.[64] "Well then, thus she spake," begins Rosindy:

> What weather of misfortune butt faire gail of good luck hath filled the sailes of hapines to bring your barck to harbour on this shore? Eaolus and Boreus especially gave place, and gentle Zephirus did breathe the blessed blast that conducted this Argesea wher the golden fleece remaines in the renowne of this most fortunate rare starrs aprochment heere. Rosindy, machles Rosindy, the terror of wicked errors, and matches Heroe for deeds of Chivallry and warr, wellcome to lowe a title; noe, nott a phrase condigne to use! Rosindy, commaunde this Iland. The Princes and all are and shall heere appeere the meanesst vasoulls to your soveraintie. Hapy arivall that thus can make Antissia a secound Niobe in tears of Joye to melt for this unlooked for hapines! Her sorrowes melted her in drops and made a stone for her self of her one self, butt I with Joyfull teares will make a flood of wellcome to swallow as a deluge the longe extinguishing darcknes sad absence brought this place. Come then, earth[s] Glory, Amphilanthus owne Image, injoye commaund as harts, soe regions to your sweete—[65]

Piling on clauses of parallel construction with the figure of *isocolon*—"weather of misfortune," "faire gaile of good luck," "the sailes of hapines"—Antissia's speech proceds in a paratactic swing between appositional clauses that amplify the single word that she ostentatiously discards: "wellcome to lowe a title; noe, nott a phrase condigne to use!" In *On Copia*, Erasmus offered an example of a schoolroom text that he also recommends. Drawing on synonyms in addition to tropes and figures including *periphrasis*, *heterosis*, *synecdoche*, *metaphor*, *enallage*, and *hyperbole*, Erasmus demonstrates over one hundred and fifty ways to vary the phrase "Your letter pleased me mightily." He describes this process as "transforming the basic expression into a Protean variety of shapes."[66] His point was not for a speaker to use all of these alternatives at once but instead to have them available as potential *formulas* from which he might selectively draw.[67] Antissia, by contrast, does not actualize potential through selection but through exhaustion: "Rosindy, matches Rosindy, the terror of wicked errors, and matches He-

roe for deeds of Chivallry . . . earth[s] Glory, Amphilanthus owne Image."
This is a Long Hello.

Antissia's greeting is an extended exercise in amplifying the single word that she openly rejects. Her dismissal—"wellcome to lowe a title; noe, nott a phrase condigne to use!"—is performed at some distance into her greeting, but its inadequacy is the point on which her speech spins (it is the central, legitimizing lack that warrants more language). The rhetorical figure known as *epanorthosis* or *correctio* is, therefore, a kind of epitome of the generative mechanisms of her speech. As Peacham explains in *The Garden of Eloquence* (1593), *epanorthosis* "is a figure which taketh away that that is said, and putteth a more nicer word in the place."[68] *Epanorthosis* is thus a performance in *decorum*. By retracting the "mightie wordes and by putting mightier in their roomes," *epanorthosis* suggests that its attribution of value is an act of calibration because the new word is (as the *Ad Herennium* describes it) "more suitable."[69] Insofar, however, as *epanorthosis* reduces *decorum* to rhetorical technique, it also enables the manipulation of values as it shifts language along an ornamental spectrum from "mightie" to "mightier." In *Directions for Speech and Style*, Hoskins suggests that the first word may even be "a word of sufficient force" but that the speaker rejects it in order to create "a greater vehemence of meaning."[70] For Hoskins, emotion (and *ethos*) warrants this performance of *epanorthosis*, but theorists remain conscious of the idea that *epanorthosis* can be used to inflate the value of the object at hand. Thus, Peacham warns that where the speaker looks "to put needlesse & fond wordes to be corrected," it "is a signe of follie."[71] *Epanorthosis* perpetrates the illusion of a misalignment between ornament and matter in order to turn one word into the occasion for many words.

Rosindy's rehearsal of Antissia's speech only comes to an end when Urania interrupts him: "'Ther is even enough,' sayd Urania, 'unles better fixed stuff.'" Urania continues by describing the peculiar capacity of Antissia's speech to torture Rosindy:

> Butt what food did she give you ore comfort after your neere suffering shipwrack? If noe other then this, itt wowld have binn to mee a greater storme then the first; this so cruell, empty blasts of senceles discourse cowld hardly fill the vaines of disaster. Farr fitter they had binn imployed in bladders to blow up her follys and fustion taulke together![72]

Likening the "empty blasts" of Antissia's "sencles discourse" to the sea storm from which Rosindy has only just escaped with his life, Urania draws on the connection, ubiquitous in both classical and early modern rhetorical theory, between excessive speech and the wind (where the breath of speech—*anima*—frequently transforms into *flautus*, the wind or breeze that can either guide a ship on its course or blow it off track).[73] Urania speaks philosophy's charge against rhetoric: the emptiness of Antissia's *poesie* is made visible by its conspicuous artifice. Yet Urania also attributes a material efficacy to the *indecorous* when she suggests that its emptiness is something like the withholding of food (a privation that affects the listener). When Urania interrupts Rosindy's rehearsal of Antissia's speech, hers is a defensive measure. Rosindy claims to have repeated Antissia's speech word for word—"I doe nott thinke I differ one word, noe, nor sillible from the originall of her, beegun"—and this repetition threatens his audience with the same torture.[74]

After Urania's interruption, Rosindy picks up his story again, and we learn something strange. Urania has interrupted Rosindy's story at the precise moment at which Antissia's husband, Dolorindus, interrupted Antissia's speech the first time around. "Dolorindus," Rosindy reports,

> released mee from her tormenting mee, she beeing just then upon that word "sweete," champing as if out of that to have more such like sweete babling to [torture] wreched mee with: all wett, hunger-sterv'd almoste, sea-and-weather-beaten, yett most wracked with her frivelous discourse and strange actions, which sertainely were bred in her owne brainsick skoole.[75]

That both Urania and Dolorindus interrupt Antissia's speech at "sweete" lends that speech a kind of autonomous logic, suggesting a strange necessity to Urania's pronouncement—"There is even enough"—as if Antissia's speech has actually reached a limit beyond which it cannot go, a limit that is something like a universal law in the world of the *Urania* (proven by its repetition). By Rosindy's account, the word "sweete" becomes the foodstuff it might otherwise describe, a morsel of a word that Antissia crushes between her teeth in order to extract "more such like sweete babling." In the *Art of Rhetoric*, Wilson criticizes those who "repeat one word so often that if such words could be eaten and chopped in so oft as they are uttered out, they would choak the widest throat in all England"; Antissia's related problem is not so much the repetition of one word as it is holding the same word in her mouth for too long—"she beeing just then upon that word 'sweete,' champing"—as if she could extract from that word the style to which she aspires: "sweete babling."[76]

As the gathered party understands it, Antissia's *indecorum* has to do with the misalignment involved in an aristocratic woman studying Ovid's verse and attempting to fly to the heights of his style. Their reading of Antissia proceeds from the qualitative dimension of *decorum*, and it reduces her rhetorical exercises to a diagnostic tool. The quantitative dimension of *decorum*, however, suggests that Antissia's style is not reducible to the symptom. The *Urania*'s characters point at Antissia and call her mad, but theirs is a fundamental misrecognition. Calling Antissia mad is something like pointing at a visual *exemplum* of gravity—the proverbial apple falling from the tree—and labeling it an anomaly rather than the illustrative demonstration of what can otherwise be an invisible but no less necessary operating condition of the world. Antissia's *poesie* is not an aberration in the world of the *Urania*; it displays how that world hangs together.

Truthless Epithets

When Rosindy rehearses Antissia's speech to his assembled audience of friends, Urania (as Dolorindus before her) interrupts that speech as it teeters on the edge of yet another *epithet*: "Rosindy, machles Rosindy, the terror of wicked errors, and matches Heroe for deeds of Chivallry and warr . . . earth[s] Glory, Amphilanthus owne Image . . . your sweete—."[77] *Epithet* (or *appositum*) is rhetoric's word for what the art of grammar calls adjective—"faire gaile," "gentle Zephyrus," "blessed blast." The *epithet* qualifies a noun by attributing an aspect to that noun. When that qualification substitutes for the noun, an *epithet* becomes the related figure *antonomasia*: when Antissia calls Rosindy the "terror of wicked errors" she produces an *antonomasia* that rings with the like endings of *similiter desinens*. What distinguishes the rhetorical *epithet* from grammar's adjective is that the *epithet* must be "fit" or "appropriate" to the thing it qualifies.[78] The rhetorical *epithet* differs from the adjective insofar as it substitutes the rule of *decorum* for the rule of syntax (or overlays the one on top of the other). The standard of "fit" or "appropriate" has the ideological force of coordinating cases. In the *Rhetoric*, Aristotle's concern with "ornamental epithets" and their violation of "appropriateness" had to do with the alignment of style to matter. To call a fig tree "queenly" is to perform a misalignment equivalent to the grammatical figure *enallage* (*hic mulier* or *haec vir*). In Antissia's speech, we have the stylistic translation of this misalignment into an excess of figures that transform her composition into a formal *paradox*—neither prose nor verse—and proceed to attack the very object that she praises, threatening Rosindy with "a shaking cold ague."

Classical and early modern discussions of the *epithet* index a broader concern about the epistemological value of figures of speech: Was the *epithet* integral to a composition because it deals in the substance of things?

Or was the *epithet* additional, primarily significant because it contributes to the aural dimension of a composition? At the most basic level of rhetorical categories, there was disagreement as to whether the *epithet* was a trope or a figure, where the difference between "trope" and "figure" identifies the power of the *epithet* in its capacity to alter meaning and, therefore, affect the mind of its audience, or in its capacity to affect the ear alone. Quintilian described the *epithet* as a trope that does not act like a trope but is "employed solely to adorn and enhance our style without any reference to the meaning."[79] Puttenham discusses the *epithet* twice: once as an "auricular" figure that "serve[s] chiefly to make the meters tunable and melodious, and affect not the mind but very little" and once among the "sensable" figures that "alter and affect the mind by alteration of sense."[80] As a trope, Aristotle's standard of "appropriateness," what Quintilian calls "suitability," established a kind of semantic circumference around the noun, suggesting that the *epithet* might alter the meaning of a noun this much (and not more).[81] For poets, Quintilian suggests that "suitability" is a sufficient standard. In a surprising formulation, however, "suitability" is not a sufficient standard for the orator because those *epithets* most suitable to the noun to which they are attached are, in fact, "redundant." At its most *decorous*, an *epithet* transforms from a trope into a figure because it fails to alter the sense: the aptest *epithet* expresses only what the noun already says. Quintilian's example for this is "white teeth." Or, calling your beverage "liquid wine."[82] This, Quintilian suggests, is to deploy a figure instead of a trope (and a figure that strides close to the vice of *pleonasm*, where to add "with my eyes" to the simple statement of "I see" is to be redundant about it). At its most *decorous*, *epithet*-as-trope becomes *epithet*-as-figure, and the standard of "appropriateness"—as measured by the alignment of ornament to matter—threatens necessarily to entail the vice of "redundancy." At its most *decorous*—where *decorum* describes the proper alignment of ornament to matter—the *epithet* threatens to become *indecorous* because it manufactures surplus.

Another way of saying this: As a figure of speech, the *epithet* is always already *indecorous*. Whereas theorists are more easily able to rehabilitate tropes because they are categorically defined as devices that alter matter or *res*, the category of figures tends to come into play when ornament is already at the threshold of a *decorous* design, tilting from moderation toward excess. Quintilian thus reserves the use of the *epithet* as a figure for the poet who enjoys a license peculiar to his craft; for the orator, "suitability" is an insufficient condition unless the *epithet* also has "some point."[83] Quintilian is vague, however, as to what constitutes this qualifying "point." Ultimately, he can only describe that "point" by the addition of yet another trope. In the case of "unbridled greed" (for example), the metaphorical "unbridled" adds something to "greed" that was not already there—a horse. The presence of *metaphor* transforms the *epithet* from figure to trope.[84] Quintilian only extracts himself from this sticky terminological debate by turning from the question of "suitability," and the threat of "redundancy," to a quantitative caveat that seems comparatively straightforward:

> But the nature of this form of embellishment is such that, while style is bare and inelegant without any epithets at all, it is overloaded when a large number are employed. For then it becomes long-winded and cumbrous, in fact you might compare it to an army with as many camp-followers as soldiers, an army, that is to say, which has doubled its numbers without doubling its strength.[85]

"Two epithets directly attached to one noun"—think, here, of Antissia's "fortunate rare starres approchement"—"are unbecoming even in verse," Quintilian concludes rather pragmatically.[86] In the end, Quintilian treats the interrelated problems of "suitability" and "redundancy" as if those problems are reducible to a simple arithmetic. Quintilian's *simile* of the "camp-followers," however, frames this quantitative standard in social terms: *lixae* included a range of individuals, from cooks and artisans to slaves and prostitutes.[87] An increase in their numbers seems to have signaled, as above, an army's descent into luxury and excess. And yet Quintilian's *simile* also encourages another perspective: *epithets* are necessary for a composition to do anything other than fight.[88] *Epithets* transform the soldier's campground into a community.

Antissia's speech puts on conspicuous display the governing logic of the world of the *Urania*, where *epithets* in the superlative degree mark out the evaluative extremities of the romance's system of virtues. One Orilena (for example) offers this description of her beloved Philarcos (unexceptional for its insistence upon the exceptional): "the loveliest that Nature framd, the valiantest that followed Mars and his exercises, the wisest that wisdom dwelt in, the sweetest that noblenesse grac'd with sweet mildnesse, and the mildest that sweetnesse honourd."[89] In Chapter 6, I will examine the work of *periphrasis* in this passage, but for now I want only to point out that these superlative *epithets* are not exclusive to Philarcos; instead, they carve out a limit that multiple characters can simultaneously occupy. The *Urania* is a world in which *epithets* are in excess, a kind of Dutch *pronkstilleven* (except the luxuries on display are abstractions): "sumptuousest," "gloriousest," and "intireliest," to cite a few.[90]

Among the large cast of characters, however, the central hero Amphilanthus is repeatedly described with an *epithet* that declares his demonstration of superlative value as such: he is the "worthiest."[91] Amphilanthus is, as our narrator declares, "the worthiest man the earth carried, the true summe for excellent light of his time, and for whose sake the Sunne would hide himselfe, in griefe hee could not shine so bright as his glory did; Fame spreading like his beames about him, rich, faire, cleare, and hott equally, and surpassing him."[92] At a curious moment in *The Second Part*, however, it seems as though Amphilanthus's position as the "worthiest" may be vulnerable. Believing Pamphilia to be married to a Tartarian king, Amphilanthus marries the first woman he comes across, but he almost instantly regrets that decision. Abandoning his new bride, Amphilanthus wanders aimlessly—"hee went every way, yett noe way; was every wher and noe wher"—until he throws himself upon a riverbank:

> "And this fruictles place," cride hee, "best beefitteth the wrechedest of man kinde and the unworthiest." A terme non els durst lay upon him, butt hee might bee bolde with him self, while noe rancorous spiritt what soever durst have presumed soe with truthles epithights to have had a thought that way, nor of any blame butt what hee layd on him self. And non durst adventure to contradict him in any thought, though aparant that if one might argue with him, in few words they might gaine the better, and say hee eclipst him self; for tow sunns can nott shine with true light att one time.[93]

Placing the negative prefix—"un-"—before his characteristic *epithet*—"worthiest"—Amphilanthus creates a linguistic bind in the world of the *Urania*. He speaks what is a lie, a "truthles epithight," but he lives in a world in which "non durst adventure to contradict him." Nobody else would dare think what Amphilanthus is thinking: "truthles epithights" throw open a channel or a direction of thought that the narrator laboriously describes as "to have had a thought that way." Our narrator, however, is able to imagine an exception to the law of not contradicting Amphilanthus. If someone could "adventure to contradict him," that person would say that "hee eclipst him self." The central image is that of one celestial body passing before and blocking another celestial body. If his status as the "worthiest man" was previously enough to make the sun want to hide, his new status as the "unworthiest" and the direction of thought that it unleashes threaten to rearrange the celestial bodies of the *Urania*. According to our narrator, the *epithet* has the status of a "sun" in the world of the *Urania* (the thing around which that world spins). In this *kosmos*, the *paradox* produced by contradictory *epithets* constitutes a physical impossibility: "Tow sunns can nott shine with true light att one time."

Eventually, Antissia will come to retract her rhetorical compositions (like the one with which she greeted Rosindy). Her husband takes her to the island of St. Maura, where she falls asleep on a mechanical bed that descends into the magical waters below and dunks her sleeping body. When the bed returns above ground and Antissia wakes, she experiences paralyzing shame.[94] Later, Antissia will tell the queen of Bulgaria that her study of *poesie* was to blame: "This new art to mee turn'd my elder braines to soe much Vanitie as I was that prettie thing itt self ore the best actor of it." Ultimately, Antissia understands her narrative as an *allegory* of vanity, and she offers two possible interpretations. Either this *allegory* turns on an Ovidian aesthetic, and what we witnessed was a metamorphosis: *poesie* directed Antissia's mind to such a quantity of "Vanitie" that she transformed into the thing itself.[95] Or, Antissia did not become "Vanitie" so much as she was its superlative "actor"; she followed Vanity's script better than anyone else. During this conversation, Antissia denies the value of her "undigested rimes," saying that she had been "taulking and ravingly throwing out undigested rimes, and to my thinking, gallant comparisons, and daintie expressions of the foulishest Vaine phansies that ever spoiled a silly braine that strained itt self, ore rather squised itt self, into foulerie in the foulishest degree."[96] If the "foulishest degree" marks out the evaluative perimeter of the world of the *Urania*, Antissia's "foulishest Vaine phansies" are significant as a kind of discursive measure of the reaches of that world. Her *poesie* articulates the evaluative threshold where both characters and their narratives take shape.[97]

Quintilian's broad categorical term for the manufacturing of conspicuous artifice is *cacozelia*:

> *Cacozelia*, or perverse affectation, is a fault in every kind of style: for it includes all that is turgid, trivial, luscious, redundant, far-fetched or extravagant, while the same name is also applied to virtues carried to excess, when the mind loses its critical sense and is misled by the false appearance of beauty, the worst of all offences against style, since other faults are due to carelessness, but this is deliberate.[98]

For Quintilian, the presence of "deliberation" distinguishes a rationally produced style, where figures of speech work toward a specifically conceived end, from a symptomatic style, where figures of speech are both the byproducts and the tokens of an unhealthy mind pursuing "the false appearance of beauty." *Cacozelia* is so offensive precisely because it is also "deliberate." *Cacozelia* is the name of the vice that is also the sign that a speaker has chosen "the false appearance of beauty" and has chosen to pursue a style in which "virtues carried to excess" cross the threshold into "vice." What is perhaps most interesting about "perverse affectation" is that it is done on purpose.

At its most conspicuous—as Cicero describes it, "with no attempt at concealment, but openly and avowedly"—artifice violates the standard of plausibility where plausibility calls for artifice that could double as nature.[99] In an early chapter of *Peculiar Language* (1988), Derek Attridge describes the paradoxical relationship between art and nature in early modern poetics, and his sense that early modern theories of *decorum* were simultaneously the solution to and distillation of this *paradox* will go some distance toward closing this chapter.[100] Attridge shows how even where art was understood as secondary to nature, crafted by men who are less than God (to whom nature owes its origins), art was also said to be the perfecter of that nature. The extent to which art might be seen as a corrective measure was justified by the fallen status of the world. Art, the product of what Philip Sidney called in the *Defence of Poesy* (c. 1580) man's "erected wit," might intervene in the natural world, but it did so as a kind of restorative, bringing the world back to what it previously *was* and ideally *should be* again.[101] Art therefore would seem to be essentially conservative, making nature more like her old self. Yet artifice was also repeatedly and routinely defined as a *departure* from nature—recognizable as such precisely where it deviated from the natural.[102] *Decorum*, as Attridge explains, functioned as the guiding artistic principle that was also natural: "to counteract the side effects of art's distance from nature—its potential viciousness, ridiculousness, and duplicity—a principle operating in the name of nature must be reintroduced."[103] *Decorum* made the guiding judgment of artificial production a property of the natural world.

These, then, were the terms under which art might become constitutive of, rather than merely supplementary to, nature. Art must operate within the bounds of a *decorum* that is itself "natural" rather than "artificial," a *decorum* that operates in concord with a judgment defined by the very ideal toward which art is meant to redirect nature: what once was and should be again.[104] Departing from the judgment of *decorum*—the "natural" reason that determines this judgment as well as the social and ontological harmony with which it was thought to tune—*indecorous* thinking describes artifice that takes on the project of world making while deviating from the moral imperative of what should be. *Indecorous* thinking conforms to neither a prior, lost ideal nor the organization of the natural world more broadly. It creates unapologetically artificially ("openly" and "avowedly," as Cicero said) not to capture the Neoplatonic recovery of a divine, transcendent ideal but to offer us an alternative to this ideal. This alternative is not always viable or even advisable—its ethics lies, instead, in its aggressive antagonism toward the normative force of *decorum* and its articulation of an alternative. Figures of speech draw implausibly artificial relations among things, but those relations also distinguish imaginary worlds and their alternative constructions of possibility.

It is frequently noted that while Cyrus served as the image that pivots poetry from *gnosis* to *praxis* in the *Defence*, Sidney's fictions provide no such model. My emphasis on the constitutive work of *indecorous* thinking in the construction of imaginative worlds allows us to describe an early modern *poesie* that is engaged with social and ethical problems even where these problems are not reducible to questions of identity or subject formation. Antissia's *epithets* are interesting not because they are symptomatic of her mind—even if she is eventually shamed into this position. They are interesting because they put on conspicuous display the assignment of value in Wroth's *Urania* and, to remember the problem of Amphilanthus's "truthles epithightes," the unthinkable directions of thought that *epithets* throw open. A good deal of the analysis in this chapter has followed Aristotle's finger as he pointed at the "ornamental epithet" in the *indecorous* alignment of "O queenly fig-tree." "*Epitheta ista*," as John Brinsley would say in his schoolroom.[105] We might have looked another way. If it is *indecorous* to address a fig tree with an ostentatious *epithet*, what of the act of address itself? What does *apostrophe* make possible simply by permitting you to speak to a fig tree? What impossible capacities do you grant that fig tree with your conspicuous artifice? What impossible capacities does that fig tree grant you?

PART II

CHAPTER 4

"Such as might best be": *Simile* in Edmund Spenser's *Faerie Queene*

Simile never quite recovered from Aristotle's subordination of the figure to *metaphor*. *Simile*, he warned, is "longer" than *metaphor*, and therefore *simile* is "less attractive" than *metaphor*: "It does not say outright that 'this' is 'that,' and therefore the hearer is less interested in the idea."[1] While *metaphor*'s act of substitution startles us by its audacity, *simile* builds hesitation, negotiation, and even accommodation into its own syntax—in English, its *as* and its *so*. *Simile*'s value as a figure depreciates accordingly: "Both speech and reasoning," Aristotle argued, "are lively in proportion as they make us seize a new idea promptly."[2] If *metaphor* presupposes an act of translation in the strictest sense of the word, a "carrying across" conceptual boundaries, *simile*'s syntax exposes the route of that translation. It forces us at length to retrace the journey—or even, the poetic labor—that *metaphor* disowns. The form of a *simile* weakens the logical end of its own comparative work by extending the time it takes for us to get from "this" to "that."[3] The very syntactical hinges, the *as* and the *so* that make *simile* identifiable as a form, also offer a peculiar organization of time.

The syntax of *simile* was marked by duration and an extension of time; the very reliability of those syntactical markers, however, also made *simile* available as a tool of poetic production in the humanist schoolrooms of the sixteenth century. Easily identified by its *as* and its *so* (or its "like," etc.), *simile* was both the sign of a piece of text ready to be gathered and a *formula* for composition. Classical and humanist rhetoricians distinguished *simile* from *metaphor* by treating it as a mechanism for generating images: in this capacity, they defined *simile* in relation to *icon*, *parable*, and the *example*.[4] In *The Art of English Poesy* (1589), George Puttenham defines *similitude* as the "common ancestor" of *icon*, *parable*, and the *example*, but he also treats it as a figure, the "bare Similitude."[5] According to this taxonomy, *simile*, or more commonly, *similitude*, appears as both a category encompassing these other figures of comparison and as a discrete figure in its own right. When discussed alongside these other figures, *simile* is often praised for its utility—the ease with which it might be found and the ease with which it might be deployed.[6] As a belabored *metaphor* (on the one hand) and a reliable tool of poetic production (on the other), *simile*'s temporal demands seem even more peculiar. The very facility with which *simile* might be handled appears to offset—but not conceal—the form's slower thinking.

As a genus encompassing other figures of comparison, *similitude* posited a separate temporal claim. In addition to being an industrious figure of *elocutio*, *similitude* was a place of *inventio* and thus participated in an increasingly spatialized understanding of knowledge and its production.[7] As I discussed in Chapter 1, while classical and early humanists were content to allow *similitude* to act as both a place of *inventio* and a figure of *elocutio*, the Ramist reforms drove a disciplinary wedge between these two functions.[8] As the Ramists began to define *inventio*—and thinking, more generally—as an operation of the silent, meditative mind, their marginalization of figures of speech exposed an anxiety concerning rhetoric's abiding commitment to language as such. As a place of *inventio* within the reformed dialectic, *similitude* marked a turn away from the temporality of dialogic exchange and a turn toward a synchronic space within the mind.[9] By contrast, as a figure of *elocutio*, *simile* carried the threat of its own excess. It carried the potential to pervert the operations of dialectic by wresting thinking out of the synchronic space of the mind and into the temporality of speaking.[10] The Ramist reforms were an attempt to preserve the art of dialectic—and the mind, for which the art had come to be a representation—from the contingencies of linguistic mutability.[11] *Similitude*'s second life as a figure of speech threatened to subject the act of thinking to its own organization of time. Simile's syntactical markers permit for a particular kind of thinking that they also slow down.

The history of *similitude* as both a place of *inventio* and a figure of *elocutio* marks *simile* as a vexed structure of composition in early modern England. As a place of *inventio*, the logical function of *similitude* facilitated an epistemological move away from the temporal experience of poetic labor and toward abstraction because it compacted the slow *simile* into an expedient interpretation. In this sense, *similitude*'s assertion of a hypothetical "as if" marked a transition into philosophy's ideal domain: what Sidney describes in the *Defence of Poesy* (c. 1580) as "what should be."[12] In her important study of figuration—for which *simile* was paradigmatic—Susanne Wofford describes this turn toward abstraction as *simile*'s ideological work. By asserting an identity between the "action" of a poem and "the poetic and cultural value attributed to it," *simile*'s claim to comparison was predicated on "the suppression of any direct acknowledgment of what could disrupt it."[13] If the very necessity of a *simile* tended to indicate that such cultural value was not inherent within the action itself, that *simile*'s aesthetic work amounted to a kind of interpretive violence on that action. By contrast, as a figure of *elocutio* the early modern *simile* also organized an experience of the indicative (Sidney called this the "bare 'was'" of history).[14] As an engine for the production of copia, *simile* provided a narrative paradigm of accumulation.[15] Slow but industrious, *simile* threatened to wrest the moralizing projections of its comparative claim back into an experience of the indicative.

In the "Letter to Raleigh" appended to the 1590 *Faerie Queene*, Edmund Spenser described his own poetic domain according to the act of negotiation outlined by Sidney—the negotiation between "what should be" and the "bare 'was.'"[16] *The Faerie Queene*, Spenser writes, offers an "ensample" of "such as might best be."[17] The early modern *simile*, with its conflicting temporal claims—its projection of an idealized domain, on the one hand, and its organization of the indicative, on the other—was among the instruments with which Spenser created "such as might best be" with the precision that such a negotiation demanded. Most discussions of narrative temporality in *The Faerie Queene* operate at the level of genre and identify the digressive force of romance as a centrifugal pull against the linear movement of epic and the *telos* of its quest.[18] *Simile* allowed Spenser to wield this digressive motion on both a local and a narrative level. On the local level, Spenser exploited *simile*'s capacity for temporal organization by suggesting that the form's syntax might itself come unhinged. In the following *simile*, Braggadochio—the vagrant pseudo-knight—climbs out from the bush in which he has been hiding. Getting himself together before Belphoebe (the beautiful huntress whose loud horn he has fled), Braggadochio reemerges as a shameless bird tending to its ruffled feathers:

> As fearfull fowle, that long in secret caue
> For dread of soring hauke her selfe hath hid,
> Not caring how her silly life to saue,
> She her gay painted plumes disorderid,
> Seeing at last her selfe from daunger rid,
> Peepes forth, and soone renews her natiue pride;
> She gins her feathers fowle disfigured
> Prowdly to prune, and sett on euery side,
> So shakes off shame, ne thinks how erst she did her hide.
>
> So when her goodly visage he beheld,
> He gan himselfe to vaunt:
>
> (2.3.36–37.1–2)

This *simile* missteps. It stumbles out of its comparative image and repeats—as if rousing itself—its own correlative: "So shakes off shame," (36.9), "So when her goodly visage he beheld" (37.1). If, as Aristotle suggested, *simile* takes more time to get from "this" to "that," from the bird resetting her "gay painted plumes" to Braggadochio reassembling himself before Belphoebe, Spenser suggests that *simile*'s syntax is itself generative of further delay (36.4). The slow thinking of *simile* is capable of resisting the process of abstraction—if only for another moment. By exploiting the correlative's capacity both to modify the bird as she gets a hold of herself—"So shakes off shame" (36.9)—and to initiate the comparative turn toward our dubious knight—"So when her goodly visage he beheld" (37.1)—Spenser allows the temporal organization of *simile* to displace the logical point of *similitude*. *Simile*'s own syntactical materials can get, as it were, in the way.

For Spenser, the local formal work of *simile* also informs the larger narrative of which Braggadochio is a part. As the thief of Guyon's horse and spear, Braggadochio's narrative is modeled after the labor of the schoolroom *simile*. Braggadochio collects, like schoolboys, other men's *ornamenta*—a word that describes both the weapons of war and the figures of rhetoric.[19] Braggadochio's entrance onto the scene of *The Faerie Queene* initiates the digressive narrative threads characteristic of romance.[20] Braggadochio's continued activity throughout the central books of *The Faerie Queene* constitutes a centrifugal pull against the *telos* of epic quest. Braggadochio proceeds through time by collecting comparative images—horse, spear, groom—and he uses them to generate his own *simile*: the likeness of a knight.[21] His accumulation of comparative images, like the early modern *simile* itself, organizes the narrative temporality that constitutes this centrifugal pull against logical abstraction. In the following pages, I attend to the paradoxical temporality of the early modern *simile* by situating it within the conflicting directives of humanist pedagogy. While I will suggest that the ideal projections of *similitude* facilitate Spenser's construction of "such as might best be" in faerie land, I will also suggest that this abstraction is never complete because of the temporal work of *simile*.[22] Figure is both instrumental to Spenser's attempt to combine the philosophical idealism of "what should be" with the historical determination of the "bare 'was'" and an abiding threat to the acceptance of "such as might best be" because the conspicuousness of figure exposes the time and labor that goes into the production of plausibility. The visibility of *poesie* challenges the very poetic domain that it also establishes. It will be the final move of this chapter to suggest that the abstraction of "such as might best be" seeks to efface the poetic labor of *simile* and—in the case of Braggadochio—the social mobility facilitated by the narrative of accumulation that underwrites this labor.[23]

The Doing and the Thing Done

At least one of Spenser's early modern readers stumbled, with the "fearfull fowle," out of Braggadochio's *simile* (2.3.36.1). In his 1617 *Spenser*, Ben Jonson marked a number of good *similes*. In fact, while Spenser's modern readers tend to take *allegory* as the defining trope (or genre, or mode) of *The Faerie Queene*, Jonson identified "<u>Simile</u>" alone among tropes and figures and schemes in the margins of his *Spenser*. Sometimes, also, and only when it was extended, he marked "An excellent simile." Once he commanded himself to memorize one of Spenser's *similes* with "M." for short.[24] In the margin beside the "fearfull fowle" *simile*, however, the kind of work that Jonson is doing shifts. Rather than simply identifying the figure, as with a notation like "<u>Simile</u>," Jonson performs the sort of abstraction against which the *simile*'s own syntax militates. Jonson's notes are reproduced to the side:

As fearfull fowle, that long in secret Caue	An excell.
For dread of soaring hauke her selfe hath hid,	Simile to
Not caring how, her silly life to saue,	expresse [word crossed out]
She her gay painted plumes disorderid,	cowardnesse
Seeing at last her selfe from danger rid,	
Peepes foorth, and soone renewes her natiue pride;	

> She gins her feathers foule disfigured
> Proudly to prune, and set on euery side,
> So shakes off shame, ne thinks how erst shee did her hide:
>
> So when her goodly visage he beheld,
> He gan himselfe to vaunt . . .²⁵

Led in at least one wrong direction, initial interpretation no sooner written than dashed quite, Jonson's careful step backward seems almost to mimic the *simile*'s own misstep. While Spenser's *simile* appears to have slowed him down along the way, Jonson's final move is to elide this temporal work. The transition to "cowardnesse" witnesses an ambition to fix meaning upon a mobile narrative image by arresting it within a synchronic framework. The interpretive act that survives looks a lot like allegoresis. By insisting that this *simile* means something "other" than what it "speaks" and by identifying this "other" as "cowardnesse," Jonson's note suggests that *simile* is only intelligible within a system of thinking that eschews time and labor in favor of erecting—and securing *simile* within—a schematic conceptual plane.²⁶

The danger in reading *similes* within an interpretive framework that prioritizes logical abstraction is that the form of *simile* can only become a measure of exegetical slack. The *as* and the *so* by which likeness and difference confront each other in a *simile* simply keep the recalcitrant materials—those images that resist abstraction from narrative—in interpretive play. Thus, in the example above, "cowardnesse" circumscribes (rather too easily) this *simile*'s somewhat problematic suggestion that "shame" is the sort of thing one simply "shakes off" (36.9). Or that "shame" persists only for as long as one "thinks" about the transgression from which it arose (36.9). Accordingly, the sort of allegoresis evidenced by "cowardnesse" offers *simile* two equally limited functions. Within what Helen Cooney calls "meaning-oriented" interpretations, the comparative image of a *simile* acts as extra figural mass, subject to abstraction's centripetal pull and reining those recalcitrant materials in by way of *so*. Within what she describes as "self-referential" interpretations, *as* and *so* mark the borders of a contained space in which to play with the potentially vagrant materials.²⁷ They produce the potential for digression only, finally, to dramatize an act of logical incorporation into an allegorical design. Such readings prioritize *simile*'s function as a place of *inventio* over its function as a figure of *elocutio*.²⁸ They prioritize the logical point of *similitude* while subordinating the materials that are produced by *simile* and are determined by their temporal relation to one another.²⁹ As Jonson's act of allegoresis prioritizes an abstraction from the "fearfull fowle" to "cowardnesse," it cancels out *simile*'s temporal work. And that, at a moment in which Spenser has dramatized *simile*'s capacity for even slower speaking—"So shakes off shame" (36.9): "So when her goodly visage he beheld" (37.1).

By arresting a *simile* in time, Jonson's act of allegoresis treats *poesie* as if it is reducible to the product that it creates and suggests that *poesie* is therefore of greatest value when it is most invisible. At least part of the hesitation evidenced by that one word, whatever it might have been, crossed out between "Expresse" and "cowardnesse," however, comes from the fact that Jonson switches, mid-note, between two different ways of reading *similes*. The first part of his annotation, "An excell. / Simile" resembles Jonson's more usual markings in the margins beside Spenser's *similes*. There, he points to the figure and names it "Simile."[30] In this capacity, his notes act like Richard Sherry's lousy "common scholemasters," lamented in "The Epistle" to *A Treatise of Schemes and Tropes* (1550), who "saye vnto their scholers: *Hic Est Figura*."[31] This first kind of reading values Spenser's poem for its *formulas* of composition and suggests (as is particularly clear with Jonson's imperative to himself, "M.") that *simile* is detachable from the poem in which it appears by virtue of its formal integrity. Detachable, *simile* becomes intelligible as an instrument of *poesie*. In the second part of his annotation, Jonson performs the kind of allegoresis we see in other moments of his reading. For example, "St. George!" inscribed above Red Crosse Knight's bumbling entrance into the poem.[32] This notation points to itself (rather emphatically) as a parody of its own reductive gesture. If "to / Expresse" does not contain the bathos of such punctuated marginalia, it does suggest that this *simile* thinks something other than what it speaks. It is not difficult to imagine that "cowardnesse" serves as a subject heading in a commonplace book, immediately preceded by "bravery." The second kind of reading prepares the *simile* for entry into this commonplace book, but this preparation requires that one read through *simile*'s *as* as well as its *so*. The first way of reading suggests that the form of *simile* itself renders the figure available for accumulation. The second way of reading suggests that the abstraction of allegoresis is a precondition for the selection and accumulation of *similes*.

As Jonson's note transitions between these two ways of reading, the object of his interpretation shifts. According to the first, Jonson locates the figure within a history of composition. "Simile" understands *The Faerie Queene* as "Poesy," defined by Jonson as "labour, and studye . . . skill, or Crafte of Making." As we have seen, Jonson also calls this "the doing."

By contrast, the abstraction by which Jonson shuffles this *simile* under the heading of "cowardnesse" takes, as its interpretive object, the "*Poeme*" or "the thing done."[33] With this transition, Jonson (to Sherry's great relief) prioritizes the "meaning of our mynd" over the "folyshe" inclination "to laboure to speake darkelye for the nonce."[34] But prior to his marginalia's shift from studying "the doing" to studying "the thing done," from endless work to completed action, Jonson locates *The Faerie Queene* within a technology of poetic labor. "Simile" registers the figure's availability for, if not other-speaking, other-makings.[35]

If Jonson's identification of "Simile" within this history of composition would seem to say more about Jonson's style than Spenser's, it says even more about the pedagogical training that pervaded the early modern schoolrooms to which Jonson and Spenser and many of their early readers belonged. Jonson's most devoted pupil, William Drummond, also marked a particularly good *simile* in his *1609 Spenser*; according to Jonson, Drummond's verse "smelled too much of yᵉ schooles."[36] One of Spenser's early modern annotators left markings pointing out only *similes*.[37] "E. K." calls attention to a number of *The Shepheardes Calender*'s *similes* in his printed annotations, and these comments are restrained in comparison to the notation's ubiquity in the printed marginalia of early modern books.[38] An entire subgenre of printed commonplace books devoted to collecting *similitudes* emerges in the sixteenth century.[39] Following the lead of humanist educators such as Erasmus, *simile* becomes a figure for which one reads in books and in the natural world as if a book. Plants, animals—all are a source of *similes*.[40] *Simile*, in turn, becomes an engine for producing your own speech or for converting someone else's speech to your own purposes. As both text and natural world become a limitless supply of *similes*, the syntax of the *simile* itself becomes a *formula* for composition. A common early modern proverb naturalizes this comparative work and distills it into the sort of pithiness you could inscribe on a ring or carve into your dinner plate: *similis simili gaudet*, "like takes pleasure in like."[41]

The underside to this naturalization is a fear of copious surfeit. The articulation of likeness might, by way of rhetoric's protean powers, transform an object into a resemblance where there was no likeness with which to begin.[42] The pilfered book of nature might run dry, as in one of John Marston's character's dreams. Here, the earth belches forth from the inside a parody of its own comparative fecundity:

> For methought I dreamt I was asleep, and methought the ground
> yawned and belked up the abominable ghost of a misshapen Simile,

with two ugly pages, the one called Master *Even-as*, going before, and the other Mounser *Even-so*, following after, whilst Signior Simile stalked most prodigiously in the midst.⁴³

In William Shakespeare's *As You Like It*, Jacques "moralize[s]" the "spectacle" of his pastoral surroundings "into a thousand similes," and the very figure meant to gauge nature, to parcel it into useful pieces, becomes a mark of man's solipsistic distance and its superfluous iteration, a means of isolating the individual.⁴⁴ If early modern pedagogy's emphasis on the sheer number of *similes* prioritizes the copious production of speech, abstractions such as "cowardnesse" emerge as a response to potential surfeit. As a place of *inventio*, *similitude* facilitates this abstraction and reins in production under the *telos* of rhetorical argumentation and its standard of persuasion.⁴⁵ Thus, the figure's apparent utility in the generation of discourse poses a particular problem for its narrative of poetic labor: If Jonson's "Simile" imagines the poetic text within a history of composition that neither climaxes nor concludes with *The Faerie Queene*, how did the exercises of early modern pedagogy determine the shape of this history? Was the form itself always alien to the context of its appearance, pointing to its origin elsewhere? What end did the accumulation of *similes* serve? What kinds of texts might the *simile* project as a continuation of its history?

The fragmentation of the text implied by "Simile" is akin to the fragmentation performed by the commonplace book, a tool through which the early modern reader produced new speech from what he read. One seventeenth-century compiler described the entries in his commonplace book as "Rhetoricall expressions, Description, or some very apt Simile," and this attention characterized his attempt to read what he called "understandingly." Reading "understandingly" meant that "he considers how aptly such a thing would fitt with an exercise of his."⁴⁶ It understands reading as part of the writing process and may, in fact, be close to what Jonson meant when he suggested that "things, wrote with labour, deserve to be so read."⁴⁷ Following the work of Lisa Jardine and Anthony Grafton, early modern scholars have understood reading with labor as "goal-orientated reading," what Eugene R. Kintgen has described as "teleological" reading: "primarily practical, aimed at some goal other than private edification, typically conceived of as private education for public action or persuasion."⁴⁸ According to this version of "active reading," the abstraction of allegoresis enables the *telos* of "goal-orientated reading." The subject headings of the commonplace book usher its user's selection into predetermined themes ("cowardnesse"), and the training *in utramque partem* for which schoolroom disputations have prepared students assures us that "Bravery" appears on a preceding page or in a preceding column.[49] Allegoresis, it would seem, is a precondition for the accumulation of *similes*.

There is, however, another kind of commonplace book proposed by humanist educators. The commonplace book organized into antithetical subject headings facilitates the "goal-orientated readings" described by Jardine and Grafton: it filters the humanist's potentially unruly investment in copia into the linear logic of argumentation and persuasion. By contrast, the commonplace books described by Juan Luis Vives and, most importantly, by Erasmus in *On the Method of Study* as well as the earlier drafts of *On Copia*, prioritize "patterns of expression" over "a method of rational thinking."[50] For Vives, Ann Moss writes:

> The organizing principle is almost entirely lexical, and the categories employed cover everyday and unusual vocabulary; obscure and familiar idioms and expressions; amusing and perceptive sayings; proverbs and tricky passages. These are the building-blocks of composition, which Vives presents as a purely linguistic exercise in which the pupil starts by arranging and rearranging vocabulary and phrases taken from his notebook in order to assemble mosaics of other men's words.[51]

Rather than facilitating the allegoresis necessary to the persuasive end of rhetoric, this kind of commonplace book enables a piecemeal, aggregative composition, primarily associative in its selections and lexical in its organization. The commonplace book of "goal-orientated readings" tends to prioritize—and even claims to represent—the world of *res* or things. By contrast, this other commonplace book presents us with an alternative epistemology in which the engine of production—the figure as *formula*—is the primary tool of a maker's knowledge. It suggests that *simile* is valued less for its capacity to represent this world than for its capacity to manufacture an altogether different world.

Braggadochio acts as just such a reader in faerie land. Like the commonplace-book compiler trolling for "some very apt simile" that "would fitt with an exercise of his," Braggadochio's acts of accumulation constitute the laborious production of a *simile*. Stealing Guyon's horse and spear, acquiring a groom in Trompart and eventually making off with another man's money and another man's snowy lady, Braggadochio moves through time by collecting the comparative images that constitute the likeness of a knight. Compiling other men's *ornamenta*, he is a version of early modern composition, the "packet of pilfries" told by Thomas Nashe. This kind of composition arrives at press in "disguised arraie" and "vaunts" other poets' "plumes as their owne."⁵² When Braggadochio crawls out from the bush in which he has been hiding and faces Belphoebe, his "plumes" (or *ornamenta*) are all in disarray. As he sets about reordering his "gay painted plumes disorderid" and refiguring his "feathers fowle disfigured," the *simile*'s emphasis on individual pieces put together ill recalls Puttenham's description of *indecorous poesie*:

> As the excellent painter bestoweth the rich orient colors upon his table of portrait: So, nevertheless, as if the same colors in our art of poesy (as well as in those other mechanical arts) be not well-tempered, or not well-laid, or be used in excess, or never so little *disordered* or misplaced, they not only give it no manner of grace at all, but rather do *disfigure* the stuff and spill the whole workmanship, taking away all beauty and good liking from it. . . . Wherefore the chief praise and cunning of our poet is in the discreet using of his figures.⁵³

As with "those other mechanical arts," bad work—the conspicuous placement of pieces, excess and superfluity—rots. They "sp[o]ill" the work because they display its labor and the time this labor implies. Conversely, the "discreet" poet, by using figures inconspicuously, produces an object that appears effortless and therefore untainted by this labor. If, according to Puttenham, the *indecorous* style produces a waste that diminishes the value of a poem, the *decorous* style disguises the action of "workmanship" by producing an ordered (rather than "disordered"), a figured (rather than "disfigured") poem. Work(manship) becomes "the thing done," at one metonym's remove from "the doing" and the verbal—or temporal—implications of this gerund.

When Puttenham suggests that "disordered" and "disfigure[d]" compositions take "good liking" away from the "whole workmanship," he may be referring to a somewhat casual aesthetic pleasure—as if a watered-down version of Horatian delight.⁵⁴ He may also be suggesting that artifice at its most conspicuous gives the lie to the likeness of a composition, betraying the boundaries of plausibility (the thing that, once done, the poetic composition *ought* to be like). In the fumbling of the "fearfull fowle" *simile*, Spenser suggests that Braggadochio's assembly resists this sort of abstraction from the history of its own composition. His process of accumulation—the collection of comparative images and the compilation of his own exercise—is visible precisely because it is ongoing ("the doing"). Spenser also suggests, as the "fearfull fowle" *simile* repeats the correlative "So," that *simile*'s form is itself capable of resisting this abstraction. A *simile*'s *as* as well as its *so* are among the recalcitrant materials bound to narrative. Thus, a more particular set of questions produced by the *simile*'s role within a history of composition emerges: How did the conflicting directives of early modern pedagogy attend to *simile*'s syntactical markers? In what ways might the form of a *simile* facilitate the very "good liking" it would also seem to resist? And how did a pedagogy preoccupied with making good use of one's time offset *simile*'s slower thinking?

Even-as *and Even*-so

Marston's "Signior Simile," who climbs up out of the earth, flanked by "Even-*as*" and "Even-*so*," suggests that the figure itself was understood to be composed of discrete parts.[55] As the schoolmaster John Brinsley instructed, the reduction of a composition into its smallest units enabled imitation. By "unmaking" a text, a student could make again another text.[56] But the Signior's parts are also moveable. Marston attributes a kind of agency to them—the agency to climb up out of the earth and the agency to fall into position (and, perhaps, to fall out of formation).[57] The "unmade" *simile* reduced to its discrete parts might come back from the dead—dismembered on a student's autopsy table—as "the abhominable ghost of a misshapen *simile*."[58]

As "pages" to a *simile*, "Even-*as*" and "Even-*so*" point to the instrumentality of *simile*'s syntax, its humdrum utility if not its labor.[59] A schoolboy's earliest formal encounter with *simile* engages with the figure's "pages" as grammatical units. Among the various classifications of adverbs in William Lily's *Shorte introduction to grammar* (1567), "some," one diagram declares, "be of Likenes: as Sic, sicut, quasi, ceu, tanquam, velut."[60] The *Grammar*'s poem, *Carmen de Moribus*, reinforces this introduction to the syntactical "pages" with a *simile* that, as does the entire poem, combines instruction in right syntax with instruction in right morals:

> For, *even as* the earth can cause neither seeds nor flowers to grow
> Unless it is made to thrive by the continuous labor of the hand:
> *Even so*, if the boy does not exercise his genius,
> He will lose, at an instant, the expectation of this genius and time itself.[61]

Extrapolating from his exemplary discussion of the first two verses of *Carmen de Moribus*, we can say that the schoolmaster John Brinsley expected each schoolboy first to translate these lines from Latin into English, assuring his teacher that he "know the meaning of them, and can construe them perfectly."[62] Next the teacher prompts his pupil to parse the text in the order of his translation; "*veluti*" would come early in this parsing, and the child should explain "why he began to construe there." The child should be able to identify *veluti* as an adverb of "Likenesse," with, perhaps, a reference to the authority of his *Grammar*, as "set down in the booke." The teacher might ask "what . . . [*veluti*] is like," and the child ought to point to "*Sic*."[63] Here, the correlative makes the comparative structure of the verse its most prominent form.

In early education, this *simile* became a kind of syntactical touchstone within the mind. Eventually, students were expected to take their own English translation and turn the verse back into Latin (the process known as double translation); then, "(which is the principall, and wherein you [the schoolmaster] will take much delight)," the children were expected to recite this *simile* "with their bookes vnder their armes."[64] Taking the poem two couplets at a time, students could move on to their afternoon lessons once, as another schoolmaster, Charles Hoole advised, "they have repeated these verses of Mr. *Lilies* so often over, that they can say them all at once pretty well by heart."[65] The syntactical "pages" of this *simile*—"*Veluti*" and "*Sic*"—retrieved the logical point of *similitude* (the necessity of diligence) even as the *simile* itself served to reinforce the student's knowledge of grammar. Memorizing the poem in fragments, a student would not have to run through the whole poem from the beginning to find his adverbs of likeness.[66] *Similitude* functions, simultaneously, in the service of abstraction and as a formal device, an engine for linguistic recollection, organization, and generation.

As a tool of intellectual labor, the slow thinking of *simile* becomes implicated in the efficiency of educational cultivation.[67] The fear expressed in these lines, perhaps even greater than that of the loss of genius, is the loss of that demonstratively produced "Time itself."[68] At the very moment that the student loses the hope of his genius, the time of his labor transforms into an object of waste. Rhetorical instruction prioritized *simile* as an instrument for the generation of discourse rather than as the expression of a point of resemblance. Its very instrumentality facilitated the temporal work of the schoolroom.[69] The schoolmaster might read a *similitude* out loud as a prompt for a writing exercise and thus generate multiple epistles from the unpacking of its comparative claim.[70] But *simile* could also be useful as a *formula* for composition, supplying the writer with an easy transition from one part of his text to another. By allowing a text to pivot from one idea to another, the syntactical hinges of the *simile* became a structure to which any student might reliably refer when he needed to get to the next topic.[71] A *simile* might also act as a closural device, lending any composition the sense of sententiousness enacted by its formulaic alternation between images.⁷² Thus, as *simile* becomes an engine of compositional productivity, it implicates its own discursive production in the economic enterprises of the classroom.⁷³ Within this economic register, the availability of a *simile*—readied, as Erasmus suggests, "in our pocket so to speak"—offsets the form's slower thinking.⁷⁴

Treatises that present themselves as "storehouses" or "treasuries" of "similitudes" translate *simile*'s potential for the timely production of discourse into the hyperbolic appraisal of precious stones. In his *Parabolae Sive Similia* or *Parallels*, Erasmus offers his reader "many jewels in one small book."⁷⁵ Shunning "barbershops" and the "tawdry conversation of the marketplace," these collections deal only in "precious stones from the inner treasure-house of the Muses."⁷⁶ If *simile* builds into its form the journey that *metaphor* disowns, these treatises claim to travel on behalf of their students.⁷⁷ They claim to act as a supplement to those bound to the discourse of "barbershop" and "marketplace" and to facilitate the journey that *simile*'s form keeps slow. When in *Astrophil and Stella* 3 Sidney's poet claims to shun the "strange similes" that "enrich each line, / Of herbs or beasts, which Ind or Afric hold," he makes the claim that Stella's face is sufficient. He also, however, rejects the very economy that these treatises maintain.⁷⁸ Like the "dictionary's methode" that allows a poem to go "running in rattling rows"⁷⁹ or like "Nizolian paper-books" containing "figures and phrases," these collections of *similitudes* place a student's text within an economy that takes its value from the journey its form organizes.⁸⁰ That these texts do not require their students to go on their own journey at once offsets *simile*'s slower form and suggests that the line between the "tawdry conversation of the marketplace" and the "inner treasure-house of the Muses" is not altogether secure.

By contrast to its productive role in the generation of discourse, *similitude* was understood to be among the weakest forms of proof. As a place of *inventio*, arguments *ex similitudine* offered abject evidence used more often by other, less rigorous disciplines ("other" to whatever discipline was at hand).⁸¹ *Similitudes* acted as both a supplement to man's weakened intellect, what Seneca called "props to our feebleness," and as a sign of this decidedly less erect wit.⁸² The Ramist redistribution of the canons belonging to rhetoric and dialectic removes *simile* from *elocutio*, thereby denying its status as a figure and suggesting that its sphere of functions is limited to the place of *inventio*.⁸³ Within this place, *similes* that are also fictions are the weakest form of proof. As Fraunce writes in *The Lawiers Logike* (1588), "fayned similitudes" can only ever contribute to the "plausible."⁸⁴

If, as Sidney suggested in the *Defence*, poets "borrow nothing of what is, hath been, or shall be," committing themselves solely to "consideration of what may be and should be," *similitude*'s demonstrative failure made it useful in the construction of a poetic domain.[85] While Sidney was ready to embrace *similitude* as the principle of likeness that giverns the poetic world, he was not altogether sure that poets should not shun *similes* as tools or *formulas*. Readily available from newly translated rhetorical taxonomies and from printed commonplace books, *similitudes* filled everybody's pockets (so to speak). The sheer number of *similitudes*—potential and actual—was itself a threat to *decorum*:

> Now for similitudes, in certain printed discourses, I think all herbarists, all stories of beasts, fowls, and fishes are rifled up, that they come in multitudes to wait upon any of our conceits; which certainly is as absurd a surfeit to the ears as is possible. For the force of a similitude not being to prove anything to a contrary disputer, but only to explain to a willing hearer, when that is done, the rest is a most tedious prattling, rather over-swaying the memory from the purpose whereto they were applied, than any whit informing the judgment, already either satisfied, or by similitudes not to be satisfied.[86]

Sidney's concern for the weak nature of the evidence supplied by *similitudes* appears to understand persuasion as its end. He treats *similtude*, that is, as a place of *inventio* (rather than a figure of *elocutio*) and locates it within the contested intersection of rhetoric and dialectic.[87] Yet his account of this weak breed of evidence takes the form of a quantitative rather than a qualitative monster. Collecting "in multitudes to wait" upon the more dignified "conceits" or thoughts, *similitudes* signify a "surfeit" that overtakes the "ears" but does not penetrate the mind or facilitate thinking. The poet with a sense of *decorum* knows to employ "these knacks very sparingly." For Sidney, the threat posed by *simile* within textual production is that it facilitates a certain kind of composition by men "more careful to speak curiously than to speak truly."[88] Easily come by and easily deployed, the utility of *simile* backfires. The figure threatens the ear with the endless iteration of its own syntactical "pages." "They come," Sidney warned, "in multitudes."

Sidney's quantitative fears at once assert an ideal of proportion and suggest that *simile*'s very utility—its capacity to act as a *formula* for composition—is a mark of the *indecorous*. In this sense, Sidney's dismissal of *similitudes* limns the normative values that classical and early modern theories of *decorum* helped sustain.[89] His fears also suggest that such ideas of *decorum* were beginning to operate within a visual epistemology.[90] Here is not so much a concern for person, time, and place as the quantification of design that I discussed in Chapter 3: Sidney registers deviation from *decorum* under the sign of "surfeit" and reduces the value of this deviation from poetry to "prattling."[91] The *indecorous* composition becomes not only a violation of proportion but also improbable.

"*Such, as he him thought, or faine would bee*"

The men who trade in these "knacks" upset not only *decorum* but also the harmonious social structure with which it coincides. The man working with these *similitudes* "doth," to quote Sidney again, "dance to his own music." "Tedious prattling" wanders outside of the realm of plausibility as that realm is determined by the places of *inventio*; the figures of *elocutio* with which *indecorous* thinking proceeds chart the parameters of a zodiac out of tune.[92] For Spenser, the crucial difference was between Plato's instruction in what "should be" and Xenophon's "ensample" of a government "fashioned . . . such as might best be."[93] While describing the "Methode" of *The Faerie Queene*, Spenser defended his use of "historicall fiction" as "most plausible":

> For this cause [the pleasing of "commune sence"] is Xenophon preferred before Plato, for that the one in the exquisite depth of his iudgement, formed a Commune welth *such as it should be*, but the other in the person of Cyrus and the Persians fashioned a gouernment *such as might best be*: So much more profitable and gratious is doctrine by ensample, then by rule. So haue I laboured to doe in the person of Arthure.[94]

That which "might best be" is a poetic domain that does not limit itself to the indicative but does understand mortal lodgings as the essential parameters of its construction.[95] What "might best be" posits a gap between its own representation and a "may be" unmitigated by the limitations of historical temporality. With the help of Demetrius, we might think of Spenser's imaginative world as restaging the difference between *metaphor* and *simile*:

> When a metaphor seems bold, convert it into a simile for greater safety. . . . The result is a simile and a less risky form of expression, while the former was a metaphor and more dangerous. This is why Plato's use of metaphor in preference to simile is thought risky. Xenophon by contrast prefers the simile.[96]

If *metaphor*'s audacity lies in its claim to substitution ("'this' is 'that,'" Aristotle said), *simile*'s caution erects a comparative structure of potential but unrealized exchange. Humanist pedagogy taught that *simile*'s syntactical "pages" might also double as negotiating caveats intended to disarm *metaphor*'s disruptive potential—"as if," "as it were," "if one may say so."[97] In these moments, the schoolboy's parsing of "*veluti*" returns: "*veluti*" might function as either the introduction to a comparative image or as an apology to hedge *metaphor*'s bet.

Insofar as Spenser's poetic world and its commitment to plausibility reassert the normative values of *decorum*, it disguises *simile*'s temporal work as an instrument of *poesie*. *Decorum* insists—like *sprezzatura*—that art disguise its artifice and produce itself as "the thing done." *Decorum* disowns the narrative of "the doing." Spenser's problem is, then, not altogether different from the problem Braggadochio faces as he generates his *similitude* of a knight. Like Spenser, Braggadochio attempts to create his own poetic domain within faerie land. After stealing a horse and spear from Guyon, this vagrant traveler "gan to hope, of men to be receiu'd / For such, as he him thought, or faine would bee" (2.3.5.5–6). Spenser's construction of "such as might best be" displaces its source of judgment onto what the letter calls "commune sence."[98] Braggadochio's world of "such, as he him thought, or faine would bee" challenges this act of displacement. Braggadochio's "would bee" suggests that individuated desire is never actually effaced, checked by, or subsumed within an appeal to the probable. The *epanorthosis* that withdraws "thought" and offers "faine" in its stead speaks to the intimate entangling of *indecorous* thinking with the pleasure of the poet-maker.

Braggadochio's history of composition also mobilizes him within the social hierarchy of faerie land. Running around collecting other men's *ornamenta*, Braggadochio imagines the generation of his *similitude* as the means of social advancement. Through a sustained *paronomasia* (or pun), *The Faerie Queene* suggests that Braggadochio's accumulation of comparative images and his ability to advance within a social hierarchy are the result of his words. When Braggadochio collects the third image of his *similitude*, he intimidates the man who will serve as his groom by waving his spear and whipping his horse. He also asserts his power over Trompart with what the poem repeatedly calls his "vaunt" (13.1). Exhaling the "smoke of vanity" (5.3), Braggadochio, as a "vaunter," offers (merely) speech without substance (2.4.1.9). This "auaunting" verbiage also constitutes a firm plan for social *advancement* (2.3.6.3). When Braggadochio first hatches his plan to construct a *similitude* of a knight, "to court he cast t'aduaunce his first degree" (5.9).⁹⁹ The narrative of Braggadochio's productive *similitude*, a tally of his comparative images over time, portrays advancement within faerie land's social hierarchy as the product of his speaking. When Braggadochio charges Trompart, he approaches "As Peacocke, that his painted plumes doth pranck," and he speaks (6.4):

> Vile Caytiue, vassall of dread and despayre,
> Vnworthie of the commune breathed ayre,
> Why liuest thou, dead dog, a lenger day,
> And doest not vnto death thy selfe prepayre.
> Dy, or thy selfe my captiue yield for ay;
> Great fauour I thee graunt, for aunswere thus to stay.
>
> (7.4–9)

Like the pun with which the poem couples Braggadochio's "vaunting" and his desire to "aduaunce," *paroemion* (or alliteration) and rhyme (also known as *similiter cadens*, the "like falling" of words) suggest associations between things that are the product of a material likeness that acts in the place of abstraction. According to Puttenham, *paroemion*—or "the Figure of Like Letter"—is a barbarism that should be used sparingly.¹⁰⁰ He continues, however, to suggest that it has this one virtue: *paroemion* saves time. The repeated letter, Puttenham writes, "passeth from the lips with more facility by iteration of a letter than by alteration," while "alteration of a letter requires an exchange of ministry and office in the lips, teeth, or palate, and so doth not the iteration."¹⁰¹ The production of like sounds is industrious because it localizes labor: *paroemion* maximizes the efficiency of the organs by which we produce speech by isolating these organs' unique "ministry" and "office." Braggadochio's "vaunts" operate within the same economy of efficient production characteristic of the schoolroom. The utility of *paroemion* suggests something strange about the syntax of *simile*—that it is the product of, rather than an imposition on, the organs with which the body generates speech.

Upon hearing Braggadochio's "vaunts," Trompart surrenders. He "cleeped" Braggadochio "his liege," thereby transforming him into a comparative image within Braggadochio's *simile* (8.9). As a comparative image, Trompart facilitates the production of what Braggadochio "thought, or faine would bee" (5.6). The poem marks Trompart's transformation into a comparative image with another *simile*. Trompart falls to the ground "as an Offall," as a piece of refuse that Braggadochio collects in order that it might participate, like horse and spear, in the production of his *simil-*

itude (8.7). And this comparative image—a waste that is a "falling off" from somewhere else—becomes a constitutive element of Braggadochio's *similitude*.[102]

By coupling the empty "vaunt" with narrative progression and social mobility, *The Faerie Queene* first fixes—and tries to contain—the threat that Braggadochio's alternative construction of "such, as he him thought, or faine would bee" poses to the poem's own construction of "such as might best be." The poet intercedes with a sententious judgment that attempts to isolate what Braggadochio "faine would bee" from two overlapping and temporarily idealized narrative paradigms. "To thinke," the poet declares disdainfully, "without desert of gentle deed, / And noble worth to be aduaunced hye" is "The scorne of knighthood and trew cheualrye" (10.6–7, 5). The thought of advancing by neither the work of "gentle deed" nor the "worth" of nobility is figured as a violation of faerie land's essential construction. "Such prayse is shame," the poet declares, prohibiting Braggoadochio's sustaining *paronomasia* (10.8).

This characterization of Braggadochio's speech as excessive allows the poem to register Braggadochio as an *indecorous* figure within faerie land. The *indecorous* is, on the one hand, a method of exorcism. Braggadochio's pretensions allow Spenser to draw a line between "such as might best be" and "such, as" Braggadochio "thought, or faine would bee" (5.6). The poem's world, however, then becomes dependent upon a difference that is quantitative rather than qualitative: Braggadochio's speech is different in degree rather than in kind. The sustainability of such a line therefore requires the perpetuation of Braggadochio's pretensions. And this is the other hand: the poem's identification of Braggadochio is not so much an exorcism as it is a goad to continuation. If Braggadochio's method for social advancement is implausible because his speech is excessive, then Braggadochio had better keep talking. His collection of comparative images becomes an imperative to the construction of "such as might best be" rather than a violation of it.[103]

After acquiring Trompart, it becomes clear that Braggadochio is missing one crucial ornament in his *similitude*—a lack that keeps him from becoming "the thing done." When Braggadochio runs into the archvillain of these early books, he is almost recognizable as a knight. Archimago is impressed by the gleam of "armour fayre" and the speed of his "goodly courser" (11.3–4). When addressing the pair, he enquires of Trompart "what mightie warriour that mote bee," recognizing him as the groom (12.2). While praising the "golden sell" (the saddle of his horse) and "spere," Archimago enquires into the "wanted sword" (12.3–4). Falling prostrate before Braggadochio (as Trompart fell before him, who himself fell "as an Offall"), Archimago hatches a plan that would revise the central revenge narrative of book 2:

> To plaine of wronges, which had committed bin
> By Guyon, and by that false *Redcrosse* knight,
> Which two through treason and deceiptfull gin,
> Had slayne Sir *Mordant*, and his Lady bright:
> That mote him honour win, to wreak so foule despight.
> (13.5–9)

The poet's straight-faced account of Archimago's revision of events reveals no sense of falsehood in its sturdy "had committed bin." This revision constitutes a kind of intersection at which Braggadochio could enter into yet another version of "what may be"—where, according to Archimago, he "mote him honour win."

In order for Archimago to use Braggadochio—"Of his reuenge to make the instrument"—he needs Braggadochio to be a complete knight with a sword (11.6). As both a reader of Braggadochio and a poet-maker attempting to reshape the central narratives of *The Faerie Queene*, Archimago recognizes that Braggadochio is incompletely assembled. Without a sword, Braggadochio is not so much a knight as someone who looks like a knight. By fixating upon the absence of a sword, Archimago suggests that Braggadochio's incompletion constitutes a centrifugal pull against his own act of allegoresis. If Braggadochio's lack of a sword marks his difference from the "instrument" of Archimago's "reuenge" and thus his resistance to abstraction, Archimago's act of allegoresis promises that the digressive force of the absent sword will succumb to his own act of allegoresis. In book 5, Artegall will become the "instrument" of Elizabeth's "iustice" after acquiring his sword from Astraea (*Proem*.11.8–9). Archimago here plays the part of Astraea: he will get the knight his sword in order to erase the labor with which he builds his own allegorical design.

Braggadochio is willing to partake of Archimago's fantasy, but only for so long. Shaking his spear and seemingly on the point of madness, Braggadochio acts "As if" Mortdant's and Amavia's "liues had in his hand beene gagd" (2.3.14.3). This "As if" effectively places Braggadochio at the court of the Faerie Queene herself, where he is "gagd" to protect the lives of Amavia and Mortdant. Charged with hunting down knights who hide "for feare of dew vengeaunce" (14.7), Braggadochio's logical incorporation into Archimago's design locates a disturbance at the center of the Faerie

"Such as might best be" 117

Queene's court where—according to Archimago and Braggadochio's collaborative revision—she issues out conflicting directives.[104] While entertaining Archimago's desires for a while, pleasing him with his boasts and swearing "dew vegeaunce," Braggadochio ultimately backs down (14.7). When Archimago tells him that he can get him the sword of the "noblest knight" (18.3) in all of faerie land (the sword of Arthur), Braggadochio trembles with fear "And wondred in his minde, what mote that Monster make" (18.9). Braggadochio "gan to quake," with Jonson's own hesitating hand, between the history of composition that has conditioned his movement through time and the final abstraction of allegoresis, incorporation into a monstrous poetic domain: the "mote" of Archimago (18.8).

I would like to conclude this chapter by returning to the *simile* with which I began. I include Jonson's notes (once again). I also include a few lines from the previous stanza and the remainder of the stanza begun by the *simile*'s stumbling correlative. Suspecting that the animal she has been chasing is making all of that noise behind the bush, Belphoebe is ready to impale her catch until Trompart fills her in, and

> She staid: with that, he crauld out of his nest,
> Forth creeping on his caitiue hands and thies,
> And standing stoutly vp, his loftie crest
> Did fiercely shake, and rowze, as comming late from rest.

> As fearfull fowle, that long in secret Caue   An excell.
> For dread of soaring hauke her selfe hath hid,   Simile to
> Not caring how, her silly life to saue,   expresse [word crossed out]
> She her gay painted plumes disorderid,   cowardnesse
> Seeing at last her selfe from danger rid,
> Peepes foorth, and soone renewes her natiue pride;
> She gins her feathers foule disfigured
> Proudly to prune, and set on euery side,
> So shakes off shame, ne thinks how erst shee did her hide:

> So when her goodly visage he beheld,
> He gan himselfe to vaunt: but when he viewed
> Those deadly tooles, which in her hand she held,
> Soone into other fits he was transmewed,
> Till shee to him her gracious speech renewed;
> All haile, Sir knight, and well may thee befall,
> As all the like, which honor haue pursewed

Through deeds of armes and prowesse Martiall;
All vertue merits praise: but such the most of all.
(2.3.35.6–37)

It appears that Spenser's poem had as much trouble getting into this *simile* as it had getting out—"as comming late from rest" (35.9), "As fearfull fowle, that long in secret caue" (36.1). If the second extended *simile* suggests that "as comming late from rest" did not quite get the job done, it also suggests the generative potency of "As." The sort of half-line *simile* that closes Spenser's hexameter is characteristic of Belphoebe's famous blazon, where the *similes* came out in succession: "Cleare as the skye" (22.3), "Like roses in a bed of lillies shed" (22.6), "Like a broad table" (24.2), to name a few. Their iterative procession attested to the inexpressibility of Belphoebe in language as each additional *simile* witnessed the failure of the previous. Their procession also, however, calls attention to the production of the blazon they constitute—piecemeal and aggregative. The fragment "as comming late from rest" reminds us that a *simile* is just the sort of thing Spenser might use to fill out his hexameter or lend it that sense of closure (35.9). In fact, when the blazon brought us to Belphoebe's skirts, we could have done worse than to have looked for a *simile* in that missing half-line. Belphoebe's "silken Camus,"

Which all aboue besprinckled was throughout,
With golden aygulets, that glistred bright,
Like twinckling starres, and all the skirt about
Was hemd with golden fringe.
(26.4.6–9)

The half-line Spenser does supply—"as coming late from rest"—suggests that the subsequent *simile* of the "fearfull fowle" is already excessive, already superfluous, but its iterative structure—like Braggadochio's own narrative—proceeds by accumulating more (35.9–36.1). Spenser tests the limits of *simile*'s syntactical industry and, in doing so, makes its labor even more conspicuous.

After reordering his "gay painted plumes disorderid," (36.4) and refiguring her "feathers fowle disfigured" (36.7), Braggadochio's assembly is precarious. Fearing Belphoebe's own *ornamenta*, Braggadochio's comparative images—what Artegall will call his "borrowed plumes"—threaten to fall again into disarray (5.3.20.7).[105] Belphoebe saves him by an act of interpellation that he will soon give her cause to regret: "All haile Sir knight" is an abstraction that proceeds from a comparative judgment, "As all the like"

(37.6–7). "All haile, Sir knight" is an act of interpellation that compares itself to greetings issued to all knights everywhere. It recognizes Braggadochio only insofar as he is like or is a likeness. We might, therefore, revise an Aristotelian conception of *simile*'s slow thinking. As Spenser exacerbates *simile*'s pace by repeating its syntactical "page"—"So shakes off shame" (36.9), "So when her goodly visage he beheld" (37.1)—he dramatizes a momentary temporal resistance to an abstraction no more monstrous and, in *The Faerie Queene*, no less monstrous than direct address.

The operations of *simile* throw into relief what is characteristic about the complexity with which *The Faerie Queene* proceeds: there are multiple and competing configurations of possibility within the world of the poem. We have Spenser's distinctive negotiation between philosophical idealism and historical reality, what he describes in the *Letter* as a "historical fiction" that deals in "such as might best be."[106] But we also have Braggadochio's personal goal of "such, as he him thought, or faine would bee," a *telos* to his accumulation that is significant because its determined deferral makes visible both Braggadochio's labor and the *poesie* of *simile* (5.5–6). According to "such as might best be," *simile*'s conspicuousness is a byproduct of the fallen world, the historical restrictions that distinguish its configuration of possibility from "what should be." In this sense, to what extent *simile* is conspicuous, to that extent is *simile* history. According to "such, as he him thought, or faine would bee," *simile*'s conspicuousness permits for a configuration of possibility that couples fiction with pleasure: Braggadochio's *faining* doubles for the *feigning* that is also the craft of *poesie*. In the alternate vocabulary provided by Jonson, we have "the thing fain'd, the faining, and the fainer."[107] That these different configurations are inextricably entangled in *The Faerie Queene* confirms the pervasive readerly intuition that the ground of faerie land, the field of possibility itself, is always moving beneath one's feet. When Archimago offers yet another account of possibility, his version picks up on the modality of poetry's "what may be" and transforms it into a "mote," a trifling speck of dust in the eye that you are not supposed to point out: "what mote that Monster make" (18.9).

CHAPTER 5

Fighting Words: *Antithesis* in Philip Sidney's *Arcadia*

Philip Sidney's revised *Arcadia* famously ends in the middle of a sentence. His elaborate rewriting of the *Old Arcadia* has just culminated in the kidnap and capture of the sisters Pamela and Philoclea as well as the Amazonian warrior Zelmane (who is also the young prince Pyrocles). We are in the castle of Amphialus, where the sisters are prisoners and Zelmane is locked into a long continuing battle with Anaxius. Each warrior is so perfectly matched against the other that neither can get the upper hand: "The Irish greyhound against the English mastiff; the sword-fish against the whale; the rhinoceros against the elephant, might be models, and but models of this combat."[1] Where one is "better armed defensively," the other "to offend had the advantage"; where one fights "most by warding," the other fights "oftenest by avoiding"; where one is big, the other is quick. While we might expect each side of this opposing pair to be entirely inscrutable to the other, the *Arcadia* instead describes the result of this play of perfect contraries as complete epistemological transparency: "as if they had been fellow counsellors and not enemies, each knew the other's mind, and knew how to prevent it" (594). Ultimately, this battle does not so much end as it simply breaks off. Anaxius goes for Zelmane's face, "but Zelmane strongly putting it by with his right-hand sword, coming in with her left foot and hand, would have given a sharp visitation to his right side, but that he was fain to leap away. Whereat ashamed, as having never done so much before in his life   "(595).

The long succession of Sidney's *antitheses* poses a problem for his narrative: If Zelmane and Anaxius are perfect contraries, how will one defeat the other? Narrative's answer to the rhythm of style's insistence on antithetical reciprocity is the introduction of an anomaly: "as having never done so much before in his life." Sidney's revision comes to a grinding halt while poised on the edge of introducing an entirely original event into the world of the *Arcadia*. To put a stop to style, something must happen that has never happened before. Though Sidney's own revisions ceased there, the editor of the 1621 folio of *The Countess of Pembroke's Arcadia* devised a bridge narrative between the first three books of the revised *Arcadia* and the final two books of the *Old Arcadia*.[2] In his "Supplement of the Said Defect," William Alexander identifies a cause for this anomaly by staging its repetition. On account of his shame—"Whereat ashamed, as having never done so much before in his life"—Alexander's Anaxius comes back stronger and for more until "the ears of Anaxius were suddenly arrested by a sound" and "his feet did so suddenly ravish away the rest of his body that even his own thoughts, much more Zelmane's, were prevented by the suddenness of his flight" (596). Marked repeatedly by a surprising temporality—"suddenly," "suddenly," "suddenness"—parts of Anaxius's body (his feet and possibly his ears, but not his mind) are overwhelmingly compelled to pursue a sound, with the result that Anaxius "vanish[es] away as carried in a cloud of whirlwind" (595–596). The hypermobility of Anaxius's feet—operating with an inexplicable agency and temporality of their own—pinpoints the problem that Sidney's revision had not yet resolved: How do you end a battle between two perfectly matched foes? The "cloud of whirlwind" in Alexander's bridge narrative doubles down on the strange agency of Anaxius's feet even as it also displaces that agency onto what amounts to an extreme weather event.

The problem with which the revised *Arcadia* ends midsentence is a problem of figure. The logic of the never-ending battle between Zelmane and Anaxius is set and determined by the long succession of *antitheses* that permit for total transparency between the minds of two foes. Even in Alexander's bridge narrative, Anaxius's feet move on but both his and Zelmane's "thoughts" remain where they were. In the rhetorical manual *Directions for Speech and Style* (c. 1601), John Hoskins selects a short chain of clauses from this battle as his illustrative example for the figure of *antithesis* (Gk. *anti*, or "against," and *thesis*, "a setting") or *contentio* (L. "a fight"). The links in this chain are artfully reinforced by the figure of *isocolon* and its equal measure of clauses: "There was strength against nimbleness, rage against resolution, fury against virtue, confidence against courage, pride against nobleness."[3] In this selection, Hoskins points to the very figure with which Sidney's style sets the conditions under which narrative cannot continue. (Note that when Alexander picks up where Sidney broke off, he does not determine a winner to this battle; his "Supplement" does not break the equal and opposing force constructed and amplified by Sidney's *antitheses*. Instead, Alexander invokes the supernatural causality of a cloud.) In this chapter, I will argue that *antithesis* establishes the conditions of possibility within the world of the *Arcadia* such that a victory of Zelmane over Anaxius or Anaxius over Zelmane would entail something like the apocalypse.

The ending of the revised *Arcadia* has more usually been described as a problem of history rather than a problem of style. Dying from a wound that he received in a battle outside Zutphen, Sidney (as John Florio wrote) "lived not to mend or end-it."[4] What Alexander described as the "unfortunate maim" of Sidney's incomplete sentence thus becomes an emblem for Sidney's fatal mutilation in the field (864).[5] Yet as several modern critics have noted, it is not so much that the revised *Arcadia* is without an end as that it seems to defy the possibility of ending.[6] In *Writing after Sidney* (2006), Gavin Alexander explains the problem of ending in the *Arcadia* by analogy to sentence structure: "Rather than the single, perfect circular period of the 'old' Arcadia," he writes, "the revised text looks set to become trapped in perpetual circles of dilatory regression." G. Alexander recasts the problem of "dilatory regression" at the level of narrative as a problem of figure at the level of the sentence. Alluding to the figure of speech that describes a speaker's act of self-correction, the revised *Arcadia* becomes "a cycle of epanorthosis."[7] G. Alexander's analogy suggests that figures of speech might serve as emblems of narrative or even *metaphors* for narrative. (For G. Alexander, the broken narrative of the revised *Arcadia* is therefore best represented by the figure of speech dedicated to interruption, the figure of *aposiopesis*.)[8] By contrast, in *Outlaw Rhetoric* (2012), Jenny C. Mann restores the *parentheses* that modern editions have elided—"Whereat ashamed, (as hauing neuer done so much before in his life)"—and argues that those *parentheses* "are typographical announcements of a practice of textual insertion operating not just at the level of the sentence, but also at that of the plot."[9] For Mann, *parentheses* do not simply reflect this "practice of textual insertion" at the local level but are, instead, capable of rearranging the causal structure of Sidney's narrative.[10] I want likewise to suggest that *antithesis* bears a causal determinacy within Sidney's narrative. Rather than understanding figure as a *metaphor* for narrative—or even as the microcosm to narrative's or genre's macrocosmic impulses—we might instead understand figures of speech as performing the constitutive work of world making.[11] Style instantiates the logic of the world of Sidney's *Arcadia* because style establishes the coordinates by which the entities of that world relate to one another. The play of opposing forces characteristic of *antithesis* establishes the parameters of possibility for the world of the *Arcadia* and serves to distinguish *what may be* from *what may not be*.[12]

My argument about *antithesis* in the revised *Arcadia* begins with a review of the vexed status of *antithesis* as both a place of *inventio* and a figure of *elocutio* in the early modern rhetorical tradition, and I suggest that the figure's combination of artifice and argument offered Sidney a peculiar approach to the construction of plausibility. I argued in Chapter 4 that what was at stake in the contested status of *simile* was the visibility of *poesie* as a temporal phenomenon: *simile* inscribed Spenser's *Faerie Queene* with its slower thinking and projected a history of composition that turned on the facility of the form in the humanist schoolroom as well as its paradigm of accumulation. The plausibility of "such as might best be" in *The Faerie Queene* was always looking to cancel the *poesie* out of which it was crafted by transforming "the doing" into "the thing done." Sidney's use of *antithesis* in the revised *Arcadia*, by contrast, tests out the idea that the conspicuousness of figure might stabilize rather than dissolve the parameters of a fictional world by making the set of oppositions that organize it both visible and perpetual. In the second section of this chapter, I return to the battle between Zelmane and Anaxius and I read it in the context of the rhetorical tradition's defensive characterization of ornament as a weapon and the figure of *antithesis* as a fight. The revised *Arcadia* lends *antithesis* a kind of agency that is not circumscribed by the agent (and its attendant structures of character, subjectivity, or personhood). Instead, the action of *antithesis* sets the terms under which each warrior cannot gain advantage over the other because each is set so perfectly against the other. The action of *antithesis* aligns stylistic copia with narrative endlessness such that Zelmane and Anaxius are themselves exhausted by the relentless figure of speech and rendered breathless. In the third section, I turn to a set of illustrative counterexamples in order to probe the relation of figure to thought in poetry's imaginative worlds. *Antithesis* and the related figures of *isocolon* and *antimetabole* establish the axes of relation that coordinate the entities populating Sidney's world. It will be the final move of this chapter to suggest that the figural logic of the world of the *Arcadia* aligns the presence of a creator with the persistence of *antithesis* such that the resolution of figure would entail the annihilation of the poet-maker.

Conspicuous and Plausible

At least as early as Abraham Fraunce's rhetorical treatise *The Arcadian Rhetorike*—published in 1588 before any version of the *Arcadia* was in print—Sidney's prose romance was read as a handbook of style. It is in this sense that Peter Heylyn, for example, describes the *Arcadia* in *Microcosmus, or A little description of the great world* (1621) as "a book which besides its excellent language, rare contriuances, & delectable stories, hath in it all the straines of *Poesy*, comprehendeth the vniuersall art of speaking."[13] This line of reception suggests an unlikely solution to the problem of ethical reading as posed by Sidney in the *Defence of Poesy* (c. 1580): If "the ending end of all earthy learning" is "virtuous action," then how does poetry pivot its readers from *gnosis* to *praxis*? According to this hermeneutic, *praxis* is not opposed to language but instead looks like more language, where the "well-doing" in which a reader of Sidney's romance might find him- or herself primarily engaged is "the doing" that Jonson describes in *Timber: Or, Discoveries* (1640) as "*Poesy*" or "skill, or Crafte of making."[14] Reading for style suggests that figures of speech in the *Arcadia* are not significant for their capacity to represent but for their capacity to generate. The identification of a figure of speech transforms a sentence from Sidney's *Arcadia* into a *formula* for composition.[15]

At its most basic, the figure of *antithesis* described the formal arrangement that renders conspicuous an opposition between *verba*, or words, as well as the *res*, or things, those words represent.[16] It is on account of its conspicuousness that Aristotle ranked *antithesis* alongside *metaphor*: because *antithesis* "impresses the new idea more firmly," it can, like *metaphor*, "make us seize a new idea promptly."[17] For Aristotle, *antithesis* served as both an instrument of style and an instrument of reason; the Roman rhetorical tradition expanded on this double capacity by describing *antithesis* as both a figure of *elocutio* and a place of *inventio*.[18] As early as the pseudo-Ciceronian *Rhetorica Ad Herennium*, what we are accustomed to calling *antithesis* actually describes a cluster of forms. Each of these forms relies on that signature oppositional force, but each of these forms is distinguished by the relative value it places on the figure's organization of either words or things and on the operations of either style or reason respectively.[19] Thus, the fourth book of the *Ad Herennium* first introduces its readers to this conspicuous oppositional force as a figure of speech called *contentio* (usually associated with the Greek *antithesis*) and defines it as "when the style is built upon contraries." "Embellishing our style by means of this figure," the author of the *Ad Herennium* continues, "we shall be able to give it impressiveness and distinction."[20] It is in this sense that Johannes Susenbrotus will describe *antithesis* in the *Epitome of Tropes and Schemes* (1562) as "among the most elegant" of schemes: "Orators hardly use any other figure more frequently to vary and enrich their discourse."[21] The *Ad Herennium* will proceed, however, to treat this oppositional force as a figure of thought named *contrarium* (sometimes associated with the Greek *antitheton*), which it describes as both elegant and argumentative: "Not only agreeable to the ear on account of its brief and complete rounding-off, but by means of the contrary statement it also forcibly proves what the speaker needs to prove."[22] The author of the *Ad Herennium* then proceeds to conflate these previously distinct rhetorical figures under the single name of *contentio*.[23] Figure of speech and figure of thought become, in this final analysis, two "kinds of Antithesis": "The first consists in a rapid opposition of words; in the other opposing thoughts ought to meet in a comparison."[24] A single rhetorical figure named *contentio* tentatively draws into conceptual proximity the elegance of style and the epistemological value of argument.

The set of provisional distinctions at play in the *Ad Herennium*—distinctions between *contentio* and *contrarium*, figure of speech and figure of thought, words and things—turns on the question of the relation of figure to thought: Is *antithesis* a form with which one ornaments thought so as to render that thought more impressive? Or is *antithesis* instrumental to the process of thinking itself? Can the form of *antithesis* establish the truth of an idea and thereby contribute to the plausibility or even the probability of that idea? The oppositions that underwrite the *Ad Herennium*'s elaboration of *antithesis* set the terms for early modern debates over the work of the figure within the arts of rhetoric and dialectic. A text like Susenbrotus's *Epitome*, for example, treats *antithesis*, *antitheton*, *contentio*, and *contrarium* as if each term is simply a synonym for the other, all of which describe a single form that "occurs when we amplify by means of contraries," adding that "it is effected by single words or ideas."[25] Other texts, like Richard Sherry's *A Treatise of Schemes and Tropes* (1550), preserve the *Ad Herennium*'s distinction between *contentio* and *contrarium*.[26] The Ramist redistribution of the canons belonging to the arts of rhetoric and dialectic, however, turns the *Ad Herennium*'s provisional distinction into the point of disciplinary separation. Because *antithesis* had been correlated with and at times conflated with the place of *inventio* that reasons from opposites (*ex contrario*), the Ramists remove *antithesis* from *elocutio* and the art of rhetoric more broadly. They reserve its formal operations for the art of dialectic. Ramus writes in *Arguments in Rhetoric against Quintilian* (1549) that "all the rules of contrariety belong to argument, and have nothing to do with style; therefore, contrast cannot be a figure."[27] He concludes that when Quintilian "makes antithesis the last of the figures of speech and he is wrong to do so, for an argument is not a figure; antithesis is of course an argument from unlikes and therefore it is not a figure."[28] This is why there is no entry for *antithesis* in Fraunce's *Arcadian Rhetorike*, in spite of the prominence of the figure in Sidney's *Arcadia*. There is no place for the figure within Fraunce's taxonomy of *elocutio* because the reformed curriculum does not recognize *antithesis* as an instrument of style.

As classical and early modern theorists shuffle *antithesis* between the categories of figure of thought and figure of speech, place of *inventio* and figure of *elocutio*, and the art of dialectic and the art of rhetoric, they are communicating something about the epistemological range of figures of speech in particular and style more broadly. As the Ramists began to define reason as an operation of the silent, meditative mind, they also limited the scope of style to what Fraunce described as "a certeine decking of speech."[29] Another Ramist, Dudley Fenner, called figure the "Garnishing of speache."[30] By removing *antithesis* from instruction in style, the Ramists reduce the range of capacities attributable to figures of speech. They also deny the peculiar combination of argument and ornament with which *antithesis* had long been associated.

Where the primary significance of *antithesis* is its capacity to make a composition elegant, that elegance is always also on the verge of stylistic excess. This is why, in *The Art of English Poesy* (1589), George Puttenham warns that "Isocrates the Greek orator was a little too full of this figure" and that "many of our modern writers in vulgar use it in excess."[31] In these accounts, the virtue of conspicuousness first introduced by Aristotle tilts toward the aesthetic and moral vice of affectation. Where, by contrast, *antithesis* is activated in its capacity to construct oppositions between the things of this world, it is primarily significant for its ability to contribute to the probability of a given argument (sometimes, by making conspicuous an impossibility).[32] The combination of these two capacities—an elegance verging on affectation (on the one hand) and a structure of reasoning (on the other)—is vexed even in the classical tradition, where Quintilian warns, "who will endure the orator who expresses his anger, his sorrow or his entreaties in neat antitheses, balanced cadences and exact correspondences?" "Wherever the orator displays his art unveiled," Quintilian continues, "the hearer says, 'The truth is not in him.'"[33] In keeping with such an account, we tend to think of artifice at its most conspicuous—the affectation into which the figure of *antithesis* is always ready to slip—as a violation of plausibility because it draws attention to the very artifice that should seem natural. When, however, *antithesis* is activated in its capacity to double as both a place of *inventio* and a figure of *elocutio*, we witness the peculiar alignment of plausibility and conspicuousness. The history of *antithesis* therefore suggests an account of "what may be" that does not disguise its origins in style but displays the *poesie* in which it is involved so as to shore up the dynamic tension of which any particular opposition is a manifestation. *Antithesis* is an interesting case study for this book because its probative value actually depends on the very visibility of form that early modern theories of *decorum* warned against.

Against

When Aristotle praises *antithesis* for its conspicuousness, he also identifies the pedagogical value of the form. Insofar as it "impresses the new idea more firmly," *antithesis* would seem to guarantee that learning stick.[34] At least since Gabriel Harvey praised the pedagogical value of the *Arcadia*'s "contraries" in his *Pierces Supererogation* (1593), readers of Sidney's romance have repeatedly hailed the formal organization of opposing entities as the signature didactic device of this sprawling prose romance, especially in its revised form.[35] Drawing on a range of humanist habits of thinking—from the schoolroom practice of argument *in utramque partem* to the dichotomizing branches of Ramus's method—Sidney's "contraries" have been variously seen as the engine for simulating what Joel B. Altman calls "the fullness of life itself" and as the organizing impulse that serves to contain what Jeff Dolven describes as "the darker possibilities" of the *Old Arcadia*.[36] What these readers share with Gabriel Harvey is an assumption that authorizes the didactic project of romance itself: that the opposing entities with which the revised *Arcadia* is most concerned are significant because they are ideas or *res* more broadly. The oppositional force of "contraries" in the revised *Arcadia* is not the mere play of rhetorical ornament or the affectation of style that has dominated our accounts of the euphuistic mode.[37] Where modern criticism defends, as Peter Mack has put it, the "intellectual basis of style" by opposing it to "mere stylistic sheen," that criticism naturalizes the very polemic that motivated pedagogical reforms like Ramism.[38] Such criticism answers philosophy's longstanding critique of rhetoric and its putatively empty ornaments, but it does so only on philosophy's terms.

In the final battle of the revised *Arcadia*, Sidney takes up a commonplace image from rhetoric's defense against philosophy: the claims that rhetoric's figures are not empty but sharp. As we saw with Braggadochio in *The Faerie Queene*, both classical and early modern rhetoricians routinely likened the *ornamentum* of rhetoric to the weapons of war.[39] Quintilian writes that the canons of *inventio* and *dispositio* "are within the reach of any man of good sense" but that facility with the canon of *elocutio* distinguishes the orator as such.[40] Without *elocutio*, "all that the speaker has conceived in his mind" is "as useless as a sword that is kept permanently concealed within its sheath."[41] Drawing on the literal meaning of *contentio* as "a contest, contention, strife (with weapons or words)," early modern theorists regularly invoke combat while describing the work of *antithesis* and the place of *inventio* devoted to contraries.[42] Dudley Fenner writes in *The Artes of Logike and Rethorike* (1584) that "Contraries are opposites whereof one is set against one. And therefore they directly fight one against another"; his examples include "Christ and Beliall, light and darkenesse, Christ and Antichriste, heauen and hell, life and death."[43] "Certain words, called opposites," Vives explains in *On the Right Way of Speaking*, "wage a war between themselves."[44] In *Directions for Speech and Style*, Hoskins imagines the signature antagonism of *antithesis* as a bloodless battle. Describing "contraries" as "one of the instruments to aggravate by way of comparison," Hoskins elaborates a "way of ordering them with interchangeable correspondencies in sentences, that though each touch not the other, yet each affronts the other."[45] The formal arrangement characteristic of *antithesis* becomes something like combat with your hands tied behind your back, where words do battle without "touch" and "every word in the latter sentence" is "aggravated by opposition to every word in the former."[46] When Hoskins exemplifies *contentio* with a passage from Sidney's battle, his act of selection follows through on the *Arcadia*'s own *allegory* of figure.[47]

It is therefore tempting to suggest that there is a third party at play in the battle between Zelmane and Anaxius. Indeed, the sense of *antithesis* as a confrontation sometimes materialized in an allegorical figure whose peculiar breed of antisociability was something like today's Negative Nelly. In *The Art of English Poesy*, for example, Puttenham's name for *antitheton* is "the Encounterer, but following the Latin name by reason of his contentious nature we may call him the Quarreler, for so be all such persons as delight in taking the contrary part of whatsoever shall be spoken." Well versed in the schoolroom exercise of argument *in utramque partem*, "the Quarreler" is a fantasy of Elizabethan education, where a student's ability to argue on either side of a question becomes a mental compulsion: "When

I was a scholar at Oxford," Puttenham explains, "they called every such one *Johannes ad oppositum*."[48] *Johannes Ad Oppositum* is the kind of which any individual might be an instance, an amorphous conglomeration of educated schoolboys motivated by what one James Howell would describe as "meer negative genius."[49] The oppositional force characteristic of *antithesis* becomes something like a pathology, and its exhibition, a form of social alienation.

Yet although Sidney's text invites attention to the agency of *antithesis*, it does not consolidate that agency within the compass of character. Instead of consolidation, what we get is copia. I quote the passage in full:

> So that they both, prepared in hearts and able in hands, did honour solitariness there with such combat as might have demanded, as a right of fortune, whole armies of beholders. But no beholders needed there, where manhood blew the trumpet, and satisfaction did whet as much as glory. There was strength against nimbleness; rage against resolution; fury against virtue; confidence against courage; pride against nobleness; love, in both, breeding mutual hatred; and desire of revenging the injury of his brother's slaughter, to Anaxius, being like Philoclea's captivity to Pyrocles. Who had seen the one would have thought nothing could have resisted: who had marked the other would have marvelled that the other had so long resisted. But like two contrary tides, either of which are able to carry worlds of ships and men upon them with such swiftness as nothing seems able to withstand them, yet meeting one another, with mingling their watery forces and struggling together, it is long to say whether stream gets the victory; so between these, if Pallas had been there, she could scarcely have told whether she had nursed better in the feats of arms. The Irish greyhound against the English mastiff; the sword-fish against the whale; the rhinoceros against the elephant, might be models, and but models of this combat.
>
> Anaxius was better armed defensively; for (besides a strong casque bravely covered, wherewith he covered his head) he had a huge shield, such, perchance, as Achilles showed to the pale walls of Troy, wherewithal that great body was covered. But Pyrocles, utterly unarmed for defence, to offend had the advantage, for in either hand he had a sword, and with both hands nimbly performed that office. And according as they were diversely furnished, so did they differ in manner of fighting; for Anaxius most by warding, and Pyrocles oftenest by avoiding, resisted the adversary's assault. Both hasty to end, yet both often staying for advantage. Time, distance and motion, custom made them so perfect in that, as if they had been fellow counsellors and not

> enemies, each knew the other's mind, and knew how to prevent it: so as
> their strength failed them sooner than their skill, and yet their breath
> failed them sooner than their strength. And breathless indeed they
> grew before either could complain of any loss of blood. (593–594)

At the opening of this battle, the repeated preposition "against" translates the logical relation of contraries into the clash of arms between warriors in battle (or gladiatorial combat, if there were "beholders"—which there are not, except for us). The succession of *antitheses* climaxes in an apparent similarity between the two fighters. The presence of "love, in both" produces the affect attached to that preposition: "mutual hatred." Zelmane and Anaxius are reversed magnets. With the "love" of one pointing toward the imprisoned Philoclea and the "love" of the other directed toward his recently slain brother, their "mutual hatred" determines the precisely calibrated difference and distance between the two fighters (a calibration disrupted only in Alexander's bridge narrative when Anaxius flees).[50] Each warrior is characterized by his ability—unbelievable to those who would have seen, were they there to see—to "resist" the other. By the time we get to the *simile* of the "two contrary tides," Sidney names the dynamic that he has illustrated at the level of the clause: "contrary." The confluence of Zelmane and Anaxius is a byproduct of the perpetual collision between two rushing streams. With the return of "against" and its successive repetitions, Sidney characterizes each link in his chain of *antitheses* as another iteration or replication of the fight that they *model*: "the Irish greyhound against the English mastiff; the sword-fish against the whale; the rhinoceros against the elephant, might be models, and but models of this combat."[51] Each clause is designed to render manageable (by reproducing on a smaller scale) the force of a "combat" that is otherwise unknowable. If, however, "sword-fish against the whale" is in part significant because it stages at the level of the clause an event that is also occurring at the level of narrative, it is also significant because it is only one among many "models," and the copious accumulation of clauses does away with the neatness of formal nesting dolls. Though this fight does not end, the warriors are compelled to call a time out. They need to catch their breath.

The breathlessness of Zelmane and Anaxius is as much an effect of figure as it is of combat. As the original unit of measurement for prose, the single breath is frequently cited in classical and early modern rhetoric as the physiological precondition for the development of a form like the periodic sentence. Aristotle, for example, uses breath to distinguish between what he calls the "free-running" style and the "compact" or "periodic" style: where the "free-running" style "goes on indefinitely" because it "has no natural stopping-places," the "compact" style is "satisfying" precisely because it is "definite" and can be "easily delivered at a single breath."[52] Cicero likewise explains that a period should not be "longer than the strength and breath can last out" and suggests that "it was failure or scantiness of breath" that "originated periodic structure."[53] As a particular species of the period, the antithetically organized sentence contains symmetrically corresponding clauses that formally organize and reward an auditor's anticipation such that an "end," as Aristotle might describe it, is always in sight.[54] Sidney's prose, by contrast, turns the figure of *antithesis* into an engine of copia. Zelmane and Anaxius are locked into a battle that each is "hasty to end" but cannot "end." Each fighter "stays for an advantage," but it is precisely an "advantage" that the figure of *antithesis*—with its relentless commitment to evenly poised contraries—denies them.

Sidney's alignment of reiterated opposition—for which that repeated "against" (and its homonym "again") might be emblematic—and narrative endlessness points up another aspect of early modern pedagogy surrounding the figure of *antithesis*. In addition to its signature ability to coordinate opposing entities, *antithesis* was also hailed as singularly useful for the simple continuation of discourse. Following Philip Melanchthon's *Elementorum Rhetorices Libri Duo* (1531), the rhetorical tradition's central defining category for *antithesis* was neither the canon of *inventio* nor the canon of *elocutio* but the "figures of amplification."[55] Melanchthon's figures of amplification were a kind of composite of *inventio* and *elocutio* because they combined the argumentative punch of the former with the latter's commitment to copia.[56] For Melanchthon, the distinction between place of *inventio* and figure of *elocutio* centered on intention rather than form. "The zealous reader," Melanchthon wrote,

> will observe that all the figures, especially those that enhance a speech, have their origin in dialectical expressions.... For the same expressions, when applied for the purposes of confirming or confuting, are bases for argument and the sinews, as they are called. When applied for the purpose of adorning, they are called rhetorical ornaments. And very many not only have been adapted to give a show of battle, but to add weight to the arguments.[57]

In its restricted sense, amplification refers to style's ability to inflate or deflate the value of the subject matter at hand. Because the inflation of value was frequently correlated with quantity of speech, discussions of amplification often veer toward a more general discussion of methods dedicated to copia.[58] As William Scott explains in *The Model of Poesy* (c. 1599), "amplification is by heaping our words and, as it were, piling one phrase upon another of the same sense to double and redouble our blows that, by varying and reiterating, may work into the mind of the reader."[59] As a figure of amplification, *antithesis* combines the work of argument and ornament.[60] The category of "figures of amplification" does not police the line between argument and ornament because its primary investment is in the simple imperative for more.

Antithesis therefore permits us to rethink both the incompletion of Sidney's revised *Arcadia* and the genre of romance. We tend to describe the endlessness of romance as a commitment to narrative: romance digresses from the *telos* of epic's quest through narratives characterized by dilation and deferral.[61] Sidney's use of *antithesis*, however, suggests that we might instead think of romance's endlessness as a commitment to style. After their brief "truce," Zelmane and Anaxius have recovered their breath, but they have also taken some time to consider the very "advantage" that *antithesis* previously denied to them: "In this pausing, each had brought to his thoughts the manner of the other's fighting, and the advantages which by that, and by the quality of their weapons, they might work themselves" (595). If we are expecting that "advantages" will emerge to upset the balance of their antithetical reciprocity, the narrator instead tells us that the two foes "so again repeated the lesson they had said before more perfectly by the using of it" (595). During the "truce," Anaxius and Zelmane exchange taunts about the latter's "weaker sex," but what we learn when they start fighting again is that this exchange was a cover. The pair was *actually* reflecting on the "lesson" of their previous battle. Neither Zelmane nor Anaxius learns from this "lesson" how to overcome the agency of *antithesis*. It does not teach either how to act differently from how he has already been acting. Instead, each fighter learns how to "repeat" the very same "lesson"—only "more perfectly." Repeating their "lesson" without fault or flaw denies the pun latent in that lesson's *perfection*. A perfect lesson in *antithesis* never ends.

How Other Battles End

In 1725, Dorothy Stanley will publish her own revised edition of *Sir Philip Sidney's Arcadia Moderniz'd*. As she states in a preface, the ambition of this edition is "not even in the minutest Point to vary from his Tract, either in the Thoughts or in the Story."[62] Instead, she translates Sidney's prose into a different style. In Stanley's hands, the extended battle between Zelmane and Anaxius is contracted to just a few sentences:

> [Anaxius] flew with eager Haste towards her, who was ready upon her Guard to receive his Fury, and tho' guided by Rage, yet he press'd not on but with the utmost Conduct; and being not only of an uncommon Size, but his Courage as Superior as his Stature, *Zelmane*, in all the battles she had ever fought, had never more Occasion for steady Courage and fortifying Conduct. Long the Contention lasted, while neither could with Justice say he had the Advantage; till all faint and breathless with the violent Exercise, and eager Thirst of Vengeance, they were constrain'd, before their ebbing Blood requir'd a Respit, to allow each other a little Space, that with recovering Breath they might renew the Fight, and try whose genius was most powerful.[63]

Stanley's revision is a studied exercise in avoiding the figure of *antithesis* (though her declaration that "Long the Contention lasted" may be a nod to the very figure she avoids). Stanley pulls apart Sidney's parallel clauses— "rage against resolution; fury against virtue"—such that "Fury" becomes the quality that Zelmane "receive[s]" (rather than "resists") and Anaxius's "Rage" is mollified by an adherence, reiterated in a subsequent description of Zelmane, to "Conduct." Though Stanley's revision insists that this is the most difficult of all of Zelmane's battles, it unilaterally attributes this difficulty to Anaxius's "Stature" and "Courage" (which it does not, as Sidney did, oppose to "confidence"). This fight translates the carefully calibrated tension of Sidney's *antitheses* into the formalism of "Conduct"—which seems to be something like the manners of combat.

After their time-out, the battle between Zelmane and Anaxius resumes, but in Stanley's revision this renewed battle measures itself against the earlier by way of a quantitative difference: "Their Courage and their Fury both, if possible, encreas'd." This resumed battle is like the earlier *but more*, and this sense of a quantitative elaboration is explained by the idea that each fighter is motivated by a competitive drive to distinguish himself as "superior" to the other: "Both exert the utmost Courage to such a high Degree." In the end, it is this quantitative move toward the superlative, "such a high degree," that permits Stanley's prose to reach a turn that Sidney's text never achieved. The closing sequence of Stanley's revision introduces the possibility of an end to this battle with the temporal relief of "At last" (as if something decisive is just about to happen): "At last, *Anaxius* finding *Zelmane* within his Reach, he summon'd all his Strength, and aim'd to strike her Head."[64] Though the possibility of victory, promised by "At last," is denied to Anaxius with an adversative turn of fortune—"but that he meanly leap'd away"—in emphasizing Anaxius's shame, Stanley suggests that the promise belongs in fact to Zelmane.[65]

Stanley's revision presumes a separation that her "Preface" makes explicit: one can do away with the *Arcadia*'s *antitheses* while leaving alone, or faithfully reproducing, "the Thoughts" and "the Story." By detailing the relation of figure to thought in Sidney's *Arcadia*, my intention is to suggest that our defenses of style frequently cede too much to approaches like Stanley's. The overlapping histories of rhetoric and dialectic, however, suggest that we should instead read the canon of *elocutio* and its constitutive figures of speech as the tools of epistemology. According to this method of interpretation, style is an instrument central to the process of coming to know a poetic world that is simultaneously generated by the form of that instrument. Figures of speech thus act as generative constraints or *formulas* for composition, where making and knowing are here—as with the mechanical arts—intimately intertwined.[66] Before William Hazlitt declared *antithesis* to be "the original sin" of the *Arcadia*, it was the vexed instrument of that text's erected wit.[67]

I would like to turn to another illustrative counterexample from Spenser's *Faerie Queene*. In book 1, Red Cross Knight does battle against Sansjoy in Lucifera's House of Pride, surrounded by inhabitants poised to turn this fight into entertainment, including "many Minstrels," "many Bards," and "many Chroniclers."[68] Whereas Sidney's *Arcadia* cleared out a space for its readers by invoking "beholders" who did not actually exist, Spenser's *Faerie Queene* gives us the sense that one from among this crowd of spectators writes what we are reading:

> The Sarazin was stout, and wondrous strong,
> And heaped blowes like yron hammers great:
> For after blood and vengeance he did long.
> The knight was fiers, and full of youthly heat,
> And doubled strokes, like dreaded thunders threat:
> For all praise and honour he did fight,
> Both stricken stryke, and beaten both doe beat,
> That from their shields forth flyeth firie light,
> And helmets hewen deepe shew marks of eithers might.
>
> So th'one for wrong, the other striues for right:
> As when a Gryfon seized of his prey,
> A Dragon fiers encountreth in his flight,
> Through widest ayre making his ydle way,

> That would his rightfull rauine rend away;
> With hideous horror both together smight,
> And souce so sore, that they the heauens affray:
> The wise Southsayer seeing so sad sight,
> Th'amazed vulgar telles of warres and mortall fight.
>
> So th'one for wrong, the other striues for right,
> And each to deadly shame would driue his foe:
> The cruell steele so greedily doth bight
> In tender flesh, that streames of blood down flow,
> With which the armes, that earst so bright did show,
> Into a pure vermillion now are dyde:
> Great ruth in all the gazers harts did grow,
> Seeing the gored woundes to gape so wyde,
> That victory they dare not wish to either syde.[69]

The narrator begins by distinguishing between "Sarazin" and "knight," but tight parallel constructions suggest something like a Mad Libs approach to the act of differentiation: the one "was stout and wondrous strong," while the other "was fiers, and full of youthly heat"; the one's "heaped blowes" were "like yron hammers great," while the "doubled strokes" of the other were "like dreaded thunders threat"; the one wants "blood and vengeance," while the other wants "praise and honour." Individuating characteristics fill in the blank spaces. While the opening would seem to set down the *antitheses* familiar from Sidney's *Arcadia*, Spenser's poem instead insists on a kind of sameness such that the strict parallelism of lines, especially in the use of *isocolon* and *zeugma*, overrides any sense of contrast. Both act, and both are acted upon. As a result, the effects of this battle—the things that it makes—are the same on both sides: dents and sparks. The figure of *antithesis*—"So th'one for wrong, the other striues for right"—might seem to pull apart what the poem has begun to conflate, except that the possible *simile* of a Gryfon devouring its unnamed prey (of one fighter gaining advantage over the other) is interrupted when a Dragon swoops in. With the repetition of that line—"So th'one for wrong, th'other striues for right"—the poem insists on the interchangeability of its fighters by turning them into an allegorical mash-up (or chimera): "with hideous horror both together smight." Their mutual destruction is so great that the crowd of observers wouldn't wish life on either one of them.

As the battle proceeds, Sansjoy briefly gets the upper hand, but Duessa's words of encouragement—"Thine the shield, and I, and all"—also give encouragement to Red Cross, who thinks that those words are addressed to him.⁷⁰ As Red Cross bends his foe to his knees, he speaks a version of what Sansjoy has just spoken to him: "Goe say, his foe thy shield with his doth beare."⁷¹ (Both Sansjoy and Red Cross understand killing the other as having a conversation with the deceased Sansfoy by proxy.) But when Red Cross proceeds to lift his sword against the stooped Sansjoy, something strange happens: "When lo a darksome clowd / Upon him fell: he no where doth appeare, / But vanisht is."⁷² We will later learn that this "darksome cloud" is Duessa's intervention on Sansjoy's behalf, but this cloud is also what keeps Red Cross from performing a kind of self-slaughter. As the strict, stylistic patterning of *isocolon* has maintained, the killing of Sansjoy amounts to Red Cross killing a part of himself and therefore fulfilling and revitalizing the very joylessness that he seeks to destroy. If not for this "darksome cloud," Red Cross, like Despair after him, would become trapped in an endless cycle of failed self-slaughter. Spenser frees his narrative from the logic of *isocolon*, but he does so only by way of Duessa and a cloud that is not unlike the one William Alexander will use to whisk Anaxius away in his "Supplement" to Sidney's *Arcadia*.

In *The Faerie Queene*, figures of parallelism—including *isocolon* and *zeugma*—establish a relation of identity between Red Cross and Sansjoy: this is not to say that one is the other but instead that the destruction of the other constitutes an act of violence against the one. If the narrative event—their battle—insists that the two fighters are separate, style and its constitutive figures of speech provide an alternative logic. Style backs narrative up into something of a tight corner where the fulfillment of its demand (the defeat of Sansjoy) amounts to a reversal of that fulfillment (the self-slaughter of Red Cross). Between the parallelism of *isocolon* and the contraries of *antithesis*, the figure of speech known as *antimetabole* (related to the more familiar *chiasmus*) articulates a strange synthesis of these diverging stylistic impulses.⁷³ In Book 1 of the revised *Arcadia*, the Arcadians and the Helots battle one another. Believing his friend drowned after a shipwreck, the Prince Musidorus (here disguised as Palladius) leads the Arcadians and takes up man-to-man combat against the captain of the Helots. From across the battlefield, the captain of the Helots identifies Palladius as "worth all the rest of the Arcadians" and "disdaining to fight with any other, sought only to join with him." Palladius thinks just the same thing—"which mind was no less in Palladius":

> And so their thoughts meeting in one point, they consented (though not agreed) to try each other's fortune: and so drawing themselves to be the uttermost of the one side, they began a combat which was so much

inferior to the battle in noise and number as it was surpassing it in bravery of fighting, and, as it were, delightful terribleness. Their courage was guided with skill, and their skill was armed with courage; neither did their hardiness darken their wit, nor their wit cool their hardiness: both valiant, as men despising death; both confident, as unwonted to be overcome, yet doubtful by their present feeling, and respectful by what they had already seen: their feet steady, their hands diligent, their eyes watchful, and their hearts resolute. The parts either not armed or weakly armed were well known, and according to the knowledge should have been sharply visited but that the answer was as quick as the objection. Yet some lighting, the smart bred rage and the rage bred smart again; till both sides beginning to wax faint, and rather desirous to die accompanied than hopeful to live victorious, the captain of the Helots with a blow whose violence grew of fury not of strength, or of strength proceeding of fury, struck Palladius upon the side of the head that he reeled astonished; and withal the helmet fell off, he remaining bareheaded, but other of the Arcadians were ready to shield him from any harm might rise of that nakedness. (98)

As it proceeds from *antimetabole* to *antimetabole*—"their courage was guided with skill, and their skill was armed with courage"; "neither did their hardiness darken their wit, nor their wit cool their hardiness"; "the smart bred rage and the rage bred smart again"—this passage traps Palladius and the captain of the Helots in an endless cycle where each fighter is a double for the other: "their thoughts . . . they consented . . . they began a combat . . . both valiant . . . both confident . . . their hands . . . their eyes . . . their hearts." The narrator describes the epistemological counterpart to this unity of body and action as "thoughts meeting at one point." The "point" or site of convergence permits for "consent" without agreement. This battle becomes something the pair makes together rather than does to the other. As both fighters lose steam, each exhibits the exact same desire: he desires not that the other fighter should die so that he might live but that they both might die together. When the captain of the Helots knocks the helmet from Palladius's head, we might expect such a "blow" to distinguish the victor: "with a blow whose violence grew of fury not of strength, or of strength proceeding of fury" (98). But what we get instead is a perfect reversal of that expectation (a reversal engineered by the figure of *antimetabole*): Palladius does not kneel before the Captain; the Captain kneels before Palladius.[74] Narrative learns something that style already knew: the Captain of the Helots is the long-lost Pyrocles. These warriors are friends.

Antithesis. Isocolon. Antimetabole. In Sidney's *Arcadia* and Spenser's *Faerie Queene*, each figure of speech establishes the conditions of possibility for narrative. The formal insistence of *antithesis* on perfectly matched contraries renders narrative's imperative for resolution impossible. The battle between Zelmane and Anaxius could go on forever, which amounts to the same thing as stopping right in the middle. Zelmane does not defeat Anaxius because she cannot defeat Anaxius. This law of the *Arcadia* brings me to my final point about this extended action sequence. While it seems as though it is Anaxius who "was fain to leap away," it is also true that the referent to our pronoun is ambiguous: Zelmane "coming in with her left foot and hand, would have given a sharp visitation to his right side, but that he was fain to leap away" (595). That "he" can belong to Anaxius or Zelmane (a proper noun that is not particular about the gender of the pronoun it accepts).[75]

In *The City of God*, Augustine attributes the beauty of the world to its being structured by contraries, "for God would never have fore-knowne vice in any worke of his" unless "hee knew in like manner, what good use to put it into." In this way, Augustine writes, God was "making the worldes course, like a faire poeme, more gratious by Antithetique figures." *Antitheses*, he continues, "are the most decent figures of all elocution," and just "as these contraries opposed doe give the saying an excellent grace, so is the worlds beauty composed of contrarieties, not in figure, but in nature."[76] At this moment, Augustine suggests that God was working with *antithesis* when he designed the world and its "course" so that it might proceed like a "faire poem." By way of *antithesis*, Augustine claims that aesthetics provides the answer to questions of morality. He also claims that the world is like a poem: the figure of *antithesis* becomes the governing structure of both. *Antithesis* is thus the form according to which the world can be said to be like a poem and a poem can be said to be like the world. And then, having posited ornament as a kind of first principle, Augustine steps back from this claim: "not in figure, but in nature."[77]

In the *Arcadia*, by contrast, the conspicuousness of figure is authorized by the natural world it is understood to structure. Held prisoner in Amphialus's castle, the sister Pamela posits the coexistence of contraries as proof for the existence of God. Arguing against her captor's skepticism, Pamela insists that something other than "chance" has "glued those pieces of this All," or "the heavy parts would have gone infinitely downward" and "the light infinitely upward" (489). Pamela argues that "there must needs have been a wisdom which made them concur; for their natures, being absolutely contrary, in nature rather would have sought each others' ruin than have served as well consorted parts to such an unexpressible harmony." "For that contrary things should meet to make up a perfection, without a force and wisdom above their powers," Pamela continues, "is absolutely impossible" (490). Pamela's proof for the existence of God is the fact that contraries coexist without annihilating one another. The coexistence of contraries makes for an unlikely but durable unity.[78] The fact that contraries in the natural world cause an "unexpressible harmony" rather than one another's ruin is the sign of "a force and wisdom above their powers." *Antithesis* is an instrument of divine artifice that keeps the formed world from returning to chaos.[79]

Imprisoned in the castle where Zelmane and Anaxius will do battle (the one against the other), Pamela pulls out the coexistence of contraries as proof for the existence of God. The figure that coordinates this coexistence, this "unexpressible harmony," is *antithesis*. Zelmane and Anaxius seek each other's ruin, but they are unable to achieve it, with the result that their continued coexistence manifests this principle of design. What keeps the one from destroying the other? The artifice of their world. Narrative incompletion becomes, paradoxically, not the sign that a work has been abandoned by its maker but proof of that maker's existence, even at the moment that this maker disappears from history.[80] Sidney puts into Pamela's mouth the criteria according to which he can live forever. Proof for the existence of the *poein* resides in the endless battle between Zelmane and Anaxius.[81] By this account, Sidney is never more dead than when Alexander attempts to suture his "unfortunate maim."

At the conclusion of this chapter, we are confronted with the one of Jonson's categories of which I have not yet had much to say: "the doer," "the feigner," "the Poet."[82] Yet the model of the *poein* that the revised *Arcadia* offers us is not, as we might have expected, the agent that is the cause of *poesie* or poem. Such a model underwrites other accounts of style in the period, like that of Puttenham, who defines style as "a constant and continual phrase or tenor of speaking and writing." He explains that style:

> showeth the matter and disposition of the writer's mind . . . therefore there be that have called style the image of man (*mentis character*), for man is but his mind, and as his mind is tempered and qualified, so are his speeches and language at large, and his inward conceits be the mettle of his mind, and his matter of utterance the very warp and woof of his conceits.[83]

Style, here, is like a tell or unrepressed facial expression. You cannot help but reveal your mind in your style. It is in this sense that John F. Danby wrote of Sidney's "balanced, antithetical, alliterative, calculated style" and suggested that Sidney "saw the world in terms of division, balance, and resolution. His style is a reflection of his vision."[84] Nancy Lindheim similarly suggests that his "use of antithesis" made "Sidney's analytical habit of mind and his temperamental need for synthesis" a "matter for literary study."[85] The work of *antithesis* in Sidney's *Arcadia*, however, suggests a reversal of cause and effect. Style is not the representation of a knowing mind that is the producer or creator of an imaginative world, and style does not reflect something like worldview, because style is instead the cause of both *poein* and the world that he makes. In his capacity as the poet-maker of this world, Sidney and his *antitheses* insist that something does not die when the body dies. Figure is both the instrument of Sidney's bid for immortality and evidence of its success.

The "unexpressible harmony" of the revised *Arcadia* is not interchangeable with the organic unity of the New Criticism. As an organizing structure of the world of the *Arcadia*, Sidney's *antitheses* defy (rather than adhere to) the proportional norms of *decorum* and design.[86] In *The Garden of Eloquence* (1593), Henry Peacham cautions that a maker ought to "moderate the number" of *antitheses* "lest they growe to too great a multitude." Having grown to a "multitude," *antithesis* will "bewrayeth affection, a fault which ought to be shunned."[87] In the battle between Zelmane and Anaxius, the figure of *antithesis* creates the very "multitude" against which the rhetorical tradition warns. Think of all of the animals that come to populate this scene—"Irish greyhound," "English mastiff," "sword-fish," "whale," "rhinoceros," "elephant"—animals that are, like the "beholders," both there and not there. It is in this sense that *antithesis* is always, relentlessly, inventing. It is precisely the affectation of figure that acts as an index of this world's constitution. *Antithesis* is the form that holds the reversed magnets of the *Arcadia*'s world in perpetual suspension. But the final battle registers a strange cost to the *indecorous* thinking of *antithesis*: the breathlessness of its warriors is also the breathlessness of its readers. In this way, both the imaginative world and the proleptic resurrection of its *poein* draw breath from the bodies of readers.

CHAPTER 6

Withholding Names: *Periphrasis* in Mary Wroth's *Urania*

In Samuel Shaw's schoolroom play *Words Made Visible* (1679), the two sons of Rhetoric compete for the love of their father and the larger share of his lands by declaring which of them has better served "to propogate the Rhetorical Dominions": Ellogus or Eclogus? The canon of *elocutio* or the canon of *pronuntiatio*? Style or delivery?[1] The bulk of the play's imperialist fantasy is devoted to Ellogus's "two great Ministers of State, *Trope* and *Figure*," who call on their own children to report back on what of the world they have conquered and how.[2] Though it postdates our period, Shaw's play is helpful to this book because its satire of the very rhetorical handbooks of which it is also an instance casts a retrospective gaze on the pedagogical tradition that I have been considering. *Words Made Visible* asks: In what way can the art of rhetoric, reduced to the canons of *elocutio* and *pronuntiatio*, make good on its traditional claim to the civilizing power of eloquence?[3] *Antithesis*, for example, steps on stage and produces a set of scales: on the one side, he places "a Catalogue of all the faults, and follies, and failings of all men that are famous in Story, together with the unhappy event and miserable issue"; on the other side, he places "a Catalogue of my own actions and the several circumstances of them."[4] Where we might expect *Antithesis* to boast a catalog of successes against the failures to which they are opposed, we instead find that *Antithesis* locates his signature work in the act of weighing itself: "In these scales I weigh them, one against the other, whereby I judge of my self, amend what's amiss, avoid the like vices and follies to prevent the like miserable conclusions." *Antithesis*, in short, claims that his dominion over the world stems from the pedagogical value of his form: "Setting before my eyes the deformity of Vice, and the ill consequences of it; encourage myself in Vertue."[5] Eclogus counters with the familiar criticism that this strategy "serves indifferently for the nourishment of *Vice* and *Vanity* in the World, as well as *Vertue*."[6] He suggests that *Antithesis* governs the world because of his pedagogical failures. *Antithesis* gives rise, equally and indifferently, to virtue and to vice.

In *Words Made Visible*, the canon of *inventio* plays the part of mere messenger. When Eclogus accuses Invention of being "a Tropes Bastard" beget by "Mounsieur *Oxymoron*" upon "Madam *Syneciosis*," Invention replies with a categorical corrective that he buries in his denial: "Those two noble persons whom your *Excellency* Names (of whom I do not account my self worthy to be the accidental Issue) are not *Tropes* but *Figures*."[7] Though Invention contests his genealogy, Ellogus subsequently confirms it: *Inventio* is the love child of the figures of *elocutio*.[8] As Trope and Figure call their various children on stage and command them to answer the question of their contribution, each of them offers us a version of world making from the perspective (quite literally, in this theatrical event) of his or her form. In the final chapter of this book, I want to turn to another of Figure's children: *Periphrase*. And, at the start of this chapter, I want to hold onto this play's genealogy for *Periphrase* because, as Invention might say, he is here not a trope but a figure. The most common definition of *periphrasis* maintains that the device offers many words in the place of one word that it does not speak.[9] When *Periphrase* walks on stage, he declares "I am that *Figure*, whereby men explain one thing in many words, and by much circumlocution."[10] In this way, *Periphrase* revises traditional definitions by excluding the act of substitution that lead to his categorization as a trope.[11] *Periphrase*'s self-definition makes explicit what both classical and early modern discussions of the device as a figure emphasize: that *periphrasis* is most significant not for the word that it withholds but for all of the words that it offers instead of that word. It is thus as an instrument of amplification that *Periphrase* stakes his claim to world domination:

> For the very life of man is *Periphrastical*; the one thing of *eating*, they
> call *Periphrase* by variety of *dishes* like diversity of *Phrases*; that one thing

of *drinking* is *Periphrastically* performed over and over again in several sorts of Liquors: they work and play the same business and sports over and over again, only with some different circumstances; and sleep the same sleep for three or fourscore years together, only with different dreams it may be. . . . In a word, the whole World is *Periphrastical*; for these five thousand six hundred and six and twenty years that came last, are nothing but else a periphrase of that first that began the World.[12]

Periphrase here claims "variety" as evidence of his dominion: we eat more than one dish, drink more than one liquid; we fall asleep every night, and we wake up every morning. It is only because of *Periphrase* that we spend the time between in "different dreams." The subsequent "it may be" is odd—"only with different dreams it may be." This oddness has to do with the referent of "it." Is *Periphrase* admitting to an uncertainty in order to hedge his bet? Or, is he saying that, as a Figure, he is the permitting condition for the "different dreams"? *Periphrase* seems to allow for the dreaming that distinguishes one night's sleep from another, but the monotony of "sleep the same sleep" clamps down on his syntax even as he tries to break it up and create the genuine "variety" that would displace the very thing he seems merely to diversify. At what point does the "variety" of *Periphrase* break with the thing of which he speaks? In order to assert his value, *Periphrase* has to hold onto the thing that he replaces, which is why his act of substitution may be no substitution at all. *Periphrase* thus diminishes the range of his capacities to the reproduction of that one "thing": the world may be many years old, but each year is "nothing but else a periphrase of that first that began the world."

When we categorize *periphrasis* as either a trope or a figure, we are saying something about how we value its form. In his *Art of English Poesy*, George Puttenham likens *periphrasis* to *allegory* (which he names "The Dissembler"): *periphrasis* "hold[s] somewhat of the dissembler by reason of a secret intent not appearing by the words, as when we go about the bush and will not in one or a few words express that thing which we desire to have known, but do choose rather to do it by many words."[13] Whereas *allegory* (and the category of tropes more broadly), however, tends to identify a symmetrical act of substitution, *periphrasis* describes the asymmetrical substitution of many words for just one word. As a trope, *periphrasis* thus appears to operate like *allegory* at its most simplistic: the one withheld word exerts a kind of centripetal pull on the act of figuration, with the result that everything that is said is reducible to the one word that is not said.[14] According to this hermeneutic, *periphrasis* might be best understood as a cipher: it both calls for and provides the means for achieving its own neutralization or undoing, its resolution into what Puttenham defines as language without figuration or "language at large."[15]

By contrast, reading *periphrasis* as a figure means that the act of withholding and the substitution that it entails are significant as the enabling conditions for the copious production of language. As a figure, *periphrasis* is the device by which one word becomes many words. In *The Garden of Eloquence*, Henry Peacham categorizes *periphrasis* as a "figure of amplification" and defines it as "a forme of spéech whereby that which might be said with one word, or at least with verie few, is declared and expounded with many, and that sundrie waies." He associates it with a "desire of copie and facilitie" as well as the place of *inventio* known as definition (when, for example, "for man" we instead say "a liuing creature endued with reason").[16] It was on account of the homology between *periphrasis* and definition that Peter Ramus removed the device from the canon of *elocutio* altogether.[17] The hermeneutic that *periphrasis* provokes as a figure is not the decoding of a cipher but the description of a device: what the many words of *periphrasis* do (that just one word could not do). In a revision of Susan Sontag's call in *Against Interpretation* (1961) for a criticism of art responsible to identifying "what [art] is, even that it is what it is, rather than to show what it means," this chapter aims *to show how periphrasis does what it does, even that it does what it does, rather than to show what it means*.[18] Where Sontag desired a criticism attuned to the question of what an art object "is," I take "the doing" rather than "the thing done" as my object of investigation. Trading in poem for *poesie*, figure indexes the history of composition that unfolds within the text that it also shapes.

In this chapter, I argue that *periphrasis* is the engine of the *indecorous* thinking of Mary Wroth's *Urania*. Through its iterative acts of withholding and the many words by which these acts of withholding are performed, *periphrasis* organizes the poetic world according to a logic of possession that grants the beholder ownership over precisely that which she does not have. Reading *periphrasis* as a figure rather than as a trope therefore also offers a corrective to a dominant trend in Wroth criticism: topical readings that take Wroth's biography and especially her love affair with her cousin, William Herbert, as the authorizing "ground-plot" of their analysis.[19] At its most reductive, the kind of criticism produced by topical readings becomes, as Marion Wynne-Davies describes it, "our search for veiled figures across Wroth's canon."[20] Its interpretive mode is that of the key, like the one George Manners began and requested that Wroth complete in his 1640 letter to her, or like the lists of personae that several seventeenth-century readers appear to have inscribed in Philip Sidney's *Arcadia*.[21] Most insistently, topical readers understand the *Urania*'s central heroine, Pamphilia, as Wroth's own "avatar"[22] (though the favored trope remains that of the "shadow" and Wroth's process, one of "shadowing").[23] The act of naming names that characterizes these topical readings opens up to broader critical questions about the modality of the *Urania* itself. For these readers, fiction is regularly regarded as a "veil,"[24] "embrodier[y],"[25] a "distorted reflection,"[26] or "a coded means of telling 'real-life stories,'"[27] and the *Urania* is "Mary Wroth's imaginative rewriting of her life."[28] Something of a test case for feminism's critical but ultimately productive alliance with the New Historicism, Wroth scholarship might be faulted in a manner similar to the ubiquitous critique of the exemplary anecdote and its synecdochic claim to a totalizing vision of history.[29] Where character acts as the formal site of correspondence between fiction and history, it tends to suggest that the representative female subject is both the cause and effect of writing; as a result, fiction is merely the instrument by which Wroth successfully consolidated herself as a historical subject.

Given the critical preoccupation with naming names, what I find so curious about Mary Wroth's *Urania* is the extent to which its characters routinely withhold names—speaking them softly, refusing to say them altogether, or talking around them (as if circling the thing or the person they would not name). Wroth's topical readers see this activity as emblematic of Wroth's strategy and as an authorization for their own critical procedure, which is to undo what Wroth has done—to speak the name that she withholds. To offer one frequently cited example from *The First Part*, Pamphilia walks with friends in a grove, where they come across "names ingraven upon the trees." The group proceeds to read these "names" though "they understood not perfectly, because when they had decipher'd some of them, they then found they were names fained and so knew them not." One member of the group, however, knows something that Pamphilia must also know: "But Perissus remembered one of the Ciphers, yet because it was Pamphilias hee would not knowe it" (*Part 1*, 490). Perissus is generally understood as a discreet reader of Pamphilia's cipher: he acknowledges to himself what he does not say aloud.[30] Perissus is a reader who knows the name being withheld but pretends as if he does not know it. The narrator describes this particular species of ignorance as "would not knowe."[31] Wroth criticism speaks the name that Perissus keeps to himself.

Yet to occupy the position in which you "would not knowe" is also to allow for the existence of obscurity; it may even suggest that obscurity is itself an object of desire. The critical strategy that withholding provokes is not the undoing of what Wroth has done but an account of "the doing" itself. A second example in which Pamphilia crafts a cipher will serve as my illustrative counterpoint. Taking a long walk in her garden, Pamphilia laments her love for Amphilanthus, and "in this estate shee stayed a while in the wood, gathering sometimes flowres which there grew; the names of which began with the letters of his name, and so placing them about her." As a cipher, the flowres with which Pamphilia surrounds herself appear to point to the lover of whose name they offer an anagram. The form that this pointing takes is *periphrasis*: these flowers substitute for the name that Pamphilia withholds. But the thing that these flowers *talk around* is not Amphilanthus but Pamphilia herself. Pamphilia sits at the center of her ring of flowers, where she addresses herself: "Well Pamphilia," she says, "for all these disorderly passions, keepe still thy soule from thought of change." Are the flowers that she has been "placing . . . about her" an expression of "these disorderly passions"? In which case, does each flower represent a passion in addition to a letter of Amphilanthus's name? Or, are these flowers an attempt to reinforce the circumscription that she commands of her self: "keepe still"? As Pamphilia continues to speak, the significance of this ring of flowers shifts again: "If thou blame any thing, let it be absence, since his presence will give thee againe thy fill of delight" (*Part 1*, 92). If we thought the circle of flowers named Pamphilia's lover, her corrective— "if thou blame anything"—suggests that she instead names Amphilanthus as the object of her "blame" (though she *now* declares the object of her blame to be "absence" rather than "Amphilanthus"). The thing to which Pamphilia's *periphrasis* of flowers points is not the name that she withholds but the physical space that it circumscribes. In the end, *periphrasis* becomes the form by which Pamphilia stages a fantasy of self-cancelation. This circle of flowers talks around that which is not there as if Pamphilia does not sit at its center.

The hermeneutic that would resolve Pamphilia's cipher by naming the name that she withholds is insufficient. In this instance, the word that Pamphilia withholds is significant as the permitting condition for an elaborate artistic creation: the act of withholding makes space for fiction. In what follows, I draw on discussions of *periphrasis* from classical and early modern rhetoric to consider the range of uses that made this figure attractive to Wroth. As a *formula* for composition, *periphrasis* allows a speaker to avoid certain words, but it is also valued for what Quintilian called its "decorative effect": its ability to make the word that it withholds even more conspicuous.[32] In the *Urania*, this "decorative effect" becomes a perverse form of possession: *periphrasis* is the device by which a speaker can lay claim to precisely what she does not have. As an alternative to philosophy's direct grasp and the stylistic ideal of clarity that is the sign of this grasp, *periphrasis* defines fiction as that space of obscure ornamentation. It is in this way that *periphrasis* provides an alternative to both history and a method of reading authorized by topicality. As a figure of speech, *periphrasis* is significant not for the history (or the historical names) to which it might have referred and from which it would derive its authority but because it permits the *Urania* to bring about the peculiar modality of fiction: what will never be.

How to Turn One Word into Many Words

By withholding a name, I mean the process by which a text avoids speaking one particular word. We tend to characterize withholding as the absence of speech and describe its form as silence—as, for example, with the omission of an *ellipsis*. But there is one figure of speech with which a speaker might withhold a word by speaking many other words in its place. The early modern rhetorical tradition called this act of withholding *periphrasis* or *circumlocutio*. The form of *periphrasis* is not silence but copia.[33] Broadly, classical and early modern rhetoricians identified three reasons why you might want to use *periphrasis*:

1. You are unable to speak the word that you withhold.
2. You wish to conceal the word that you withhold.
3. You wish to offset—to highlight or make *more* conspicuous—the word that you withhold.

As we progress through these three categories of use, the idea that *periphrasis* is reducible to or resolved by naming the name that it withholds becomes more difficult to maintain. In the end, I want to suggest that, from the perspective of *periphrasis*, figurative language turns on a quantitative rather than a qualitative distinction from "language at large," with the effect of aligning eloquence with the simple imperative for more.

1. The word that *periphrasis* withholds is unspeakable if you do not know it (you cannot form its shape in your mind or on your tongue). Instead of speaking that word, you talk around it—as if working away at the surrounding marble in order to find the statue waiting within. In this sense, it is only as if you know the word that you do not speak and the act of withholding is a posture (an appearance or a cover). As Johannes Susenbrotus explains in *Epitome of Tropes and Schemes* (1562), you are using a *periphrasis* "if you should say, 'our neighbor's daughter, a very lovely girl, desires to get married,' when her name may not be known to you."[34] In *The First Part*

of the *Urania*, Polarchos (formerly disguised as the Knight of the Spear and currently disguised as a stranger) asks his beloved Orilena "who the knight of the Spear was":

> "Alas my Lord," said she, "you lay too hard a taxe on me, since I cannot pay it, without yeelding as tribute many teares, and even the breaking of my heart to say he is, and is not now here: but yet to deny nothing to you, who so freely have granted my request, I will say what I know of him; He was, and (I hope) is the true image, or rather masculine vertue it selfe; the loveliest that Nature framd, the valiantest that followed Mars and his exercises, the wisest that wisdome dwelt in, the sweetest that noblenesse grac'd with sweet mildnesse, and the mildest that sweetnesse honourd: excellent in eloquence, true in profession, and making his actions still the same with his word: but for his name, or birth, I can say nothing." (*Part 1*, 204)

While it seems at first as if Orilena will provide a simple answer to Polarchos's question by naming his name—"to say he is"—what could have been a copula becomes, instead, the mere assertion of existence: "he is." The past tense of Polarchos's question implies that the Knight of the Spear is dead, but Orilena's corrective suggests that the Knight's existence is only qualified by the apparently heart-wrenching admission that though "he is," he "is not now here." He exists, but not by her side. (The fact that Orilena's language also casts Polarchos's disguise into a *paradox* of being—"he is, and is not now here"—suggests that she may know that she addresses the very man whose name she does not know.) Orilena then proceeds to supply a series of *periphrases*—"what I know of him"—as a substitute for the name of which, she declares, "I can say nothing": "the loveliest that Nature framd, the valiantest that followed Mars, etc." In response to the question of who someone is, you might offer a single name like Polarchos. If you do not know the name of that person, you might instead say everything you do know of that person. The extreme version of this second response would be something like the life story (which is also the primary form of narrative in the *Urania*).

Because *periphrasis* allows you to identify a thing for which you have no name, *periphrasis* was an especially useful tool for students learning Latin in early modern grammar schools. In *Ludus Literarius* (1612), John Brinsley advises schoolmasters "if there be any phrase, which" their students "cannot expresse; to resolue & expresse it by some other easier words & phrases of speech, with which they are better acquainted, & to do it by Periphrasis, that is moe words, if need be."[35] The one withheld word is the word that you want—you do not have it and you wish you did have it—with the result that *periphrasis* becomes both the form of desire and the form of compensation. Lack, in this sense, is the cause of *periphrasis*. Lack might also, however, be an effect of *periphrasis*. By talking around a word, you can produce the illusion that the word is beyond all naming (the deficit is in language rather than in your knowledge of language).[36] This is why, as one early reader marked in his copy of *Ludus Literarius*, *periphrasis* was also among "wayes of verying the Superlatiue degree."[37] *Periphrasis* in this mode is the companion of *hyperbole*, and the lack that is its effect suggests that the word being withheld does not exist in any language.[38] When Orilena provides that parade of *periphrases*—"the loveliest that Nature framd, the valiantest that followed Mars . . . the wisest . . . the sweetest . . . the mildest, etc."—she imitates the hyperbolist who possesses something that she does not: a name.

2. The word that *periphrasis* withholds might be unspeakable for social reasons. In this case, you use *periphrasis* to conceal that word. If the word that you would speak is what Quintilian called "indecent" (*deformia* or misshapen) or what Susenbrotus called "unsightly or sordid or repulsive," *periphrasis* will hide that word and protect you from its shame.[39] The favored example, here, is Sallust's *ad requisita naturae* (or, "nature calls") for urinating.[40] When Richard Sherry includes this example in *A Treatise of the Figures of Grammer and Rhetorike* (1555), he offers a blank space in lieu of the word that his exemplary *periphrasis* withholds:

> Periphrasis is, to hide thinges that
> be foule: as when we saye, I wyl goe to
> the priuie, for.
> I will make water, for   [41]

Examples also regularly include genitals—as in Martial's epigram where he disingenuously declares that he will not "by Periphrasis describe that thing / That common parent whence we all doe spring; / Which sacred Numa once a Prick did call."[42] As Henry Peacham explains in *The Garden of Eloquence* (1593), a "cause" of *periphrasis* "is desire to shunne obscenitie and naked telling of bashful matters, which is a part of modestie, much to be commended." This is why *periphrasis* can, for Peacham, preserve "chastitie."[43]

The Second Part of the *Urania* features an episode in which both the narrator and her characters use *periphrasis* to conceal the name of incest. When one mother correctly believes that her husband desires their daughter, she turns to the daughter and "tolde her what she feared she discerned in her fathers loose and bacely wicked desires towards her." In response, the daughter "tolde her all she demanded. Yett as seeming desirous to saulv her fathers faults as well as she cowld, hateing as much to relate his shame in the shamefullnes of his sinn as to speake that foule expression of his desired-to-bee-committed sinn." The daughter's telling of "all" that her mother "demanded" becomes a bizarre form of cover for that father. The daughter may seem as if she is looking to prop up her father's virtue by withholding the relation of his desire, but, really, she does not want to speak the language of his desire (she hates that language as much as she hates the act to which that language refers). Because the act has not yet been attempted, it is as if her speaking would wrest that act from the realm of fantasy ("desired-to-bee-committed") and bring it into the present (the having-already-been-committed). The mother subsequently removes both her daughter and herself to "a delicate wood" where they might "more freely discourse." That wood soon becomes the site of the father's attempted rape of his daughter ("hee commaunded his wyfe to hold her, while hee tooke his full pleasure of her").[44] The sequence of events implies a causal structure to which the narrative does not fully own: the space in which mother and daughter "more freely discourse" becomes the occasion for the father's attempt of the very act that the daughter's *periphrasis* previously withheld and that the narrator continues to withhold. The son interrupts the father before he can succeed and attempts "mildely and respectively . . . to winn him from his ill" (*Part 2*, 311). When the sister steps between the father's sword and the brother's body, she "had the blowe her self, which was ment to her brother," and the narrator gives us a version of the act that the narrative has been talking around (*Part 2*, 312).

3. You might also use *periphrasis* to make a word not less but more conspicuous. As Thomas Wilson explains in *The Art of Rhetoric* (1560), you can use *periphrasis* to "hide" a word "if the ears cannot bear the open speaking," but you might also use *periphrasis* "to set forth a thing more gorgeously."[45] It is in this sense that *periphrasis* acts as what Sherry called a "garnyshe," but the exact nature of this "garnyshe" is surprisingly difficult to pin down.[46] Whereas "garnish" usually points to the presence of figures as a kind of added decoration, the language that makes up the act of *periphrasis* might equally be plain. That is, while tropes like *metaphor* tend to deal in language marked by a deviation from the everyday (a norm that is itself posited by *metaphor*'s pretense of deviation), the language of *periphrasis* did not assume this same orientation away from the plain.[47] The characteristic distinction of *periphrasis* is, instead, quantitative rather than qualitative. Elegance may be a feature of *periphrasis*, but it does not necessarily or even ordinarily

substitute an ornamental style for a plain style. Instead, *periphrasis* necessarily entails only the substitution of more language for less, of more words for fewer. From the perspective of *periphrasis*, the defining characteristic of figurative language can be counted using a basic arithmetic.

It is for this reason that *periphrasis* was sometimes described as a figure of amplification.[48] The emphasis, in this case, is not on *periphrasis* as an act of substitution but as an engine for generating copia. Rhetorical theorists from Puttenham to John Hoskins maintain that it should not be difficult for a reader to discover the word that *periphrasis* withholds.[49] Though *periphrasis* requires the trope's characteristic act of substitution, this act is merely the cause of the "decorative effect" toward which *periphrasis* points. At the close of *Directions for Speech and Style* (1601), Hoskins struggles with precisely this point. He writes that *periphrasis* is "a vein of speech wherein the vulgar conceits are exceedingly pleased":

> For they admire this most, that there is some excellency in it and yet they themselves suspect that it excels their admiration. In some examples I would gladly discover the reason thereof. It cannot be but if either the meaning or the words be obscure or unfamiliar unto a man's mind, that the speech so consisting should be much accepted; and yet it is impossible that there should be any extraordinary delight in ordinary words and plain meaning. How then shall we determine? It is as it is in many dishes at our tables: our eyes and taste give them commendation, not for the substance but for the dressing and service.[50]

The pleasure of "vulgar conceits" is a problem for Hoskins. Not even they know, he suggests, why they like *periphrasis* so much. As he goes on to say, "*when they had slept awhile* is ordinary; but *when they had a while hearkened to the persuasion of sleep* is extraordinary." Break it down into vocabulary, and "all the words of it, by themselves, are most known and familiar, yet the bringing-in and fetch of it is strange and admirable to the ignorant."[51] Hoskins calls this *periphrasis*, yet he also attributes the recognizable act of figuration—what is "strange and admirable to the ignorant"—to another trope altogether: "It is much helped by metaphors; as before, *inclined to sleep* is expressed by a metaphor taken from an orator, who moves and inclines by persuasion, and to be so moved is *to hearken*."[52] Of what, then, does *periphrasis* as such consist?

Hoskins's account suggests that what the "vulgar" reader appreciates most about *periphrasis* is precisely that aspect of the figure that functions like *allegory*: "They admire this most: there is some excellency in it and yet they themselves suspect that it excels their admiration." What "they admire most" is how *periphrasis* points beyond itself. Yet according to Hoskins, the more to which *periphrasis* points is not the "other-speaking" of *allegory* (it is not the word that the figure withholds). Instead, *periphrasis* points to a thing outside of the ken of their admiration ("it excels their admiration") but the existence of which they "suspect." *Periphrasis*, that is, points to a quality of ornamentality that is not reducible to the words on the page or even to a particular formal arrangement of those words (as, say, with a figure like *gradatio*). As a result, when you try to pin it down, you find *metaphor* where you thought to find *periphrasis*. At its most expansive, what "vulgar conceits" love so much about *periphrasis* cannot be identified on the page, because it is an effect of the readers themselves (what they "admire" most is what they cannot see); at its most restricted, it is "the dressing and service" (how you would describe a meal if you were forbidden from naming any of its ingredients).

The word that *periphrasis* withholds is thus neither the source of its obscurity nor the key to undoing its obscurity. The absence of that word is simply the condition under which *poesie* might produce its "decorative effect." In the end, *periphrasis* is only explicable in quantitative terms. What do you get when you use *periphrasis*? More words than one. *Periphrasis* withholds a word that may be, as Quintilian describes it, *deformia*, but it does so only to produce another deformity or dis-formity in its stead.[53] The danger into which *periphrasis* always drives is the danger of saying too much (because you are really saying nothing at all). "Employed solely for decorative effect," *periphrasis* is, as Quintilian explains it, the name we lend to "whatever might have been expressed with greater brevity, but is expanded for purposes of ornament."[54] Precisely because *periphrasis* describes an amplification of words rather than an amplification of things, it is always threatening to go on, as Peacham warns, for "too long, whereby it may make the speech both tedious and barren."[55] Even the name—*periphrasis* or *circumlocutio*—and its implication of circling about (aimlessly) gave Quintilian cause for concern: "a term scarcely suitable to describe one of the virtues of oratory." Quintilian rescues *periphrasis* by pointing to yet another term: "It is only called periphrasis," he concludes, "so long as it produces a decorative effect: when it passes into excess, it is known as *perissology*" (the vice that Puttenham dubs "Long Language").[56] *Perissology* is the name for the superfluous speech that is both the style into which *periphrasis* ought not to wander and the very characteristic that describes *periphrasis* as such. As we saw with the category of vices in Chapter 3, *perissology* is both the distillation of *periphrasis*'s signature excess and an attempt to purge that excess from *periphrasis* itself.

Periphrasis turns philosophy's critique of rhetoric—that it is all style and no matter—into an engine for creative production by disrupting the ideal alignment of words to things. Think of the terms according to which Thomas Sprat will characterize "the Mathematical plainness" of the Royal Society's stylistic project in *The History of the Royal Society* (1667): "to reject all the amplifications, digressions, and swellings of style: to return back to the primitive purity, and shortness, when men deliver'd so many *things*, almost in an equal number of *words*."[57] *Periphrasis* takes up the one word that would fulfill Sprat's ideal of "Mathematical plainness," holds it back, and offers many other words in its place. The pedagogical reforms of Peter Ramus sought to resolve the problem of *periphrasis*'s elusive figuration by removing it from the art of rhetoric. As with *simile* and *antithesis*, *periphrasis* does not appear in any of the Ramist rhetorical textbooks. For Ramus, *periphrasis* was redundant of the place of *inventio* known as definition. Because "periphrasis can be devised in all cases through proper words," Ramus wrote in *Arguments in Rhetoric against Quintilian* (1549), "it does not involve any trope at all but a class of argument from the dialectical topics of definition."[58] Because *periphrasis* deals in "plain" language it does not, Ramus suggests, describe an operation of *elocutio*. The act of substitution that led some to classify *periphrasis* as a trope is not significant to Ramus; instead, he suggests that *periphrasis* is nothing but the place of definition. A definition, Fraunce writes in *The Lawiers Logike* (1588), "is that which declareth what a thing is": it does so either by identifying that thing's formal cause or by description.[59] Both kinds of definition "limit and circumscribe, or, as it were binde in the nature of that which is defined," but where the first is valuable for its "breuity," the second is valued for "copious amplification."[60] Fraunce adds this one caveat: "yet so as swelling superfluitie bée alwayes auoyded."[61] Lack and excess sit on either side of the spectrum of acceptable definitions. Reason becomes sophistry "if it eyther want, or haue too much."[62]

To think with *periphrasis* therefore requires an inversion of the mental "grasp" that characterizes philosophical thinking.[63] The kind of thinking that *periphrasis* permits suggests that you best come to know a thing not when you name its name but when you encompass the space that could hold a name by talking around that name. This is a form of thinking through encircling (not the grasp of the hand but an embrace of the arms). And this way of thinking is valued according to standards other than clarity and efficiency. This is not the elegance of simplicity, reductionism, or Occam's razor; to borrow a word from Thomas Wilson, *periphrasis* trades in elegance for *gorgeousness*.[64]

How to Possess Your Love

In the *Urania*, some words are more precious than others. The value of these words and the things that they name rises or falls in inverse proportion to their iteration. For example, where "every one" is "discoursing of poor Love," Love himself is "made poore by such perpetuall using his name" (*Part 1*, 321). To repeat the name of Love is to empty out Love's pockets. This is why Amphilanthus will confide the fact of his amorous distress to his friend but will not "for all his trust in him, impart his Mistresses name, holding that too deare, even for his friend to heare" (*Part 1*, 349). According to Amphilanthus, the act of withholding preserves the value of his lover's name: the image is of guarding your treasure. What is perhaps most peculiar about this image, however, is the fact that Amphilanthus's knowledge of that name does not diminish its value. Under this model, a name at its most valuable can belong to only one person, but it does not belong to the person we might expect (in this case, Pamphilia). Instead, Pamphilia's name belongs to her lover, and if he repeats it to anyone else, he diminishes its value. Your name is most valuable when your lover keeps it to him- or herself. In the *Urania*, characters are never more in possession of their lovers as when they walk around refusing to speak their names.

Pamphilia routinely returns the favor by withholding the name of "Amphilanthus." As we saw with her *periphrasis* of flowers, this withholding is also a kind of artistry. *Periphrasis* is significant, then, not only for its act of concealment but as an expression of value. In another episode, Pamphilia again takes a walk in her garden and begins to speak aloud:

> "Sweete wood," said she, "beare record with me, never knew I but this love."
> "Love," answered the wood being graced with an Echo.
> "Soft," said she, "shall I turne blabb? no Echo, excuse me, my love and choyce more precious, and more deere, then thy proud youth must not be named by any but my selfe, none being able to name him else, as none so just, nor yet hath any eare (except his owne) heard me confess who governs me; thy vast, and hollow selfe shall not be first, where fondest hopes must rest of secresie in thee, who to each noise doth yeeld an equall grace. As none but we doe truely love, so none but our owne hearts shall know we love." (*Part 1*, 318)

Pamphilia calls on the woods—"beare record with me"—to witness the singularity of "this love." But when the woods speak back—"Love"—what she hears is a question and a request that she quickly denies: "no Echo, excuse me."⁶⁵ Pamphilia constructs a *periphrasis* of her "love"—"my love and choice"—by asserting that his relative value is "more precious and more deere" than Echo's love (whose name she also withholds—"thy proud youth"). Two circumscribed absences sit on either side of this comparative structure, but the fulcrum tilts toward the greater value of "Amphilanthus" because there is also a sense in which Pamphilia's *periphrasis* for her lover utilizes and absorbs the *periphrasis* of another lover. Though Pamphilia wants a record that she has only ever loved this one man, she also insists that only she has the right to name him. No one else can name him because no one else has a "just" claim over him. Echo's capacity to repeat is a problem for Pamphilia's possession. In a curious reversal of cause and effect, Pamphilia fears that by speaking Amphilanthus's name aloud and thereby permitting Echo to speak his name, she will surrender her claim on him. If she speaks the name of her "love," she will have to share him as he sits on the tongues of other women (Echo standing in for all the women who would speak his name).

Pamphilia suggests that she saves Amphilanthus's name from Echo because Echo is promiscuous: her "hollow selfe" treats every "noise" with "equall grace," and so Echo's speech cannot provide an accurate measure of the value of "Amphilanthus," which is "more precious, and more deere" than other names (including Narcissus). But Pamphilia displaces Amphilanthus's own promiscuity onto Echo. The real problem that Pamphilia confronts in this scene is that other women have the right to speak—are equally "just" in their claim to speak—Amphilanthus's name. Pamphilia's *periphrasis* thus becomes a perverse engine for the preservation of Amphilanthus's fidelity and her possession of him. If nobody but Amphilanthus knows that she loves him, then nobody can dispute Pamphilia's claim by asserting that she is equally "just" and justified in naming him. When Pamphilia withholds the name of Amphilanthus, she thereby inflates its value—he is only "more precious, and more deere, then thy proud youth" so long as nobody speaks his name. In order to maintain the value of her possession, Pamphilia must deny herself the privilege to which she also claims right. In this light, Pamphilia's *periphrasis* for Narcissus might be a kind of offering to Echo—*I won't name the name of your lover if you don't name the name of mine.*

To withhold a word, to refuse to speak a name, is a form of possession in the *Urania*: it allows a speaker to take hold of precisely that which she does not have. *Periphrasis* permits Pamphilia to maintain her grip on the very thing it does not name, even as it also suggests that she does not have it all. This model of possession is a *paradox*, but it is not a trick of self-delusion. As is made explicit in the episode of Alarinus and Myra, it is a logic of possession that exceeds even the lifespan of a lover. Duped by a false double, Myra believes that she has just witnessed her beloved Alarinus throw himself from a window and plummet to his death. As if in imitation of this action, she "withdraw[s] her selfe from the windowe" and proceeds to "threwe her selfe upon her bed"; she "cryed out only against misfortune, and so brake her heart, and dyed, her last words being, 'Yet though honour, and life bee lost, I dye just, and truely thine, my onely deare Ala—'" (*Part 1*, 595). Myra does not finish her sentence or even her lover's name.[66] "And this Ala—was all," Alarinus tells his audience, "for all my name shee spake, death either then wholly possessing her, or shee desirous still to hold mee neere her, kept that last part in her" (*Part 1*, 595–596). The syllables that Myra withholds go with her where she goes. This may be an accident of death or an expression of desire. Had Myra fully spoken "Alarinus," she would have released him; had she never said his name at all, he would have died with her. "Yet truely," he continues, "had I like to have gone with her, with her (though asunder) I may say, for our soules united had gone together: but alas, I was not so happy" (*Part 1*, 596). Though physically separated from one another at the time of her death, the lovers would have died "united" had Myra withheld his name. The broken form that Myra speaks—"Ala—"—breaks Alarinus "asunder": Myra continues to possess half of him in death. The half that remains alive—"Ala—"—is bound to rehearse their story over and over again at the monument dedicated to her exemplarity, each word a variation on the homonym that he cannot help but repeat: "alas."[67] Only half-alive, "Ala—" becomes an allegorical figure for grief.

The episode of Myra and Alarinus suggests that the kind of possession that comes from withholding your lover's name is not exclusive to the material conditions of the world. But it also suggests that lovers might become shared property in death. When Myra dies, it may be that she speaks only half of her lover's name in order to maintain possession of half of him, or it may be that she is trying to release him fully before death seizes her— "wholly possessing her." Death possesses Myra who—unable to finish her lover's name—still possesses half of Alarinus. An extreme version of this phenomenon is at stake when we meet "the widow of Polidorus" only after her husband has been killed. We never learn her name. The *Urania*, instead, refers to her with *periphrases*: "thy other selfe," "her, that lives to dye," (*Part 1*, 352), and in her final moments, "I am, and was, his wife, deerely beloved of him" and "I was Daughter to a King" (*Part 1*, 353). The widow believes that her husband is dead because he has not come home from the war. She sits in their tomb and subsists wholly on a word that she eats but does not speak (which means we never hear it). She "feed[s] on the sweetest word thou gavest mee when we parted," and she waits: "A dying life doe I continue in, till thou or thine release me unto thee" (*Part 1*, 352). Although she repeatedly calls on death—"let this bee my last minute of unquietnesse"—the widow does not enjoy Myra's success. She insists, "I know that thou art dead," yet that knowledge cannot precipitate her death (*Part 1*, 350). She must know for "certaine," which means she must hear it from someone else (*Part 1*, 352). Amphilanthus has firsthand knowledge of Polidorus's death, but Amphilanthus hesitates to speak the word that the widow desires to hear: "The Army is overthrowne, and your beloved Lord, who wee have heard you so much speake of—." Amphilanthus stops short. The widow supplies the word that he withholds: "'Slaine,' said shee, 'I see it in your face, though you will not in pitty speake it.'" Amphilanthus's face becomes a *periphrasis* for the word that he will not utter. And then the widow makes her final request: "Lay me then brave Sir, with my Lord, and only deere Polidorus, and thus my deere, my soul to thine doth flye" (*Part 1*, 353). With that, the widow gains "the excellent libertie of dying" that she has been seeking (*Part 1*, 350). There is a general expectation in the world of the *Urania* that language can kill, and that expectation is here fulfilled: "She stretched her selfe straight out, and by curious Art laid her selfe forth, fit to be carried to her buriall, dying as if the word dead had kild her" (*Part 1*, 353).[68] But what is perhaps most strange about this moment is that nobody has spoken the word that kills her: "the word dead." When Amphilanthus tried to say as much, he went silent (and she supplied "Slain" in its stead). And when the widow wills herself to death—"and thus my deere, my soule to thine doth flye"—what she speaks is a *periphrasis* for that death. At this moment, the word that nobody speaks is also that which possesses Polidorus, who possesses the name of his widow.

In his essay "That to Philosophie, is to learne how to die," Montaigne (as translated by John Florio) considers the ways in which men divert themselves from knowledge of the inevitability of death. Among them, withholding the word: "For so much as this sillable sounded so unpleasantly in their eares . . . the Romans had learned to allay and dilate the same by a Periphrasis. In liew of saying he is dead, or he hath ended his daies, they would say he hath lived. So it be life, be it past or no, they are comforted."[69] Montaigne opposes *periphrasis* to philosophy insofar as the figure becomes a mechanism for avoiding the thought on which the mind ought to fix.[70]

What the *Urania* suggests, by contrast, is that *periphrasis* offers a different way of thinking death: the way of the lover's embrace.

Not Yet

For a romance that gets so much of its stylistic energy from *periphrasis*, *The First Part* of the *Urania* opens with a surprising economy of diction: "When the Spring began to appear like the welcome messenger of Summer" (*Part 1*, 1). Wroth begins her romance by featuring the very character—Urania—whose absence gave rise to the laments of Sidney's pair of shepherd-lovers in the revised *Arcadia*. In the *Urania*'s opening sentence, Wroth appears to redouble her emulative claim to presence by speaking the word that the *Arcadia* withheld in the *periphrasis* of its opening sentence: "It was in the time that the earth begins to put on her new apparel against the approach of her lover, and that the sun, running a most even course, becomes an indifferent arbiter between the night and the day."[71] Where Sidney offered what one early reader marked down in the margin as a "Periphrasis of the Spring," Wroth rather matter-of-factly names "the Spring" (see Figure 2 in Chapter 2).[72] By naming the name that Sidney withheld, Wroth's sentence repeats the claim to presence enacted by her titular character's opening lament and walk in the woods. In the *Urania*, the absent ideal of the *Arcadia* speaks, goes on walks, and hands off her companion-lamb to the hungry for dinner.

Wroth's romance, however, rather quickly complicates this revision when it suggests that Urania's name is the only thing about her that *is* known. Abandoned as a baby and left to the care of a shepherd and his wife, Urania knows nothing else about herself: "For my selfe I can say nothing, but that my name is Urania" (*Part 1*, 22). Throughout the early episodes of the romance, Urania is also known as "the X Sheperdess": "the sweet and tender-hearted Shepherdesse" (*Part 1*, 3), "the excellent Shepherdesse" (*Part 1*, 4),[73] "faire Shepherdesse" (*Part 1*, 5),[74] "rare Shepherdesse" (*Part 1*, 15),[75] "the Prime of Shepherdesses" (*Part 1*, 20), "Admired Shepherdes," "incomparable Shepherdesse," (*Part 1*, 21), "most delicate Shepherdes," (*Part 1*, 24), "sweet Sheperdes" (*Part 1*, 25), etc. Even when Urania's first lover, Parselius, reveals her current habit to be the disguise that everybody already knows it is, he still calls her by the language of that disguise: "You most faire Shepherdesse are the lost Princesse" (*Part 1*, 23). These examples reference the full range of functions we have come to expect from *periphrasis*. A speaker will call Urania "faire Shepherdess" when he does not know her name (*Part 1*, 5);[76] *periphrasis* can serve as a linguistic counterpart to the shepherd's weeds that conceal her true identity (the narrator will refer to Veralinda as "the delicatest Shepherdesse, now Urania had left that habit" [*Part 1*, 427]); the *epithets* perpetually attached to "Shepherdess" can also serve to offset or make more conspicuous what cannot be concealed: Urania's superlative status as "the matchlesse Shepherdesse" (*Part 1*, 28).

While Wroth's opening scene turns on Urania's insistent presence, she returns to Sidney's *Arcadia* once again to revise its inaugural lament (though this time tilted at a slightly new angle). Urania's lover, Parselius, has just rescued Limena from her husband and tormentor and has returned her to her grateful lover, Perissus. Parselius then rushes to tell both Limena and Perissus that he knows exactly who they are:

> Then did Parselius tell them how infinitly happy he esteemed himselfe, in having come so luckily to serve them, of whom, and whose unfortunat affection hee had heard, having had it from the rare Shepherdesse. Name her he could not, his breath being stopp'd with sighes, and his teares falling down in all abundance.

Parselius's inability to name the name of Urania is physiological: the copia he supplies instead of that name is an "abundance" of tears. The breath that would have gone into speaking her name is repurposed for sighing. It is at least slightly odd, then, that Perissus knows immediately and exactly just who Parselius is talking about:

> Perissus seeing his sorrow, made hast to ask the cause, fearing some great harme had befalne that Divine Creature, of whom he gave such praises, as Limena thought they were too much, which hee perceiving left, with demanding of her safety, and why his greeving was; which Parselius having passionatly, and truely related, he desired most earnestly, to heare the rest of Limena's story. (*Part 1*, 87)

At first it may seem as if Perissus's *periphrasis*—"that Divine Creature, of whome he gave such praises"—is an expression of Perissus's own ignorance (like Susenbrotus's example of the neighbor's daughter, he does not know the name that Parselius withholds). But with Limena's response—"that Divine Creature, of whome he gave such praises, as Limena thought they were too much"—we learn that that pronoun "he" refers to Perissus rather than Parselius. As if compelled by Perissus's awkward slip, Parselius's subsequent turn to the remainder of Limena's story looks like covering for his new friend. As the narrative proceeds, Limena augments her story of psychological and physical torture with the visual aides of her devastating scars (as if securing Perissus's affection by reminding him of all that she has suffered on his behalf).

The escalating *periphrases* of Urania's two would-be lovers threaten to turn Perissus and Parselius into Strephon and Claius, the pair of lovers whose devotions to Urania opened Sidney's revised *Arcadia*. Except for Limena's response—one that Perissus "perceiv[ed]" but to which we are not privy—these lovers might have continued with their praises forever. At this moment, Limena becomes a measure of the difference between the *Urania* and the *Arcadia*, a kind of embodiment of what keeps the *Urania* from becoming the *Arcadia*. As is the case with most female characters in the *Urania*, Limena is not wrong to be suspicious of Perissus.[77] And, as Parselius continues on in his adventures, he will forget all about Urania (he marries another woman before he even remembers who he has left behind). *The Second Part* of the *Urania* plays out the problem of Parselius's abandonment onto the next generation. Urania's son, Floristello, falls in love with a seeming shepherdess. Urania's own story is so well known that everyone in the narrative seems to note the similarity. Casting himself down "under the shadow of a well-spredd beech" (the shade of the very species of tree under which Urania opened *The First Part*), Floristello maintains that the social rank of his shepherdess is not a problem because he knows her to be more than she seems: "Yett why may she, O why may she nott be other? Her spiritt is as high as an Emperess. Was not my mother a shepherdes? Yes, and the fairest, loveliest Urania, yett she proved a kings daughter, and sister to the most renowned Emperour" (*Part 2*, 92).[78] The new shepherdess herself notes the parallel.[79] The union of Floristello with this shepherdess would therefore provide a kind of intergenerational form of closure to one of *The First Part*'s loosest narrative ends by staging Urania's rediscovery (in the person of this shepherdess) and her lover's fidelity (in the person of her son). Eventually, we will learn that Floristello's unnamed shepherdess is the daughter of Parselius and his wife. A prophecy reveals that because Parselius broke "bands" with Urania, "one of hers shall have this throne with your daughter, the true picture of your dearest Dalinea" (*Part 2*, 322). There is a symmetry to this prophecy: Urania's child will get precisely what he would have gotten if Parselius were his father. But this symmetry is only achieved by that child's repetition of his would-be father's betrayal: Floristello must marry the woman who is the spitting image of the woman Parselius married instead of his mother.

If we were expecting, then, that the union of Floristello and the shepherdess might wrap up this storyline, what we find instead is that Floristello never learns her name. The next time we see Floristello, he has lost his shepherdess: "Wher, O wher, is my deerer self? . . . You, O you, the darling of the worlde, the ornament of Nature, the glory and onely miroir of her sex, wher O wher, shall I seeke, thee." Though Floristello's question is *where*, his speech is structured by the problem of *who*. As the series of *periphrases* suggest—"the darling of the worlde, the ornament of Nature, the glory and onely miroir of her sex"—Floristello still does not know the Shepherdess's name. What is more, it seems that the answer to the question of where is wrapped up in the question of who she is:

> Did nott I see a clowde take her violently from mee then? Why did I lose my self soe willfully? Why went I from this place of hapines, and stayed nott heere to expect her coming? Or why, rather, did I nott goe in her search, but follow adventures? Yes, to adventure my parpetuall loss and shame in leaving her. Who, if unknowne, why then did nott I adventure rather to find out her parents, and assist her in her greatest miserie, which she ever esteem'd to bee in nott beeing knowne? (*Part 2, 332*)

There are many parts to Floristello's self-loathing. The shepherdess was "taken away as ravisht from him in a clowde." Instead of either looking for her or staying put until her return, Floristello went on "adventures." And not an "adventure" on her behalf (he does not spend this time in search of her or her parents). Soon after this lament, Floristello stumbles across the very enchantment that has trapped his shepherdess. He is permitted to see her but cannot touch her (his arms go right through her). At this enchantment, "a Voice" speaks the following: "This adventure is reserved for you, and you shall have this lady you soe much covett, butt you must follow other, and pass many other adventures first" (*Part 2, 333*). Before leaving the enchantment Floristello asks "the Voice," "May I nott know who she is?" To which "the Voice" replies: "Nott yett, but fortunately advance" (*Part 2, 334*).

The closure that "the Voice" promises is the closure of *periphrasis*: "Nott yett." It posits the necessary fulfillment of Floristello's desire—he will learn the shepherdess's name—while dilating the space prior to that moment.[80] We have seen the *Urania*'s lovers refuse to speak the names of their beloveds, but in this instance it is as if the narrative—speaking through a disembodied and otherwise unnamed "Voice"—withholds the name of Floristello's lover on his behalf. When the agency of withholding your lover's name is displaced onto narrative, the act of withholding looks a lot like not knowing. Narrative's act of withholding is not a riddle to be solved.

The "Voice" advises Floristello against tracking down the shepherdess's parents. Narrative's act of withholding is, instead, an enabling condition for adventures. The "Voice" advises Floristello to "fortunately advance."

The next time we see the shepherdess, she knows her name. In fact, everybody seems to know her name (though the narrative does not represent this moment of revelation). Everyone, that is, except for Floristello. Instead of reuniting with his shepherdess, Floristello's adventures latch onto the deferred union of yet another couple. Floristello can reunite with Candiana (and, presumably, learn her name) once the knight known as "Faire Design" meets up with his lover. "Faire Design" takes his name from a cipher on his heart. As he explains, "I know no parents, nor have I a name more then the unknowne. I have a sipher on my hart, which is sayd to bee her name whom I must by many hard adventures att last gaine, and knowe her by having a sipher likewise, which shall discover my name, and then I shalbee knowne" (*Part 2*, 297). The logic of the cipher would seem to push Faire Design in the direction of her "whom I must by many hard adventure at last gaine," but the cipher instead reveals a different capacity. Instead of traveling toward the woman who bears the key to his cipher, Faire Design heads in the direction of Amphilanthus (who once went by the name of the Knight of the Cipher).[81] As Andromarko explains before *The Second Part* cuts off, midsentence:

> "your Faire Designe hath now left all things (beeing certainly informed by severall wisards, especially the sage Melissea), that the great Inchantment will nott bee concluded thes many yeeres; nay nev[er], if you live nott to assiste in the concluding. For his search is for you, resolving nott to leave you if once found. Till that hapy hower come, in this Island hee is seeking adventur; the best and hapiest, I assure my self, wilbee in finding you."
>   Amphilanthus was extreamly   (*Part 2*, 418)

Faire Design looks for his model, Amphilanthus. Mary Ellen Lamb has argued that Faire Design is a figure for Mary Wroth's illegitimate son by William Herbert. Ending the romance where she does, Wroth offers a cipher—Faire Design—for one topical reader whose formal act of recognition would necessarily entail the decoding of that cipher. Lamb describes this ending as "a benevolent maternal instinct":

> to move the Earl to acknowledge his natural son through writing its desirability into a text—through pointing to what could be, if this nar-

rative of recognition were continued to its expected ending not only in Wroth's romance but in her son's life.[82]

By the logic of the cipher, Wroth's romance cannot move forward because history does not provide it with anywhere to go. William Herbert never acknowledges his son, and thus this moment "encodes a lost opportunity." The scene in which Faire Design finds Amphilanthus, this "moment of mutual acknowledgment," is "forever deferred because it never happened."[83] Wroth's interrupted ending tethers the fortunes of fiction to history: "what could be" binds the possibilities of fiction to the historical determinism of a specific action in time.[84] In this instance, that specific action is the interpretation of a topical reader in the person of William Herbert.

The promise of the cipher is the promise that all of the narrative threads will succumb to the centripetal pull of reunion and recognition. The promise of the cipher is that the name revealed will prove the key to unlocking all obscurity. The undoing of obscurity will end romance. The promise of *periphrasis*, by contrast, is that it is precisely in the withholding of the name of Faire Design that the *Urania* brings about what will never be.[85] The intense focus on Faire Design at the close of *The Second Part* recasts the entirety of the *Urania* as an elaborate art of withholding. The *Urania* is the conspicuous artifice of *periphrasis*: its words are the many words that it offers instead of this name. At its most stark, I am suggesting that the *Urania* is not a cipher for Mary Wroth, because it is a *periphrasis* for the name of her son. It is not that an absence in history marks the limit point of fiction. It is, instead, that Wroth retroactively posits a historical act of withholding as the permitting condition for her fiction: a "Faire Design" that is also an elaborate expression of that fiction's value.[86] It is not, finally, that fiction stops because history gives it nowhere to go. It is, instead, that history's withholding permits fiction to bring about its own peculiar modality: what will never be.

CODA

Indecorous Forms

When Ben Jonson transcribed Francis Bacon's famous disavowal of the "affectionate study of eloquence" into his *Timber: Or, Discoveries* (1640), he did away with the figure of speech that organized it. Jonson systematically dismantled Bacon's dramatic swing of *antitheses* and the suspect priorities of men who "hunt more after words than matter."[1] Curiously, Jonson's undoing of Bacon's *antitheses* transforms a passage that is most familiar to us as evidence of the turn against *elocutio* into a surprising defense of figure.[2] In Jonson's hands, Bacon's condemnation becomes an imperative command:

> Then make exact animadversion where style hath degenerated, where flourish'd, and thriv'd in choicenesse of Phrase, round and cleane composition of sentence, sweet falling of the clause, varying an illustration by tropes and figures, weight of matter, worth of Subject, soundness of Argument, life of Invention, and depth of Judgement.[3]

Jonson's revision is as close as the *Discoveries* gets to advocating for the schoolroom practice of figure pointing: Bacon's oppositions become a continuous catalog of "where" style has "flourish'd, and thriv'd." Yet Jonson's defense of style achieves its reversal of Bacon's corrective by undoing the very *antitheses* that previously pit "the varying and illustration of their works with tropes and figures" against the "life of invention."[4] Jonson's revision flattens Bacon's hierarchy and turns his account of perversion into a program for learning that reinforces the very pedagogy Bacon condemned.[5] Jonson's revision only articulates this program, however, by doing away with one of the figures of speech that was among humanist pedagogy's signature objects of study.

In *Ben Jonson and the Language of Prose Comedy* (1960), Jonas Barish reads Jonson's revision of Bacon as an example of his deep-rooted antipathy for any symmetrical syntactical forms but especially *antithesis*.[6] "'Asymmetrical' seems to define the shape of Jonson's prose so exactly," Barish writes, "that one is tempted to use it to describe the topography of his mind."[7] This account of Jonson's style continues to underwrite a literary history that tracks the rise of the "plain style" in the seventeenth century, or, as Barish called it, "antirhetorical rhetoric that seeks to disguise itself almost as nonrhetoric."[8] This history, for example, informs the standard reading of the conspicuous artifice of Jonson's *Every Man Out of His Humour*, according to which the figure pointing of the play's many characters betrays their unthinking participation in a style that is really a social scene. This history also solidifies figure's position as a target of Jonson's early experiments in "comical satire."[9] At the close of this book, however, I want to offer a reading of *Every Man Out* in order to signal the complexity of Jonson's relationship to the canon of *elocutio* and its figures of speech. The category of figure was irrelevant to Barish's study of style because Barish was invested in those movements of prose that might reveal the mind thinking "at a deeper level than by the conscious employment of stylistic devices."[10] Where Jonson engaged with figure as such, he was therefore revealing something other than his mind (and doing something other than thinking). In this book, by contrast, I have been tracking the particular kind of thinking that only figure makes possible. In both Jonson's revision of Bacon and in the pervasive figure pointing of *Every Man Out*, Jonson holds open the possibility of an alternative conception of style, one in which figures of speech drive thinking and act as the constitutive engines of imaginary worlds.

My reading of Jonson's play will fall into three brief sections. First, I will consider the bizarre structure of *Every Man Out* so as to frame Jonson's experiment in what I am calling, after Katherine Eisman Maus's parallel formulation, "the law of the conservation of forms."[11] Against Sidney's claim in the *Defence* that the poet can make "forms such as never were in nature" and in contrast to Spenser's chamber of *Phantastes*, which contains "Infinite shapes of thinges dispersed thin; / Some such as in the world were neuer yit," Jonson sets out to satirize Elizabethan eloquence by restricting himself to figures of speech already in existence and to which his characters repeatedly point.[12] From Fastidius Briske's appreciation of figure wherever he can find it—"By Minerva, an excellent figure!"—to Macilente's aside—"I ne'er knew tobacco taken as a *parenthesis* before"—*Every Man Out* performs the figure pointing of the sixteenth-century schoolroom so as to put these forms before our eyes.[13] The play explicitly describes Sidney's *Arcadia* as a source of these figures (and at least one copycat courtier runs off in mid-play to read the *Arcadia*), but Jonson is also thinking about Spenser's *Faerie Queene* (in the ineffective hanging of Sordido, in the vision of the Queen that concluded the original production, and in Carlo Buffone's insistence that men are pigs and the eating of roast pork, cannibalism).[14] Mary Wroth had not yet written the *Urania*, but the manner in which Fastidius, Mistress Fallace, and Sogliardo labor with *epithets* offers a proleptic display of Antissia's art.[15] These acts of figure pointing create a condition to which they restrict the play itself: the set of forms with which Jonson will work is closed, though it is not exhausted, and this closure is a problem of literary history.

I argue that in *Every Man Out* Jonson's parody turns against itself. Targeting two aspects of figure's conspicuousness—its instrumentality and its overuse—Jonson's satire unleashes the inventive capacities of figure. In the second and third sections of this coda, I read two figures of speech that represent the range of figure's world-making capacities in the play: the "vainglorious knight" Puntarvolo uses *periphrasis* to transform his estate into an artful enclosure dedicated to the pleasure of one ("List of Characters," 13); Carlo Buffone's *similes*, by contrast, threaten to rearrange the world of the play at large by remaking the entities that populate that world into deformities or disformities.[16] In a climactic scene, the disguised playwright pits Carlo and his "stabbing similes" against Puntarvolo, following the death of his dog (4.3.227). It will be the final move of this coda, and the book as a whole, to suggest that Carlo's *poesie* on the occasion of Puntarvolo's dead dog offers an anatomy of form and its capacities in early modern literature and its criticism.

The Law of the Conservation of Forms

Widely regarded as unperformable, *Every Man Out*'s unwieldy structure and size is propelled by two organizational extravagances. First, the play moves along a chain of scenes that do not contribute to a recognizable plot so much as they elaborate on the given humor from which each of the play's characters suffer—that "peculiar quality" that "doth so possess a man that it doth draw / All his affects, his spirits, and his powers / In their confluxions all to run one way" (*In.* 103–106). The play's characters therefore resemble wind-up toys that won't quit, and the discreteness of episodes is determined by the artifice with which each character remakes his or her immediate environment into the conspicuous elaboration of his or her "peculiar quality."[17] Second, the play contains a play-within-a-play, but the outer play refuses to remain where it ought: a chorus composed of Cordatus and Mitis perpetually interrupts the performance while the playwright, Asper, plays the part of Macilente. Rather than standing outside of the play, the characters of the chorus are subject to the same stringent logic of the "peculiar quality." The combination of these two eccentricities has led Helen M. Ostovich to describe *Every Man Out* as "a seemingly formless play about dramatic form."[18] As the play piles observers on top of observers (chorus on top of chorus, critic on top of critic, audience on top of audience), it initiates an unmistakable and endless motion in which it is constantly folding in on itself only to reconstitute itself as precisely that folding in.[19] As a result, the play becomes an experiment in a *poesie* that seeks to become its own criticism.

Asper gets the play going by acerbically railing against the world he inhabits: "Who is so patient of this impious world / That he can check his spirit, or rein his tongue?" (*In.* 2–3). Cordatus and Mitis take turns trying to silence Asper until Cordatus sets him this one condition: "Unless your breath had power / To melt the world and mould it new again, / It is in vain to spend it in these moods" (*In.* 46–47). "Unless" deposits the "power" that Cordatus describes on the other side of a line that it also draws. ("Unless" drains the virtue from the related "if.") Cordatus thinks that his condition is impossible, but it is at precisely this moment that Asper realizes he is in a theater: "I not observed this throngèd round till now" (*In.* 49). The articulation of Cordatus's impossible condition transforms a crowd into an audience.[20] "Throngèd round," the audience circumscribes an ideal theatrical space in which Asper will put on a play and justify the expenditure of his labor by virtue of the fact that his "breath" can "melt the world and mould it new again."[21] Asper's world making emerges as a combination of radical and restricted components: he destroys the world as it is in order to make another world, but this new world is nonetheless constrained to the same set of finite resources. Asper proposes to "prodigally spend myself, / And speak away my spirit into air," which means he will empty himself out and cannot replenish what is lost (*In.* 202–203).[22] The image is of one giant inhale followed by a single, continuous exhale burdened with the entirety of the play. He proposes to "melt my brain into invention" and "Coin new conceits" (*In.* 204–205). Whereas we have been thinking of invention as an activity in which the mind engages, Asper here reveals "invention" to be something like the material cause of the mind itself, the thing into which his "brain" can be melted. The metal of "invention" that gave rise to Asper's "brain" will now be repurposed for the play; the "coin[ing]" of "new conceits" requires the eradication of the "brain," which is also, by implication, merely an old "conceit."

Asper's brand of satirical theater destroys the world as it is in order to make a new world out of it: it can repurpose all of the old world, but it cannot add to it. This is what Katherine Eisman Maus has described, by way of a productive anachronism, as "the law of the conservation of matter" in Jonson's "satiric economy": "He represents a world that contains a predetermined quantity of substance, a quantity not subject to increase."[23] I want to suggest that in *Every Man Out* Jonson is also engaging what we might call "the law of the conservation of forms": the redistribution of matter that defines Asper's world making can only proceed by virtue of forms that already exist. The play's acts of figure pointing establish this constraint even as they ask early modern romance's conspicuous figures of speech to represent metonymically the full range of available forms. When Asper promises the audience that he will "hang my richest words / As polished jewels in their bounteous ears," he both literalizes Sidney's emblem of *indecorous poesie* from the *Defence* and proposes a new measure of *decorum* (*In.* 205–206). Complaining of "the diligent imitators of Tully and Demosthenes" and the "Nizolian paper-books of their figures and phrases," Sidney likens the *indecorous* poets who "cast sugar and spice upon every dish that is served to the table" to "those Indians, not content to wear earrings at the fit and natural place of the ears, but they will thrust jewels through their nose and lips, because they will be sure to be fine."[24] Asper will place his bejeweled words in the ears where they belong, but he will not place them in his own ears. He offers them instead as the ornaments of his audience. The *decorum* of this transaction resides in the alignment of Asper's "richest words" with the size of his audience's "bounteous ears." "Bounteous" also suggests, however, that those ears will reciprocate with their own form of wealth. Asper's promise conceals a transaction that will close the loop of this play: Let's see the generosity of those ears. The *decorum* of Asper's new world depends on the audience and its criticism.

Every Man Out would seem explicitly to reject "the law of the conservation of forms" when Cordatus claims the maker's right to innovation against the critical expectation that it adhere to "the laws of comedy" as defined by Terence (*In.* 231): "We should enjoy the same *licentia* or free power to illustrate and heighten our invention as they did, and not be tied to those strict and regular forms which the niceness of a few (who are nothing but form) would thrust upon us" (*In.* 261–265). Cordatus rejects adherence to "strict and regular forms" by making the critics who enforce such forms into another object of the play's satire of humors: the critics who police "strict and regular forms" are themselves "nothing but form." As Carlo Buffone suggests when he walks into the Induction, the title of the play promises to deliver each and every one of its characters from the "peculiar quality" that defines and controls them.[25] Cordatus's rejection of "the law of the conservation of forms" thus raises the specter of yet another humor for the play to exorcise. In his defense of poetic license, Cordatus describes a character of the Critic who does not materialize on stage and who is not featured among "The List of Characters" at the play's start but who is nonetheless a recipient of the play's guiding promise. This Critic begins as an expression of her "peculiar quality": devoted to "strict and regular forms," she is "nothing but form." If the play is successful, it will knock her out of that "peculiar quality." The Critic's "bounteous ears" will guarantee the *decorum* of the play because the play will transform that Critic into what it needs her to be. In a move characteristic of the strange operations of this play, the organizing system that is *Every Man Out* reaches out across space and time by scripting a type that any particular can fill.

The Periphrastical Fantasia

Carlo Buffone points his finger at *periphrasis* before we have met Puntarvolo or arrived at his estate. Witnessing a fumbling conversation between Sogliardo and Macilente, who has been lounging on Sogliardo's land, Carlo determines that when Macilente answers Sogliardo's question, "Why, who am I, sir?" with "One of those that fortune favors," the form of his speaking is "the periphrasis of a fool" (1.2.178–180). Macilente's *periphrasis* permits him to withhold Sogliardo's name and to remake Sogliardo as the object of his own all-consuming envy. The act of naming with which Carlo points to this figure has the curious effect of lending a name to the very device that withholds names. The preposition of his formulation, "periphrasis of a fool," also raises these questions: To whom does a *periphrasis* belong? Does the figure belong to the speaker who wields it, or to the object that it treats? In other words, whom does a *periphrasis* possess?

When we meet Puntarvolo, this earlier exchange has prepared us to recognize *periphrasis* as the form that organizes his fantasy, though no one points directly at it. A collection of characters including Carlo, Sordido, and Fastidius hide themselves nearby as they watch Puntarvolo enact a scene that he has scripted and that he performs every morning: Puntarvolo stands outside of his own house and commands his forester to signal his arrival there as if he were a stranger to that house; Puntarvolo then mistakes his wife's maid for his wife, as if he does not know either one of them; finally, Puntarvolo proceeds to woo his wife as if he were someone other than her husband. When Puntarvolo asks his Lady's maid, "What call you the lord of the castle, sweet face?" she answers rather directly: "The lord of the castle is a knight, sir: Signor Puntarvolo" (2.1.216–218). The maid does not withhold the name of the man in front of her. But Puntarvolo's response becomes the occasion for a *periphrasis*, like the "sweet face" with which he addressed the maid, when he refuses to take on that name as his own: "Puntarvolo?" he echoes, "Oh" (2.1.219). By refusing to recognize his own name, Puntarvolo withholds his name from himself.

In what ensues, *periphrasis* permits Puntarvolo the bizarre opportunity of hearing about himself as if he is not himself but with the ears of someone who is just like him. He solicits from the maid an account of his attributes, what Carlo calls "an inventory of his own parts" (2.1.242). Puntarvolo asks, for example, "What years is the knight, fair damsel?" and he hears in response, "Faith, much about your years, sir" (2.1.227–229); Puntarvolo asks, "What complexion or what stature bears he?" and he hears, "Of your stature, and very near upon your complexion" (2.1.230–232). This exchange goes on for some time. By withholding his name from himself, Puntarvolo is able to hear at length about how remarkably like he is to himself. Puntarvolo is able to speak about himself in the third person—"What stature bears he?"—even as the maid's response—"Of your stature"—insists that he is the very measure of himself. When Puntarvolo expresses the desire to see himself—"Would I might see his face!"—Carlo thinks that this desire can be satisfied by a mirror (2.1.258). He suggests in an aside, "She should let down a glass from the window at that word, and request him to look in't" (2.1.259–260). According to Carlo, Puntarvolo simply desires to see himself.

But Carlo offers an incomplete account of what is happening in this episode. On the face of it, Puntarvolo's fantasy is to commit adultery with his own wife, and *periphrasis* is a device of defamiliarization. By showing up at his house as a stranger, Puntarvolo's role playing is a single elaborate instance of his attempt to recreate the world within his estate according to the conventions of romance. This is why Carlo likens him to Saint George: "When he is mounted, he looks like the sign of the George, that's all I know—save that instead of a dragon, he will brandish against a tree, and break his sword as confidently upon the knotty bark as the other did upon the scales of the beast" (2.1.145–149). But the operations of *periphrasis* suggest that Puntarvolo desires something else. He wants to hear himself spoken of as the very measure to which he can also hear himself held. He wants to be both the thing evaluated and the measure of evaluation. By withholding his name from himself, Puntarvolo remakes the world within his estate according to the geometry of what he calls "the perfection of compliment" (2.1.207).[26] Puntarvolo withholds his name from himself so that he can be told: You are just as yourself. Or, You are your own *simile*! The desire expressed by "Would I might see his face!" cannot be satisfied by a mirror because Puntarvolo wants to see his own face on somebody else's body so that he can compare it to himself. *Periphrasis* is the closest Puntarvolo can get to fulfilling this specific configuration of desires.

Carlo is an impatient audience to this episode. He wants to interrupt: "Pox on't! I am impatient of such foppery" (2.1.343). But Fastidius wants to hear more: "O, let's hear the rest" (2.1.344). Eventually, when Puntarvolo's wife descends, she sees the hidden audience, and the jig is up, but the competing desires of Carlo and Fastidius are significant. Fastidius wants to know the extent of the conceit, to find its borders, "the rest." In the Chorus, Mitis cannot believe its extensions: he asks, "Is't possible there should be any such humorist?" (2.1.320). In response, Cordatus insists that the event provides evidence of itself: "Very easily possible, sir. You see there it is" (2.1.321). Fiction provides evidence of its own reality. Fastidius's desire to "hear the rest" suggests what this exchange in the Chorus makes explicit. Mitis's question implies that it is impossible that any man can create such a conspicuously artificial construction and take it this far, inhabit it for this long. Carlo calls this impossibility "foppery."[27] Fastidius, by contrast, wants to see the new boundary it will draw.

Transform, Adulterate, Confound

Periphrasis permits Puntarvolo the impossible experience of looking at himself as if he were someone other than who he is. As with characters like Fastidius, Sogliardo, Mistress Fallace, and Mistress Salviolina, an enclosed environment like the estate doubles as a space within the world of the play in which a character rearranges the artifice of his environment in order to gratify his or her "peculiar quality." Carlo's *similes*, by contrast, do not build an artificial world from within the world of the play (distinct and fantastical) but instead transform the world around him by activating each of their targets in their capacity to look like the things they are said to be like. *Every Man Out* and its characters discuss Carlo's *similes* more than any other figure of speech in the play. I want to highlight here three activities that they attribute to them: Carlo's *similes* transform, adulterate, and confound. By these accounts, figure is primarily significant for the unexpected axes of relation that it draws. Figure pulls the field of possibility out from under our feet.

The "List of Characters" at the start of the play describes Carlo as "a public, scurrilous, and profane jester that, more swift than Circe, with absurd similes will transform any person into a deformity" (23–25). This description suggests that Carlo's *similes* initiate a metamorphosis that they do not complete (as if someone arrested Actaeon just after his horns sprouted but before his skin turned to hide). *Simile* can "transform any person" into a "deformity" because it produces an indiscreet mixture of forms that do not settle into a whole: this is the multiplicity of forms characteristic of disformity. Cordatus calls this procedure of mixing "adulterate": "No honourable or reverend personage whatsoever can come within the reach of his eye but is turned into all manner of variety by his adulterate similes" (*In.* 355–357). The thing into which Carlo's *simile* transforms a person is "variety" itself. Carlo's *similes* are "adulterate" because they have the power to mix the substances that they treat, and the logic of this intermixture is that of an impurity ("debased or made impure by intermixture or admixture").[28] The "variety" into which Carlo's "adulterate *similes*" transform a man is thus something like a chimera.

Simile's ability to mix—to "transform" and "adulterate"—lies with the word that introduces the figure: "like." "Like" renders *simile* simultaneously recognizable and usable: "Like" renders *simile* a *formula* for composition. In one episode, Fastidius presents Carlo with his servant and asks, "How lik'st thou my boy, Carlo?" (2.1.14). Fastidius means "how do you like him?" or "how do you desire him?" (and also "this object of desire is mine and not yours"). Carlo, however, hears Fastidius differently and offers a handful of *similes*: "O well, well," he begins, warming himself up and buying himself just a little time, "He looks like a colonel of the pygmies' horse, or one of these motions in a great antique clock" (2.1.15–16). When Fastidius responds with the exclamation, "How he confounds with his similes!" he means that Carlo confuses but also that he mingles elements together (see the Latin *confundo*, "to pour, mingle, or mix together") (2.1.19–20).[29] Carlo's *similes* violate the integrity of the boy by mixing him together with the things that Carlo says he is "like." When Carlo retorts, "better with similes than with smiles," he distinguishes his *poesie* from the flattery that Fastidius initially requested (2.1.21). To confound with smiles is to complement in parasitic service to an auditor. To confound with *similes* is to redistribute and recombine elements; it is to make something that is new only insofar as it is an aggregate or an assemblage of preexisting forms.[30] In the subsequent conversation about his horse, Fastidius will try to imitate Carlo's *poesie*, but he fails, breaking off mid-*simile*: "A fine little fiery slave, he runs like a—O! excellent, excellent—with the very sound of the spur" (2.1.44–46). Unable to complete his *simile*, Fastidius points to it by appraising it.

In Carlo's hands, *simile* exerts an organizing force on the world around him and remakes the elements of that world according to "like." Carlo, for another example, describes Macilente as "that salt villain, plotting some mischievous device, and lies a-soaking in their frothy humors like a dry crust, till he has drunk 'em all up" (5.3.25–28). Macilente's primary function within the play is to rid each character of his or her humor, but this *simile* suggests that what appears to be a disappearing act is actually just some tricky reshuffling. Macilente cannot make a humor disappear from the world; he can only move it around. Macilente rids someone else of a "peculiar quality" only by taking it into himself (his cure is really a consolidation). Carlo's *simile* renders this process visible, but it also articulates a relation between Macilente and the other characters in the play. Critics have long noted the isolation of characters in *Every Man Out* and the model of the social world attendant on this isolation: "Society," Barish writes, "is conceived as a collection of disconnected atoms, in which each character speaks a private language of his own, pursues ends of his own, collides from time to time with other characters, and then rebounds into isolation."[31] Carlo's *simile*, however, articulates a relation that organizes this social world: Macilente soaks himself in and absorbs qualities from the men with whom he lives. He does not become more like those men, because his act of absorption drains them of those qualities.

Barish understands Carlo's speeches as unique for stimulating what he called "live language" and "live thinking"; reading Carlo's *similes* for their accumulative syntax rather than as a figure of *elocutio*, Barish concludes, "at such moments, Jonson reproduces the accent of living speech so convincingly that he seems to have abandoned rhetorical artifice."[32] Barish and I both call the work of Carlo's *similes* "thinking," but for Barish, Carlo's prose only becomes thinking because the artifice of his *similes* is invisible. The characters of *Every Man Out*, however, see Carlo's *similes* and see them for what they are. They point to the artifice that he wields, and they call it out by name. For these characters, Carlo's prose is most alive precisely where it is figured. "Come," Macilente jokes, upon hearing Carlo unleash his *similes* on Puntarvolo, "you'll never leave your stabbing similes. I shall ha' you aiming at me with 'em by and by" (4.3.227–228); Fastidius tries to imitate *Carlo's similes*; Puntarvolo tries to collaborate with Carlo in the production of a *simile*.[33] The conspicuous artifice of Carlo's *poesie* is an invitation to participate.

Here is another way of thinking about this: in *Every Man Out*, Jonson plucks Braggadochio out of Spenser's *Faerie Queene* and pulls him apart. In one hand, Jonson holds up the pseudo-knight who desires to create an imaginary world built around "such, as he him thought, or faine would bee."[34] Jonson calls this character Puntarvolo: a "vainglorious knight" who uses *periphrasis* to construct a world in the image of his own pleasure ("List of Characters," 13). In the other hand, Jonson takes hold of *simile* and makes the virtuosic capacity to wield this *formula* of composition the "peculiar quality" that propels Carlo Buffone and that must be undone by the play's close. Carlo's practice of *poesie*, however, exceeds the satiric frame of the humor, and Carlo threatens to take over Asper's role as poet-maker. In the person of Macilente, Asper watches this all unfold.

Ultimately, Macilente silences Carlo by sealing his lips shut with candle wax. That Macilente can do so only by the proxy of Puntarvolo speaks to the strange mixture of loathing and admiration with which Macilente relates to Carlo and his *similes*. Is that forecast, "I shall ha' you aiming at me with 'em by and by," an expression of fear or desire (4.3.228)? Just after Puntarvolo has found his very expensive dog dead, he goes to dinner with Carlo. Egged on by Macilente, who periodically shouts encouragements like, "Upon 'em Carlo! Charge, charge!" Carlo likens Puntarvolo's grieving face to a series of objects: "'S'blood, he looks like an image carved out of box, full of knots. His face is for all the world like a Dutch purse with the mouth downward; his beard's the tassels" (5.3.211–214). Carlo does not seem to be getting the response he requires—"Do you hear, Sir Puntar?"—and so, in spite of Puntarvolo's increasingly menacing warnings, Carlo develops a program for canine revitalization (5.3.216). Carlo goes from likening Puntarvolo's grieving face to a Dutch purse to an account of what would be similar enough to the dog Puntarvolo has lost:

> CARLO: I would ha' you do this now: flay me your dog presently—but in any case, keep the head—and stuff his skin well with straw, as you see these dead monsters at Bartolomew Fair—
>
> PUNTARVOLO: I shall be sudden, I tell you.

CARLO: —or, if you like not that, sir, get me somewhat a less dog and clap it into the skin. Here's a slave about the town, here, a Jew, one Yohan, or a fellow that makes periwig, will glue it on artificially; it shall ne'er be discerned. Besides, 'twill be so much warmer for the hound to travel in, you know.
MACILENTE: Sir Puntarvolo, 'sdeath, can you be so patient?
CARLO: Or thus, sir: you may have (as you come through Germany) a familiar, for little or nothing, shall turn itself into the shape of your dog, or anything—what you will—for certain hours. [*Puntarvolo threatens.*] God's my life, knight, what do you mean? You'll offer no violence, will you? [*Puntarvolo draws his rapier and beats Carlo with the hilt.*] Hold, hold! (5.3.220–238).

Carlo's guiding question is: What can we make that would look like Puntarvolo's dog? His series of answers to that question is also an escalating meditation on how to do things with form. First, flay the form: disarticulate that form from its previous incarnation. Second, stuff the form with straw: inflate the form so that it occupies the same space that it previously occupied. Combined, Carlo's first two directives suggest that form becomes reproducible only at the moment at which it has been made empty. Third, replace the straw with another instance of the very thing that form used to be. This will allow the form to retain the range of capacities that characterized its previous incarnation while also transforming it into an ornament akin to the highly stylized "periwig." At this stage, craft is foregrounded in the artisan, "a slave about the town, a Jew" who "will glue it on artificially." If dogs-within-dogs begins to sound redundant (why not just find a new dog that looks like the old dog?), Carlo offers the benefit of an unintended consequence: the new dog will be kept warm by the coat of the old. I take warmth, here, to be significant as a beneficial byproduct. In the fourth and final step of Carlo's program, you abandon the outward form of the flayed dog in favor of an entity, "a familiar," that can assume the shape of the dead dog as one among many.

Puntarvolo will proceed to melt candle wax onto Carlo's lips, and, once those lips are sealed, they do not speak again. In the person of Macilente and through the proxy of Puntarvolo, Asper must close Carlo's lips lest he take over the role of poet-maker. Curiously, Asper does to Carlo exactly what Carlo proposed in the Induction that the audience do to itself: "If any here be thirsty for it, their best way that I know is to sit still, seal up their lips, and drink so much of the play in at their ears" (*In.* 345–347). As an alternative poet-maker who threatens to rearrange the world of the

Coda 177

play with his *similes*, Carlo's final action is his own transformation: Carlo becomes an audience member who opens only his ears. He is now the guarantee of the play's *decorum* because his ears provide a place for Asper to hang his treasure. But before they can seal his lips, Carlo's *poesie* offers us a vision of how the play finally imagines optimally operating within "the law of the conservation of forms": discover the principle, the impulse, the thing by virtue of which you can move among any and all forms. While it might seem as if the "familiar" is a mystification of the artisan's craft, Carlo's attention to payment, "for little or nothing," reminds us that this ability to assume the shape of the dead dog as one among many is yet another form of labor. Carlo's time limit on the spirit's shape—"for certain hours"—is a restriction: this new dog will not last forever. But this restriction is also a gift: the temporality of form is precisely what admits for flux across the field of possibility. It is why the new form can be anything other than the dead dog. Carlo's theory of *poesie* transforms the condition that says *you can only use these forms* into its virtuosic expression: *You can use all of these forms.*

ACKNOWLEDGMENTS

At the close of a book about the value of conspicuous labor, I am acutely conscious of how this project has benefitted from the labor of others both as individuals and as collectives: advisors, friends, colleagues, mentors, departments, reading groups, participants in and audiences of colloquia and symposia and conferences and workshops and talks, librarians, panelists, speakers, students, and teachers. It is in the spirit of their conversation and its dynamism that I send this book off.

Jackie Miller was the first reader of this project and its biggest fan. Her keen intelligence helped me get it off the ground, and her sharp readings in the intervening years have helped me push my ideas as far as I am able. The community of Medieval and Renaissance faculty at Rutgers University put together a vibrant environment for dreaming up the early contours of this project, and I am especially grateful to Emily Bartels, Ann Baynes Coiro, Thomas Fulton, Stacey Klein, Ron Levao, Larry Scanlon, and Henry Turner. Mary Crane offered an incisive intervention into early formulations, for which I am grateful. Jeff Dolven has been the most generous of interlocutors, always reflecting my ideas back to me with a clarity and ease of thinking that are uniquely his own. At a crucial stage of revisions, Roland Greene offered insightful comments on the manuscript and its organization, for which I am thankful. Chris Warley is one of my favorite readers of poetry, and I am lucky to have had his eyes on the book: his insistence throughout that I was writing about art helped train my focus. Friends and colleagues have read parts, including Michael Clody, Darryl Ellison, Joshua Gang, Carrie Hyde, Sarah Kennedy, Brian Pietras, Debapriaya Sarkar, Scott Trudell, Michael Ursell, and Jacque Wernimont. Three friends deserve special thanks: the wonderful Katherine Schaap Williams helped me see this book through to its very last reading by shedding her bright light in its mustiest of corners; the amazing J. K. Barret always kept me pointed in the right direction with her gentle but firm reminders that this is a book about poetry for people who care about poetry; and the spectacular Alison Annunziata provided me with her keen perspective on the organization and methodology of this book while also helping me think through more than one tortured expression. My *epithets* are not enough, too low a title (as Wroth's Antissia might say).

At Pomona College, I have benefitted from the generous readings of colleagues including Kevin Dettmar, Jordan Kirk, Kyla Tompkins, and my late, dear friend Hillary Gravendyk. My conversations with Aaron Kunin have been the single most important influence on this book during my years at Pomona; they have also been the source of my single greatest professional pleasure. Here's to you and to many more conversations and many more books. A year's research leave from Pomona allowed me to finish the project, as did short-term fellowships from the Folger Shakespeare Library and the UCLA Clark Memorial Library. I am grateful to the staff of the Folger, the Clark, the Newberry Library, and the Huntington Library for making my time in their reading rooms so productive. I have shared work from this book with the English Department at the University of Texas–Austin, the Early Modern Reading Group at UCLA, and the Medieval & Renaissance Colloquium at Rutgers University: I am grateful for those lively discussions. I have presented the ideas of this book at the conventions of the Renaissance Society of America, the Modern Language Association, the Sixteenth-Century Society, Spenser at Kalamazoo, the Group for Early Modern Cultural Studies, and the Shakespeare Association of America: I am grateful to the questions of all of those audiences and, especially, to the generous and welcoming community of Spenserians who populate them.

Melissa Sanchez, Jenny C. Mann, and an anonymous reader provided me with thoughtful and clarifying reports, for which I am truly thankful. A series of undergraduates have acted as research assistants over the years, many of whom traveled down dead ends on my behalf, and I would like to thank both them and their source of funding, the Summer Undergraduate Research Program at Pomona College: Alana Friedman, Emily Brotman, Aliza Nur Lalji, and Katherine Snell. More recent RAs have been burning the late-night oil with me while tirelessly proofing: Claire Eldridge-Burns, Peter Brown, Andy Reishcling, Shai Goldberg, and John Flanagan. Thanks to all of my students for allowing me to test out new ideas in seminar. And thanks to all of those teachers in whose seminars I was a student—from my early years of reading with Ben Benskin to my time at Reed College with Robert Knapp, Nathalia King, and Pete Rock. An earlier version of Chapter 4 was published as "Braggadochio and the Schoolroom Simile," *English Literary Renaissance* 41, no. 3 (Autumn 2011): 429–461.

I save my most heartfelt thanks for my family, whose peculiar combination of complete confidence, and utter lack of interest, in my book has been key to my happiness. I think the world of my parents, Terry and Steve, who lead by example. (They also looked the other way when I faked sick to stay home from school and read.) My brothers, Lenny and Eli, remain my favorite friends. Felix has been trying to climb inside of books since before he could walk—reading and playing with him in the final stages of this project has been so much fun. (I promise to look the other way when you fake sick.) Instead of naming my love and partner in all things, I offer a *periphrasis*. This book is dedicated to him.

NOTES

INTRODUCTION. THE SPECTACLE OF CARE: FROM FIGURE TO FORM

1. Spenser, "Muiopotmos," lines 437–440.
2. Spenser, "Muiopotmos," lines 90–91.
3. See Dundas.
4. Spenser, "Muiopotmos," line 94. For a catalog of figures of speech in *Muiopotmos*, see Kearns. His essay is characteristic of the midcentury work that Heinrich F. Plett has described as the "encyclopedic" approach to rhetoric, including Sister Miriam Joseph, *Shakespeare's Use of the Arts of Language*; and Herbert David Rix, *Rhetoric in Spenser's Poetry* (Plett, *Rhetoric and Renaissance Culture*, 416).
5. Clarion, after all, can even take his wings on and off. He is a fly parading as a butterfly. Or, all butterflies are ultimately reducible to the fly because their wings are ornamental. For handheld fans, see: "Full manie a Ladie faire, in Court full oft / Beholding them, him secretly envide, / And wisht that two such fannes, so silken soft, / And golden faire, her Love would her provide; / Or that when them the gorgeous Flie had doft, / Some one that would with grace be gratifide, / From him would steale them privily away, / And bring to her so precious a pray" (*Muiopotmos*, lines 105–112).
6. "Conspicuous" is a key term for this book, and my use is informed by Harry Berger Jr.'s sense that something (in his study, "irrelevance," frequently aligned with "ornament" as opposed to "argument") can be "so very conspicuous that it ought to make us suspect the poet is more than merely clumsy or naïve" (*The Allegorical Temper*, 122). See also Isabel MacCaffrey's modification, where she writes of *allegory* that "its significant feature is its conspicuousness—the force with which it asks us to notice peculiarities of modes of being within the poem" (*Spenser's Allegory*, 90).
7. On early modern *poiēsis* and a maker's knowledge, see Parker, "Rude Mechanicals," 43–82, esp. 49–53; Turner, *The English Renaissance Stage*; Kalas. On the productive materiality of language, see Anderson, *Words That Matter*; and Burckhardt, *Shakespearean Meanings*, 22–46.
8. Jonson, *Discoveries*, 120–121. See Scaliger's different articulation of this distinction: "For *poema* is the very work itself, the material, I might say,

which is used in the making. *Poesis*, on the other hand, is the plan and form of the poem" (*Select Translations from Scaliger's Poetics*, 18). [*Nàmque Poema est opus ipsum: materia, inquam, quae fit. Poesis autem, ratio ac forma Poematis*] (Scaliger, *Poetices Libri Septem* [1561], 5).

9. Sidney, *The Defence of Poesy*, in *The Major Works*, 224. My emphasis on "how" is also cued by Sidney, who suggests that a poet's capacity to "bestow a Cyrus upon the world" turns on the reader's pursuit of two questions: "why and how that maker made him" (*Defence*, 217).

10. On humanist pedagogy, see Halpern, esp. 19–100; Crane; Bushnell; Mack, *Elizabethan Rhetoric*; Dolven, *Scenes of Instruction*; and Enterline, *Shakespeare's Schoolroom*. On the canon of *elocutio*, see Vickers, *In Defence of Rhetoric*, esp. 294–339; *Renaissance Figures of Speech*; Mann; and Nicholson, *Uncommon Tongues*, esp. 59–99.

11. Sherry, *A Treatise of Schemes and Tropes* (1550), A_6v. As Rosemond Tuve describes it, "Indecorous obscurity is the kind which prefers rich confusion to illuminating a meaning, prefers intricacy (whether of syntax or of ornament) to clear formal relations" (228–229).

12. Grafton and Jardine, *From Humanism to the Humanities*. See also I. A. Richards's review of Joseph's *Shakespeare's Use of the Arts of Language*, where, writing of her "concern with establishing—through laborious and systematic collation—a close parallelism or equivalence between logical and rhetorical teaching and the work of the figurists of Shakespeare's time," he concludes that "Rhetoric and Dialectic, quarreling with one another, jointly forgot their common aim. And now it is not easy to see in these by-products of scholastic drudgery the issue of an original concern with the salvation of man" (18, 30).

13. Aristotle advises that "a writer must disguise his art and give the impression of speaking naturally and not artificially": "Naturalness is persuasive, artificiality is the contrary; for our hearers are prejudiced and think we have some design against them, as if we were mixing their wines for them" (*Rhetoric*, trans. Roberts, 1404^b15-25).

14. See Hutson, *The Invention of Suspicion*, esp. 104–145.

15. Sidney, *Defence*, 235. On Sidney's "ground-plot," see Anderson and Linton, 3, 8; Turner, *English Renaissance Stage*, 111–113 and *passim*; Hutson, *Invention of Suspicion*, 94–95 and "Fortunate Travelers," where she explains, "'Plot' or 'ground plot' then seems to be able to refer both to the conceptual organization of a scheme and to its effective communication or probability in discourse" (88). Gavin Alexander has suggested that Sidney "is using the lexicon of rhetoric and poetics to describe not composition but interpretation and *praxis*. He means . . . 'make use of the story in building in your own mind the foundations of some useful idea or course of action'" (in *Sidney's 'The Defence of Poesy' and Selected Renaissance Literary Criticism*, 342n169). I would

modify this to suggest that Sidney's use of this lexicon is significant precisely because it suggests that "composition" and "interpretation" are inextricable. As Turner writes, "by 'imitating' the poetic model . . . the reader intuitively imitates also the very deliberative process that was constitutive of that model in the first place and that continues to reside within it" (*English Renaissance Stage*, 111). See also George Gascoigne's related "platforme of . . . inuention" in "Certayne Notes of Instruction" (1575), 1:51.

16. The approach offered here is not intended to compete with but to augment, through a distinct archive and methodology, accounts of world making that take the history of colonialism or the history of science as the "ground-plot" for their analysis (as with Spiller, esp. 24–58, and Campbell). See also Ayesha Ramachandran's study of "the processes by which the world is remade in the early modern period through a combination of rhetoric, aesthetics, *poiēsis*, and the speculative imagination" (*Worldmakers*, 10). I share Ramachandran's sense of the conceptual value of "world" because it "offers an alternative order and alternate means of identification that both resists and transcends the hegemonic energies of empire—even though it threatens to be co-opted into displays of imperial ambition" (*Worldmakers*, 17).

17. Sidney, *Defence*, 218. On poetry as the language of contingency, see Heller-Roazen, esp. 11–28. He writes that in poetry "figures of speech are displaced onto a terrain in which they no longer function in the service of the consolidation of meaning. . . . No longer speaking of what exists, speech now concerns itself solely with what might, or might not, take place, dedicated entirely to what can and cannot be. In this sense, poetry may be defined precisely as the language of contingency: that form in which language, speaking of what is merely possible, shows itself to be something other than what it has been thought to be at least since its canonical, Aristotelian determination in terms of reference and signification, predication and assertion" (26). On the relation of the contingent and the probable in the art of rhetoric, see Gaonkar, 5–21.

18. I borrow the term "capture" from Gordon Teskey's theory of *allegory*, where "capture" is "an act" that "turn[s]" personification "inside out." He continues: "What the act of capture exhibits is the truth over which allegory is always drawing its veil: the fundamental disorder out of which the illusion of order is raised" (*Allegory and Violence*, 19). See also Dolven's elaboration of "stanzaic capture": "the fiction that the stanza is imposed upon some antecedent matter that once had a shape of its own" ("The Method of Spenser's Stanza," 23).

19. For overviews of the art of rhetoric in the humanist schoolroom, see Wroth; Vickers, *Classical Rhetoric in English Poetry*, 36–54; and Mack, *Elizabethan Rhetoric*, 11–48.

20. Brinsley, O$_4$v. See Dolven, *Scenes of Instruction*, 15–64.

21. I take my key term here, "*formula*," from Susenbrotus, *Epitome Troporum Ac Schematum*, trans. Brennan, e.g., "formulas for writing and speaking" (2) [*scribendi dicendique formulas*] (A$_2$r). Ascham's exercise in double translation understands proximity to the exemplary text as the standard of success: "lastly, the measure and compass of every sentence, must needs by little and little draw unto it the like shape of eloquence as the author doth use which is read" (*The Schoolmaster* [1570], 87).

22. On the Ramist reforms, see Ong; Wilbur Samuel Howell; Jardine; Reiss, *Knowledge, Discovery, and Imagination*; Reiss, "From Trivium to Quadrivium"; and Dolven, *Scenes of Instruction*, esp. 178–180.

23. Fenner, D$_1$v.

24. Keilin, 26–28. See, for example, Keilin's reading of the nightingale's "warbling": "warbling is indissociable from the liberties that it takes with language. It is, if you will, a form of a poetic license that violates the very limits that it posits. And in this sense it serves to think contradictions like silent singing and bestial eloquence" (123). See also Mann, 2–3; Nicholson, *Uncommon Tongues*, 11.

25. See Blank, *Broken English*; Ferguson, *Dido's Daughters*; Mazzio, *Inarticulate Renaissance*; Mann; and Nicholson, *Uncommon Tongues*.

26. Nicholson, *Uncommon Tongues*, 70.

27. Mann argues that the rhetorical canon of *inventio* "moved *inside* the catalog of figures of speech," with the result that the English manual's "explication of the figures is animated by a sense of place that provides a covert content, the subject matter (*res*) animating what is in effect an explosion of words (*verba*)." But whereas *Indecorous Thinking* examines the places of *inventio* and figures of *elocutio* as a method of thinking, Mann argues that "the English 'country' provides the topoi or loci of vernacular eloquence—or, put another way, the commonplace material of vernacular rhetoric is 'England'" (19). See esp. 29–54. In its focus on epistemology, this book is deeply indebted to work in early modern rhetoric and language by Anderson, including *Words That Matter* and *Translating Investments*, as well as Parker, especially *Literary Fat Ladies*.

28. Mazzio, *Inarticulate Renaissance*, 56. As with *Inarticulate Renaissance*, the line between "fault" and "figure" is important to this book because "the apparently ineffectual utterance could direct attention to the fault lines of articulate speech so that new constellations of meaning, and communities of interaction, might emerge into view" (55).

29. On the ethics of thinking entailed by the genre of the Defense in Renaissance and modern criticism (where the value of what is defended is not taken for granted), see Ferguson, *Trials of Desire*, esp. 1–17. See also Chris-

Notes to pages 6–7

topher Warley's sense of the value of "hesitation": "to hesitate is to insist that criticism happens in history and that it has no clear beginning and no clear end. The hesitation of literary criticism embraces a certain slow-motion description of life that imagines, sometimes, that things might be different than they are. Every now and then, it might even make things change" (27–28).

30. For an overview of early modern discussions of *decorum*, see Tuve, 192–247; McAlindon, 6–16; Attridge, 17–45; and especially Rebhorn's useful "Outlandish Fears," 3–24. See also related discussions of "discretion": Hillman, 73–90; J. Miller, 452–473. On this set of terms, see Puttenham, *Art of English Poesy* (1589), 348; McAlindon, 6–7; Attridge, 29–30.

31. MacKay, 312.

32. Leff, 62. Leff describes *decorum* as "the rhetorical counterpart of poetic *muthos*": in Aristotle's *Poetics*, *muthos* or plot is that "element of the poetic process that simultaneously attunes the internal constituents of poetic discourse and directs them toward the final goal of mimesis" (59). Thus, Leff argues that where *muthos* guarantees poetry's way of being by managing a poem's mimetic project, *decorum* similarly regulates the rhetorical artifact's relation to the world as it manifests in the particularity of the given "occasion."

33. Leff, 62, 58.

34. Ramus, *Arguments in Rhetoric against Quintilian*, trans. Newlands, 158. [*Quare quod tam late pateat, ridiculum sane est rhetoricae veluti proprium subiicere*] (227).

35. Ramus, *Arguments in Rhetoric*, 158. [*Nec tamen separatum de decoro et distinctum ullum praeceptum erit, quia decorum ipsum conueniens ea perfectio est, quam artes suis praeceptis, quam ipsa humanitatis ratio et sapientia demonstrat*] (227).

36. Ramus, *Arguments in Rhetoric*, 158. [*quid vere deceat, quid non deceat.... Decorum in sermonis puritate et elegentia ex grammatica, in elocutione et actione ex rhetorica, in numerorum supputatione et magnitudinum diuisione in concentibus et sonis, in astrorum motibus ex arithmetica, geometria, musica, astrologia: in stirpibus et plantis atque animalibus ex physica*] (227).

37. On the idea of disarticulation, I am indebted to Warley's idea that it is precisely in its scrupulous attention to form that literary criticism distinguishes itself from what Jameson called the utopian "program." Warley writes: "This possibility of the impossible comes about ... through strict adherence to form, to a constant respect for and return to the lucidity, organization, and structure of dreams. To see the border you must always see beyond the border; but to see beyond the border you always have to look at the border" (7).

38. Demetrius, trans. Innes, 114–115. Drawing on design theory, Levine suggests that we read form for its "affordances," where "*affordance* is

a term used to describe the potential uses or actions latent in materials and designs" (6–7).

39. It is worth remembering here what Erich Auerbach described as Lucretius's "most brilliant, though not the most historically important" (because apparently unique) use of *"figurae"* to describe "atoms": "The numerous atoms are in constant motion; they move about in the void, combine and repel one another: a dance of figures" (17–18).

40. See "figure" in the *Oxford English Dictionary*.

41. Auerbach, esp. 11–28. See also Anderson and Linton, 2–6.

42. Auerbach, 16. On *figura* and Ovidian metamorphosis, see Enterline, *Rhetoric of the Body from Ovid to Shakespeare*, esp. 1–90.

43. See Wolfson, "Reading for Form." See also the special issue of *Modern Language Quarterly* coedited by Wolfson and Brown (and the edited collection based on this issue, *Reading for Form*); Dubrow, "Guess Who's Coming to Dinner? Reinterpreting Formalism in the Country House Poem," 60. See also Wolfson, *Formal Charges*, especially her illuminating chapter "Formal Intelligence: Formalism, Romanticism, and Formalist Criticism" (1–30). For one account of "new formalism," see Marjorie Levinson's "What Is New Formalism": her distinction between "activist formalism" and "normative formalism" has been important for situating work on form in relation to the New Historicism (on the one hand) and the New Aestheticism (on the other) (558–569). In early modern studies, Dubrow has been at the center of new formalist conversations: her contribution to the *MLQ* special issue, "Guess Who's Coming to Dinner?" as well as "'You may be wondering why I called you all here today': Patterns of Gathering in the Early Modern Lyric" are exemplary of her practice, but see also *Echoes of Desire*, *Shakespeare and Domestic Loss*, *The Challenges of Orpheus*, and, most recently, *Deixis in the Early Modern English Lyric*. Warley's account of form in *Reading Class* is particularly compelling, esp. 73–95. In addition to the essays collected in *The Work of Form* (2014), see the contributions to *Shakespeare and Historical Formalism*, ed. Stephen Cohen, and *Renaissance Literature and Its Formal Engagements*, ed. Mark David Rasmussen.

44. For Parker's work, see especially *Literary Fat Ladies* and "Preposterous Events." For Alexander, see *Writing after Sidney*, "Sidney's Interruptions," and "Prosopopoeia."

45. By contrast, Anderson and Linton (1–18) demonstrate the entangled histories of figure and form in classical and early modern conceptions of the terms. Teskey's *Allegory and Violence* is also an important exception to this characterization as his theory of *allegory* is deeply rooted in Aristotelian conceptions of the relation of form to matter. Explorations of the concept of "form" in literary studies include La Drière; a special issue of *New Literary History* entitled "Form and Its Alternatives," ed. Ralph Cohen, including

Chapman; Bruster; Turner, "Lessons from Literature"; Leighton, who offers a helpful account of the word, though she does not think much about "form" before the eighteenth century (1–29); Levine.

46. They write: "exploring the prehistory of form can help us gain fresh perspective on our own perceptions of formalism, providing an opportunity to reassess the challenges and contradictions, as well as the promise and potential of literary scholarship conducted in its name" (7). Like Burton and Scott-Baumann, this book is interested in how the range of meanings of "form" in the period include how "form is associated with the literary artefact as well as the process of its creation and reception" (8).

47. See Vickers, *In Defence*, 83–213.

48. See Rebhorn, *The Emperor of Men's Minds*.

49. See Vickers, *In Defence*, 294–339; Alexander, "Prosopopoeia," 97–112; Enterline, *Shakespeare's Schoolroom*, esp. 120–152. See also Berger's critique of what he calls the "psychological function" of figures in "Narrative as Rhetoric in *The Faerie Queene*," 175.

50. In the *Art of English Poesy*, Puttenham warns against a vice that he lists among "deformities in speech and writing." Puttenham translates *periergia* (Gk. *peri*, "exceedingly" and *ergon*, "work") as the "Over-Labor" and suggests that its "Surplusage lieth not so much in superfluity of your words as your travail." An excess of words is significant as an index to an excess of labor: "Ye over-labor yourself," Puttenham writes, "in your business" (344). See also Sherry (1550), C_1r–C_2v.

51. See Timothy Morton's attempt to "revise formal causation while unplugging it from teleology": "Poems," he writes, "are records of causal-aesthetic decisions," and a poem's "shape," as with blown glass, "is the trace of what happened to it" (219–220). My account of form departs from those influenced by Bruno Latour because I do not posit a flat ontology: early modern poetics privileged figures of speech precisely for their capacity to assign value.

52. Turner writes, "'form' should be understood as a verb rather than as a noun, as an active relation among significant parts that are apprehended through a transaction between that artifact and its readers, viewers, listeners, or speakers" ("Lessons from Literature," 582).

53. Campion writes: "By Rime is vnderstoode that which ends in the like sound, so that verses in such maner composed yeeld but a continual repetition of that Rhetoricall figure which we tearme *similiter desinentia*, and that, being but a *figura verbi*, ought (as Tully and all other Rhetoritians have iudicially obseru'd) sparingly to be vs'd, least it should offend the eare with tedious affectation" (*Observations in the Art of English Poesie* [1602], 2:330).

54. Campion, 2:330. See also Gascoigne, who advises the novice poet: "I would exhorte you also to beware of rime without reason: my meaning is

hereby that your rime leade you not from your firste Inuention, for many wryters when they haue layed the platforme of their inuention, are yet drawen sometimes (by ryme) to forget it or at least to alter it" (1:51).

55. Daniel, *A Defence of Rhyme* (1603), 216.
56. Jarvis, 931.
57. La Drière, 170.
58. La Drière, 170. See also Susan Stewart's sense that "until such a mark or note is struck, and then the next and the next, the form is replete with any number of choices, and each choice then exercised is dense with its relation to what otherwise could have been" (30).
59. On the power of figures (*hyperbaton*, *parenthesis*, etc.) to shape literary plots, see Mann, esp. 87–117. On the relationship between "the conceptual thought of the English Renaissance and its 'fabulous thinking' . . . [how] classical fables about Orpheus, Philomela, and Circe provided the context and texture of the emergent category of vulgar eloquence," see Keilin, 27.
60. Puttenham, 221.
61. For a brief but illustrative survey of the concerns that motivate distinctions between "figure" and "trope," see Barthes, *Semiotic Challenge*, 85–86. "There is always a stake," Barthes wrote, "in how things are placed: *tell me how you classify and I'll tell you who you are*" (47).
62. Burke's "master tropes" included *metaphor*, *metonymy*, *irony*, and *synecdoche* (*A Grammar of Motives*, 503). As Vickers has shown, from Vico to Burke to Roman Jakobson to Paul de Man, literary theorists consolidated the canon of *elocutio* by reducing it to a small number of tropes understood to encompass (and therefore, explain) the vast array of figures that populated classical and early modern rhetoric textbooks (*In Defence*, 439–469). This reduction tends to reproduce the very distinction between thought and style that these same theorists seek to overturn because its focus on the tropes quietly reproduces the art of rhetoric's uneasy distinction between those forms that alter *res* and the mind and those forms that alter *verba* and the ear. The story of this book is how the very articulation of that line generates a productive crossing, whether in the provisional distinctions drawn by Quintilian and Erasmus or in the polemical oppositions imposed by Peter Ramus and his followers. What distinguishes the methodology of this book is therefore its commitment to the idea that a history of figures of speech is significant to our understanding of what writers of the early modern period thought poetry might think and do, of what poetry of the early modern period might have been capable of thinking and doing, and of what we understand early modern poetry to be capable of thinking and doing today.
63. In *Shakespeare after Theory*, David Kastan distinguishes the work of literary scholars from their counterparts in departments of history by sug-

gesting that while historians are interested in what was "*thought*" at a given moment in time, literary scholars are interested in what was "*thinkable*" (50). While his primary concern in this moment is to consider how different evidentiary standards for the "thought" and the "thinkable" tend to treat the literary text as either "exemplary" (on the one hand) or "idiosyncratic" (on the other), Kastan's distinction implies a wider disciplinary acknowledgment of the unique modality of knowledge in literary studies. Dimock has described this modality as the "subjunctive": "if works of fiction are always subjunctive to some extent, dwellers in some counterfactual universe," she writes, "literary *scholarship* can also afford to go some length in that direction" (244). The "thinkable"—that which can be thought or may be thought—is itself authorized by early modern definitions of poetry that embrace the art's defining capacity to speak of "what may be."

64. For this reorientation toward the pleasure of makers, see also Barret.

65. See Ramus, *Peter Ramus's Attack on Cicero* (1548), trans. Newlands, 97; and *Arguments in Rhetoric*, 139, 149, 163.

66. Praising the figure of speech *symploce* (the repetition of the same words at the beginning and end of a succession of clauses), Peacham writes that "this figure may serue to any affection"; he adds, however, a caveat: "Too many members of this figure do much blemish the beautie of it, and bewrayeth the affectation, for this ornament is much deformed if it be stretched with the tenters of foolish fancie, as oft it is, and likewise many others" (*Garden of Eloquence* [1593], H$_2$v). See also his "caution" for *epizeuxis* (H$_4$v).

67. Peacham, *Garden* (1593), H$_4$v.

68. As Mann argues in her reading of the figure of *parenthesis* and its striking typography, "The marks thus function epistemologically (as cues for the reader) and also ontologically (altering the status of the words they enclose)" (98).

69. As Adamson, Alexander, and Ettenhuber write in their introduction to *Renaissance Figures of Speech*, "one cause of the taxonomic confusion may be a recurrently felt need to discriminate between figurative operations that *represent* thought and those that actually *provoke* it" (8).

70. Puttenham, 281.

71. My understanding of romance is indebted to Parker, *Inescapable Romance*; and Dolven, *Scenes of Instruction*.

72. This book is therefore in sympathy with Barbara Fuchs's sense that we ought to read romance as a "strategy": "Focusing on what romance does and enables within a narrative not only reveals its bones, but shows most clearly how it appears within a variety of genres" (2).

73. Mann suggests that the example of Sidney's eloquence in the *Arcadia* "authorizes the translation of academic rhetorics into the vernacular, and

his contribution to the culture is expressed as the foundation of a universally accessible common field of English eloquence" (47). When Fulke Greville published a version of Sidney's romance in 1590, selections had already been published by Abraham Fraunce in his *Arcadian Rhetorike* (1588), which also incorporates selections of Spenser's verse, including material that would appear in the 1590 *Faerie Queene*; Fraunce's *Lawiers Logike* (1588) illustrates the places and arguments of dialectic with verse from Spenser's *Shepherds Calendar* (1579). John Hoskin's manuscript manual, *Directions for Speech and Style* (c. 1601), written for a young student at law, also exemplifies the tropes and figures by way of Sidney's *Arcadia* (1593); two later manuals, Thomas Blount's *The Academie of Eloquence* (1654) and John Smith's *The Mysterie of Rhetorique Unveil'd* (1656), are strongly indebted to Hoskin's work.

74. Sidney, *The Countess of Pembroke's Arcadia*, ed. Evans, 176.

75. On *aposiopesis* in Sidney's *Arcadia*, see Alexander, *Writing after Sidney*, esp. 1–55; and "Sidney's Interruptions." This passage is discussed by Sherman, *Used Books*, 44; Alexander, *Writing after Sidney*, 54.

76. Mann tells this history (171–218). Vickers argues that figure remains crucial to the theories and practices of the emergent empiricism in spite of well-known disavowals by Francis Bacon, Thomas Spratt, and John Locke (*In Defence*, 201).

77. See Daston, 283. See also Eggert, 7. This book's sense of the role of figure in the construction of possibility, plausibility, and probability contributes to a history of probability that precedes and is not extinguished by the mathematical quantification of probability in the seventeenth century. See Patey; Hutson, *The Invention of Suspicion*.

78. Fahnestock, 24. Fahnestock describes figure as "a condensed or even diagram-like rendering of the relationship among a set of terms, a relationship that constitutes the argument and that could be expressed at greater length" (24). Like Fahnestock, I am interested in that curious, productive intersection between *inventio* and *elocutio*: "there has always been an undertow working against the separation of invention and style," she writes; "It is even possible to discover arguments stylistically . . . by using the figures generatively, allowing the form to find the content" (31).

79. White writes that "the historian performs an essentially *poetic* act, in which he prefigures the historical field and constitutes it as a domain upon which to bring to bear the specific theories he will use to explain 'what was *really* happening' in it" (xxx). See 1–41; esp. 21, 28–30. As Michael S. Roth writes, *Metahistory* was "meant to lift the burden of history qua burden of realism" by considering how "conventions of realism were solidified as 'criteria of plausibility'": "Respectable plausibility was meant to restrict the imagination—especially to foreclose the possibility of radical change or sublime

meaninglessness. White's work, especially in *Metahistory*, frees us to rethink the enormous range of choices available to us as we establish our connection to our past and make our way in the present" (xvii).

80. Erasmus, *Copia*, trans. Knott, 302. [*Hoc igitur tantum malum facile vitabit, cui promptum erit sententiam eandem in plureis formas vertere quam Proteus ipse se transformasse dicitur*] (*De Copia*, ed. Betty I. Knott, 34).

81. Spenser, "Muiopotmos," lines 140–144.

82. See Ramachandran, "Clarion in the Bower of Bliss."

83. Spenser, "Muiopotmos," lines 330–332, 339.

84. Anderson connects these flowers to the figures of *elocutio* when she writes that "the presentation of the 'gay gardins' involves rhetorical flourishes; indeed the gardens *are* in some sense such a flourish" ("'Nat worth a boterflye,'" 100).

85. James, "Flower Power." Like James, I am interested in passages in which "Spenser collects flowers with abandon and in abundance and yet refuses to surrender them to allegorical significance." "Instead," James writes, "he keeps them for himself."

86. On trefoils, or the floral marker in manuscript marginalia, see Sherman, *Used Books*, 27. James reports that Jonson would sometimes add a little mark to the flowers in the margins of his Martial, "perhaps to suggest that a particular rhetorical ornament or flower had an especially sweet smell" ("Ben Jonson's Light Reading," 251–252).

87. Sherry (1550), A_8v. The full passage reads: "For as lyke plesure is not to him whiche gooeth into a goodlye garden garnyshed wyth dyuers kindes of herbes and flowers, and that there doeth no more but beholde them, of whome it maye be sayde that he wente in for nothynge but that he wold come out, and to hym which be syde the corporall eie pleasure, knoeth of eueri one the name & propertye: so verelye much difference is there in readynge good authors, and in sundry sortes of menne that do it: and muche more pleasure, and profit hath he which useth arte and judgement, then the other, whiche wyth greate studye indede turneth them ouer but for a lacke of the knowledge of preceptes wanteth also the fruite and delectacyon that he more amplye myghte obtayne" (Sherry [1550], A_8r–A_8v).

1. INVENTING FIGURES OF SPEECH

1. Sidney, *Defence*, 215–216.

2. Sidney, *Defence*, 216, 218. See Aristotle, *Poetics*, trans. Bywater, 1451^b 1–20. See also William Scott's distinction between "*imitators*" and "*poets*" in *The Model of Poesy* (1599): "They that lay down things as they be, more precisely tying themselves to true narration, may more properly be called *imitators*. . . . The other, that feign, by following their own conceits, how

things may or should be, which make new or perfecter works than corrupted nature bringeth forth, who, with the silkworm, spin their web out of their own bowels, may by a more peculiar privilege challenge the title and honour of *poets* or makers" (12); and Richard Willis, who writes that poetry "imitates in words not only such actual things as exist, but also things which do not exist, as if they did; and represents either how they might be or how they ought to be" (*De Re Poetica* [1573], trans. Fowler, 53). [*Poeisque dicitur, propterea quod non solum vocibus res ipsas imitaretur quae essent, verum etiam quae non essent, quasi essent, & quomodo esse vel possent, vel deberent, repraesentaret*] (52).

3. Sidney, *Defence*, 216.

4. See Spiller, 24–58; Berger, *Second World and Green World*, 3–40; Levao, *Renaissance Minds and Their Fictions*, 134–156.

5. Sidney, *Defence*, 224.

6. On the ideal of Xenophon's Cyrus, see Sidney, *Defence*, 216. See also Spenser's "Letter to Raleigh," in *The Faerie Queene*, 716. On the nationalist and imperialist ambitions of Sidney's theory of poetry, see Spiller, 40–44.

7. Sidney, *Defence*, 216. Berger puts the difference most starkly: "Is the goal an ethical ideal (what *should* be) or a hedonist idyll (what *could* be)?" (Berger, *Second World and Green World*, 7). For the potential mood, see De Grazia; Magnusson. For the language of contingency, see Heller-Roazen, esp. 11–28.

8. Sidney, *Defence*, 216–217.

9. Spiller, 38. See also Berger's definition of "second world" as "the playground, laboratory, theater, or battlefield of the mind, a model or construct the mind creates" (*Second World and Green World*, 11–12).

10. For *heterocosm*, see Berger: "The concept of *heterocosm* entails no assumptions about the quality of experience to be found in such a world, its content is neutral or indeterminate. . . . Modern thought commonly reserves the term universe for organized wholes of this sort and understands them as hypothetical in that they are constructed by thought rather than given in experience. . . . It is rather a frame of reference or coordinate system originally chosen with a view toward exploring a concrete problem or fulfilling a specific desire. . . . In this radical context the term *heterocosm*, which literally means *other world*, will serve primarily to remind us that disjunction or difference is the basic relation between universes" (*Second World and Green World*, 16).

11. On the word "invention" as "a kind of palimpsest, with some of its senses in the foreground and others barely visible but available," see Greene, *Five Words*, 21. On *inventio* and "the creation of a heterocosm," see Levao, 115.

12. In other words, that the poetic field will be partly defined by questions formulated from the places of *inventio* is fixed by the humanist training

to which Sidney alludes; the array of answers with which any particular poem might reply to those questions is vast and varied.

13. Wilson, *Art of Rhetoric* (1560), 49.

14. As Wilson elaborates in a subsequent discussion of *narratio*, "We shall make our sayings appear likely and probable, if we ... frame our invention according as we shall think them most willing to allow it that have the hearing of it" (*Art of Rhetoric*, 140). See Nicholson, *Uncommon Tongues*, esp. 45–71; and "Othello and the Geography of Persuasion," 56–87. On the rhetorical invention of probability, see Hutson, *Invention of Suspicion*, esp. 104–145; and Patey, esp. 3–34, 266–273.

15. See Vickers's account of "the expressive function of rhetorical figures" (*In Defence*, 294–339) as well as Berger's critique of what he calls the "psychological function" of figures ("Narrative as Rhetoric," 175). For a more thorough discussion of *aposiopesis*, see Alexander, "Sidney's Interruptions"; and *Writing after Sidney*, 1–55.

16. Quintilian, *Institutio Oratoria*, trans. Butler, 9.3.102. [*ubi vero atrocitate, invidia, miseratione pugnandum est, quis ferat contrapositis et pariter cadentibus et consimilibus irascentem, flentem, rogantem? cum in his rebus cura uerborum deroget adfectibus fidem et ubicunque ars ostentatur, veritas abesse videatur.*]

17. On affiliates of the Sidney Circle including Abraham Fraunce and William Temple, see Alexander, *Writing after Sidney*, 128–148, esp.134–135. For Gabriel Harvey and the Sidney Circle, see Anthony Grafton and Lisa Jardine, "'Studied for Action,'" esp. 35–40.

18. The influence of these reforms on English pedagogy is less important to my argument than the perspective they afford. I understand Ramism as the distillation and intensification of a much more pervasive set of anxieties about the relation of figure to thought in humanist pedagogy and poetics at large.

19. See Vickers, *In Defence*, 83–214.

20. Sidney, *Defence*, 235.

21. In his reading of Sidney's description of poetry as a "figuring forth," Walker suggests that Sidney almost invokes "a kind of tropological fantasia, or an unsystematic system of poetical invention" (327). Walker, however, backs away from this claim and emphasizes Sidney's more explicit and conservative stance: "But this is not quite so. For 'philosophy,' and the authoritative moral truths identified by philosophy, provide the *materia* that preexists and in effect predetermines poetical invention ... poetry is conceived in such passages not as a medium of genuine invention or of ideological contestation but as a medium whose rhetorical and inventional possibilities are more or less limited to finding ways to ornament or 'figure forth' already received opinion and authoritative dogma for nonphilosophic minds" (327–328). This chapter is in sympathy with Walker's subsequent claim that "what Sidney

really has in view, if unsteadily, is a more thoroughly rhetorical poetics, one that is more consistent with the oft-remarked rhetoricity of his own poetic practices" (328).

22. Fraunce, *Lawiers Logike*, B_4v.

23. As a series of scholars have sought to recover Ramus from the critique of Walter J. Ong's *Ramus, Method, and the Decay of Dialogue*, this claim has become controversial. For example, see Mack, *A History of Renaissance Rhetoric*, 142–145; see also his "Ramus and Ramism: Rhetoric and Dialectic." As I understand it, this debate turns on two points: First, does it matter what a given movement within a historical period calls "rhetoric" and what it calls "dialectic"? That is, are disciplinary distinctions meaningful to a synchronic understanding of the art of rhetoric—of what canons and practices the art did or did not consist at a given moment in time and from the perspective of a given movement? My answer to this question in Chapter 1 is "yes." (For the contrary view, see what Mack calls the "rhetoricized approach to logic" [*A History*, 51] and what Vickers calls the "rhetoricization of logic" [*In Defence*, 267]). Second, what is the relationship between theory and praxis? What, that is, is the difference between what Mack calls a "properly Ramist scheme of teaching" and the ways in which other habits and forms of knowledge production—pedagogical trends and exercises, media for the transmission of knowledge, etc.—made possible and even encouraged the improper or incomplete use or manifestation of that scheme? (Mack, *A History*, 145). This tension between theory and practice, between schematic representation of the art and the habits or modes of analysis and genesis, is the subject of Chapter 2. The following account of Ramism is largely informed by Ong; W. S. Howell; Jardine; Reiss, *Knowledge, Discovery, and Imagination*; Reiss, "From Trivium to Quadrivium"; and Dolven, *Scenes of Instruction*, esp. 178–180.

24. Fenner, D_2v. Vickers writes of Fenner and figures that he "has no awareness of their emotional function" and of Fraunce's *Arcadian Rhetorike* that "there are a few signs of a more intelligent awareness" (*In Defence*, 324, 328). Vickers writes that the Ramists, more generally, were "the least interested in stressing the imaginative potential of rhetoric . . . surprisingly so in view of the fact that they illustrated their textbooks with examples taken from contemporary poetry. One looks in vain for any advance on the generalized concept of rhetoric as being ornament or 'garnishing'" (*In Defence*, 327).

25. Harvey, *Ciceronianus*, trans. Forbes, 7; and *Rhetor* (London, 1577). I will be citing the Latin text and English translation of *Rhetor*, from *Rhetor*, trans. Mark Reynolds (2001), http://comp.uark.edu/~mreynold/engtran.pdf. For Harvey's lectures on rhetoric, see H. S. Wilson.

26. Harvery, *Ciceronianus*, 69. [*Pluris verba, quam res; linguam, quam mentem*] (68). See also W. S. Howell, 251–252.

27. See Ong, 61–63. For a discussion of the *Summulae* and the "corpuscular view of reality and the mind, a kind of epistemological or psychological atomism" that it bestowed upon the reformed dialectic, see Ong, 72, 58–74. See also W. S. Howell, 17; Jardine, 20–24.

28. For Agricola's *De Inventione*, see Crane, 17–25; for its importance to Ramus, see Ong, 92–130; for the prevalence of Agricola at Cambridge, see Jardine, 29–30. For Agricola's influence on Juan Luis Vives and Philip Melanchthon, see Monfasani, esp. 196–201; and Ong, 101–104.

29. Fraunce, *Lawiers Logike*, C_2v. See also Ramus, *Dialectique* (1555), 3–4 (quoted by W. S. Howell, 154–155).

30. Relatively neglected even in classical accounts of rhetoric, *pronuntiatio* drops out almost entirely from reformed accounts of rhetoric (Ong, 281). See Fraunce's discussion in *The Arcadian Rhetorike*, L_2v–M_5r. The fourth canon of *memoria* (or memory) drops out of the Ramist account of dialectic "on grounds that to follow Method was necessarily to set concepts in their natural rational order, requiring no special memory skill" (Reiss, "From Trivium to Quadrivium," 45).

31. Ramus, *Attack on Cicero*, 63. [*haec cogitat & perpendit omnia: illae cogitata pure & ornate pronuntiant*] (63). Harvey praises Agricola for his reforms in *Rhetor*, H_2r–H_3v.

32. While Ramus's definition of the arts resembles both Agricola's and Melanchthon's (his reforms are indebted to the various textbooks written by these men), Ramus worked to divorce figures of speech from the canons of *inventio* and *dispositio* in treatises like *Brutinae Quaestiones* (1548) and *Rhetoricae Distinctiones in Quintilianum* (1549). By contrast, Agricola's *De Inventione Dialectica* admitted figures of repetition and figures of emphasis into the same discussion of arguments as it did the syllogism and the enthymeme (Mack, *A History*, 67). Similarly, Melanchthon created a subdivision of rhetorical figures, "figures of amplification," that he organized according to the dialectical topics of invention from which he derived each figure. In his *Elementorum Rhetoricae Libri Duo*, Melanchthon writes that "the zealous reader will observe that all the figures, especially those that enhance a speech, have their origin in dialectical expressions" (*Elementorum Rhetorices Libri Duo*, trans. La Fontaine, 263); [*Observet autem studiosus lector figuras omnes, praesertim has, quae augent orationem ex locis dialecticis oriri*]. See Mack, *A History*, 118–119, 121, 122, 216–217; Baldwin, 2:20–21. See also Schanze. Where earlier humanists allowed for an overlap between the invention and arrangement of knowledge (on the one hand) and the genesis of style (on the other), Ramism drew a disciplinary border between these activities with the effect of divorcing rhetorical figures from the production of knowledge.

33. According to Ramus, a neat division of the trivium boils down to the following: "The whole of dialectic concerns the mind and reason, whereas rhetoric and grammar concern language and speech" (Ramus, *Arguments in Rhetoric*, 104). [*Dialectica mentis et rationis tota est, rhetorica et grammatica sermonis et orationis*] (184). "The curious drift in Ramus's thought," Ong writes, is "his tendency to be 'objective' not by turning to the outside world but by treating the contents of the mind as a set of objects. Here this tendency joins the pedagogical tradition, for Ramus assumes that the primary units which the mind 'contains' are the subjects in the curriculum" (197–198).

34. On how Ramus "firmly identified the rules of dialectic with the operations of natural reason," see Jardine, 41.

35. In Ramus's *Training in Dialectic* (1543), "natural dialectic" is "aptitude, reason, mind, the image of God, the light rivaling the eternal light" (quoted by Ong, 177; see also 189–190). On the Platonism underwriting the claim that "dialectical method must mirror our apprehension and classification of natural phenomena," see Jardine, 28, 42–44, 47; Reiss, *Knowledge*, 28, 49.

36. As Patey succinctly summarizes: "Invention, the power of finding probable arguments, Ramus derives from the Latin *in rem venire*, a laying open of the arguments which reside in things themselves. These arguments arise to invention in a natural order, an order which is itself an echo of the larger order of nature: the *arguments* which are the stuff of dialectic are simply the *relations* which obtain in nature, made present to the mind. Invention thus becomes a kind of natural reasoning, a kind of memory even, since according to Ramus its following out of the connections which reside in nature is in large part a remembering of the same patterns already encountered in other circumstances" (22).

37. Fraunce explains: "Logike was deseruedly called the Art of Arts, the instrument of instrumentes, the hand of Philosophie, because by the helpe thereof, not onely the groundes of naturall reason are artificially put downe, but all other Arts also are made to be Arts" (*Lawiers Logike*, B$_2$v–r).

38. Ong, 280, 195.

39. Ramus, *Attack on Cicero*, 16. [*breviter artium omnium fines & institutiones separentur: usus tamen coniungatur: sicuti in hominum fundis & agris fieri videmus: ut meus ager in tuum non incurrat nec tuus incidat in meum: rerum tamen nostrarum vendendo, emendo, permutando usus communicetur*] (16). See Ong, 280–281.

40. Trans. Reynolds, *Rhetor*, 48–49. [*cur me proprijs ornamentis, insignibusque, contentam, sororum mearum opibus, atque gazis locupletas? cur me inuitam in alienas possessiones detrudis? cur extra praestitutos fundi mei terminos, atque limites euagari facis? cur mea praedia, quae ego semper amoena potius, & pulchra, & belle aedificata esse volui, quam ampla atque vasta; pro arbitrio tuo dilatas? . . .*

cur mihi meo regno, non magno illo quidem, sed splendido, & florentissimo contentae, mare, terras, aërem, coelum, omnia subijcis? cur quibus ipsa & debeam, & velim morigerari, eas sub meum imperium, dictionemque subiungis?] (*Rhetor*, G$_1$r–G$_1$v).

41. For female corporeality and *copia*, see Parker, *Literary Fat Ladies*, 8–35.

42. As Harvey writes: "But tell me please, suppose you commissioned an Apelles, or a Zeuxis, for a large sum to paint a portrait of your little Tullia and he, from an overabundance of love I am sure, instead of a soft and delicate and slender girl, portrayed a woman—not entirely grotesque, except for her great size, or even otherwise very lovely, with the fairest complexion—but nevertheless a woman who was big and tall and stout and masculine, with a large head, a heroic face, prominent eyes, an elongated neck, broad shoulders, bulging arms, a huge, muscular chest, and an enormous, almost Cyclopean body. Would this painting meet with your approval? . . . But by the gods, to me you have behaved like this painter . . . Marcus Tullius, by making me much larger, and in a way plumper and stouter than I really am, and investing me with all things, as if I were the daughter of some Polyphemus, and wished to vie in size with the giants of Etna" (trans. Reynolds, *Rhetor*, 51–52). [*Sed dic mihi, amabo te, siquem Apellem, aut Zeusim, magno precio conductum, ad Tulliolae tuae simulacrum pingendum, efformandumque adhiberes; & is abundantia quadam amoris scilicet, pro tenera, & delicata, & gracili puella, foeminam, non illam quidem, excepta magnitudine, admodum deformem, aut etiam caeteroqui valde sane formosam, & candidissima cute praeditam, sed tamen grandem, & proceram, & crassam, & virilem, magno capite, vultu heroico, eminentibus oculis, oblongo collo, latis humeris, validis lacertorum toris, ingenti, & musculoso pectore, toto corpore vasto, & prope Cyclopico exhiberet: an eam tu imaginem probares . . . At per Deos, talem te mihi pictorem . . . M. Tulli: multo me grandiorem, & quodammodo pinguiorem, crassioremque, reddens, quam reuera sim, & ita mihi circundans omnia, quasi Polyphemi cuiusdam essem filia, & magnitudine vellem cum Aetnaeis gygantibus concertare*] (*Rhetor*, G$_2$r–G$_{3,r}$). Contrast this with the "Eloquentia" Harvey promises (more familiar from Petrarchan blazons): "her lovely face, her rosy complexion, her enchanting eyes," which students will "fly to kiss and embrace" (trans. Reynolds, *Rhetor*, 6). [*Cuius vbu faciem pulcherrimam, coloremq[ue] roseum, & peruenustos oculos aspexerint (aspicient autem propediem, nisi ego fallor) non dubito, quin ad illius complexum sint, atque osculum, non dico cursuri, ut ille, sed plané aduolaturi*] (*Rhetor*, A$_4$v). See also the extended blazon that concludes his journey to *Eloquentia* (*Rhetor*, P$_2$r–P$_2$v; trans. Reynolds, *Rhetor*, 115).

43. Trans. Reynolds, *Rhetor*, 42. [*alieni corporis adumbrata membra, & ad eloquentiae, tanquam ad Veneris caput affixa sunt*] (*Rhetor*, F$_2$r).

44. Ramus, *Attack on Cicero*, 16. [*Duo vero sunt universa deorum munera hominibus tributa, unde alia fere omnia profecta sunt, ratio & oratio: rationis*

doctrina, Dialectica est: ideoque quicquid rationis ac mentis proprium fuerit, quod sine oratione tractari & exerceri possit, id proprie dialecticae arti attribuito] (16). See also Ramus, *Arguments in Rhetoric*, 86.

45. Ramus, *Attack on Cicero*, 44. [*quanto enim mens praestantior lingua, tanto inventio dispositioque (quae mentis sunt) excellentiores sunt elocutione*] (44). He continues, "Surely, since the mind is more excellent than the body, invention and arrangement are then more noble and excellent than style" (44). [*nempe quanto sit animus corpore praestantior, tanto inventionem & dispositionem elocutione esse nobiliorem & excellentiorem*] (44). On "representations of the disruptive and autonomous tongue," see Mazzio, "Sins of the Tongue," 97.

46. Ramus, *Attack on Cicero*, 80. [*unus est in hominis natura senatus, unum consilium, ratio est: cuius explicationem & doctrinam Dialectica sibi vendicat: duo sunt in vestibulo curiae praecones, ad ea quae senatus decreverit proferenda atque enuntianda, sermonis puritas, quam sibi Grammatica declarandam sumit: orationis ornatus, cuius artem sibi Rhetorica tribuit*] (80).

47. Ramus, *Attack on Cicero*, 29. [*ut Rhetorica, quae abs te saepe famula & administra sapientiae dicitur, nunc videatur eius domina constitui*] (29).

48. Ramus, *Attack on Cicero*, 42. [*in Republica optimis legibus moribusque constituta, fundos & possessiones singulorum civium certis finibus regi, terminari, & circunscribi . . . tu cum ad alienum dialecticae artis fundum, rhetoricum murum aedifices, non modo intermedium pedem nullum relinques, sed mediam fundi partem occupabis & intercipies?*] (42).

49. Ramus, *Attack on Cicero*, 77. [*at tu rhetoricam hanc, si Palladi placet, oleam cum plantes, iuxta philosophorum fundum, non modo pedem nullum intermedium relinquis, sed radicibus arboris totam philosophiae regionem complecteris*] (77). Harvey alludes to these unruly roots when he contrasts the classical account of rhetoric "joined and sewn together from many, like a quilt from many rags and skins (way too many rhetoricians have given this sort of art to us, if indeed one may call art that which conforms to no artistic principles)" with one "that is concise, precise, appropriate, lucid, accessible" so "that it might stand more firmly grounded, secured by deeper roots" (trans. Reynolds, *Rhetor*, 31). [*non vnam ex multis tanquam pannis, atque pellibus coagmentatam, & consutam: (qualem nobis artem nimis multi Rhetores dedere: si tamen artem nominare licet, quae ad nullam est artis rationem redacta:) sed breuem, sed enucleatam, sed commodam, sed dilucidam, sed popularem . . . vt altioribus defixa radicibus haereat firmius*] (*Rhetor*, D_4v).

50. Ramus, *Attack on Cicero*, 74. [*non modo ex academiae spatiis, sed ne ex rhetorum quidem officinis haec profecta esse*] (74). This distinction is originally from Cicero, *Orator*, trans. Hubbel, 12. See also Harvey, *Rhetor*, E_4v–r.

51. Ramus, *Attack on Cicero*, 80. [*utroque carere potest disputatio, quia mente fieri & exerceri sine ullo sermonis vel orationis commercio potest*] (80).

52. Ramus, *P. Rami Dialecticae Libri Dvo* (1584), Ar [*Dialectica est ars bene disserendi*]. Ong describes the respective orientations as "a polar difference: rhetoric was concerned with what was resonant and closer to the auditory pole; dialectic with what was relatively silent, abstract, and diagrammatic" (280).

53. Jardine, 41.

54. Fraunce, *Lawiers Logike*, Br. See also Fenner's definition of "Logike" as "an Art of reasoning" (Br).

55. Fraunce, *Lawiers Logike*, Br. He attributes the emphasis on language to the art's other name, dialectic (Gk. "to speak or talke").

56. Fraunce, *Lawiers Logike*, B_2v.

57. In *Ramus, of Vermandois, the King's Professor, his Dialectica in two books* (1632), R. F. imagines a reader who will protest: "I live privately, converse not in the world; what neede have I of this Science? It seemeth to consist chiefly in disputing, but I imploy my selfe most in silence and meditation." To which objection R. F. responds, "Well friend, thou mayest have great benefit by this science, even in that likewise" (A_4r). See also, the "sweete delight of meditation" (A_7r). There are, however, more inclusive accounts of reason, such as defining logic as "an Art of reasoning well ... also called Dialectick." Anthony Wotton glosses "reasoning" as "Vsing reason, that is considering, debating, discoursing, disputing, either with our selues, or with other: by speaking, writing, meditating of any matter whatsoeur" (*The Art of Logick* [1626], Br–B_2v). See also Ramus, *A Compendium of the Art of Logick and Rhetorick* (1651), Br; *Peter Ramus His Logic* (1636), B_2r; *Peter Ramus ... his Dialectica* (1632), B_2r.

58. Ramus, *Arguments in Rhetoric*, 105. [*quae mentis omnino sunt et intus sine ullo linguae aut orationis auxilio exerceri possunt: ut in plerisque mutis, ut in multis populis, qui sine sermone ullo vivunt*] (184).

59. Fraunce, *Lawiers Logike*, Cc_2r–Cc_3v.

60. Ong argued that such thinking looked increasingly like geometry or even Newtonian physics. Ramism was thus a kind of pivot on which thinking turned away from speech and turned toward the arrangement of "noiseless concepts or 'ideas' in a silent field of mental space" (291). This mind is indebted to the supposition theory of medieval Scholasticism, a projection of what Ong described as "a corpuscular view of reality and of the mind, a kind of epistemological or psychological atomism" that "regards reality as coming in little chunks—like tiny men or asses or troops of little Socrateses—and intellectual activity as the marshalling and maneuvering of corresponding little chunks of mind-stuff" (72). See Dolven, *Scenes of Instruction*, 177–181. On schematic representations of learning and knowledge more generally and the temporality of the mind and its activities, see Dolven, *Scenes of Instruction*, esp. 15–64.

61. Aristotle's account of the concept in his *Categories* is dropped from the reformed dialectic (Ong, 104–112); Nelson, 5–7. Reiss suggests that early modern grammarians and rhetoricians were unable "to distinguish between communicative and cognitive functions of language, even though a distinction was made between grammar and rhetoric on the one hand and dialectic on the other," but that "the clearer the distinction became, the more stripped language was of *any* cognitive function whatsoever: at least to the extent that this might involve anything like 'discovery'" (*Knowledge*, 61). At moments like these, Fraunce sounds like he is approaching something like a universal language theory as described by M. M. Slaughter: the "mental deep structure of which individual languages are but the less interesting surface manifestations" (87; see, more generally, 85–103).

62. See Ong, 107–112, 129, 184–185; on Ramus's reorientation of reason away from language and toward mathematics, see Reiss, *Knowledge*, esp. 53–55.

63. Ong, 110. See also what Ong calls "psychological mechanics" (185) and his description of a "mental world as made up of something like physical corpuscles" (196).

64. Sidney, *Defence*, 216.

65. Temple, 81. [*Vis tu poeseos naturam fictione quadam comprehendi. Ecquid fictio ista aliud est quam inventio rei quae nondum extitit?*] (80).

66. Temple, 81. [*Qui fingit, is logica argumenta fingit, nempe causas, effecta, subjecta, adjuncta, dissentanea, comparata aut caetera quae ex istis oriuntur. Sic Ovidius fingens regiam Solis finxit efficientem causam a qua constructa* [*est*], *materiam ex qua conflata est, adjuncta quibus ornata est. At fingere Causas, effecta, subjecta, adjuncta, caeteraque argumenta, nihil aliud est quam invenire causas, effecta, subjecta, adjuncta. Quamobrem fictio erit idem quod rei quae nondum extiterit, inventio*] (80).

67. Temple, 81–83. [*Dum igitur Aristoteles poesin fictione definit, collocat poesin velut in domicilia logicae inventionis violata lege χαθ'αυτό. Ac proinde quoties fingunt poetae, non id faciunt aliquo proprio munere poeseos sed dialecticae artis facultate*] (80–82).

68. See Webster's analysis of Temple on poetry and lying, 30–33.

69. Temple, 81. [*At ipsa fictio perinde ac excogitatio horum argumentorum est actio nativae vel artificiosae rationis in inveniendo*] (80).

70. Temple's use of the verb *fingere* and the noun *fictio* throughout this analysis and even, as Webster points out, his use of *ars fictionis* as a gloss for Sidney's "art of imitation" contribute to his emphasis on poetry as an interventionist making rather than a removed imitation (see ed. Webster, 30, 182n25).

71. Ong suggests that while "Ramist arts are constituted of an all but palpable 'matter,'" what he calls the "*simpliste* economy" of their topical logic

could not be put usefully to questions of metaphysics (262–263). "Thus when questions concerning knowledge are touched on explicitly by Ramus or Talon, they are likely to have as their background some unhappily misleading question such as, Is the universal in the mind or the world of things? Indeed, this well-known *simpliste* formulation is weighted in the same way as the Ramist dialectic for it supposes a 'universal' as a kind of object which could commute between a real and a mental world, annihilating any meaningful difference between the two worlds by implying that being 'in' the mind and being 'in' the extramental world is a mere matter of position, so that legitimate epistemological considerations such as, What happens when we know? appear degraded to the order of questions such as, Is the pea under the right-hand or the left-hand walnut shell?" (209).

72. Hoskins, 2. See also Ben Jonson's incorporation of this passage into his *Discoveries*: "Disordered speech is not so much injury to the lips that give it forth, as to the disproportion, and incoherence of things in themselves, so negligently expressed" (109). See Plett's related discussion of an "ontological conception of style" (*Renaissance Eloquence*, 356–375).

73. Ramus's critique of Cicero's "poetic madness" [*Poeticus est iste furor*, 27] in his search for the ideal orator "whom Anthony never saw, who, all in all, never existed" is illustrative of this claim (*Attack on Cicero*, 26) [*quem nunquam vidit Antonius: qui omnino nullus unquam fuit*] (26). His primary point is that such an ideal does not exist and can never exist because the art of rhetoric cannot account for anything other than a man who speaks well. Having limited the ideal to a "man who has excelled equally" [*quibus in omnibus qui peraeque praestiterit*] in each of the three styles, Ramus declares, "we possess the definition of the orator which we are seeking." He imagines his interlocutor to reply, "We possess it, you will say, in our imagination but not in fact," to which Ramus then states, "We have grasped the ideal, truly defined, of perfect eloquence with our imagination and intelligence; we seek an example of its outward appearance with our ears" (31). [*definitum igitur oratorem tenemus, quem quaerimus. Tenemus, inquies, animo, reipsa non tenemus . . . perfectae eloquentiae speciem & definitam veritatem mente & intelligentia complexi sumus: effigiem & exemplum auribus quaerimus*] (31). Ramus declares the invention of a definition of an ideal orator to be a kind of existence for that orator (he is "possessed" and "grasped"). If Antony (or anyone) never sees him, he nonetheless exists by virtue of that definition; the only thing left to seek is "an example" of that ideal's "outward appearance." See also *Attack on Cicero*, 76. For a related claim, see Goeglein: "As Temple told Sidney, Ramist invention creates 'something that has never existed'—or more accurately, Ramist invention creates natural relations where none were previously *understood* to exist. By coupling the subject and predicate, invention acts as a logical

signifier, namely as a copula, which makes claims for existence" (92). These "natural relations" inhere in what Goeglein calls (via Thomas M. Greene) "the '*mundus*' of Ramist invention," in which the relations prescribed by the places of *inventio* "forged metonymic associations among semantic entities (the subject and predicate) which were exemplified in the poetic snippets, and it averred these metonymies as 'naturally' there" (93).

74. Temple, 111–113. [*Virtutis vitiique effigiem eminentem fateor a poetis proponi nobis ob oculos. sed effigiei istius prima lineamenta omnesque colores, quibus variatur & distinguitur, sunt logicae inventionis argumenta vestita rhetoricis ornamentis*] (110–112).

75. "Fiction-making" belongs to "dialectical invention, through which are conceived not only true things, but fictions as well" (Temple, 81). [*id si ita est, ars fictionis non ad poesin sed ad dialecticam inventionem pertinebit: qua non solum res verae sed etiam fictitiae cogitantur*] (80).

76. Temple, 81. [*Qui fingit, is logica argumenta fingit*] (80).

77. Hacking, 146, 145.

78. Fraunce, *Lawiers Logike*, B₄v.

79. Quintilian, 8. pr. 6. [*orationem porro omnem constare rebus et verbis; in rebus intuendam inventionem, in verbis elocutionem*].

80. At the beginning of his discussion of style, for example, Quintilian finds himself "compelled to offer the most prompt and determined resistance to those who would at the very portals of this enquiry" proceed by "disregarding the subject matter which, after all, is the backbone of any speech" and "devote themselves to the futile and crippling study of words" (even though Quintilian regards style as "the fairest of all the glories of oratory") (8. pr. 18). [*occurram enim necesse est et, velut in vestibulo protinus apprehensuris hanc confessionem meam, resistam iis qui, omissa rerum (qui nervi sunt in causis) diligentia, quodam inani circa voces studio senescunt, idque faciunt gratia decoris, qui est in dicendo mea quidem opinione pulcherrimus, sed cum sequitur non cum adfectatur.*] For teachers like Quintilian and Erasmus, a division between *res* and *verba*, between *inventio* and *elocutio*, constituted a provisional organization of material. It allowed for the arrangement of material and for the intelligibility of difference; it enabled the conceptual distinctions according to which a discussion of the art of rhetoric might proceed.

81. Ramus, *Attack on Cicero*, 98. [*rhetorica elocutio hic tractatur: rerum igitur inventio non admisceatur . . . Elocutio est orationis conformatio ut in singulis verbis tropus, in coniunctis figura: argumenta igitur nec misceantur*] (98).

82. Quintilian, 8.3.83. [*vicina praedictae sed amplior virtus est ἔμφασις altiorem praebens intellectum quam quem verba per se ipsa declarant.*]

83. Ramus, *Arguments in Rhetoric*, 146. [*At hoc Quintiliani ratiocinationis cuiusdam et conclusionis est, figurae nihil. Neque enim est noua orationis forma, sed vis quaedam cogitationis solers et acuta*] (217).

84. Quintilian, 8.3.84. [*idem, Cyclopa cum iacuisse dixit* per antrum, *prodigiosum illud corpus spatio loci mensus est.*]

85. Ramus, *Arguments in Rhetoric*, 133. [*cuiusmodi capita duo proxima sunt de amplificatione et de sententiarum generibus, quorum capitum artem nullam omnino Quintilianus intelligit. Praecipit hoc libro de elocutione, At ista genera amplificationum et sententiarum non elocutione verborum, sed rerum inuentione fiunt*] (207).

86. Ramus, *Attack on Cicero*, 97. [*omnia enim haec sine ulla figura esse possunt*] (97). Definitions are quoted from *Silva Rhetoricae* (http://rhetoric.byu.edu).

87. Ramus, *Attack on Cicero*, 97. Temple writes: "A simile (most eminent Sidney) is not an ornament of rhetorical eloquence, but an argument of logical invention, since there is in simile a certain force for arguing and explaining something" (163). [*Similitudo (clarissime Sidneie) non est Rhetoricae elocutionis ornamentum, sed Logicae inventionis argumentum: quia inest in similitudine vis quaedam ad rem arguendam et declarandam*] (162).

88. "He makes antithesis the last of the figures of speech and he is wrong to do so, for an argument is not a figure; antithesis is of course an argument from unlikes and therefore it is not a figure" (Ramus, *Arguments in Rhetoric*, 149). [*Postremam e figuris verborum facit* antitheton, *in eoque fallitur: argumentum enim figura non est*, antitheton *autem ex dissimilibus argumentum est: non igitur figura*] (220). See also *Attack on Cicero*, 97.

89. "Quintilian makes periphrasis the tenth class of trope. But periphrasis can be devised in all cases through proper words. For this reason it does not involve any trope at all but a class of argument from the dialectical topics of definition" (Ramus, *Arguments in Rhetoric*, 139). [*Decimum tropi genus periphrasin Quintilianus facit. At periphrasis omnibus proprijj verbis effici potest: nec idcirco tropus ullus est omnino, sed argumenti genus ex dialectico definitionis loco*] (212).

90. Ramus, *Arguments in Rhetoric*, 111.

91. Ramus, *The Logike of The Most Excellent Philosopher P. Ramus Martyr* (1574), 29–30. Notation describes an argument from etymology and offers the "true reason of the word, how it commeth to signifie this, or that"; conjugation describes an argument from "names diversly derived from the same beginning ... Those that are joyned, as it were, by kindred; as Iust, Iustice, Iustly" (Wotton, *The Art of Logick* [1626], G_3v, G_2r). Wotton supplies a Spenserian example for his illustration of notation: "*From Court, it seemes, men courtesie doe call / For that it there most useth to abound*" (G_4v).

92. For a description of Fraunce's and Fenner's logic, see W. S. Howell, 219–229. The dismissal of the places of notation and conjugation is not so much a departure from Ramism as it is faithful to the fundamental premises of the movement. Fraunce and Fenner proceed from a desire to divide *inventio* from *elocutio* and a desire to strip the art of dialectic of all but its most essential precepts. The dismissal of notation and conjugation follows these premises through to their logical conclusion (they out-Ramus Ramus).

93. Granger, 159. Granger writes: "Notation is the interpretation of a name or word from the originall thereof; whereby a reason is shewed, why such a name is giuen to such a thing, that by the name, the thing it selfe may be interpreted, explicated, and knowne. For as the nature of the thing giueth a semblable name: so the name is a note, signe, image, or symbol noting, and representing the nature of the thing. So that to interpret a name or a word (according to Logik) is to explicate the reason, and originall thereof from some prime argument of the thing named or noted. . . . Notation therefore hath place, and vse in explicating of thinges to which names are giuen and agree by some certaine reason, by which we are brought to the knowledge of the thing so named" (164–165). For Granger's Ramism, see W. S. Howell, 229–232, 284.

94. Wotton writes of conjugation that "these words, and the like belong to Grammar; but it is *Logike*, that teacheth vs to reason by them" (G_2r).

95. "For that *iust* and *iustlie* are formed one of an other," Fenner writes, "appertaineth to Gramer." "*Notation*, which is the interpretation of a name," he suggests, "appertaineth not to Logike but to Dictionaries" (*Lawiers Logike*, A_4r).

96. Fenner declares that in notation there "is neyther reason, nor new force of reason" (A_4r). Fraunce similarly writes: "As for Coniugates, I sée in them no new different force of arguing, as hée is iust, for hée dealeth iustly: héere is nothing in effect, but the cause and the effect. For as for the deriuation of this woord Iuste, from Iustice, it séemeth altother [*sic*] grammaticall. . . . So in Notation, the interpretation of the name, séemeth rather the dutie of the dictionary, then of any Logicall institution, as Argumentum ab arguendo: where againe there is no force of arguing but from the cause and the thing caused" (*Lawiers Logike*, O_2r–O_3v). In *The Art of Logick* (1628) Spencer also suggests that while the arguments supplied by conjugation and notation are logical (and thus belong in dialectic), they are already covered by the first arguments from which they derive and therefore should not receive a separate treatment. He writes, "if wee should multiplie the seates of arguments, according to the varietie that our vnderstanding doth apprehend to be in them, then wee must haue an endles (at least) a fruitles number: seeing it is in vaine to set ten men to doe the labour of one" (140–141).

97. Fenner, A_4r.

98. Fraunce, *Lawiers Logike*, O_3v (Fraunce's term for *paronomasia* is "Rhetoricall Agnomination"); Fenner, A_4r.

99. Fenner, A_4r; Fraunce, *Lawiers Logike*, O_2r–O_3v.

100. Wary of departing too dramatically from Ramus, Fraunce determines that he will "giue them leaue for a time to soiourne among the annotations" of his handbook though he "dare not admit them into the text" (*Lawiers*

Logike, K₄v). Fenner goes further. He banishes any discussion of notation or conjugation from his account of the art of dialectic and sends them back to *Eloquentia*'s hearth: "let vs keepe them no longer, nowe the owner claymeth them, but according to the law turne them home againe" (Fenner, A₄r).

101. Fallacies occur on account of the ambiguity of a single word ("the diuers signification of any one woord") or on account of the ambiguity of multiple words ("the ambiguous construction of many woordes") (Fraunce, *Lawiers Logike*, H₄v). For this division, see also Granger, 348 (fallacies of "homonymie," 353; and fallacies of "amphiboly," 354); Wilson, *Rule of Reason* (1551), 162–167. Blundeville defines equivocation as "when the deceit consisteth in the doubtfulnesse of some one word, hauing diuers significations" (*The arte of logick* [1617], Bb₄v).

102. Fraunce, *Lawiers Logike*, H₃v. Fraunce departs from the Ramist line by providing an account of fallacies even though (as was the case with notation and conjugation) he "reserued" discussion of them for his "annotations" rather than "thrusted them in among the precepts" for fear he should "iniury the art by ioyning sophistical fallacians with Logicall institions" (*Lawiers Logike*, H₂r–H₃v). Macilmaine describes the presence of sophistry within logic as a violation of Ramus's law of truth (or "veritie") according to which "all the rules and preceptes of thine arte be of necessitie tru." "Thou shalt violate this document," he continues, "whensoeuer amongest thy precepts in writing or teaching, thou shalt myngle any false, ambiguous, or vncertaine thing: as if in teaching me my logicke, which consistethe in rules to inuente argumentes, and to dispone and iudge the same, thou shouldest begyn to tell me some trickes of poysonable sophistrie" (5). For Fraunce's treatment of fallacies as dispersed through the *Lawiers Logike*, see Pomeroy.

103. Fraunce, *Lawiers Logike*, H₃v–r.

104. Peacham, *Garden of Eloquence* (1593), 56. In his anatomy of the figure *paronomasia*, Quintilian warns that "Gorgias carried the practice to an extravagant pitch" and that Isocrates "was much addicted to it." *Paronomasia* is "unattractive," Quintilian explains, when "carried to excess": "when it goes hand in hand with vigour of thought, it gives the impression of natural charm, which the speaker has not had to go far to find." "In itself," however, "this artifice is a flat and foolish affectation" (9.3.74). [*Gorgias in hoc immodicus, copiosus aetate utique prima Isocrates fuit. delectatus est his etiam M. Tullius, verum et modum adhibuit non ingratae, nisi copia redundet, voluptati et rem alioqui levem sententiarum pondere implevit. nam per se frigida et inanis adfectatio, cum in acres incidit sensus, innatam gratiam videtur habere non arcessitam.*]

105. Hoskins continues: "Sir Philip Sidney would not have his style be much beholding to this kind of garnish," and John Lyly, who first thrust the fad of this figure upon us all, "hath outlived this style and breaks well from

it" (16–17). Hoskins uses the Latin synonym "agnomination" for *paronomasia*. On euphuism and conspicuous artifice, see Nicholson, *Uncommon Tongues*, 72–99.

106. Ong wrote that the historical distinction of Ramism lies not so much in a single proposition or procedure as in a "special concentration of items, most of which can be discerned individually outside Ramist circles. Because of its curiously amateurish cast," Ong continues, "it does not repress the crude conceptualizing tendencies which more astutely controlled philosophies block or disguise." Ong therefore likens Ramism to a prism, one that "makes it possible to discern the nature of subconscious drives which have been obscured elsewhere" but "call for radical revision in our ways of viewing intellectual history" (8).

107. Sidney, *Defence*, 218; Temple, 89. [*si dimensione soni comprehenditur natura poeseos. id quod necesse est esse, si fictione non includitur*] (88).

108. I discuss this most fully in Chapter 3. For Ramus's account of *decorum*, see the introduction to this book.

109. Fraunce, *Arcadian Rhetorike*, Cv.

110. Fraunce, *Arcadian Rhetorike*, D$_7$r.

111. Fraunce, *Arcadian Rhetorike*, E$_3$r.

112. Fraunce, *Arcadian Rhetorike*, E$_3$r.

113. Quintilian, 9.3.35. [*est et illud repetendi genus, quod simul proposita iterat et dividit*].

114. Fraunce, *Arcadian Rhetorike*, Cv. *Epanodos* is "regression, turning to the same sound, when one and the same sound is repeated in the beginning and middle, or middle and end" (Fraunce, *Arcadian Rhetorike*, D$_4$r). George Puttenham's defintion of *epanodos* in *The Art of English Poesy* (1589) retains these two understandings: "This Figure of Retire [*epanodos*] holds part with the Propounder, of which we spake before (*prolepsis*), because of the resumption of a former proposition uttered in generality, to explain the same better by a particular division. But their difference is, in that the Propounder resumes but the matter only. This Retire resumes both the matter and the terms" (306).

115. See A. Stewart, 84–121.

116. Spenser, *The Faerie Queene*, 2.4.33.9.

117. Spenser, *The Faerie Queene*, 2.4.34–35.

118. Spenser, *The Faerie Queene*, 2.4.33.9.

119. Spenser here sounds more like George Gascoigne, as in Puttenham's example of *epanodos* (from Gascoigne's *Adventures of Master F.J.*): "Love, hope, and death do stir in me much strife, / As never man but I lead such a life: / For burning love doth wound my heart to death, / And when death comes at call of inward grief, / Cold ling'ring hope doth feed my fainting breath /

Against my will, and yields my wound relief, / So that I live, but yet my life is such / As never death could grieve me half so much" (Puttenham, 306).

120. Berger, "Narrative as Rhetoric," 199.
121. Puttenham, 239.
122. Shelby, 247.
123. See also the related moment of Phaedria's "chosen plott of fertile land" (2.6.12.1), where Spenser's *incrementum* culminates in a review of its degrees and the consolidation of its *telos*. Conspicuous art here works to undo thinking: "No tree, whose braunches did not brauely spring; / No braunch, whereon a fine bird did not sitt: / No bird, but did her shrill notes sweetely sing; / No song but did containe a louely ditt: / Trees, braunches, birds, and songs were framed fitt, / For to allure fraile mind to carelesse ease" (2.6.13.1–6).
124. Spenser, *The Faerie Queene*, 2.12.70–71.
125. On form and affordance, see Levine, 6–7.
126. Hollander, "Spenser and the Mingled Measure," 235.
127. Hollander, "Spenser and the Mingled Measure," 237.
128. For *poesie* and joints, see Parker, "Rude Mechanicals," 43–82.
129. For Stephen Greenblatt, Spenser's open art—"art that constantly calls attention to its own processes"—ultimately constitutes a renunciation of the epistemological value of world making (190). This is why "Spenser's art does not lead us to perceive ideology critically, but rather affirms the existence and inescapable moral power of ideology as that principle of truth toward which art forever yearns" (192). Where Greenblatt, however, takes the image as Spenser's central artistic tool, I am suggesting that we read for figure because it is the instrument of *poesie* with which Spenser's poem radically redefines what constitutes thinking and the assessment of its truth-value.
130. Greene has described the bower as "a paradigm for the world-making procedure of the entire epic, which is to bring a site into view, develop it into an emergent world that vies with the originary world of the poem, pose directly or not the matter of how one world relates to the other—and then subduct the second world back into that singular world, making unitary what was plural and evanescent what was concrete" ("A Primer of Spenser's Worldmaking," 27). My reading of *epanodos* confirms Greene's sense that in *The Faerie Queene* movement into another world within the poem is simultaneously a burrowing deeper into the world of the poem, but I want to suggest that this burrowing entails a rearranging of constitutive axes such that it no longer seems right to describe the world as a "unitary" construct, because it is never fixed. In the Bower, Spenser revises the poem's axes of relation such that the world of *The Faerie Queene* becomes another version of itself.

131. The Ramist account of *metonymy* stands as the singular exception to the movement's separation of *inventio* from *elocutio* by insisting on their perfect conflation: it offers the places of *inventio* as subdivisions of the trope of *metonymy* (see Fraunce, *Arcadian Rhetorike*, A₃r–A₇v). See also Blundeville's *Art of Logike*, which features his original place of *inventio*, called "translation": "Otherwise called a Metaphor, is a figure of speech, whereby the proper signification of a worde is changed into an other vnproper." His subsequent elaboration registers the ambivalence at the heart of this chapter: "It is rather a Trope, or figure of Rhetoricke, more meet to adorn speech then to proue any thing thereby" (O₂r).

132. Eggert, 31. On "alchemical language" as "singularly devoted to examining figuration as a process rather than just a rhetorical fillip" (32–33), see esp. 25–38. Eggert's focus is primarily on tropes (and the logic of substitution).

133. Eggert, 53.

134. Eggert, esp. 207–247.

135. Eggert writes: "Alchemy undertakes the work of literature by marrying a specifically literary language, the language of metaphoric substitution, to a certain laxness about truth claims. So too does Sidney's poetry substitute a golden world for a world of brass; and this literary golden world is the one in which we are presented, not with what is or what should be, but what *might* be" (220).

136. Greene, *Five Words*, 33.

137. Gascoigne, 1:48. See also Greene, *Five Words*, 29–33.

138. Gascoigne, 1:47–48.

139. On "capture," see Teskey, 19; Dolven, "The Method of Spenser's Stanza," 23.

140. See Hutson, *Invention of Suspicion*, esp. 104–145.

141. See Nicholson, *Uncommon Tongues*, esp. 45–71.

2. FIGURE POINTING IN THE HUMANIST SCHOOLROOM

1. Susenbrotus, 1. [*Ego sane, quo id praecauerem, huius modi orationis ornamenta uobis ac caeteris discipulis olim meis, pro uirili ac ingenii captu, etsi non omnia semper quae occurrebant, pleraque; tamen quae elegantiora uidebantur, inter praelegendum uelut digito commonstraui: quo sensus illius, quod praelegebatur, a uobis certius de citra obscuritatem perciperetur, simulque haberetis scribendi dicendique formulas, quas assiduo usu imitari liceret*] (A₂r). See also the 1529 statutes for Ipswich (quoted by Mack, *Elizabethan Rhetoric*): "Lastly, you are carefully to mark out to your pupils every striking elegance of style, every antiquated expression, everything that is new, every grecisised expression, every thing that is obscure, every etymology, derivation or composition that

may arise, whatever is harsh or confused in the arrangement of the sentence. You are to mark every orthography, every figure, every graceful ornament of style, every rhetorical flourish, whatever is proverbial, all passages that ought to be imitated and all that ought not" (15). See Latour, 24–79, esp. 29–30; Sherman on the manicule in *Used Books*, 25–52.

2. For example, Puttenham in *The Art of English Poesy* (1589) describes *decorum* as "the line and level for all good makers to do their business by" (347). See also his suggestion that the poet "may both use and also manifest his art to his great praise, and need no more be ashamed thereof than a shoemaker to have made a cleanly shoe, or a carpenter to have built a fair house" (382). On the intersection between *poiēsis* and the mechanical arts, see Kalas; Turner, *The English Renaissance Stage*; Parker, "Rude Mechanicals." On the materiality of language, see Anderson, *Words That Matter*; Burckhardt, 22–46.

3. Susenbrotus, 2 [*scribendi dicendique formulas*], A$_2$v.

4. Sidney, *Defence*, 218.

5. E.g., Peacham in *The Garden of Eloquence* (1593) says of *ecphonesis* or *exclamatio*: "The principal end and vse of this figure is by the vehemency of our voice and utterance to express the greatnesse of our affections and passions, and thereby to moue the like affections in our hearers" (K$_4$r). For what he calls "the expressive function of rhetorical figures," see Vickers, *In Defence*, esp. 294–339, also 50, 77–79, 208, 225–226, 276–286. In his briefest formulation, Vickers describes this as "the doctrine of the figures and tropes, which were seen as recording powerful emotions in normal speech, recreating those emotions in a speaker, and so arousing them in the audience" (x). Berger calls this the "psychological function" of figures in "Narrative as Rhetoric," 175. See also Enterline, *Shakespeare's Schoolroom*, esp. 120–152; Alexander, *Writing after Sidney*, 39–40. Understanding *metaphor* ("a 'bearing across or going over'") as the archtrope for the relationship between orator and audience, Rebhorn writes: "In the rhetorical transaction those boundaries are the ones between selves, between the orator and the auditor, and what gets transported through the space separating the two is the mind or will of the former, which impresses itself on the mind or will of the latter" (*The Emperor of Men's Minds*, 43).

6. On the "natural" source of figures, see Susenbrotus's praise of rhetoric textbooks: "It is [inspiriting] to perceive the marvelous industry of rhetoricians in collecting these figures, who, as Melanchthon testifies, have so diligently observed the various formulas of human speech and even pronunciation (as in irony, epiphonemata, interrogation and the like), as well as the nuances of meaning conveyed by our very mouth, eyes, and physiognomy, and who have in this way at length reduced them to an art" (46). [*Atque*

miram Rhetorum in his colligendis industriam est cernere, vt Philippus testatur, qui tam uarias humanae locutionis formulas, adeoque, & pronunciationis (ut in Ironia, Epiphonemate, Interrogatione, &c.) ac ipsius oris nostri, oculorum & uultus discrimima haud oscitanter obseruarunt, ac ita tandem in artem redegerunt] (C₈v). A similar fiction underwrites the production of dramatic character; see Berger, *Imaginary Audition*, 147.

7. "If there is anything that excites the contempt of all," Harvey explains in *Rhetor* (1577), "it is surely affectation. In the realm of Eloquence its very name is anathema" (trans. Reynolds, 102) [*Siquid enim communibus omnium fastidiis adhaerescit, id quidem certe Affectatio est: cuius vel nomen ipsum in Eloquentiae regno maxime esse solet odiosum*] (N₃v). Though Harvey himself advises his students to mark every trope and figure that they come across—"You will pass over in silence no stylistic excellence"—he also warns against what he calls "that Maeotic swamp of Hermogenes, an endless and overly ambitious 'fool's art'": "It was written of him that he was so keen-eyed and meticulous in his art that he boasted he could find hundreds of figures and rhetorical subtleties in a single period" (94). Harvey calls those "who have not been nourished on food but are filled with the wind and air of rhetoric ... either sophists, or pseudo-rhetoricians, or even rhetorical chameleons" (95). [*Nullam eloquendi virtutem, nullam elegentiam, nullam denique machinam sine piaculo praeteribitis. Ita tamen, vt ne in Hermogenis illius, at Maeotidem paludem nati, infinitam, & ambitiosam nimis* ματαιοπονίαν *incumbatis; de quo literis proditum est, adeo eum fuisse in sua arte oculatum, atque curiosum, vt in vna, eademque periodo sexcentas se figuras, atque subtilitates Rhetoricas deprehendere posse gloriaretur ... ego hoc tempore Pseudohermogenes non inscite vsurparim; alias fortasse, vt videbitur, vel sophistas, vel Pseudorhetores, vel etiam Camaeleontes quosdam Rhetoricos apellaturus; non tam cibo illos quidem pastos quam vento, vt ita dicam, atque aëre Rhetorico saturatos*] (M₃v–M₄r).

8. In "Preposterous Events," Parker shows how "condemnations of 'preposterous' inversion appear repeatedly in the texts of an emerging neoclassical orthodoxy devoted to order, decorum, and proper sequence," arguing that Shakespeare's own preposterous reversals expose "the very bases of discursive, of social, and of political ordering—and their power when naturalized into narratives of authority or plausibility" (190, 212). See also Parker's more recent discussion of *hysteron proteron* as "a term from the discourse of rhetoric for an inversion that reversed the order of 'things' themselves, including in both temporal and logical sequence" ("*Hysteron Proteron*," 135) and *Literary Fat Ladies*, esp. 8–35, 67–96, 97–125.

9. Udall, *Floures for Latine* (1533), E₆v.

10. For readings of this scene that emphasize "sympathy" and "friendly harmony and rivalry" (respectively), see McFaul, 20–21; and Alexander, *Writing after Sidney*, 13.

11. Sidney, *Old Arcadia*, 148.

12. According to the normative paradigm of rhetorical composition, the "transactional division" of rhetoric, as Berger describes it, "consists in mastering the strategies of linguistic communication, the relations of senders to receivers, and it includes the two forms of 'artificial proof' Aristotle called *ethos* and *pathos*: the first, focused on the speaker's self-representation, the second on the skills by which he moves the audience" ("Narrative as Rhetoric," 175–176). Vickers defines this network as the relations among "artist, artefact, and audience" (*In Defence*, 64).

13. Sidney, *Old Arcadia*, 148.

14. Sidney, *Old Arcadia*, 148–149.

15. Sidney, *Old Arcadia*, 149.

16. Demetrius writes of an example of *climax* in *On Style* : "This sentence seems almost to be climbing higher and higher at each step" (270); *Rhetorica Ad Herennium*: "Climax is the figure in which the speaker passes to the following word only after advancing by steps to the preceding one" [*Gradatio est in qua non ante ad consequens verbum descenditur quam ad superius ascensum est*] (trans. Caplan, 4.25.34); Augustine, *On Christian Doctrine*: "Yet we recognize there the figure generally designated by the Greek word 'Climax'—though some people, not wishing to speak of a 'ladder,' prefer the Latin word *gradatio*—whereby words or ideas are linked with one another" (trans. Green, 209) [*Et tamen agnoscitur hic figura quae climax grace, latine vero a quibusdam est appellata gradatio, quoniam calam dicere nolverunt, cum verba vel sensa conectuntur alterum ex altero*] (208); Sherry, *Treatise of Schemes and Tropes* (1550): "Gradacio, is, whe~ we rehearse again the word y^t goth next before, & desced to other things by degrees thus" (D$_5$v), with an emphasis on "degree" (Lt. *de-gradus*), meaning "a step in an ascent or descent; one of a flight of steps; a step or rung of a ladder" (see "degree" in the *Oxford English Dictionary*); in his 1555 revision, Sherry makes this allusion to the ladder more explicit: "Gradation is, when the wordes that goe before, be forthwith repeted, and so runneth as it wer from steppe to steppe" (*A Treatise of the Figures of Grammer and Rhetorike* [1555], E$_6$r); Wilson, *Art of Rhetoric*: "Gradation is when we rehearse the word that goeth next before and bring another word thereupon that increaseth the matter, as though one should go up a pair of stairs and not leave till he come at the top" (228); Fenner: "A pleasaunt clyming is a redoubling continued by diuers degrees or steppes of the same sounds" (D$_3$v); Peacham, *Garden* (1593): "Climax is a figure which so distinguisheth the oration by degrees" (T$_3$r; see also *The Garden of Eloquence* [1577], Q$_3$r); Fraunce, *Arcadian Rhetorike*: "Climax, gradation, is a reduplication continued by diuers degrees and steps, as it were, of the same word or sound" (C$_8$v); Hoskins: "Climax is a kind of anadiplosis leading by degrees and making the last word a step to the further meaning" (12; see also Blount, B$_4$r; J. Smith: "*Climax* . . .

Gradatio, Gradation, or a climbing by steps; derived from . . . [*clino*] *reclino*, *acclino*, to bend towards or incline to, for that its ascending is rising upwards, and its descending, declining or turning away. *Gradation* is a kind of *Anadiplosis*, by degrees making the last word a step to a further meaning" [94]). In "Revolution by Degrees: Philip Sidney and *Gradatio*," Alex Davis argues that *Astrophil and Stella* 2 alludes to its own *gradatio*, as well as the *gradatio* of the opening sonnet, by way of its play on "degree" and "decree" (494).

17. Puttenham, 292.

18. For a similar moment of figure pointing, see Rosalind in Shakespeare's *As You Like It* as she recounts the courtship of her cousin with Orlando's brother: "Your brother and my sister no sooner met but they looked, no sooner looked but they loved; no sooner loved but they sighed; no sooner sighed but they asked one another the reason; no sooner knew the reason but they sought the remedy; and in these *degrees* they have made a *pair of stairs* to marriage, which they will climb incontinent or else be incontinent before marriage" (5.2.31–38). On this moment of figure pointing, see ed. Dusinberre, 321; Joseph, 180.

19. For the civilizing power of eloquence, see Peacham, *Garden* (1593), AB$_2$r–AB$_3$v. In an important corrective to more idealistic accounts of eloquence and community formation, Rebhorn has persuasively argued for the imperial logic of this claim. What one student described in his commonplace book as a "lively contagion" is, for Rebhorn, something like germ warfare: "Every time a rhetor uses a figure of speech . . . he both expresses his identity and impresses that identity on his auditor. It amounts to a *translatio imperii*, an imperial sallying-forth beyond the boundaries of the self in order to occupy the alien terrain of the Other and to plant one's banner there as conqueror and ruler. Figures and tropes constitute mini-dramas of invasion and domination" (*The Emperor of Men's Minds*, 44). See also Enterline, *Shakespeare's Schoolroom*, 132.

20. Robert Stillman has argued that Sidney's *Old Arcadia* "gives an unusually forthright analysis of what the poet does badly when misusing his art: of poetry's capacity for constructing solipsistic worlds which corrupt as they multiply desires, alienating humanity from Nature and trapping it within a painfully responsive landscape" (14). Nicholson describes this tension between the abundant style's humanist claims to sociability and friendship (on the one hand) and its tendency toward extravagancy and alienation (on the other) in *Uncommon Tongues*, esp. 92–99.

21. Quintilian, *Institutio Oratoria*, 9.3.99–100. The larger passage reads: "With regard to genuine *figures*, I would briefly add that, while, suitably placed, they are a real ornament to style, they become perfectly fatuous when sought after overmuch. There are some who pay no consideration to the

Notes to pages 53–54

weight of their matter or the force of their thoughts and think themselves supreme artists, if only they succeed in forcing even the emptiest of words into *figurative* form, with the result that they are never tired of stringing *figures* together, despite the fact that it is as ridiculous to hunt for *figures* without reference to the matter as it is to discuss dress and gesture without reference to the body." [*ego illud de iis etiam, quae vere sunt, adiiciam breviter, sicut ornent orationem opportune positae, ita ineptissimas esse, cum immodice petantur. sunt qui neglecto rerum pondere et viribus sententiarum, si vel inania verba in hos modos depravarunt, summos se iudicent artifices ideoque non desinant eas nectere, quas sine substantia sectari tam est ridiculum quam quaerere habitum gestumque sine corpore.*]

22. In *On Copia*, Erasmus writes: "But to return to the main point, style is to thought as clothes are to the body. Just as dress and outward appearance can enhance or disfigure the beauty and dignity of the body, so words can enhance or disfigure thought" (*De Copia*, trans. Knott, 306). [*Sed ad rem: quod est vestis nostro corpori, id est sententiis elocutio. Neque enim aliter quam forma dignitasque corporis cultu habituque, itidem et sententia verbis vel commendatur vel deturpatur*], (*De Copia*, ed. Knott, 36). On style and clothing, see: Quintilian, 8.Pr.27; J. Smith, B_3v, Mv; and Purchas's amazing quibble on "Word-Robe" (*Purchas his Pilgrimage* [1613], $\P_5r$). See also Hazard, 15–32; and Mahadvi Menon, who writes: "tropological language clothes, and therefore makes physical, a body that does not signify outside the realm of rhetorical interpellation. The existence of a body beneath the clothes, in other words, is a purely *hypothetical* (or metaphorical) assertion, conceived in order to provide a point of contrast to 'mere' ornament" (23).

23. Sidney, *Old Arcadia*, 148.

24. Sidney, *Old Arcadia*, 149.

25. See Peter Stallybrass and Ann Rosalind Jones, who describe the single glove, "released from the 'utility' of the pair," as an "external organ" (131). It is on this sense that Puttenham's illustration of the *enigma* turns: "I have a thing and rough it is / And in the midst a hole iwis, / There came a young man with his gin, / And he put it a handful in." Puttenham concludes that this "riddle is pretty but that it holds too much of the cacemphaton, or foul speech, and may be drawn to a reprobate sense" (273).

26. Sidney, *Old Arcadia*, 148–149.

27. Dorus's song literalizes a commonplace criticism of *elocutio*'s tropes and figures: that they are sweet nothings designed to arouse the beloved. John Johnson parodies this method of wooing in *The Academy of Love* (1641), where Cupid guides our narrator on an admissions tour of the "most populous, most ample, and most famous Vniversitie in the world" (C_1v). When Cupid enters the schoolroom of rhetoric, he describes their lesson in *elocutio* as follows:

"the women courtiers, although they endure not delayes, yet they are much addicted to the figure *Gradatio*, especially if their pretendent rhetorize in *Conduplicatio*, and through the faithful solution and sweet series of consent they couple and lovingly rest themselues upon the pallade *Polysindeton*, or *Multiplex conjunctio*" (F₂v). Foreplay and consummation. As in Dorus's poem, both sets of students are primarily interested in and wield figures in the service of their own pleasure.

28. "Debate and dispute are the function of the logicians; the orator's function is to speak ornately. Zeno, the founder of the Stoic school, used to give an object lesson of the difference between the two arts; clenching his fist he said logic was like that; relaxing and extending his hand, he said eloquence was like the open palm" (Cicero, *Orator*, 113). [*disputandi ratio et loquendi dialecticorum sit, oratorum autem dicendi et ornandi. Zeno quidem ille a quo disciplina Stoicorum est manu demonstrare solebat quid inter has artis interesset; nam cum compresserat digitos pugnumque fecerat, dialecticam aiebat eiusmodi esse; cum autem deduxerat et manum dilataverat, palmae illius similem eloquentiam esse dicebat.*] See also Ong, 16, 322n24; Martin Crusius's annotations to Melanchthon's *Elementorum Rhetorices Libri Duo* (1567), C₅r; Bacon, *The Advancement of Learning*, 239; Bryskett, *The discourse of ciuill life* (1606), 105.

29. Rainolde, A₂v. In Rainolde's formulation, "Logike is like saith he the fiste, for euen as the fiste closeth and shutteth into one, the iointes and partes of the hande, & with mightie force and strength, wrappeth and closeth in thynges apprehended" (A₁r). Parker, "*Othello* and *Hamlet*," 60. Dorus's song echoes this commonplace: when tucked inside his bosom the glove "didst preserve" what it was "hiding," and when removed form that bosom the glove, "opened forth," acts as a source of "comfort" (*Old Arcadia*, 148–149).

30. Sidney, *Astrophil and Stella*, in *Major Works*, Sonnet 1, lines 3–4. A. Davis writes that "*Gradatio* is the figure that deals with the 'causeful' nature of things": *gradatio* "deals with processes" in that it both "divides them into a series of perceptibly separate steps" and "articulates the connection between them so powerfully that one sometimes has the sense that they exist simultaneously, because each is continually implicit both in its predecessors and in its successors. The end of the process already *exists in potentia*, contained in its beginning; or, conversely, the beginning is to be understood as the mere prospective echo of its achieved end" (493).

31. Hoskins writes: "Climax is a kind of anadiplosis leading by degrees and making the last word a step to the further meaning. If it be turned to an argument, it is a Sorites. . . . Now to make it a sorites, or climbing argument, join the first and the last with an *ergo*" (12–13). Blundeville writes that *gradatio* "is much like to *Sorites*, sauing that the Subject of the first Proposition

is not rehearsed in the Conclusion, for they vse it rather as an ornament of speech, then as a proofe" (Aa₁r).

32. Reading *gradatio* in a 1948 speech by Lenin, Burke writes: "Regardless of these doubts about it as a proposition, by the time you arrive at the second of its three stages, you feel how it is destined to develop—and on the level of purely formal assent you would collaborate to round out its symmetry by spontaneously willing its completion and perfection as an utterance. Add, now, the psychosis of nationalism, and assent on the formal level invites assent to the proposition as doctrine" (*A Rhetoric of Motives*, 59).

33. Something like the difference between "affect" and "affectation" is at stake in the moving target that distinguishes "figures of words" from "figures of sentences" in early modern rhetoric textbooks. Fraunce divides figures of "word" from figures of "sentence" according to whether they delight or move: where figures of word (e.g., *anaphora*) are "pleasant and fit to delight," figures of sentence (e.g., *exclamatio*) "expres some motion of the minde" and are "apt to perswade" (*Arcadian Rhetorike*, E₄v–E₅r). Peacham declares, "The difference betwéene the figures of wordes, and the figures of sentences is great, found both in their formes and effects, for the figures of words are as it were effeminate, and musicall, the figures of sentences are manly, and martiall, those of words are as it were the colour and beautie, these of sentences are as the life and affection" (*Garden* [1593], K₃r).

34. Wilson, *Art of Rhetoric*, 187. See Menon, 21–26.

35. Baldwin, 2:23–25. The following discussion of grammar school practices is indebted to Dolven, *Scenes of Instruction*, 15–64; Vickers, *In Defence*; and Baldwin. On the primacy of *inventio* in the humanist schoolroom, see Dolven, *Scenes of Instruction*, esp. 45–48; and Crane, 12–38. Dolven is representative of histories of humanist pedagogy that "take *inventio* . . . as a synecdoche for the problem of method in composition generally"; he suggests that "the other stages seem to have much less of a hold on the poetic imagination" (*Scenes of Instruction*, 45). The account below is intended to expand our sense of "method" with respect to "the poetic imagination."

36. Sturm suggests that the student record a "copy of words" and "formulas of *sententiae*" from "rhetorical books," including those by Cicero and Hermogenes. These "formulas," he continues, "bring with them style, and *sententiae*, and arguments themselves; and often are shaped and figured" (*De Literarum Ludis Recte Aperiendis* [1538], E₃v; quoted by Baldwin, 2:23). The knowing schoolmaster in Brinsley's *Ludus Literarius* complains that "to follow the Logicke places in Apthonius in a Philosophical discourse, doth require both some insight in Logick, and reading in such Authors as haue written of such morall matters. And therfore herein many a Master deserues rather to be beaten then the schollar, for driuing the childe by cruelty, to doe that

which he himself can see no reason how the poor child should be able to do it" (Z_3v). *Contra* Vickers, who writes: "No school teacher would have taught *elocutio* or *memoria* without having first introduced *inventio*, the finding of materials, and *dispositio*, their arrangement" ("Rhetorical and Anti-Rhetorical Tropes," 117).

37. See Green.

38. Lily, [*A short introduction of grammar*] (1567), G_4r. [*FIGURA, est nouata arte aliqua dicendi forma.*] English translation is from Charles Hoole's *The Latine Grammar Fitted for the Use of Schools* (London, 1651), S_3v. For *elocutio* as a practice of the art of grammar, see Green. The six species of *metaplasm* are *prosthesis, aphaeresis, epenthesis, syncope, paragoge, apocope*. This category will sometimes also include *diæresis, synæresis, metathesis, antithesis, tmesis, enallage, archaismus*, and *metaplasmus* (e.g., Hoole, *Examinatio Grammaticae Latine in usum scholarum adornatae* [1661], 125). The eight "figures of construction" in Lily are *appositio, evocatio, syllepsis, prolepsis, zeugma, antiptosis, synthesis, and synecdoche*. This category will sometimes also include *ellipsis, pleonasmus, asyndeton, polysyndeton, anastrophe, synchysis, hypallage*, and *hellenismus* (e.g., Hoole, *Examinatio*, I_8r).

39. Brinsley, O_3r.

40. Brinsley, O_3v.

41. Though introduced in Lily's *Grammar*, these figures will also appear in rhetorical treatises and textbooks as a subgroup of *elocutio*. The individual members of this subgroup will change (the category expands and contracts): Susenbrotus calls them "Schemata Grammatica Syntaxeos" (B_5r); Sherry (1550), "Figure Lexeos or of worde" (B_5v); and Peacham, "Schemates Gramatical" (*Garden* [1577], B_1r).

42. Forshall, 416–417.

43. Brinsley, Dd_2r. Students need not memorize the remaining examples, but "the wordes wherein the force of the examples consist, would bee marked as in the Grammar" (Dd_2r). "Talaeus Rhetorick" refers to the Ramist textbook that was also the source for Fraunce's *Arcadian Rhetorike* and Fenner's *Artes of Logike and Rhetorike*. While Brinsley's account of schoolroom practices is consistent with the second half of the sixteenth century, his designation of schoolbooks is probably more idiosyncratic. The two most popular schoolroom books in *elocutio* in the sixteenth century were Susenbrotus's *Epitome* and Book 4 of the *Ad Herennium* (Baldwin, 1:82).

44. Brinsley, Dd_2r–Dd_2v. Statutes for the Rivington Grammar School describe the parsing of figures as "long painful exercises," and thus they encourage schoolmasters to begin situating "figures of grammar and phrase" within larger organizational patterns, like the three genres (i.e., judicial, deliberative, epideictic) as well as the six parts (i.e., *exordium, narratio*,

partitio, confirmatio, refutatio, peroratio): "And now daily the Master must more diligently than before, teach his Scholars to note and observe the figures of grammar and phrase, how the verbs and nouns be joined together after the fashion that such an author useth. . . . That all these long painful exercises may have some better show of learning, with stronger kinds of persuading and teaching others, the Master may now enter his Scholar into the rules of Rhetoric . . . to let him understand the divers kinds, and parts of an Oration, giving him examples out of other Authors, and how to furnish his sentences with figures of all sorts, as they be plainly set forth in the fourth book [*Ad Herennium*], which will be more easy to follow by daily practice" (quoted by Baldwin, 1:349).

45. Vives, *De Tradendis Disciplinis* (quoted by Vickers, *In Defence*, 261).

46. Brinsley, T$_3$r. Harvey advises students in *Rhetor:* "Mark too all those passages which are ornamental, elaborate, and highly polished. Then compare your findings with a carefully formulated artistic theory. Illustrate the rules with examples, and fit the examples to the rules. . . . As soon as you come upon some trope in the Philippics of Cicero or Demosthenes, or in the comedies of Terence or Aristophanes, I want you to identify it immediately by name, and without hesitation to say something like 'This is a remarkable metonymy.'" Harvey then advises the same with figures: "If not individual words, but rather the whole discourse is figurative (or as the Greeks say, 'schematized'), I think even here you should do the same thing, so that you can easily point out the embellishments of language, and immediately expose the brilliant figures of thought" (trans. Reynolds, *Rhetor*, 92–93). [*& quae sunt ornata, elaborata, perpolitaque omnia, cum arte accuratissime tradita comparate: praecepta exemplis illustrate: exempla praeceptis accommodate . . . Quam primum in tropum aliquem in Ciceronis, aut Demosthenis Philippicis, in Terentii, aut Aristophanis Comoediis incideritis, volo ego vos illico artis vocabulum recitare; atque ita sine vlla haesitatione dicere: haec insignis est Metonymia . . . Si non verba singula modificata, sed tota oratio ἐσηματισμένη vt Graeci vocant, vt nostri, figurata fuerit; idem etiam hic vobis sentio faciendum, quod prius: vt exornationes dictionis facillime indicare; sententiarum ardentiora lumina confestim exponere valeatis.*] (M$_2$v–M$_3$r).

47. Brinsley, V$_1$v. An account of the curriculum at Hertford suggests that such figure pointing required an expertise reserved for the schoolmaster himself. While more advanced scholars were allowed to lecture to their younger counterparts, a detailed account of "Figures and Order of composicion," as well as attention to synonyms and idiomatic differences between Latin and English, would be produced by "the master, observed by the schollers and inserted by them into their paper books" (V.C.H., *Hertfordshire*, 2:90–91; quoted by Baldwin, 1:373).

48. Trans. Reynolds, *Rhetor*, 83. [*Sic . . . in Gallica, aut Italica, aut etiam quauis veste, probene, an secus confecta, & quam illa apta corpori, quamque vel magnifica, vel venusta sit, cum intuendo, dispiciendoque inquirimus: vel etiam consutam iam vestem, introspiciendi causa, dissuimus: Analysis quaedam est. At vero cum nosmetipsi praeliamur, simulachra pingimus, in poculis, vasisque crustas, aut emblemata illigamus; cum vestes ipsi conficimus, Genesis est*] (L_1v–L_2r).

49. Brinsley describes *analysis* as "vnmaking" and *genesis* as "making it againe iust after the same manner" (O_4v).

50. Ascham, 87. Dolven, *Scenes of Instruction*, 38. For example, Harvey in *Rhetor* writes that "the chief purpose of this instrument [*genesis*]—its best and most important function—is to write as much as possible, and as precisely as possible. And of course you should apply in your writing a certain skillful imitation, and in your own compositions . . . you should express with great care and diligence what you have recognized as most splendid and remarkable in the works of Cicero and Demosthenes. . . . Use their . . . brightest metaphors . . . their choicest synecdoches, and their most colorful tropes. Match them, and sometimes even surpass them in refined and elegant stylistic charms, in smooth, flowing periods, and in tasteful repetitions of the same words and sounds. Decorate your speech, as if with sparkling little stars, with appropriate and energetic epizeuxis, with unstrained anadiplosis, with smooth gradation, with splendid anaphora . . . and with any other stylistic ornaments that exist" (trans. Reynolds, 99–100). [*instrumenti istius pars optima, atque praecipua, quam plurimum, et quam accuratissime scribere. Ita nimirum, vt Imitatio quaedam adsit eximia; & quae in M. Tullio, quae in Demosthene . . . clarissimis Metaphoris . . . lectissimis membri, & integri; generis, & speciei modis; singulorum vocabulorum ornatissimis immutationibus vtamini. Non minus comptas, exquisitasque dictionis venustates, non asperiores, & dissolutiores periodos, non ineptiores eorundem verborum, sonorumue repetitiones adhibeatis, quam illi; nonunquam etiam vincatis. Apta, & vehementi Epizeuxi;, non coacta Anadiplosi; gradatione limata; illustri Anaphora . . . siqua sunt adhuc alia dictionis lumina, ijs, tanquam stellulis quibusdam splendentibus orationem distinguatis*] (N_2r–N_3r).

51. Jonson, *Discoveries*, 120–121. Consider the following exercise described by Brinsley, an advanced experiment in *metaphrasis*. After taking a dozen verses out of Virgil or Ovid and converting hexameters into pentameters (or vice versa), the students are then asked to "contract" their lecture, "drawing seauen or eight verses into foure or fiue, or fewer." Here's the trick (the challenge, if you will): though he reduces the original lecture by half (twelve lines become six), the student should be "still labouring to expresse the whole matter of their Author in their owne verse, and euery circumstance, with all significant Metaphors, and other tropes and phrases, so much as they can" (Cc_1v). The exemplary lecture models an ideal of proportion by

its "shape of eloquence," but this exercise encourages dalliances in excess: the exercise that maintains fidelity to the "matter" is successful, but the exercise with the *most* tropes and figures wins. Only one limit is placed on the number of figures in the condensed verse lines: the virtuosic talent of the student. When it comes time to pronounce verse out loud, whether of his own composition or of Virgil's, even the student's voice ought to emphasize those parts of the line that he knows to derive from *elocutio*, "those words in which the chiefe Trope or Figure is" (Ee$_3$v). The act of pronunciation encourages both the student and his audience to perceive the patterns of repetition, balance, and *antithesis* produced by the tropes and figures of *elocutio*. In Fraunce's discussion of pronunciation in *The Arcadian Rhetorike*, this emphasis sometimes has to do with tone (i.e., "without this change of voyce, neither anie *Ironia*, nor liuely *Metaphore* can well bee discerned"); it sometimes has to do with affect (i.e., with respect to "figures of affections, the voyce is more manly, yet diuersely, according to the varietie of passions that are to bee expressed"); and finally, it sometimes has to do with form: "in figures of words which altogether consist in sweete repetitions and dimensions, is chiefly conuersant that pleasant and delicate tuning of the voyce, which resembleth the consent and harmonie of some well ordered song" (H$_7$r).

52. For a "goal-orientated reading," see Grafton and Jardine, "'Studied for Action,'" 30–78. Eugene R. Kintgen defines such reading as "teleological": "primarily practical, aimed at some goal other than private edification, typically conceived of as private education for public action or persuasion" (*Reading in Tudor England*, 92, 148).

53. *Sententia* was a figure in its own right, described by Puttenham as "the Sage Sayer" (321). *Sententia* was also, however, understood as an occasion for other figures or even as a kind of protean shapeshifter. Thus, Peacham describes a category of *sententia* or "a figured sentence, wherof there be as many kindes, as there be figures: If it be figured, it beareth the name of the figure wherewith it is ioyned" (*Garden* [1593], Cc$_3$v–Cc$_4$r). On the relation of figure to *sententiae*, see Crane, 44–46.

54. Cicero, *M.T. Ciceronis Orationum volumen primum-tertium* (Pariis: Apud Simonem Colinaeum, 1532) [Newberry Wing ZP 539 .C674]. "*Articulus*" is roughly equivalent to the compositional unit of the phrase and is sometimes synonymous with *asyndeton* (the lack of conjunction), which is how this reader deploys the term: e.g., "*articulus*" next to the underlined "*violarint, vexarint, perturbarint, euerterint*" (1r); see also: 2v, 4r, 5r. "*Repetitio*" is a Latin term for the more familiar *anaphora* and describes the repetition of a word at the beginning of a series of clauses, sentences, or poetic lines: e.g., "*repetitio*" beside "*& quos lapidibus, quos ferro, quos facibus, quos vi*" (1r); see also: 1v. "*Occupatio*" describes the practice of drawing attention to a topic even as you

declare to pass over that topic: e.g., "*occupatio*" alongside, "*Possum multa dicere de liberalitate, de domesticis oficiis, de Tribunatu militû, de pronuinciali in eo magistratu abstinêtia. sed mihi ante oculos obuersatur reip. dignitas, quæ me ad se rapit. haec minora relinquere hortatur*" (2r–2v). "I can say much of his noble spirit, of his kindly services at home, of his military tribunate, of his incorruptibility in the discharge of that office. But it is the dignity of the State which confronts me, which seizes my attention, and urges me to pass over these less important matters" (Cicero, *Orations: Pro Sestio. In Vatinium*, trans. Gardner, 3.7); for *occupatio*, see also *Ciceronis Orationum*, 3_r.

55. Erasmus, *De Copia*, trans. Knott, 635–648. In his briefest formulation: "Having made up your mind to cover the whole field of literature in your reading (and anyone who wishes to be thought educated must do this at least once in his life), first provide yourself with a full list of subjects. These will consist partly of the main types and subdivisions of vice and virtue, partly of the things of most prominence in human affairs which frequently occur when we have a case to put forward, and they should be arranged according to similars and opposites" (*De Copia*, trans. Knott, 635–636). [*Ergo qui destinuit per omne genus autorum lectione grassari (nam id omnino semel in vita faciendum ei qui velit inter eruditos haberi), prius sibi quam plurimos comparabit locos. Eos sumet partim e generibus ac partibus vitiorum virtutumque, partim ab his quae sunt in rebus mortalium praecipua, quaeque frequentissime solent in suadendo incidere. Eaque conueniet iuxta rationem affinitatis et pugnantiae digere*], (*De Copia*, ed. Knott, 258).

56. [*& quod erat eo nomine, vt ingenerata familiae frugalitas videretur, fauebant, gaudebant, et ad integritatem maiorum spe sua hominem vocabant, materni generis obliti.*] "and because he bore a name which seemed to have made frugality the hereditary virtue of his family, they favoured him, they rejoiced, they encouraged him to prove to be as honest a man as his ancestors, forgetting his mother's blood" (*Orations*, 9.21).

57. "I've heard a worthy man approv'd for learning, / Say," writes Nathaneel Whiting in his verse epistle to the reader, "that *Sidney*-prose / Outmusickes *Tully*, if it scape the nose" (*Le hore di recreatione* [1637], A₆v). After praising the "lightes of speach" of biblical verse, John King complains that "insteed of the writings of Moses and the prophets, and Evangelistes, which were wont to lie in our windowes as the principall ornaments, & to sit in the vppermost roumes as the best guests in our houses, now we haue Arcadia, & the Faery Queene, and Orlando Furioso, with such like frivolous stories: when if the wanton students of our time (for all are studentes, both men and women in this idle learning) would as carefully read and as studiously obserue the eloquent narrations and discourses contained in the Psalmes of David and other sacred bookes, they would finde the~ to be such, as best deserued

the name & co~mendation of the best Poets" (*Lectures upon Jonas* [1599], Z₂r–Z₂v). See also Harvey, *A New Letter of Notable Contents* (1593), Br; Henry Peacham recommends reading the *Arcadia*, an example of the "best and purest English" while studying other languages (lest you forget your own) (*The Compleat Gentleman* [1622], I,); Henry Reynold's praise of the "smooth and artfull *Arcadia*" in *Mythomystes* (1632), 8; Thomas Fuller's praise of Sidney as "a compleat Master of Matter and Language, as his *Arcadia* doth evidence" in *The History of the Worthies of England* (1662), Ll₂r. See also Anthony Scoloker's parodic rendering of such praise in the epistle to *Daiphantus* (1604): "the *Neuer-too-well read Arcadia*, where the *Prose* and *Verce*, (*Matter* and *Words*) are like his *Mistresses* eyes one still excelling another and without Coriuall for to come home to the vulgars *Element*" (A₂r).

58. Sidney, *The Countess of Pembroke's Arcadia* (1598), 2 [Newberry Case Y 1565-.S556]. A page from this copy is the frontispiece of *Renaissance Figures of Speech* and is discussed by Mann, 93.

59. Drawing on Galenic theories of the passions, Daniel T. Lochman argues that at this moment, Urania "is inwardly present to the shepherds due to visceral, imprinted memories . . . memories that inspire a chaste, friendly, and impassioned *ménage à trois*." He describes this sentence as "a climax of joy that displaces pain" (69).

60. Susenbrotus writes: "For if anyone should use these figures sparingly and as the situation demands—as some added condiment—his discourse will be more agreeable." He proceeds to warn against a dish made up wholly of "condiments": "but he who shall have affected too much will miss that same grace of variety" (6). [*Quod si quis hisce figuris parce & cum res poscet utetur, uelut asperso quodam condimento, oratio iucundior erit: at qui nimium affectauerit, ipsam illam gratiam uarietatis amittet*] (A₄v).

61. In the *Defence* Sidney complains of those who "keep Nizolian paperbooks of their figures and phrases" with the result that they "cast sugar and spice upon every dish that is served to the table" (246). See also Aristotle, who complained that "the epithets of Alcidamas seem so tasteless; he does not use them as the seasoning of the meat, but as the meat itself, so numerous and swollen and aggressive are they" (*Rhetoric*, 1406a, 15–20).

62. Folger V.b. 83. Brayman Hackel describes this volume in greater detail, 187–192.

63. Brayman Hackel, 189.

64. Brayman Hackel, 188.

65. Brayman Hackel, 188n153.

66. For a more detailed discussion of Markham's work with Sidney, see Alexander, *Writing after Sidney*, 268–273. Alexander writes that "Markham has two purposes: to set up a world dependent on the memory of Sidney's,

a self-consciously secondary experience; and to offer more—if only quantitatively, with more corpses or antimetaboles—and to overgo" (*Writing after Sidney*, 271–272).

67. Markham, B$_2$v-B$_3$r. I suspect this is a reference to the sentence "O *Vrania*, blessed be thou *Vrania*, the sweetest fairnesse and the fairest sweetnesse." Markham's prose offers a *chiasmsus*—"induring constancies & forlorne indurances"—and then names the grammatical category of the "degree superlative."

68. Markham, B$_3$r.

69. In *The Model of Poesy*, Scott compares the poet's love of ornaments to a parent's love for his child: "They ordinarily offend in loving them too much. . . . So I had need first to warn the poet how he should avoid that fond love and affectation which too evidently shows they too often catch at shadows, with Aesop's dog, and lose by neglecting the substance." He continues: "when with the orators they should consider that words are invented for the thing's sake and that they are of no worth nor estimation farther than as they serve to express our conceits" (46–47). Puttenham compares a "high style . . . disgraced and made foolish and ridiculous by all words affected, counterfeit, and puffed up" to "a wind-ball carrying more countenance than matter." His subsequent comparison of the "wind-ball" to "midsummer pageants in London" and their exhibition of "great and ugly giants marching as if they were alive and armed at all points" is also revealing of Cleophila's position: she is like those "shrewd boys" who discover that "within they are stuffed full of brown paper and tow," exposing the construction of the artifact "to a great derision" (237–238).

70. Scott, 47.

71. See Hartman, 337–355, esp. his discussion of figure's creation of "a breach or space" a "mini-phenomenon" that "dramatizes the differential or, as Saussure calls it, diacritical relation of sound to meaning" (340–341).

72. As Gérard Genette writes, "We know that on certain jukeboxes one can get, for the same price as the latest tune, a period of silence equal to that of a record: it may in fact be a blank record specially made for this purpose. But whatever the means, the lesson of this invention is clear, namely, that in a civilization of noise silence must also be a *product*, that it is the fruit of a technology and a commercial object" (43n52). See also Berger's discussion of *eros*: "*Eros* involves an urge to create an emptiness, a sense of something missing, and project it toward a future. . . . Unlike nature, *eros* demands a vacuum, a permanent *tohu bohu* without which no new creation or revision would be possible" (*Second World and Green World*, 99).

73. Sidney, *Old Arcadia*, 149.

74. See "vaunt" in the *OED*.

75. See "*vanus*" in *Lewis and Short*.
76. Quintilian, 9.2.33. [*falsa enim et incredibilia natura necesse est aut magis moveant, quia supra vera sunt, aut pro vanis accipiantur, quia vera non sunt.*]
77. Moss, "Horace in the Sixteenth Century," 67. Udall's reiteration of Donatus (from which I quote in this paragraph) reads in total: "*Sin falsum aut uanum, aut fictum est, continuo palam est.* But if it be fals or a lie, or els unlikely & to no purpose, or els feined by subtyltie. *Donatus in comentarijs. Falsum est, quo tegitur id quod factum est. Vanum quod fieri non potest. Fictum, quod non est factum, et fieri potuit. Vel, Falsum est fictum mendatium simile ueritati: Vanum, nec possibile nec uerisimile: Fictum, totum sine uero, sed uerisimile. Falsum loqui, mendacis est: Vanum, stultifictum, callidi. Falsum loqui, culpae est. Fictum, uirtutis: Vanum, uecordiae. Falsis decipimur, Fictis delectamur, Vana contemnimus*" (E₆v). In Terence's *Eunuch*, the source of all of this commentary is Parmeno the slave, who claims that his ability to keep a secret is conditional upon the truth-value of that secret. If it is true, he retains it faithfully, but "if anything's false or fanciful or fictional," he cannot help but let it out immediately: "I'm full of cracks, I leak all over" (trans. Barsby, 1.104–105). [*Sin falsum aut vanum aut fictumst, continuo palamst; / plenus rimaraum sum; hac atque illac perfluo*] (1.104–105).
78. See "*vanus*" in *Lewis and Short*.
79. See "*contemnimo*" and "*stultifictus*" in *Lewis and Short*.
80. See Moss, "Horace in the Sixteenth Century," 66–67.
81. Sidney, *Old Arcadia*, 149.
82. Walker, 327.
83. Sidney, *Defence*, 235, 219.
84. Horace, trans. Fairclough, lines 6–9. [*credite, Pisones, isti tabulae fore librum / persimilem, cuius, velut aegri somnia, vanae / fingentur species, ut nec pes nec caput uni / reddatur formae.*] Melanchthon likens the use of affected Latin to the production of "empty dreams" (*inania somnia*). He warns that "those who fashion a new type of speech, generally let important things fall by the wayside. For, while they are thinking up the new speech, they dream up new things, while they inefficiently hanker after praise for their subtlety. And despite that, when we look close at those things, then they are found to be nothing but empty dreams" (trans. La Fontaine, 228). [*Plerunque etiam isti, qui novum sermonis genus fingunt, res amittunt. Ut enim novum sermonis excogitant, ita nouas res somniant, dum inepte affectant laudem subtilitatis. Et tamen res illæ inspectae, nihil esse deprehenduntur nisi inania somnia.*]
85. Quintilian, 9.3.54. [*gradatio, quae dicitur κλῖμαξ, apertiorem habet artem et magis adfectatam ideoque esse rarior debet.*]
86. Hoskins, 13.
87. This point of distinction is most explicit when *gradatio* was measured against the figure known as *anadiplosis*: what *gradatio* describes over a

succession of clauses, *anadiplosis* describes over just two clauses. The formal difference between *gradatio* and *anadiplosis* was therefore a measure of degree rather than kind. See Hoskins, 12; Blount, B$_4$r; J. Smith, 94.

88. Peacham, *Garden* (1593), T$_3$r–T$_3$v.

89. From this perspective, *gradatio* is most like (and discussed in relation to) a method of amplification known as *incrementum*, "words that progress, step by step, from the least important points to the most important ones" as well as the chain of reasoning known as *sorites* (what Hoskins called the "climbing argument" [12–13]) (Melanchthon, trans. La Fontaine, 283). [*Incrementum est, cum non eiusdem significationis verba coniungimus, sed per gradus ab infimis ad summa imus*]). Peacham describes *incrementum* as "the Orators scaling ladder, by which he climeth to the top of high comparison" (*Garden* [1593], Aar).

90. In his discussion of "order" in composition, Quintilian suggests that "there is also another species of order which may be entitled natural, as for example when we speak of 'men and women,' 'day and night,' 'rising and setting in preference to the reverse order'" (9.4.23–24). [*est et alius naturalis ordo, ut* viros ac feminas, diem ac noctem, ortum et occasum *dicas potius quam retrorsum.*] In *Arguments in Rhetoric against Quintilian*, Ramus does not disagree, though he relocates the authority of that order in "subjects" rather than "words": "But if, as usually happens, a dignified order must be observed, certainly it should be observed from the subjects themselves, not from the order of the words" (151). [*Veruntamen si quid ordinis ista dignitas ut plerunque obseruanda est, certe de rebus ipsis, non de verborum ordine obseruanda est*]. Peacham, writing of *incrementum*, suggests the reversal of values: "When we make our saying grow and increase by an orderly placing of our words, making the latter word always exceede the former, in force of signifycation, contrary to the naturall order of thinges, for that euer putteth the worthyest and wayghtiest wordes fyrst, but this placeth them alwayes last." "In this fygure," he cautions, "order must be dilligently obserued, that the stronger may follow the weaker, and the worthyer the lesse worthy, otherwise, you shal not increase the Oration, but make a mingle mangle, as doeth the ignoraunt" ([1577], O$_2$v). Peacham adds the following caution to "climax" in his 1593 revision: "In using this figure we ought to obserue a meane, that there be not too many degrees and also to forsee that the degrees following, may rather increase then diminish in signification and lastly, that they ascend that they may end with a clause of importance" (*Garden* [1593], L$_3$v). See Parker, *Literary Fat Ladies*, 97–125.

91. As Melanchthon writes: "The same expressions, when applied for the purpose of confirming or confuting, are bases for argument and the sinews, as they are called. When applied for the purpose of adorning, they

are called rhetorical ornaments" (trans. La Fontaine, 264). [*Nam iidem loci cum confirmandi aut confutandi causa adhibentur, argumenta sunt ac nervi, ut vocant. Cum adhibentur illuminandi causa, dicuntur ornamenta.*] After defining *gradatio* as when "we proceed by steps from one thing to another, and so forth, in such a way that the nearest (last) word will be repeated in each case," Melanchthon refers his reader to his discussion of causes in his chapter on dialectic: "But we have explained in the Chapter on Logic, that causes and effects, general and specific facts are connected in that manner" (trans. La Fontaine, 290). [*cum per gradus itur ab aliis ad alia, ita ut semper proximum verbum repetatur . . . Diximus autem in dialecticis hoc modo connecti causas et effectus, genera et species.*]

92. J. Smith understands *polyptoton* to be related to *gradatio* and *anadiplosis*, describing it as "a kinde of Gradation" (110).

93. Aristotle, *Topica*, trans. Forster, 2.9.114a. On *polyptoton*, see Fahnestock, 168–172. As we saw in Chapter 1, *polyptoton* was correlated with the place of *inventio* known as conjugation, which is why Abraham Fraunce and Dudley Fenner banished conjugation from the art of dialectic.

94. Aristotle writes: "If 'justice' is something praiseworthy, then 'the just man' and 'the just action' and 'justly' will be something praiseworthy" (*Topica*, 2.9.114b).

95. Puttenham, 288.

96. The following discussion of *hyperbole* is indebted to Ettenhuber and Adelman.

97. Hoskins, 29. He adds, "this figure is more credit to your wit than to your speech" (29).

98. *Hyperbole* asserts what is, to cite Susenbrotus, "beyond belief" but not "beyond measure" [*Est autem omnis Hyperbole ultra fidem, non tamen esse debet ut ita modum*]: it "says no more than the situation warrants, but still what is true is understood from what is false" (17). [*Breuiter plus dicit Hyperbole quae res habet, attamen quod verum est, ex falso intelligitur*] (B_2r).

99. Peacham, *Garden* (1577), D_4v. He defines *hyperbole* as "a sentence or saying surmounting the truth onely for the cause of increasing or diminishing, not with purpose to deceiue by speaking untruly, but with desire to amplifie the greatnesse or smalnesse of things by the exceeding similitude. The use hereof serueth most fitly for amplification, and that especially when matters require either to be amplified in the greatest degree, or diminished in the least" (*Garden* [1593], F_4r). Both *hyperbole* and *gradatio* are therefore concerned with quantity and proportion: "By this figure," Peacham writes of *hyperbole*, "the Orator either lifteth up high or casteth downe low, either stretcheth things to the uttermost length, or pressenth them to the least quantitie: so high is the reach, & so wide is the compasse of this figure, that it

mounteth to the highest things, compasseth the widest, and comprehendeth the greatest" (*Garden* [1593], Gr.).

100. J. Smith, $E_3v–E_4r$. Ettenhuber argues that for Sidney, *hyperbole* "drives the process of poetic idealization," but she also reserves for *hyperbole* a function independent of the ideology of what "should be": "it also provides," Ettenhuber writes, "the dynamic moral principle—the process of *moving beyond* the boundaries of our own moral self—that forms the foundation of Sidney's defense" (212). It is in this sense that *hyperbole* "fosters a sense of perspectival mobility, and an enhanced awareness of the ways in which boundaries, norms, and conventions are constructed" (212–213). See also Adelman, who argues that *hyperbole* "presents the spectacle of man making his own imaginative universe in despite of all reality, in despite of all human limitation" (115); she says of Antony's *hyperboles*: "Antony's words assert his access to a hyperbolical world where such things actually happen, a world beyond the reach of metaphor. . . . His words do not give us the protection of regarding them merely as apt metaphors: they make their claim as literal action. We may choose to disbelieve their claim; but in doing so, we are rejecting a version of reality, not the validity of a metaphor" (106).

101. As Jonas Barish describes it, "A logical style, to say it summarily, is one that marks out divisions of thought, that inspects things in order to classify and subdivide them either into antithetic or into complimentary components, which strives for clarity of syntax by opposing clause to clause, phrase to phrase, and word to word . . . and which, furthermore, tends to develop its ideas in terms of some of the traditional topics of logic still felt as logical today: definition, cause and effect, antecedent and consequent, alternative hypotheses, and the like" ("Prose Style of John Lyly," 28). Jonathan Crewe's critique of Barish is exacting and concise: "Instead of healing the split between ornamental figures and meaningful words, he assigns a semantic role to syntax and thus in one stroke transforms a pure rhetorical excess (or redundancy) into a pure economy of representation. The 'world,' even if it is only that of the artist, becomes that which is *signified* by a given syntactical order, and any apparent lack of significance in Lyly's mechanical euphuism is more than adequately redressed. This success is paid for, however, by the transformation of reading into a Sisyphean allegorization of syntax" (16). I find A. Davis's sense that *gradatio* points "toward Sidney's interest in a world of temporality and incessant change" compelling (496; see esp. 500–501, 505–506).

102. Crewe, 22–23.

103. Warley, 7.

104. Sidney, *The Countess of Pembroke's Arcadia*, 291. In both the *Old* and *New Arcadia*, the glove is significant for a "proportion" that "shewed well" what once was but no longer is there: a body part.

105. Fraunce, *Arcadian Rhetorike*, C₈r. While I have retained most of the formatting of the original, the line "Pleasure might cause her read, reading might make her know" ran long on the page, forcing the compositor to place the final word "know" at the end of the next line, marked off by a *parenthesis*. I have silently smoothed that out in the above.

3. QUEENLY FIG TREES: FIGURES OF SPEECH AND *DECORUM*

1. The passage reads: "If a painter chose to join a human head to the neck of a horse, and to spread feathers of many a hue over limbs picked up now here now there, so that what at the top is a lovely woman ends below in a black and ugly fish, could you, my friends, if favoured with a private view, refrain from laughing?" [*Humano capiti cervicem pictor equinam / iungere si velit, et varias inducere plumas / undique collatis membris, ut turpiter atrum / desinat in piscem mulier formosa superne, / spectatum admissi risum teneatis, amici?*] (Horace, lines 1–5).

2. See Attridge, 17–45. As Angel Day glosses in *The English Secretorie* (1586): "*decorum*, the very direct square and measure wherof, conduceth all thinges with such exquisite performance, as whereunto neuer afterward ensueth any iust reprehension, willeth (as *Horace* in his booke *de arte poetica* excellentlie deliuereth) that vnto euery thing bee geuen his true nature, collour and proportion, aswel with pen as pencill, abhorring as monstrous, and enemie unto skill, what otherwise vnaduisedly shall be portrayed or described, by reason whereof, whatsoeuer carryeth wyth it selfe a iust *decorum*, is sayde to be neate, apte, and comelie, the contrarie whereof as altogeather impugned, is sayde to be vnmeete or vnseemely" (B₄r).

3. On the involuntary nature of laughter, see Herrick, 50–52. Cicero describes this physical compulsion as the ground that he will not cover in his discussion of laughter in *De Oratore*: "how it comes into being, and bursts out so unexpectedly that, strive as we may, we cannot restrain it, and how at the same instant it takes possession of the lungs, voice, pulse, countenance, and eyes" [*quomodo exsistat, atque ita repente erumpat, ut eum cupientes tenere nequeamus, et quomodo simul latera, os, venas, vultum, oculos occupet*] (Cicero, *De Oratore*, trans. Sutton and Rackam, 2.58.235).

4. See also Horace's laughter as a response to poetry that fails to arouse the emotions: "Not enough is it for poems to have beauty: they must have charm, and lead the hearer's soul where they will. As men's faces smile on those who smile, so they respond to those who weep. If you would have me weep, you must first feel grief yourself: then, O Telephus or Peleus, will your misfortunes hurt me: if the words you utter are ill suited, I shall laugh or fall asleep" (lines 99–105). [*Non satis est pulchra esse poemata; dulcia sunto / et quocumque volent animum auditoris agunto. / ut ridentibus arrident, ita flentibus adsunt / humani voltus : si vis me flere, dolendum est / primum ipsi tibi : tunc tua*

me infortunia laedent, / Telephe vel Peleu; male si mandata loqueris, / aut dormitabo aut ridebo.]

5. For this two-part approach to *decorum* as a shift in relative emphasis between "audience" and "artifact," see Vickers, *In Defence*, 64, 80–81. Drawing on Panofsky, Vickers helpfully likens the distinction between the *decorous* and the *indecorous* modes to the difference between hypotactic and paratactic sentences or between classical and romanesque sculptures (*In Defence*, 244–253).

6. For an overview of the various axes of *decorum*, see Tuve, 192–247; T. McAlindon, 6–16; and especially Rebhorn's useful discussion in "Outlandish Fears," 3–24. For examples of an emphasis on person, time, and place, see Vives, *On Education*, 181; and *De Ratione Dicendi*, trans. Cooney, 164–202; Puttenham, 347–378; E. K.'s "Epistle" to Spenser's *Shepheardes Calender* (1579), in which E. K. praises the poet for "his dewe observing of Decorum everye where, in personages, in seasons, in matter, in speach, and generally in al seemely simplycitie of handling his matter, and framing his words," in *The Yale Shorter Poems*, 13–14. For praise of Spenser's *decorum* in the *Shepheardes Calender*, see also Webbe, *A Discourse of English Poetry* (1586), E$_4$v. See also the following related discussions of "discretion": Hillman, 73–90; J. Miller, 452–473.

7. Mantuan, A$_3$v–A$_4$r.

8. See Vickers's widely accepted account of "the expressive function of rhetorical figures" (*In Defence*, 294–339); see also Berger's critique of this account and its privileging of the "transactional" dimension of rhetoric in "Narrative as Rhetoric," 173–217. The master trope for the *decorous* alignment of *ethos* and speech act is *prosopopoeia*: insofar as exercises like those in Apthonius's *Progymnasmata* trained schoolboys to animate absent persons linguistically with careful attention to "'the motions' of the speaker's 'mind in every respect,'" those same exercises constituted a structural pivot between rhetoric's *ethos* and drama's character. See Enterline, *Shakespeare's Schoolroom*, 92–93, esp. 62–94). See also Alexander, "Prosopopoeia," 97–114; A. Kinney, 22–23 and *in passim*.

9. Robert Roche's description of his heroine's face in *Eustathia* (1599) is illustrative of this quantitative approach to *decorum*: "And this decorum sitting in her face: / The whole and partes, resembled and were like / To perfect numbers, in Arithmetike" (B$_5$v).

10. Scott, 35. It is in this sense that Quintilian uses Horace's image as a visual illustration of the stylistic vice known as *soraismus* or *cumulatio*. Warning against "the indiscriminate mixture of grand words with mean, old with new, and poetic with colloquial," Quintilian suggests that by thrusting such a mishmash of languages into a single period, the misguided orator

combines horse and human right at the neck. [*si quis sublimia humilibus, vetera novis, poetica vulgaribus misceat*] (8.3.60). In *De Officiis*, Cicero appeals to the vice of *cumulatio* to explain the "uniform consistency" demanded by *decorum*: "If there is any such thing as propriety at all, it can be nothing more than uniform consistency in the course of our life as a whole and all its individual actions. . . . For as we ought to employ our mother-tongue, lest, like certain people who are continually dragging in Greek words, we draw well-deserved ridicule upon ourselves, so we ought not to introduce anything foreign into our actions or our life in general" [*Omnino si quicquam est decorum, nihil est profecto magis quam aequabilitas cum universae vitae, tum singularum actionum . . . Ut enim sermone eo debemus uti, qui innatus est nobis, ne, ut quidam, Graeca verba inculcantes iure optimo rideamur, sic in actiones omnemque vitam nullam discrepantiam conferre debemus*] (Cicero, *De Officiis*, trans. Miller, 1.111–112). For a discussion of *cumulatio* and the vernacular, see Mann, 171–200.

11. In his defense of a teleological oration, according to which "nothing can be explained, stated or grasped in an orderly fashion, except some proposition be formulated which includes the sum total of the case," Philip Melanchthon invokes Horace's chimera: "And it can often be perceived in meetings of the unskilled how great the significance of this precept is when, with no definite proposition having been expressed as the subject of debate, their speeches no more hang together than that picture in Horace where the painter attaches a horse's neck to a human head, etc." [*Nihil ordine explicari, dici, aut percipi potest, nisi constituatur aliqua propositio, quae summam causae comprehendat . . . Ac saepe in concionibus indoctorum iudicari potest, quanta huius praecepti vis sit, ubi, postquam nulla certa propositio constituta est, de qua dicendum sit, oratio non magis cohaeret, quam illa apud Horacium pictura, in qua humano capiti cervicem pictor equinam addit etc.*] (trans. La Fontaine, 115–116).

12. For the relation of form to organicism in twentieth-century criticism, see Wolfson, esp. 1–30. Other important genealogies of form and formalism include Leighton and Levine.

13. Puttenham, 109. On "mulitformity uniform" and the difference between icastic and fantastic art, see Kalas, 136–144.

14. Della Casa, 102. See also Scott on "*beauty*" (32).

15. Della Casa, 102–103. Cicero's Caesar describes "deformity" [*deformitate*] as an object of laughter in *De Oratore*, 2.58.236. See also Sidney's critique of comedy that deals in laughter rather than delight, in the *Defence of Poesy*: "For delight we scarcely do but in things that have a conveniency to ourselves or to the general nature; laughter almost ever cometh of things most disproportioned to ourselves and nature . . . we laugh at deformed creatures, wherein certainly we cannot delight" (245).

16. See "deform" and "difform" in the *Oxford English Dictionary*.

17. "The embellishment of oratory is achieved in the first place by general style and by a sort of inherent colour and flavour; for that it shall be weighty and pleasing and scholarly and gentlemanly and attractive and polished, and shall possess the requisite amount of feeling and pathos, is not a matter of particular divisions of the framework, but these qualities must be visible in the whole of the structure." [*Ornatur igitur oratio genere primum et quasi colore quodam et suco suo; nam ut gravis, ut suavis, ut erudita sit, ut liberalis, ut admirabilis, ut polita, ut sensus, ut dolores habeat quantum opus sit, non est singulorum articulorum: in toto spectantur haec corpore*] (Cicero, *De Oratore*, 3.24.96). See also the discussion of "the opening passage" of an oration, which "should be so closely connected with the speech that follows as to appear to be not an appendage, like the prelude to a piece of music, but an integral part of the whole structure" [*Connexum autem ita sit principium consequenti orationi ut non tamquam citharoedi prooemium affictum aliquid sed cohaerens cum omni corpore membrum esse videatur*] (Cicero, *De Oratore*, 2.80.325).

18. Wilson, *Art of Rhetoric*, 194. Quintilian writes: "For my own part I regard these particular ornaments of oratory to be, as it were, the eyes of eloquence. On the other hand, I should not like to see the whole body full of eyes, for fear that it might cripple the functions of the other members, and, if I had no alternative, I should prefer the rudeness of ancient eloquence to the license of the moderns" [*Ego vero haec lumina orationis velut oculos quosdam esse eloquentiae credo. Sed neque oculos esse toto corpore velim, ne cetera membra officium suum perdant; et, si necesse sit, veterem illum horrorem dicendi malim quam istam novam licentiam*] (8.5.34). See also Jonson, *Discoveries*, 32–33.

19. Puttenham, 239; Gascoigne, 1:52.

20. On *sprezzatura*, see Berger, *The Absence of Grace*, 9–25; Whigham, esp. 88–136; Javitch, esp. 18–75.

21. Cited by *Part* and page number: *Part 2, 36*.

22. *Part 2, 41*. "If you did, Madame, butt see her speake," Antissius reiterates, "you wowld say you never saw soe direct a mad woeman" (*Part 2, 41*).

23. E.g., Naomi Miller, who writes that Antissia's "inability to frame a harmonious lyric bears witness to her failure to establish a stable position as a subject, so that her texts give voice to the disintegration rather than the emergence of female subjectivity" (175); Sheila T. Cavanagh, who writes that "as Antissia exits the narrative, the reader is left with images of a wildly-clad woman storming the beaches, filling both air and paper with evidence of her mental wanderings" (76). By contrast, see Melissa Sanchez, who understands Antissia's style as an effect of her political position: "Although Antissia is eventually cured of her madness, the clumsy, uncontrolled poetry that she writes up until that point registers the impotence of the courtier

who can express anger and opposition only indirectly in fiction and poetry" (138–140).

24. See Fletcher, 70–146; Fumerton, 21–22; Brown, 32–36.

25. Carson, 98a.3.

26. Fletcher, 110.

27. It is in this sense that Fumerton argues that "we must open up the cosmos of Renaissance ornaments to reveal the great allegory of history they harbor": "Whenever we see a piece of such ornament—a jewel, an epic simile, any peripheral fact or artifact that merely 'adorns' the center—behind it lies the historical. There is no such thing, in other words, as 'pure' ornament. Pure ornament, pure aestheticism, always hangs around the bespangled neck of history; and, reciprocally, history never appears naked of ornamentation" (22).

28. Demetrius, 114–115.

29. See Brown on "prodigality": "The very negative aspects that define it as reprehensible, such as peripherality and ornamentality, are explored as ways of articulating change and of rewriting inherited hierarchies of value" (24).

30. Aristotle, *Poetics*, 1457^b. See also *Poetics*, ed. and trans. Halliwell, 1457^b, n. "e": "It is assumed that an explanation of 'ornament,' *kosmos*, has dropped out here" (107).

31. On the constellation of these terms, see Puttenham, 348; McAlindon, 6–7; Attridge, 29–30.

32. Aristotle, *Rhetoric*, 1408^a.

33. As Day explains, it is an "*indecorum* . . . when vppon a grosse conceite: a trifling toye a matter of no valewe, wee seeke to frame high and loftie sentences" (B_4r).

34. As Wilson states, "Such are thought apt words that properly agree unto that thing which they signify, and plainly express the nature of the same" (*Art of Rhetoric*, 191).

35. The *locus classicus* for this critique is Plato's *Gorgias*, where Socrates says of "the rhetor, and rhetoric": "It does not at all need to know how the matters themselves stand, but to have discovered a certain device of persuasion so as to appear to know more than those who know, to those who don't know" (trans. Nichols, 459^b–459^c).

36. *De Oratore*, 1.5.17. [*Est enim et scientia comprehendenda rerum plurimarum, sine qua verborum volubilitas inanis atque irridenda est.*]

37. *De Oratore*, 1.11.50–51. [*Unum erit profecto, quod ei, qui bene dicunt, adferant proprium: compositam orationem, et ornatam, et artificio quodam et expolitione distinctam. Haec autem oratio, si res non subest ab oratore percepta et cognita, aut nulla sit necesse est, aut omnium irrisione ludatur. Quid est enim tam furiosum,*

quam verborum, vel optimorum atque ornatissimorum, sonitus inanis, nulla subiecta sententia, nec scientia?]

38. In *A direction or preparatiue to the study of the lawe* (1600), William Fulbecke writes that "Wordes if they bee not vested with the substaunce of thynges, are of no force: Rhetoricke which is the Artificer of perswasion . . . if it bee bestowed in vayne and superfluous matters, it may bee tearmed *Mataeotechina*, a friuolous labour, and a tryflyng arte" (F_8r).

39. Bacon writes in *The Advancement of Learning* (1605) that "for minds empty and unfraught with matter" an education in logic or "judgement" and rhetoric or "ornament" is like teaching someone "to weigh or to measure, or to paint the wind," with the result that "the wisdom of those arts, which is great and universal, is almost made contemptible, and is degenerate into childish sophistry and ridiculous affectation" (173). See also Harvey, *Rhetor*, M_3v; Puttenham, 237–238.

40. See Poole, 237–251. Quintilian's treatise on the vices, *De Causis Corruptae Eloquentiae*, is no longer extant, but he provides a discussion of the vices in Book 8 of the *Institutes* (8.3.42–48).

41. [*Totidem autem generibus corrumpitur oratio quot ornatur*] (Quintilian, 8.3.57–58). Demetrius makes a similar point at the level of the types of style: "But just as in the sphere of ethics certain bad qualities lie close to certain good ones (rashness, for example, next to bravery, and shame to modest respect), so too the types of style have neighbouring faulty styles" (114–115).

42. E.g., Puttenham on *sententia*: "Heed must be taken that such rules or sentences be choicely made and not often used, lest excess breed loathsomeness" (321); on *antithesis*: "Isocrates the Greek orator was a little too full of this figure . . . and many of our modern writers in vulgar use it in excess and incur the vice of fond affectation" (296). Aristotle advises that "strange words, compound words, and invented words must be used sparingly and on few occasions. . . . The reason for this restriction has been already indicated: they depart from what is suitable, in the direction of excess" (*Rhetoric*, 1404^b 28–32).

43. Puttenham, 259.

44. Puttenham, 340–341. On the overuse of alliteration, see also Gascoigne, 1:52.

45. This approach to *decorum* shares with early modern theories of prosody Neoplatonic appeals to harmony and proportion that frequently invoke Pythagoras as an authority. E.g., Willis in *De Re Poetica* (1576): "The origin of metrical form is from God the Almighty Creator, in that He created this universe and whatever is contained in its sphere with a fixed design, as it were by measure; to such an extent that Pythagoras has asserted that there is a harmony in celestial and in earthly things. For how could the universe exist, un-

less it were governed by a fixed order and established harmony? Again, all the instruments we use are made with certain proportions—that is, by *measure*. If this happens with other things, how much more so with language, which gives expression to all things?" [*Metri origo a Deo opt. max. est, quippe qui hunc mundum & quaecunq; eius ambitu continetur, certa ratione, quasi metro composuit, vsq adeo vt harmoniam in coelestibus terrenisq; rebus Pythagoras confirmarit. quo enim pacto mundus consisteret, nisi certa ratione ac definitis numeris ageretur? omnia quoque instrumenta, quibus vtimur, mensura quadam. i. metro fiunt. quod si hoc caeteris in rebus accidit, quanto magis in oratione, quae res omnes interpretatur?*] (63–65). For a discussion of Pythagorean harmony and *musica speculativa* in early modern England, see Ortiz; Hollander, *The Untuning of the Sky*, 20–51. The close relationship between meter and figures is most visible in those grammatical figures that, in describing the alteration of a letter at the beginning, middle, or end of a word, bear directly on the construction of quantitative verse in Latin. Though the relationship is different in vernacular meter, they remain intertwined. Puttenham makes the connection between figure and meter explicit: "A word as he lieth in course of language is many ways figured, and thereby not a little altered in sound, which consequently alters the tune and harmony of a meter as to the ear" (245).

46. Puttenham, 267.

47. See Cicero's *De Officiis*, where *decorum* is aligned with temperance: "For, as physical beauty with harmonious symmetry of limbs engages the attention and delights the eye, for the very reason that all the parts combine in harmony and grace, so this propriety . . . engages the approbation of our fellow-men by the order, consistency, and self-control it imposes upon every word and deed" [*Ut enim pulchritudo corporis apta compositione membrorum movet oculos et delectat hoc ipso, quod inter se omnes partes cum quodam lepore consentiunt, sic hoc decorum, quod elucet in vita, movet approbationem eorum, quibuscum vivitur, ordine et constantia et moderatione dictorum omnium atque factorum*] (1.100). For Cicero, *decorum* sets one on the path to "harmony with Nature and the faithful observance of her laws" [*ad convenientiam conservationemque naturae*] (1.100). Though Cicero is primarily concerned with "conduct" more broadly conceived, the *decorous* style that he describes in his rhetorical treatises is here a kind of model and ideal: "The conduct of our life shall balance and harmonize," he writes, "as in a finished speech" [*ut, quem ad modum in oratione constanti, sic in vita omnia sint apta inter se et convenientia*] (1.144). In distinguishing the divine efficient cause from the formal cause practiced by artificers such as the potter or carpenter, an early modern translation of Augustine's *City of God* (1610) reads: "for from that . . . all diuiding, and all effectiue diuine power, which cannot be made, but makes, and which in the beginning gaue rotundity both to the Heauens & Sunne, from the same,

had the eye the apple, and all other round figures that we see in nature their rotundity not from any externall effectiue, but from the depth of the creators power that said, *I fill heauen and earth*: and whose wisdome reacheth from end to end, ordering all in a delicate *Decorum*" (trans. Healey, R$_5$r–$_6$v).

48. E.g., Puttenham, 239–240, 281–282; Wilson writes: "When we have learned usual and accustomable words to set forth our meaning, we ought to join them together in apt order, that the ear may delight in hearing the harmony. . . . Composition, therefore, is an apt joining together of words in such order that neither the ear shall espy any jar, nor yet any man shall be dulled with overlong drawing out of a sentence, nor yet much confounded with mingling of clauses, such as are needless, being heaped together without reason and used without number" (*Art of Rhetoric*, 192).

49. As Puttenham explains in his discussion of *decorum*, if the mind and the ear "discover any ill-favoredness or disproportion to the parts apprehensive, as, for example, when a sound is either too loud or too low or otherwise confused, the ear is ill-affected; so is the eye if the color be sad or not luminous and recreative, or the shape of a membered body without his due measures and symmetry. . . . These excesses or defects or confusions and disorders in the sensible objects are deformities and unseemly to the sense" (347). See Blank, *Shakespeare and the Mismeasure of Renaissance Man*, esp. 15–40.

50. Hoskins, 39.

51. "For everybody is able to discriminate between what is right and what wrong in matters of art and proportion by a sort of subconscious instinct, without having any theory of art or proportion of their own" [*Omnes enim tacito quodam sensu sine ulla arte aut ratione quae sint in artibus ac rationibus recta ac prava diiudicant*] (*De Oratore*, 3.50.195). For *decorum* as the province of the aristocracy, see Attridge; Rebhorn, "Outlandish Fears"; and Taylor, 127–150.

52. "A writer must disguise his art and give the impression of speaking naturally and not artificially," Aristotle explains: "Naturalness is persuasive, artificiality is the contrary; for our hearers are prejudiced and think we have some design against them, as if we were mixing wines for them" (*Rhetoric*, 1404^{b}15–22). Puttenham writes that "the well-tuning of your words and clauses to the delight of the ear maketh your information no less plausible to the mind than to the ear—no, though you filled them with never so much sense and sententiousness. Then also must the whole tale (if it tend to persuasion) bear his just and reasonable measure, being rather with the largest than with the scarcest" (281). Cicero says that "the ear, or rather the mind which receives the message of the ear, contains in itself a natural capacity for measuring all sounds. Accordingly it distinguishes between long and short,

and always looks for what is complete and well proportioned: certain phrases it feels to be shortened, mutilated as it were, and is offended by these as if it were cheated of its just due; others are too long and run beyond reasonable bounds; the ear rejects these still more; for in this as in most things excess is more offensive than deficiency" [*Aures ipsae enim vel animus aurium nuntio naturalem quandam in se continet vocum omnium mensionem. Itaque et longiora et breviora iudicat et perfecta ac moderata semper exspectat; mutila sentit quaedam et quasi decurtata, quibus tanquam debito fraudetur offenditur, productiora alia et quasi immoderatius excurrentia, quae magis etiam aspernantur aures; quod cum in plerisque tum in hoc genere nimium quod est offendit vehementius quam id quod videtur parum*] (*Orator*, 177–178).

53. Fumerton, 29–66. Grateful for the king of Romania's friendship, the king of Achaia requests his daughter: He "sent Embassadours to demand his daughter in marriage for his sonne, and withall to have the Princesse sent unto him, to be brought up together, to the end, that conversation (a ready friend to love) might nurse their affections so wel, as she might as contentedly be his daughter, as it was affectionately desired of him" (*Part 1*, 30).

54. Fumerton, 37. "Through circulation," Fumerton explains, "the child underwent translation from mere trifle to polished ornament—from being peripheral, detached, and primitive to being central, connected, and cultivated" (44).

55. Fumerton, 44.

56. For romance as a "form which simultaneously quests for and postpones a particular end, objective, or object," see Parker, *Inescapable Romance*, 4, esp. 54–113. Hearing of "the noise of Antissia's losse, the likelihood of her beauty, the griefe of Parents, and the wrong done to my selfe," the betrothed Leandrus sets out to recover his intended: "These did not only invite, but command me to be diligent, in making all these pieces joyne again in the first body of content" (*Part 1*, 41). Leandrus is said to be "afflicted with the losse of Antissia" and means to go "straight into Morea to finde her" (*Part 1*, 49); under the influence of charms and forgetting to wait for a boat to convey him, Leandrus throws himself into the sea, "crying out he would have Antissia in spite of the valiantest black Knight" (*Part 1*, 59). Fortuitously rescued by a few friends, the next we hear of Leandrus's heart it belongs to Pamphilia (*Part 1*, 101).

57. *Part 2*, 33.

58. *Part 2*, 40. Antissia's "poeticall furies" are the direct result of her having taken up with a private tutor fluent in Ovidian poetry, a "skoller ... who had binn mad in studying how to make a peece of poetrie to excell Ovid, and to bee more admired then hee is" (*Part 2*, 33, 40). For Ovid's exilic poetics generally and their relation to questions of metamorphosis and stylistic

degeneration, see Gareth Williams; Dickenson. For Ovid's exile elegies in the sixteenth century, see Pugh, 152–202; Stapleton, 41–73. On Ovid and poetic license, see James, "The Poet's Toys," 103–127; James, "Ovid and the Question of Politics in Early Modern England," 343–373.

59. *Part 2*, 41.
60. *Part 2*, 35.
61. For the interrelatedness of style, dress, and gesture, see Seneca, "Epistle 114 [On Style as a Mirror for Character]," in *Epistles 93–124*, trans. Gummere, 300–319.
62. *Part 2*, 33.
63. *Part 2*, 33.
64. Rosindy describes Antissia's hybrid compositions as disturbing formal anomalies, but the indistinction of prose from verse doubles as both stylistic ideal and pejorative in early modern rhetorical theory. In a letter to Andrew Ammonius (1513), for example, Erasmus declares: "Just as Philoxenus delivered the opinion that the sweetest-tasting fish were those that were not fish, the most delicious flesh that which was not flesh; and reckoned, again, that the most delightful sea-voyages were those close to the shore and the most delightful land walks those by the seaside; so do I take the greatest pleasure in rhetorical poems and in poetical rhetoric, such that one can sense the poetry in the prose and the style of a good orator in the poetry" (Erasmus, *The Correspondence of Erasmus: Letters 142–297 [1501–1514]*, trans. Mynors and Thomson, 270–271). [*Quemadmodum Philoxenus suauissimos iudicauit pisces qui pisces non essent, et iucundissimas carnes quae carnes non essent, rursus amoenissimam existimauit nauigationem iuxta littus, ambulationem iuxta mare; ita me vehementer delectat poema rhetoricum et rhetor poeticus, vt et in oratione soluta carmen agnoscas et in carmine rhetoricam phrasin*] (*Opus Epistolarvm Des. Erasmi Roterodami*, ed. Allen, 545). While we might expect meter to generate the formally patterned intersection of this Venn diagram, that intersection was instead defined by figures of speech that conditioned the rhythm of both prose and verse more broadly, including *isocolon, parison, polyptoton, similiter cadens, similiter desinentes*, and *paroemion* (those figures that we now use to describe the "euphuistic mode"). In Wilson's *Art of Rhetoric*, the composition that conflates prose with verse becomes the sign of the excessive use of figures of speech. In his discussion of *similiter cadens* and *similiter desinens* (figures routinely likened to the vernacular rhyme), Wilson cautions: "Some end their sentences all alike, making their talk rather to appear rimed meter than to seem plain speech, the which as it much delighteth being measurably used, so it much offendeth when no mean is regarded. I heard a preacher delighting much in this kind of composition, who used so often to end his sentence with words like unto that which went before, that in my judgment there was not a dozen sentences in

Notes to pages 84–86

his whole sermon but they ended all in rime for the most part. Some not best disposed wished the preacher a lute, that with his rimed sermon he might use some pleasant melody and so the people might take pleasure diverse ways and dance if they list. Certes there is a mean, and no reason to use any one thing at all times, seeing nothing delighteth—be it never so good—that is always used" (193–194). On the euphuistic mode, see Croll, 241–295.

65. Part 2, 34–35.

66. Erasmus, *De Copia*, trans. Knott, 348. [*eandem veluti Proteum in omnem speciem vertere*] (*De Copia*, ed. Knott, 76). Of the first word of his expression, for example, Erasmus begins, "There is no synonym for 'your,' but a periphrasis is possible: Your excellency's, your highness's, your majesty's." [*Tvae non admittit synonymiam; 'tuae amplitudinis,' 'tuae celsitudinis,' 'tuae maiestatis' periphrasis est*] (*De Copia*, ed. Knott, 76).

67. Responding to critiques of "the Hellenistic period's as well as the Roman period's increasingly refined analysis of style in rhetoric manuals," Walker argues (via Quintilian) that such instruction facilitated the orator's ability to improvise in public: "Just as a musical trainee could practice finger exercises and particular sequences, runs and trills that later could be recombined in musical performances or musical invention," Walker writes, "so too the would-be civic orator could practice and acquire a ready repertoire of styles and figures that eventually would enable copious, fluent, and appropriate stylistic improvisation in public forums" (58).

68. Peacham, *Garden* (1593), Aa$_2$v. See also Fraunce, *Arcadian Rhetorike*, F$_5$r.

69. Peacham, *Garden* (1593), Aa$_2$v. "Correction retrats what has been said and replaces it with what seems more suitable" (*Ad Herennium*, 4.26.36). [*Correctio est quae tollit id quod dictum est, et pro eo id quod magis idoneum videtur reponit.*] See also Susenbrotus, 72–73.

70. Hoskins, 29. J. Smith writes: "*Correction*[:] having used a word of sufficient force, yet pretending a greater strength of meaning, refuses it, and supplyes the place with one of more extension" (Kv). See also Puttenham, 300–301.

71. Peacham, *Garden* (1593), Aa$_2$v.

72. Part 2, 35.

73. See Cave, 144–156; Anderson, *Words That Matter*, 7–13; Bloom, 66–110. Quintilian, for example, advises slow and cautious openings, warning that "such a procedure is preferable to yielding ourselves to an empty torrent of words, that the storm may sweep us where it will" (10.7.23). [*hoc, dum egredimur e portu, si nos nondum, aptatis satis armamentis aget ventus . . . Id potius quam se inani verborum torrenti dare quasi tempestatibus quo volent auferendum.*] Quintilian also advises revision because "we may spread our sails before the

favouring breeze, but we must beware that this indulgence does not lead us into error." The orator must be attentive to "any passage where we have reason to regard our fluency with suspicion" (10.3.7). [*interim tamen, si feret flatus, danda sunt vela, dum nos indulgentia illa non fallat . . . sed redeamus ad iudicium et retractemus suspectam facilitatem.*]

74. Part 2, 35.
75. Part 2, 35.
76. Wilson, *Art of Rhetoric*, 192–193. On the alignment of female garrulity with female corporeality, see Parker, *Literary Fat Ladies*, 8–35.
77. Part 2, 34.
78. As Thomas Knell explains in his *An answer at large, to a most hereticall, trayterous, and papisticall byll in English verse* (1570), replying to a description of "preachers" as "knaues": "The Preacher is the Trumpe of God, this sure is spoke amis. / A lying knaue, a brauling knaue, a romish knaue more fyt: / But sure thys *Epithite* thou adst without reason or wyt. / For *Epithites* we adde to shew the nature, force, and kinde: / Of men, of things, and wordes as we in Rethoricke rules do finde. / But contraries for *Epithites*, wyse men do neuer place: / *Epithetons* of lyke must be, to shew of wordes the grace. / Preaching a woord of Maiestie, and Knaue, doo disagrée: / Although a Knaue hath ioynd them thus, from wyt and learning frée. / A sclaunderous knaue, a foolish knaue, a foule malicious knaue: / These *Epithites* may sound more fyt, for him that thus doth raue" (A$_4$v).
79. Quintilian, 8.6.40. [*Cetera iam non significandi gratia sed ad ornandam et augendam orationem assumuntur.*]
80. Puttenham, 257, 262.
81. See also Peacham, who defines *epitheton* as "a figure or form of speech, which joyneth Adiectiues to those Substantiues, to whom they do properly belong," warning that "a Speciall regard ought to be had in the frame & coniunction of this figure, that y^e Epithets be not unproperly or peruersly applied, as to say: A valiant Phisitian, a reuerend labourer, a coragious Counseller, which is a form of speech very unproper and also very absurd" (*Garden* [1593], Iv–I$_2$r).
82. The passage from Quintilian reads in full: "Poets employ it with special frequency and freedom, since for them it is sufficient that the epithet should suit the word to which it is applied: consequently, we shall not blame them when they speak of 'white teeth' or 'liquid wine.' But in oratory an epithet is redundant unless it has some point. . . . There are some writers who refuse to regard an *epithet* as a *trope*, on the ground that it involves no change." [*Eo poetae et frequentius et liberius utuntur. Namque illis satis est convenire id verbo, cui apponitur, itaque et 'dentes albos' et 'humida vina' in iis non reprehendemus; apud oratorem, nisi aliquid efficitur, redundat. Tum autem*

efficitur, si sine illo, quod dicitur, minus est: qualia sunt 'O scelus abominandum,' 'O deformem libidinem'... Sunt autem, quibus non videatur hic omnino tropus, quia nihil vertat] (8.6.40–43).

83. Erasmus calls the *epithets* permitted to poets "natural descriptive phrases" (e.g., "white snow"), writing that they "should not be employed in prose unless they carry some particular emphasis and are relevant to what we are trying to achieve" (*De Copia*, trans. Knott, 591). [*In poematis licebit naturalibus epithetis vti, vt: 'candida nix'... In oratione prosa non oportebit adhiberi, nisi emphasim quandam habeant, et ad rem propositam pertineant*] (*De Copia*, ed. Knott, 217). See also Susenbrotus, who writes that "poets use this figure the more frequently and liberally, for an orator it is superfluous unless something is effected by it, that is, unless what is said would be less effective without it" (39). [*Eo poetae & frequentius & liberius utuntur, apud Oratorem nisi cum aliquid efficitur, redundat. Tum autem efficitur, si sine illo quod dicitur minus est*] (C_5r). Scott warns: "You must not have idle attributes only to fill up your metre (saith Scaliger): 'The endless date of never-ending woe'—a very idle, stuffed verse in that very well-penned poem of Lucrece her rape" (53).

84. Erasmus also associates *epithets* with *metaphor* (*De Copia*, trans. Knott, 335). Demetrius suggests that *epithets* are a way of taming a "risky" metaphor: "When they consider their metaphors risky, some writers try to make them safe by adding epithets; for example Theognis refers to the bow as a 'lyre with tuneless strings,' when describing an archer in the act of shooting. The image of the bow as lyre is bold, but it is made safe by the qualification 'with tuneless strings'" (85).

85. Quintilian, 8.6.41–42. [*Verumtamen talis est ratio huiusce virtutis, ut sine appositis nuda sit et velut incompta oratio, oneretur tamen multis. Nam fit longa et impedita, ut* [*in quaestionibus*] *eam iudices similem agmini totidem lixas habenti quot milites, cui et numerus est duplex nec duplum virium.*]

86. Quintilian, 8.6.43. [*duo vero uni apposita ne versum quidem decuerint.*]

87. See Whittaker, 133–137.

88. Scott also sees *epithets* within a social world: "Being as pages to the substantives, we account this the best general rule, to make them suitable to their leaders: if they mourn, these followers go sad; if they fight, these are bloody; when they be merry, these are cheerful; when they grave, these sober" (52).

89. *Part 1*, 204.

90. *Part 2*, 141, 153.

91. At a climactic moment in *The First Part*, for example, Amphilanthus and Pamphilia are able to free their friends from an enchantment because she is the "Loyallest, and therefore most incomparable Pamphilia," and he is "Amphilanthus, the valliantest and worthiest of thy sexe" (*Part 1*, 169–170).

92. *Part 1*, 363.
93. *Part 2*, 136.
94. *Part 2*, 52–53.
95. See Burrow, "Original Fictions"; Fox.
96. *Part 2*, 251.
97. Amphilanthus, for example, spends some time "miserable in the trebble degree" after he is banned from Pamphilia's conversation, where "trebble" refers to the highest notes a human being can produce and hear (*Part 2*, 256).
98. Quintilian, 8.3.56. [κακόζηλον id est mala adfectatio, per omne dicendi genus peccat. Nam et tumida et pusilla et praedulcia et abundantia et arcessita et exultantia sub idem nomen cadunt. Denique κακόζηλον vocatur, quidquid est ultra virtutem, quotiens ingenium iudicio caret et specie boni fallitur, omnium in eloquentia vitiorum pessimum. Nam cetera parum vitantur, hoc petitur.]
99. I am quoting from Cicero's description of epideictic rhetoric (believed to be the origin of the charming, middle style practiced by Gorgias and Isocrates and understood as the classical precursor of the euphuistic mode): [de industriaque non ex insidiis sed aperte ac palam elaboratur] (*Orator*, 38).
100. Attridge, 17–45.
101. Sidney, *Defence*, 217.
102. Puttenham, 222, 238.
103. Attridge, 31.
104. As Attridge suggests, this account of the poet-maker is itself transgressive and, in the *Defence*, Sidney seems to back away from its articulation even at the moment that he steps right up to it: "But these arguments will by few be understood, and by fewer granted" (217). "Were Sidney to follow this argument through," Attridge writes, "he would replace religion with poetry as the way back to God's grace" (38). We have tended, following work like Attridge's, to consider nature as most vulnerable to art precisely where artifice is no longer distinguishable from nature. Where art mimics nature, it successfully usurps its primary status, wresting divine transcendence into the contingency and mutability of secular time and substituting the poet-maker for Maker.
105. Brinsely, V_1v.

4. "SUCH AS MIGHT BEST BE": *SIMILE* IN EDMUND SPENSER'S *FAERIE QUEENE*

1. Aristotle, *Rhetoric*, 1410^b 15–20. For the mitigating syntax of *simile* (in contrast with *metaphor*), see Demetrius, 2.89; Hobbes, "A Briefe of the Art of Rhetorique" (1637), 110. See also Longinus, in which these correlatives are grouped with the modest, "as it were," etc., in *On the Sublime*, trans. Fyfe and rev. Russell, 2nd ed., 32.4.

2. Aristotle, *Rhetoric*, 1410^b 20–25.

3. For temporal difference between *metaphor* and *simile*, see also Quintilian, 13.6.8; Cicero, *De Oratore*, 3.39.157; Erasmus, *De Copia*, trans. Knott, 337.

4. See Susenbrotus, 95–99; Sherry (1550), F$_5$v–F$_7$r.

5. Puttenham, 326.

6. See Erasmus, *De Copia*, trans. Knott, 641–646; *Rhetorica Ad Herrenium*, 4.47.61.

7. For treatments of the "places" as producing a spatialization of thinking, see Crane, 12–38. Marsh H. McCall tracks the origins of *similitude*'s division into (or conflation of) figure and place in a survey to which the present chapter is indebted. McCall concludes that while we can separate *simile* from other figures of comparison on the basis of form, we cannot separate it "in sphere and method of use" (259). I will suggest that *simile*'s unique form led to a celebration of its utility (on the one hand) and a fear of its overuse (on the other) and thus conditioned both its "sphere" and "method of use" in early modern England.

8. Sherry, for example, writes: "Neyther skylleth it that we haue rehearsed ficcion and comparacion amonge argumentes, for there is no cause why that amplificacion and ornacion shuld not be taken out of the same places from whence ther commeth probacion" ([1550], E$_5$r). The very fact that Sherry found the need to anticipate and refute such an objection to the organization of his discourse, however, is itself evidence that the objection existed and that it had produced a certain anxiety or ambivalence among pedagogues. See also Quintilian, 8.3.72–75.

9. Dolven writes of the results of humanist pedagogy's emphasis on *inventio* more generally: "*There will be something fundamentally atemporal, anarrative, even ahistorical about the arguments you make.* Even when you draw the words of the question through the place *a causa* you are seeking after commonplaces rather than a narrative, and seeking in a space of memory that is not stratified or sedimented with time, but laid out in a topical field. The mind so represented is a timeless place" (*Scenes of Instruction*, 48; see also 178–181).

10. Ong describes the Ramist relation to language as the "drive to tie down words.... Words are believed to be recalcitrant insofar as they derive from a world of sound, voices, cries; the Ramist ambition is to neutralize this connection by processing what is of itself nonspatial in order to reduce it to space in the starkest way possible" (89). See also J. N. Smith.

11. See also Gerard Passannante's account of the "containment mechanisms" with which Ramus's method attempted "to quarantine the problem of chance and contingency" (821).

12. Sidney, *Defence*, 218. "'As' modulates with 'as if,'" Catherine Addison writes, "a copula which extends perception and knowledge into the realms of the hypothetical, the imaginative, and the fantastic" ("From Literal to Figurative," 405). See also Wolfson, 88. Many critics have suggested that *similes* provide a view into a world that is not that of the poem proper. See Fletcher, 117; Ferry, 78. For Linda Gregerson, writing of Milton's *similes*, "the grammatical suspension gives the reader a little sampling of Limbo itself" (138). Later, she calls this a "conceptual space" (140). Stephanson, 29. For A. D. Nuttall, Milton's *similes* are "rests, holidays," "an inhalation of air": "The very excursiveness . . . gives it the character of a window unexpectedly appearing in the wall of a long corridor" (75); Addison, "'So Stretched Out Huge in Length,'" (499).

13. Wofford, 42–43.

14. Sidney, *Defence*, 224.

15. I understand this alternative as a complement to what Wofford describes as *simile*'s "metonymic" tendencies, though where she separates *simile* from "action," I am suggesting that *simile* participates in narrative action (43–44). See also Wolfson's suggestion that, for Coleridge, *simile* is among those "poetic processes [that] . . . are resistant, often devoted to fragments, disjunctions, and revisions" (*Formal Charges*, 69).

16. Sidney, *Defence*, 218, 224.

17. Spenser, *The Faerie Queene*, 716. Poetry from *The Faerie Queene* is cited parenthetically in the text by book, canto, and stanza. Where the whole stanza is not cited, I also provide line numbers.

18. See Burrow, *Epic Romance*; Parker, *Inescapable Romance*.

19. Rebhorn, *Emperor of Men's Minds*, 35.

20. For example, James Nohrnberg writes that Braggadochio's theft of Guyon's horse "opens a serial that is not closed" until Artegall returns the horse to Guyon and "the interlacement of Books III and IV cedes its functions in organizing the narrative to a more linear kind of parallelism" (355, 357). In what follows, I read Nohrnberg's claim that Braggadochio's groom, Trompart, "proceeds to *amplify* his master" more literally than he perhaps intended (355, emphasis mine). *Similitude* is among the figures wielded for the amplification of discourse in Wilson, *Art of Rhetoric*, 214–215.

21. James V. Holleran describes Braggadochio's acquisitions as a "comic subplot" to the epic quest, reversing the paradigm whereby knights lose their accessories and come to rely on the intervention of "a superior agent of good" (20). See also Huston, 212–217. For Braggadochio as a figure from the Italian *commedia dell' arte*, see Quilligan.

22. Spenser, *The Faerie Queene*, 716.

23. In my suggestion that the collection of comparative images also doubled as a means of social mobility in early modern England, I am indebted to Crane's *Framing Authority*. See also Halpern. David Quint reads Braggadochio as a "courtly upstart" who embodies, by way of his bragging, a new version of the aristocrat: "In his case, clothes literally make the man" (414–415, see 391–430).

24. All references to Jonson's marginalia refer to the transcriptions provided by Riddell and Stewart. For the annotation "Simile," see 164 (1.2.16.1) and 165 (1.3.31.1, 1.5.8.1). That a *simile* was only marked as "excellent" when it might be considered "epic" is Riddell and Stewart's, 78. For the annotation "An excellent simile" (including autographical variants), see 168 (2.5.10.3), 175 (2.8.42.1), and 184 (3.4.17.4). For "M." next to a *simile*, see 175 (2.8.50).

25. Riddell and Stewart, 167. Text of the *Faerie Queene* is here quoted from the folio: *The faerie queen: The shepheards calendar: together with the other works of Englands arch-poët, Edm. Spenser: collected into one volume, and carefully corrected* (1617), G$_1$v.

26. I understand my account of *simile*'s abstraction and the moral register of this abstraction as a complement to what Dolven has called (via Jerome Bruner), "*paradigmatic understanding*, which satisfies us by providing some kind of detemporalized paradigm . . . to which we can contract and compare the flux of experience" (*Scenes of Instruction*, 53). In this instance, "cowardnesse" enables just such a contraction.

27. Cooney outlines these two major interpretive approaches to Spenserian *allegory*, 171.

28. Stephen A. Nimis reports that allegoresis was among the strategies wielded by Homer's ancient commentators, who found his *similes* "to be diffuse, loosely constructed and full of digressions and illogic" (2–3). Such prioritization has been a defining feature of *simile*'s critical reception. Whether in the early modern preference for Virgil's *similes* over those belonging to Homer or in the modern critical vocabulary of "relevance" versus "irrelevance" (Empson), "homologation" versus "heterogeneity" (Whaler), or "argument" versus "ornament" (Ferry), these oppositions prioritize the logical point of *similitude* over the figure's productive capacities. For the early modern preference, see its rebuttal in *Chapman's Homer: The Iliad*, 69. See also Empson, 170; Whaler, "The Miltonic Simile"; Whaler, "Grammatical Nexus of the Miltonic Simile"; Whaler, "Similes in 'Paradise Lost,'"; Ferry, 68–69. Berger offers a critique of the polemical subordination of "ornament" as "irrelevant," highlighting instead "conspicuous irrelevance" as a strategy the poet might wield (*Allegorical Temper*, 120–160; esp. 120–132). If, however, an earlier insistence on logical incorporation reined seemingly irrelevant images in via *prolepsis*, Berger places the burden of

similitude in and on literary history via allusion. Without denying the importance of the logical point of *similitude*—and indeed, the model of intertextuality it might sustain—it is my argument that such a focus solves only half of *simile*'s problems.

29. Boethius offers a concise explication of this difference with reference to *similitude*: "Dialectic discovers arguments from qualities themselves; rhetoric, from things taking on a quality.... The dialectician [discovers arguments] from similarity; the rhetorician, from a similar, that is, from the thing which takes on similarity" (*De topicis differentiis*, trans. Stump, 95). See Moss, *Printed Commonplace-Books*, 15–17.

30. This notation is the most frequent identification of *simile* in Jonson's *Spenser*. See 167 (2.2.24.2–3), 168 (2.4.7.8, 2.5.2.5), 175 (2.7.48.4–5), 176 (2.9.16.5), 180 (2.11.19.4–5, 2.11.32.4), 181 (2.11.36.6–9).

31. Sherry (1550), A_6v.

32. Riddell and Stewart, 164.

33. Jonson, *Discoveries*, 120–121.

34. Sherry (1550), A_6v–A_7r.

35. For a discussion of the maker's knowledge as an alternative epistemology, see Parker, "Rude Mechanicals," 43–82, esp. 49–53; Turner, *English Renaissance Stage*; Kalas, *Frame, Glass, Verse*. On the productive materiality of language, see Anderson, *Words That Matter*; and Burckhardt, 22–46.

36. Fowler and Leslie, 821; "Conversations with Drummond," in *Ben Jonson*, 1:135.

37. Fowler, 417.

38. Spenser, *Yale Edition of the Shorter Poems*, 84, 181, 196, 211. See Slights, 690–691.

39. Shirley Sharon-Zisser refers to "the compendium of similes" as a "sub-genre" in her Lacanian reading, 13. The most famous of these must be Erasmus's *Parabolae Sive Similia* (1514). For medieval manuscript precedents, see Moss, *Printed Commonplace-Books*, 26–48.

40. See Erasmus, *De Copia*, trans. Knott, 641–646.

41. See Erasmus, *De Ratione Studii*, trans. McGregor, 685; *Letters and Exercises of the Elizabethan Schoolmaster John Conybeare*, 23.

42. On figure's participation in alchemical transmogrification, see Eggert, 25–38, esp. 33–37.

43. Marston, *Antonio's Revenge*, 1.3.61–67.

44. Shakespeare, *As You Like It*, 2.1.44–45. This leads Watson to ask: "Capturing the deer is certainly more brutal, but captioning its picture may be no less appropriative. Which has done more insidious violence to pristine nature as a collectivity, during its long siege by humanity: shooting it with arrows or shattering it into similes?" (*Back to Nature*, 82).

45. For the fear of copious discourse and cultural containment strategies, see Parker, *Literary Fat Ladies*, 8–35. See also Cave, 3–34. His account tends toward the celebratory rather than the anxious.

46. Folger V.a. 381, 86–87. Quoted by Braymen Hackel, 147; and Sherman, *Used Books*, 61–62.

47. Jonson, *Discoveries*, 124–125. For a discussion of reading as part of the writing process, see Agricola, "Letter 38," 203–219.

48. Grafton and Jardine, "Studied for Action," 30–78; Kintgen, 92, 148.

49. For the humanist training in arguing both sides of a question, see Kahn.

50. Moss, *Printed Commonplace-Books*, 104–105, see more generally 101–130. Moss constructs a spectrum, at one end of which we might find the logical organization taught by Agricola and Melanchthon, at the other end of which we find Vives's lexical organization, and, as a pivot between the two, Erasmus's revisions of *De Copia*, which move increasingly toward the linear organization of copious material.

51. Moss, *Printed Commonplace-Books*, 117. See also her description of Jesuit commonplaces books in Europe, 166–185, esp. 176–177.

52. Nashe, "The Gentlemen Students of both Vniversities," 1:308–309. Quint writes: "What the upstart lacks in physical courage he makes up in his finery and swagger: his borrowed plumes are themselves a form of boasting" (415).

53. Puttenham, 222. My emphasis.

54. Puttenham, 222.

55. Marston, 1.3.65–67.

56. Brinsley, P$_1$v. See also Dolven, *Scenes of Instruction*, 36–38.

57. The apparent corpulence with which "the misshapen simile . . . stalks prodigiously" is reminiscent of Parker's fat ladies, who were made to embody—and contain—the threat of copious surfeit in *Literary Fat Ladies*. Baines reads Balurado's dream as a parody of Antonio's figurative excess (284).

58. Marston, 1.3.64.

59. Marston, 1.3.65–66. See also Scott's description of *epithets* "being as pages to the substantives, we account this the best general rule, to make them suitable to their leaders" (52).

60. Lily, C$_2$v.

61. [*Nam veluti flores tellus nec semina profert / Ni sit continuo victa labore manus: / Sic puer ingenium si non exercitet ipsum / Tempus & amittet, spem simul ingenii*] (Lily, D$_5$v).

62. The specific directives concerning the schoolmaster's examination of the pupil are taken from John Brinsley, R$_4$r.

63. Brinsley, R$_4$r.
64. Brinsley, S$_2$r.
65. Hoole, *A new discovery of the old art of teaching* (1661), 49.
66. See Carruthers, 7.
67. For the relationship between Georgic imagery, pedagogy, and poetic labor, see Wallace.
68. Lily, D$_5$v.
69. See Wilson's illustration of how *similitudes* allow one to "dilate" matter "with poesies and sentences" so that "we may with ease talk at large." There he offers an extended *exemplum* comparing the lesser value of money to the greater value of time, which, in wasting or "losing of time we lose all the goodness and gifts of God which by labor might be had" (*Art of Rhetoric*, 214–215). See also Erasmus, *De Copia*, trans. Knott, 622–623.
70. Erasmus, *De Conscribendis Epsitolis*, trans. Fantazzi, 27; *De Copia*, trans. Knott, 236.
71. Erasmus, *De Conscribendis Epsitolis*, 33.
72. Erasmus, *De Conscribendis Epsitolis*, 107.
73. When Erasmus demonstrates how multiple figures can allow you to amplify on any topic, such as "iron," his *simile* brings us back to the value of time: "Or the simile: just as iron is worn away by use, yet if not used it is eaten away by rust, so ability is consumed by over-working, yet if not exercised it is further atrophied by disuse and neglect" (*De Ratione Studii*, trans. McGregor, 677). [*Aut similitudinem, vt, quemadmodum ferrum si exerceas, vsu atteritur, si non exerceas, exeditur rubigine, ita ingenium si exerceas, labore absumitur, si non exerceas, magis ocio situque laeditur*] (*De Ratione Studii*, ed. Jean-Margolin, 129).
74. Erasmus, *De Copia*, trans. Knott, 635. [*ac velut in numerato possimus habere indicabimus*] (*De Copia*, ed. Knott, 258).
75. Erasmus, *Parabolae*, trans. Mynors, 130. [*plurimas in vno libello gemmas mitto*] (*Parabolae*, ed. Margolin, 88). For discussion of the place of the *Parabolae* in sixteenth-century English schooling and literature, see Lizette Islyn Westney's introduction to *Parabolae Sive Similia: Its Relationship to Sixteenth-Century English Literature*, 1–45.
76. Erasmus, *Parabolae*, trans. Mynors, 131. [*equisitas aliquot gemmas ex abstrusis musarum thesauris deprompsimus. Neque enim haec a tonstrinis aut sordidis fori conciliabulis petuntur, quae doctorum aures et oculos morentur*] (*Parabolae*, ed. Margolin, 92).
77. See Nicholson, *Uncommon Tongues*, esp. 45–71.
78. Sidney, *Astrophil and Stella* 3 (lines 7–8), in *Major Works*, 154.
79. Sidney, *Astrophil and Stella* 15 (lines 5–6), in *Major Works*, 158.
80. Sidney, *Defence*, 246.
81. E.g., Cicero, *Topica*, trans. Hubbell, 10.45.

82. Seneca, "Epistle LIX," in *Epistles 1–65*, trans. Gummere, 413. [*inbecillitatis nostrae admincula*] (412). See also J. Smith, who warns: "Note that similitudes are rather to make dark things plain, then to prove any doubtful thing; similitudes are not argumentative" (N₇r).

83. Ramus, *Attack on Cicero*, 97.

84. Fraunce, *Lawiers Logike*, U₁v. See also Cicero, *Topica*, 10.45.

85. Sidney, *Defence*, 218.

86. Sidney, *Defence*, 247.

87. As Temple writes in his *Analysis* of Sidney's *Defence*: "A simile (most eminent Sidney) is not an ornament of rhetorical eloquence, but an argument of logical invention, since there is in simile a certain force for arguing and explaining something" (163). [*Similitudo (clarissime Sidneie) non est Rethoricae elocutionis ornamentum, sed Logicae inventionis argumentum: quia inest in similitudine vis quaedam ad rem arguendam et declarandam*] (162).

88. Sidney, *Defence*, 247.

89. See Attridge, 17–45; Taylor, 127–150; Hillman, 73–90; Rebhorn, "Outlandish Fears," 3–24.

90. For the reorientation of conceptions of *decorum* toward a visual epistemology, see Ong, 212–213.

91. Sidney, *Defence*, 247.

92. Sidney, *Defence*, 247.

93. Spenser, *The Faerie Queene*, 716.

94. Spenser, *The Faerie Queene*, 716. My emphasis.

95. For a reading of the subjunctive and the imperative in Protestant debates concerning the will, see Cummings, 159–167.

96. Demetrius, 2.80.

97. Longinus, 32.4.

98. Spenser, *The Faerie Queene*, 716.

99. Quint points to this pun, 415.

100. Puttenham, 258. *Paroemion* becomes the vice of *tautologia* "when our maker takes too much delight to fill his verse with words beginning all with a letter" (Puttenham, 340).

101. Puttenham, 341.

102. Ed. Hamilton, *The Faerie Queene*, 181n.

103. Spenser, *The Faerie Queene*, 716.

104. It may be interesting to remember here that *The Faerie Queene* provides diverging origin stories for Guyon's quest: while book 2 has Guyon stumble across a dying Amavia in the woods, the *Letter* has him engaged by the Faerie Queene at the Palmer's request. We could think of this discrepancy as something like the byproduct of Braggadochio and Archimago's unrealized counternarrative.

105. This moment of discomposure will be repeated as the violence of Talus's dismantling of the "counterfeits" in book 5 (which is also the last time we see Braggadochio) (5.3.39.1).

106. Spenser, *The Faerie Queene*, 716.

107. Jonson, *Discoveries*, 121.

5. FIGHTING WORDS: *ANTITHESIS* IN PHILIP SIDNEY'S *ARCADIA*

1. Sidney, *Countess of Pembroke's Arcadia*, 593. Hereafter cited parenthetically in the text by page number.

2. On the early publication history of Sidney's *Arcadia*, see J. Davis.

3. Hoskins, 37.

4. Florio, "Epistle to the Second Book, dedicated to Elizabeth, Countess of Rutland," 168.

5. "What conclusion it should have had," the 1621 Folio reads, "or how far the work have been extended (had it had his last hand thereunto) was only known to his own spirit, where only those admirable Images were (and no where else) to be cast" (863–864).

6. See McCoy, 212–217; Roche, 3–12.

7. G. Alexander, *Writing after Sidney*, 48.

8. G. Alexander writes: "There is therefore a particular potency to the breaking off of the revised *Arcadia* mid-narrative, and mid-sentence: two sorts of structure, each of which can serve as a metaphor for the other, are broken together, 'without full point,' as Spenser puns at a related moment" (*Writing after Sidney*, 39). Alexander will proceed to suggest that "the way aposiopesis hovers over Sidney's endings, and over the efforts of others to understand or complete him, suggests to me that figurative rhetoric may present a framework for thinking about these endings" (53). Though Alexander does not "propose to try and explain why the revised *Arcadia* ends where it does and how it does," he does suggest that the "seeds of the revised *Arcadia*'s end are, I believe, not accidental but structural" (52–53). I understand this chapter to be an engagement with and contribution to these crucial insights. See also G. Alexander, "Sidney's Interruptions," 184–204.

9. Mann, 90–91.

10. Mann writes: "These *parentheses* signify one of the *Arcadia*'s primary narrative mechanisms, a compositional logic that inserts episodes into one another in a series of grafts that reverse the hierarchies of cause and effect" (102). See also 103–108.

11. See John Carey, "Structure and Rhetoric in Sidney's *Arcadia*," where he argues that "the prolific display of figuring in which Sidney's narrative is embodied is not ornate but functional, a linguistic equivalent of a particular and tragic world view" (245). Michael McCanles writes: "Far from veiling be-

hind its artificial style a fictive world of 'real' characters and actions, the new *Arcadia* gives us a world in which both characters and actions are structured rhetorically, and what is not structured rhetorically is not there. A basic argument of this study is that in the fictive world of the *New Arcadia* all realities, both human and natural, are structured according to the resources of verbal figuration" (11; see also 3, 17, 85–110).

12. On contraries as the dynamic "that acts as a creative and generative force in the cosmos," see Wolfe, esp. 20–33, 146–155.

13. Heylyn, Cc$_4$v. On this point, see McCanles, 2; Mann, 47–49.

14. Jonson, *Discoveries*, 120–121.

15. Contra pervasive readings of the affective dimension of figure: e.g., Carey's sense that "figures that waver and oscillate and hover over redoubled antitheses" or that "the shaking delicate syntax . . . has the function of portraying in words, in wavering figures of speech, the fragility and delicacy of what is going on, of the lovers' inner disturbance and indecision and mutual embarrassment" (261).

16. For the basic definition of *antithesis*, see the useful website *Silva Rhetoricae* (http://rhetoric.byu.edu), though even this entry records the associations through which any basic definition of *antithesis* is necessarily reductive. The following discussion of *antithesis* is indebted to Fahnestock, 45–85.

17. Aristotle, *Rhetoric*, 1410^b 20–25. Aristotle writes: "The more briefly and antithetically such sayings can be expressed, the more taking they are, for antithesis impresses the new idea more firmly and brevity more quickly. . . . The more a saying has these qualities, the livelier it appears: if, for instance, its wording is metaphorical, metaphorical in the right way, antithetical, and balanced, and at the same time it gives an idea of activity" (1412^b 20–35).

18. Aristotle writes that antithetical members in a single sentence are "satisfying, because the significance of contrasted ideas is easily felt, especially when they are thus put side by side, and also because it has the effect of a logical argument" (*Rhetoric*, 1410^a 20–25). Cicero discusses the place of *contrarium* in *Topica*, 10.47.

19. The *Rhetoric to Alexander*, contemporaneous with Aristotle's *Rhetoric*, suggests that *antithesis* can have "simultaneously contrary wording or meaning, or both," offering examples of "wording alone" and where "the words are not contrary, but the actions are." It concludes its discussion by suggesting that "Antithesis in both ways would be finest" (trans. Mirhady, 26). Fahnestock writes: "This dissociation of the antithesis into stylistic and probative aspects, the one a figure of diction and the other a figure of thought, first mentioned in the *Ad Alexandrum* and repeated in the *Ad Herennium*, will persist in the rhetorical tradition for centuries" (55). On "contraries" in the *Rhetoric to Alexander*, see Montefusco.

20. *Rhetorica Ad Herennium*, trans. Caplan, 4.15.21. [*Contentio est cum ex contrariis rebus oratio conficitur . . . Hoc genere si distinguemus orationem, et graves et ornati poterimus esse.*]

21. Susenbrotus, 70. [*Hoc schema cum primis elegans est, quo uix alio crebrius in uarieganda locupletandáque oratione Oratores utuntur*] (E_4v).

22. *Rhetorica Ad Herennium*, 4.18.25–26. [*Contrarium est quod ex rebus diversis duabus alteram breviter et facile contraria confirmat . . . et cum commodum est auditu propter brevem et absolutam conclusionem, tum vero vehementer id quod opus est oratori conprobat contraria re.*]

23. "Through Antithesis contraries will meet" (*Rhetorica Ad Herennium*, 4.45.58). [*Contentio est per quam contraria referentur.*]

24. *Rhetorica Ad Herennium*, 4.45.58. [*Inter haec duo contentionum genera hoc interest: illud ex verbis celeriter relatis constat; hic sententiae contrariae ex conparatione referantur oportet.*]

25. Susenbrotus, 69. [*est cum per contraria amlificamus: sit cum singulis uerbis tum sententiis*] (E_4r).

26. Sherry (1550), D_4r. Although (to confuse the matter), Sherry associates the first with *antitheton* and the second with *antithesis* in a reversal of the more usual translation from the Greek.

27. Ramus, *Arguments in Rhetoric against Quintilian*, 148. [*At tota ratio contrariorum argumenti est, elocutionis nihil est, ideoque figura esse non potest*] (220). Ramus similarly says of the activity of the related figure *synoeciosis* that it has "nothing at all to do with style, nor for that reason with any figure" (148). [*quod elocutionis nihil est omnino, nec ideo figurae quicquam*] (219).

28. Ramus, *Arguments in Rhetoric*, 149. [*Postremam e figuris verborum facit* antitheton, *in eoque fallitur. argumentum enim figura non est,* antitheton *autem ex dissimilibus argumentum est: non igitur figura*] (220). He is referring to Quintilian, 9.3.81. See also Ramus's critique of Cicero's *Orator* in *The Questions of Brutus* (1549), where he writes: "Among figures of speech you place antithesis, which is a name of an argument, both of class and species" (*Attack on Cicero*, 97). [*In figuris verborum contrarium ponis, quod argumentis nomen est, ut generis, ut speciei.*]

29. Fraunce, *Arcadian Rhetorike*, B_8r.

30. Fenner, D_2v.

31. Puttenham, 296.

32. As in Hobbes's succinct epitome of Aristotle, where he writes that "A *Period* with *opposition of Parts*, called also *Antithesis*, and the parts *Antitheta*, is when *contrary Parts* are put together. . . . *Antitheta* are therefore acceptable; because not onely the *Parts* appeare the better for the *opposition*; but also for that they carry with them a certaine appearance of that kind of *Enthymeme*, which leades to impossibility" (114–115). He writes that "*Enthymemes* that

leade to *Impossibility* please more than ostensive: for they compare, and put contraries together, whereby they are the better set off, and more conspicuous to the Auditor. Of all *Enthymemes*, they be best, which we assent to as soone as heare. For such consent pleaseth us; and makes us favourable to the speaker" (101).

33. Quintilian, 9.3.102. [*quis ferat contrapositis et pariter cadentibus et consimilibus irascentem, flentem rogantem? cum in his rebus cura verborum deroget adfectibus fidem, et ubicunque ars ostentatur, veritas abesse videatur.*]

34. Aristotle, *Rhetoric*, 1410^b 20–22.

35. Harvey, *Pierces Supererogation* (1593), G$_3$v. Harvey's praise of the pedagogical value of "contraries" in the *Arcadia* includes learning how to fight: "He that would skillfully, and brauely manage his weapon with a cunning Fury, may finde liuely Precepts in the gallant Examples of his valiantest Duellists; especially of Palladius, and Daiphantus; Zelmane, and Amphialus; Phalantus, and Amphialus: but chiefly of Argalus, and Amphialus; Pyrocles, and Anaxius; Musidorus, and Amphialus; whose lusty combats, may seeme Heroicall Monomachies. And that the valor of such redoubted men, may appeere the more conspicuous, and admirable, by comparison, and interview of their contraries; smile at the ridiculous encounters of Dametas, & Dorus; of Dametas, and Clinias" (G$_3$v).

36. Altman, 104–105; Dolven, 191. Altman demonstrates that "the ancient tradition of arguing *in utramque partem* clearly informs both the structure and the spirit of the work" (89). For Altman, the kind of "inquiry" shaped by *antitheses* in the *Arcadia* is not reductive because the text never finds the "general principle" sufficient to understanding fully a "particular case" (95); ultimately, the *antitheses* that underwrite argument *in utramque partem* are significant to Sidney as a device for simulating real-world experience. G. Alexander similarly understands "schemes and tropes—antimetabole, antithesis, synoeciosis—that work by strictly managed contrasts" as formal evidence of "a basic dialogical or dialectical principle at work in Sidney's language" (*Writing after Sidney*, 3). See also McCoy, 43–45; Lindheim, esp. 7–8, 13–41, 76–77; McCanles, 41. On argument *in utramque partem* more broadly, see Kahn. By contrast, attending to what he calls "the methodizing impulse of the *New Arcadia*," Dolven understands Sidney's romance as a turn away from contingent, dialogic knowledge and a turn toward the schematic organization of knowledge characteristic of the encyclopedia, with its attendant claims to exhaustion and objectivity (*Scenes of Instruction*, 191). See also Lanham, who writes of Sidney's tendency to "organize his sentences in balanced and antithetical elements": "He aims, I think, to create on an elementary stylistic level the same division into opposites which on a higher level we have called a dialectical method" (345).

37. Dolven, *Scenes of Instruction*, 194–195.

38. See Mack's conclusion that "Shakespeare makes forceful and meaning-laden a figure which in *Euphues* is mere stylistic sheen. And that surely is the point. Shakespeare uses the figure because of the way equal intensity of opposites can prepare for the overcoming of contrariety which will be the climax of the play. There is nothing decorative about it. The figure makes possible the action of the scene" ("Synoiceosis and Antithesis in *The Winter's Tale*," 197). While my argument is in sympathy with Mack's insights regarding figure's ability "not just to produce emotional intensity, as the manuals would suggest, but actually to generate the intellectual basis for the scene," it is my sense that to oppose such an "intellectual basis" to "mere stylistic sheen" is to naturalize the very polemic between reason and style that was itself a historical production of those manuals (188). See also McCanles, 98–100.

39. See "*ornamenta*" in *Lewis and Short*. E.g., Peacham in *The Garden of Eloquence* (1593): "They are as martiall instruments both of defence & inuasion, and being so, what may be either more necessary, or more profitable for vs, then to hold those weapons alwaies readie in our handes, wherewith we may defend our selues, inuade our enemies, reuenge our wrongs, ayd the weake, deliuer the simple from dangers, conserue true religion, & confute idolatry?" (AB$_4$r). See Rebhorn, *Emperor of Men's Minds*, 35; Vickers, *In Defence*, 312–313. See also Bernard Lamy's extended comparison "betwixt a Soldier's fighting, and an Orator speaking" ("The Art of Speaking" [1676], 240–242). On the mutually informing logic of physical and discursive battles in the Homeric tradition, see Wolfe, esp. 78–104, 146–155. On strife at court, see Whigham, 87.

40. Quintilian, 8.Pr.14. [*Et Marcus Tullius inventionem quidem ac dispositionem prudentis hominis putat, eloquentiam oratoris, ideoque praecipue circa praecepta partis huius laboravit.*]

41. Quintilian, 8.Pr.15–16. [*Eloqui enim est omnia, quae mente conceperis, promere atque ad audientis preferre; sine quo supervacua sunt priora et similia gladio condito atque intra vaginam suam haerenti.*]

42. See "*contentio*" in *Lewis and Short*.

43. Fenner, B$_3$r. He is here discussing the place of *inventio* under which *antithesis* is subsumed in the Ramist classification.

44. Vives, *De Ratione Dicendi*, 83. He concludes after a series of examples: "These antitheses give elegance and beauty and are generally graded according to the degree of the conflict in the warring elements, similar to the natural composition of the conflicting elements of the human body" (85).

45. Hoskins, 21–22.

46. Hoskins, 22.

47. Hoskins, 37. Though Hoskins divides his discussion between "contraries" and "contentio," he also cross-references the discussions (see 21–22).

48. Puttenham, 295.

49. In his *Epistolae Ho-elianae* (London, 1650), James Howell explains: "But ther are some men that are of a meer negative genius, like *Iohannes ad oppositum*, who will deny, or at least cross and puzzle anything though never so cleer in itself, with their but, yet, if, &c. they will slap the lie in Truths teeth though she visibly stand before their face without any visard, such perverse cross-gartered spirits are not to be dealt withall by argumente, but palpable proofs, as if one should deny that the fire burns, or that he hath a nose on his face" (C_4r).

50. In his taxonomy of Lyly's *antitheses*, Barish writes that the form "may be broken down . . . according to the force of mutual attraction and repulsion between the terms. . . . Antithetic terms thus considered resemble atomic particles or heavenly bodies: the gravitational pull between them varies inversely as the square of the distance" ("Prose Style of John Lyly," 17). Vives says of *antithesis*: "In diversity there is beauty, but only if the two elements are not so far apart and far-fetched as to destroy the likeness between them. Beauty consists precisely in the likeness and proportion we find in the two things put side by side" (*De Ratione Dicendi*, 83).

51. On the range of meanings of the word "model," see G. Alexander's "Introduction" to Scott, esp. liii and lxix, and his Commentary 1.1 (85–86). Alexander writes that Sidney exhibits a tendency "to use different orders of form as metaphors for each other," with the result that one order of form becomes a "model" for another order of form (liii). On the model as an instrument of thinking and practice, see Turner, who describes "the role of the reader" in Sidney's account of *poiēsis* as "to treat these artificial images like the 'models' or 'groundplats' that they are: to reconstruct from the methods of reasoning that they demonstrate, using the imagination to vivify the image on the page and judgment to produce action in the substantial world" (*English Renaissance Stage*, 112). See also 71–75.

52. Aristotle, *Rhetoric*, 1409^a 20–1409^b 20.

53. Cicero, *De Oratore*, 3.191 [*ne circuitus ipse verborum sit aut brevior quam aures exspectent aut longior quam vires atque anima patiatur*]; 3.181 [*Clausulas enim atque interpuncta verborum animae interclusio atque angustiae spiritus attulerunt.*] Cicero continues to say that the artifice of the period is so admirable that "now that this has once been discovered . . . even if a person were endowed with breath that never failed, we should still not wish him to deliver an unbroken flow of words" [*id inventum ita est suave ut, si cui sit infinitus spiritus datus, tamen eum perpetuare verba nolimus*] (3.181). See also Quintilian's claim that delivery requires "strength in the lungs, and breath that both holds out well and will not easily give way to fatigue" (11.3.40). [*et toto, ut aiunt, organo instructa; cui aderit lateris firmitas, spiritus cum spatio pertinax, tum labori non facile cessurus.*]

54. Aristotle, *Rhetoric*, 1410^a 1–25.

55. For an excellent account of the innovations of Melanchthon's second rhetoric and the residual force of these innovations in his *Elementorum*, see Weaver, 367–402. Melanchthon divides figures into three "types": the first and second fall roughly into the categories of figures of speech and figures of thought, while the third "for the most part, concerns the speaker and comprises the manner of enlarging, that is, the figures which embellish the speech and make it broader and more extended" (trans. La Fontaine, 248–249). [*Postremus ordo maxime ad oratorem pertitinet, qui continet rationem amplificandi, hoc est, figuras, quae augent orationem, et longiorem atque ampliorem efficiunt.*] Hoskins first discusses "contraries" under the section of "To Amplify" (21–22) and then discusses "contentio" in the section entitled "These Figures Following Serve Properly for Amplification" (37–38).

56. To this place of *inventio* belongs the question, "*Quae cognata et pugantia*" [What things are related to it and what things are opposed to it?] (Melanchthon, trans. La Fontaine, 99; see also 105–106, 110). On the places and amplification, see 112, 140, 193; on *antithesis* as a figure, see 290–291.

57. Melanchthon, 263–264. [*Observet autem studiosus lector figuras omnes, praesertim has, quae augent orationem ex locis dialecticis oriri . . . Nam iidem loci cum confirmandi aut confutandi causa adhibentur, argumenta sunt ac nervi, ut vocant. Cum adhibentur illuminandi causa, dicuntur ornamenta.*] (See also Melanchthon, 279, 297; Mack, *A History of Renaissance Rhetoric*, 118–119, 121, 122, 216–217; Baldwin, 2:20–21).

58. For amplification and the inflation of value, see Melanchthon, trans. La Fontaine, 202, 220.

59. Scott, 66.

60. The categories used to partition the activities of *antithesis* become instead units of composition like the word, the clause, and the sentence. "Contrasting statements," Melanchthon writes, "may be brought together in various ways, but we include the various types under the one name *antithesis*. For that subdivision into special types, which is all too much chopped up into little pieces, is an obscure one" (291). [*Varie conferuntur contraria, sed nos uno titulo antithesis plerasque alias species comprehendimus. Nam illa nimis exiliter concisa specierum partitio obscura est.*] The question for *antithesis* becomes—not its relation to thought—but the formal level at which it might enlarge discourse. See also Quintilian, 9.3.81.

61. Parker, *Inescapable Romance*.

62. Stanley, Br. On Stanley's adaptation, see C. Kinney, "The Gentlewoman Reader Writes Back"; Mitchell.

63. Stanley, 396.

64. Stanley, 397.

65. Stanley, 397. Unlike William Alexander, Stanley does not supply a bridge narrative ("*I must beg to be excus'd*"); instead she invites her "*Readers to raise the Structure of a Supplement in their own Imaginations, and give them an Opportunity of trying the Strength of their Fancies, as also the pleasure of adding something to Sir* Philip Sidney" (397).

66. On *poiēsis*, the materiality of words, and a maker's knowledge, see Burckhardt, 22–46; Anderson, *Words That Matter*; Parker, "Rude Mechanicals," 43–82, esp. 49–53; Turner, *English Renaissance Stage*; Kalas.

67. Thinking of the early description of a shipwrecked Pyrocles, Hazlitt writes: "If the original sin of alliteration, antithesis, and metaphysical conceit could be weeded out of this passage, there is hardly a more heroic one to be found in prose or poetry" (322).

68. Spenser, *The Faerie Queene*, 1.5.3.4, 6, 8.
69. Spenser, *The Faerie Queene*, 1.5.7–9.
70. Spenser, *The Faerie Queene*, 1.5.11.9.
71. Spenser, *The Faerie Queene*, 1.5.13.4.
72. Spenser, *The Faerie Queene*, 1.5.13.6–8.

73. On *antimetabole*, see Puttenham, 293–294; Susenbrotus, 78–79; Wilson, *Art of Rhetoric*, 228–229; Hoskins, 14–15. By some accounts, *antimetabole* is even a species of *antithesis* that generates an efficient inversion of words while expressing an opposition: Quintilian says that "Antithesis may also be effected by employing that *figure* known as ἀντιμεταβολή, by which words are repeated in different cases, tenses, moods, etc., as for instance when we say, *non ut edam, vivo, sed ut vivam, edo* (I do not live to eat, but eat to live)" (9.3.85). [*Fit etiam adsumpta illa figura, qua verba declinata repetuntur, quod* ἀντιμεταβολή *dicitur; Non, ut edam, vivo, sed, ut vivam, edo.*] Susenbrotus writes: "Commutatio . . . occurs when some idea is transposed through its antithesis" (78) [*Commutatio . . . est cum inueritur aliqua sententia per contrariam*] (E_8v). See also *Rhetorica Ad Herennium*, 4.28.39; Peacham, *Garden* (1593), Z_2r.

74. Puttenham describes *antimetabole* as a device for place shifting or place swapping: "Ye have a figure which takes a couple of words to play with in a verse, and by making them to change and shift one into other's place, they do very prettily exchange and shift the sense" (293).

75. In T. Roche's reading (via *Orlando Furioso*), the "pronominal adjectives behave in a perverse manner (almost Spenserian) that will not allow us (or at least me) to make them sit where we want to find their meaning": "The logical referent of that 'he' is, of course, Anaxius, who would, of course, jump away from any such thrust and would, of course, be ashamed at doing something he had never done before, but I would like to suggest that the 'he' is not Anaxius but Zelmane who finds himself aiming at Anaxius's loins (reins) and leaps back out of embarrassment because of this very unknightly pursuit" (11).

76. Augustine, *Of the citie of God*, trans. Healey, Oo₁v.

77. In his notes to Augustine, Vives relates this passages to the *Ad Herennium* and Quintilian before saying (of Augustine's *exempla* from Corinthians) that "*Augustine* makes *Paul* a Rhetorician. [Well it is tolerable, Augustine saith it: Had one of us said so, our eares should ring of heresie presently, heresies are so ready at some mens tongue ends, because indeed they are so full of it themselves]" (Oo₁v).

78. See also Montaigne's idea that "in nature one contrarie is vivified by another contrarie" (trans. Florio, 30).

79. See Daniel's related celebration of the sonnet in his *Defence* as "a just form": "For the body of our imagination being as unformed chaos without fashion, without day, if by the divine power of the spirit it be wrought into an orb of order and form" it becomes "pleasing to nature" (216).

80. At the start of his chapter on *antithesis* in *S/Z*, Roland Barthes writes that "the several hundred figures propounded by the art of rhetoric down through the centuries constitute a labor of classification intended to name, to lay the foundations for, the world" (26). Distinguishing the work of *antithesis* from "dialectical movement," he continues: "Antithesis is the battle between two plentitudes set ritually face to face like two fully armed warriors; the Antithesis is the figure of the *given* opposition, eternal, eternally recurrent: the figure of the inexpiable." What is important to Barthes is that narrative can only begin with an act of "transgression" that destroys figure's "harmoniously closed loop" (27). In *Sarasine*, the act of transgression is the body of the narrator. Barthes writes: "It is by way of this *excess* which enters the discourse after rhetoric has properly saturated it that something can be told and the narrative can begin" (28). In the *Arcadia*, by contrast, *antithesis* brings about the stylistic revival of the *poein*.

81. At the opening of *The Art of English Poesy*, Puttenham defines the poet as a "maker": "Such as (by way of resemblance and reverently) we may say of God, who without any travail to his divine imagination made all the world of nought . . . even so the very poet makes and contrives out of his own brain both the verse and matter of his poem" (93). This chapter is a serious reading of Puttenham's *simile* as he aligns the "verse and matter" of the poet's "poem" with God's "world." As Erasmus would say, however, this *simile* limps (it does not walk on all fours): where God makes "without any travail," the poet makes with labor.

82. Jonson, *Discoveries*, 120–121.

83. Puttenham, 233.

84. Danby, 50; Lindheim, who suggests that Sidney's "use of antithesis" makes "Sidney's analytical habit of mind and his temperamental need for synthesis" a "matter for literary study" (6).

85. Lindheim, 6.

86. They therefore also depart from the Pythagorean justification that underwrites Gorgias's defense of style (and which will later inform Cicero's account of *decorum*). Nancy S. Struever writes, concerning the Gorgian claim, that "stylistic has its epistemological basis in the axiom that meaning in human experience can only be apprehended and communicated aesthetically": "Thus Gorgias, rejecting the pretensions of pure reason, holds that only the incantatory power of words can overcome subjectivism or solipsism; through measure in rhythm and sound the artists convey measure or proportion in meaning according to patterns of thought which are primordial—the patterns of identity and antithesis—and therefore universally appealing. . . . This is a Pythagorean concept which had its foundation in Pythagorean ontology; a thing is not a single pure essence but is a unity or harmony of contraries" (12). See also 29.

87. Peacham, *Garden* (1593), Zr.

6. WITHHOLDING NAMES: *PERIPHRASIS* IN MARY WROTH'S *URANIA*

1. Shaw, H_3r–H_3v.

2. Shaw, H_4r. Eclogus's part is restricted to pointing out repeatedly that no trope or figure could have done what it did without having been pronounced; Eclogus's children, Voice and Gesture, refuse to come on stage when called for (see N_5r–N_6r).

3. See Mann's discussion of the play, 208–217.

4. Shaw, L_6r–L_6v.

5. Shaw, L_6v.

6. Shaw, L_7r.

7. Shaw, H_5r

8. Shaw, H_5v.

9. E.g., Puttenham, 277–279.

10. Shaw, M_2r.

11. For a discussion of the contested status of *periphrasis* as trope or figure, see Quintilian, 9.1.3–7.

12. Shaw, M_2v.

13. Puttenham, 277–278. Puttenham also suggests that *periphrasis* is a species of *allegory* when he defines *allegory* as, "we may dissemble, I mean speak otherwise than we think . . . by long ambage and circumstance of words" (271). Puttenham categorizes *periphrasis* among what he calls "figures sensable," a category that also includes *hyperbole* and *irony* (27).

14. It is for this reason that Grant Williams argues that *periphrasis* is "a perfect match for the paranoid construction": "The periphrasis is a figure semiotically out of proportion with what it purports to represent . . . whereas

with common tropes a single signifier yields either one or many signifieds, periphrasis works in the opposite direction. Multiple paradigmatic and syntagmatic relations yield only one signified. Periphrasis presupposes the one behind the many and thereby proclaims the one to have been responsible for the redundant prolixity" (208–209). Another way of saying this would be that *periphrasis* works like *allegory* at its most successful (and least literary), where the apparent ease with which it veils the rift at its center maintains the trope's ideological investments in the seamless transition from material to ideal. See Teskey, *Allegory and Violence*.

15. Puttenham, 279.

16. Peacham, *Garden* (1593), X$_2$v. For his discussion of figures of amplification, see R$_4$r–Sr.

17. Ramus, *Arguments in Rhetoric against Quintilian*, 139.

18. Sontag, 14.

19. Sanchez's recent characterization of Wroth criticism suggests that "by interpreting the well-documented topical references of the *Urania* according to a logic that limits female autobiography to romantic or gendered concerns, we have magnified Wroth's female marginalization in order to show how she resisted it. As a result, we have effectively denied Wroth a voice in larger political debates of early seventeenth-century England" (118). On the conflict with Edward Denny that paradoxically authorizes these topical readings, see Roberts; Salzman, "Contemporary References in Mary Wroth's *Urania*"; Hackett; Carrell; Salzman, "The Strang[e] Constructions of Mary Wroth's *Urania*"; Kinney, "'Beleeve this butt a fiction.'" Nona Fienberg, for example, understands Denny as a kind of ideal reader: "Having identified the subversive tenor of Wroth's imagination as well as her method of indirection, of working by ways, Denny invited readers of the *Urania* to seek the *roman à clef* references in the prose romance" (123).

20. Wynne-Davies, 82. Wynne-Davies refers to Wroth's writing as "autobiographical" throughout her essay, arguing: "While her writings may not be clearly categorised as 'autobiography' in the straightforward manner of Ann Clifford's diaries, her literary texts are so replete with familial allegory and multiple reworkings of her own life that they demand to be classified within an autobiographical framework" (79).

21. For Manners's request, see Carrell, 87. For keys to the *Arcadia*, see Alexander, *Writing after Sidney*, 301.

22. Hannay, 237.

23. E.g., Lamb, 109; Wynne-Davies, 82; Alexander, *Writing after Sidney*, 285. Initially introducing the concept via her reading of Edmund Spenser's *Letter to Raleigh*, Roberts prefers the word "shadowing" to "topicality," arguing that this Spenserian project more "accurately describes the intermittent

nature of the references" (*Part 1*, lxxi). While "shadowing" maintains historical persons as the referents of Wroth's *roman à clef*, it trades in an older historicism's tendency "to decipher texts in order to *fix* their meaning" for what she describes as a New Historicist criticism "based on a more interactive model of how literary and historical texts relate" (*Part 1*, lxx).

24. See, e.g.: Hackett, 61, 62, 64; Alexander, *Writing after Sidney*, 285; Wynne-Davies, 82; Luckyj, 269.

25. Hannay, 237.

26. Carrell, 100.

27. Hackett, 61.

28. Alexander, *Writing after Sidney*, 148. Comparing the published *Part 1* to the manuscript continuation of *Part 2*, Alexander argues that where "autobiographical elements" are "displaced on to minor characters and inset narratives" in *Part 1*, they are restored to "the central narrative of Pamphilia and Amphilanthus" in *Part 2* (294n28). As a result, Alexander finds that "where Part 1 finds its way, conscious of generic example and genealogical origin, Part 2 seems more convinced of the reality of the world it has created" (294). This is an odd claim. Where autobiographical elements become the measure of a narrative's confidence in "the reality of the world it has created," the created world is only as strong as the historical referent that stands as its origin. For Kinney, any insistence on the unique modality of fiction—that it is something other than a vehicle for personal history—undercuts both the authority of female speakers and the personal histories encoded within their fictions. By this view, the *Urania* is only as transgressive as it is historical: insofar as it is a vehicle for Wroth's own "erotic history," it authorizes both female desire and female speech ("'Beleeve this but a fiction,'" 242).

29. Howard, esp. her critique of "the illustrative example," 38–39.

30. Lamb, 127. See also when Pamphilia finishes telling the story of Lindamira and reciting a sequence of sonnets to conclude; Dolorina "admired these Sonnets, and the story, which shee thought was some thing more exactly related then a fixion, yet her discretion taught her to be no Inquisitor" (*Part 1*, 505).

31. This species of knowledge is related to what Eggert has called "disknowledge": "the conspicuous and deliberate setting aside of one compelling mode of understanding the world—one discipline, one theory—in favor of another" (3).

32. "Employed solely for decorative effect," *periphrasis* is, as Quintilian explains it, the name we lend to "whatever might have been expressed with greater brevity, but is expanded for purposes of ornament" (8.6.61). [*Quicquid enim significari brevius potest et cum ornatu latius ostenditur.*]

33. As in the medieval *Poetria Nova* by Geoffrey of Vinsauf: "In order to amplify the poem, avoid calling things by their names; use other designations for them. Do not unveil the thing fully but suggest it by hints. Do not let your words move straight onward through the subject, but, circling it, take a long and winding path around what you were going to say briefly. Retard the tempo by thus increasing the number of words. This device lengthens brief forms of expression, since a short word abdicates in order that an extended sequence may be its heir" (trans. Nims, 24).

34. Susenbrotus, 39–40. [*Item vicini nostri puella haud iuvenusta nupturint, cum nomen eius tibi non sit cognitum*] (C_5r–C_5v).

35. Brinsley, X_2v. See also where Brinsley advises that when a student comes across a "phrase or word they cannot utter in Laitine . . . let them bethinke themselves how they would first vtter and vary it in English, and some of the English words will bring Latine wordes or phrases to their remembrance; or else how they can expresse it by periphrasis, or circumlocution in the words, by some description, or by the generall, or the contrary, or by some property, or the like" (Bb_2r).

36. See Rosindy's address of Sophy of Persia: "Nor indeed can I tell what title to give you, who in excellencies excell excelence itt self" (Wroth, *Part 2*, 170. Hereafter cited parenthetically in text by Part and page number).

37. Brinsley, marked by Thomas Barney in the Huntington Library [HEH RB 29028]. I originally came across these notes thanks to William Sherman's guide to marked copies at the Huntington (a manuscript in his possession entitled "HEH MARG"). Sherman discusses these notes in *Used Books*, 4. This early reader's marginalia shares the page with Brinsley's reiteration of the utility of *periphrasis*: "Where none can giue a fit word . . . describe the thing by some Periphrasis or circumlocution of words or phrases mentioned" (Ffv). John Cleveland concludes "Hecatomb to His Mistress," in which he insists at length, "From pole to pole, I could not reach her worth / Nor find an Epithet to set it forth" that "She, she it is, She that contains all blisse, / And make the world but her Periphrasis" (*Poems* [1651], 5–7).

38. In an interesting twist on this idea, the *Urania* contains an episode in which one of Pamphilia's rejected lovers, Steriamus, withholds Pamphilia's name from her rival, Nereana, because he does not believe she is worthy of it: "I will assure you that I love a Princesse, whose feete you are not worthy to kisse, nor name with so fond a tongue, nor see, if not (as the Images in old time were) with adoration; nor heare, but as Oracles; and yet this is a woman, and indeed the perfectest." While Steriamus resists naming Pamphilia for some time, eventually Nereana wins out: "perplexing him still, leaving him in no place quiet, till she got your name" (*Part 1*, 192–193).

39. Quintilian: "It is sometimes necessary, being of special service when it conceals something which would be indecent, if expressed in so many words" (8.6.59). [*qui nonnunquam necessitatem habet, quotiens dictu deformia operit.*] Susenbrotus: "It comes about, moreover, almost unavoidably, when we would conceal in our speech what is either unsightly or sordid and repulsive" (39) [*Fit autem, uel neccessitatis causa, cum videlicet aut turpia, sordida dictumque deformia operimus*] (C₅r). Sherry: "if it bee foule to hyde it" ([1550], C₆v). As in the didactic verse of Mancinus: "Abstayne from vyle wordes in speche and communyng / Whan thou hast to common of thyng of grauyte / For oft tyme vyle wordes corrupteth good lyueng / And are thou shamefast lyfe / nat small difformyte / But whan thou must in speche touche of necessite / Such matters vnclenly use circumlocucion / And let thy mynde and tonge be honest all season" (*Here begynneth a right frutefull treatyse*, trans. Bercley [1518], G₆v).

40. Quintilian, 8.6.50; Susenbrotus, 39.

41. Sherry (1555), D₁v. I have represented the prose here with its original line breaks.

42. Martial, *Ex otio negotium. Or, Martial his epigrams translated*, trans. Fletcher (1656), 98. [*nec per circuitus loquatur illam, / ex qua nascimur, omnium parentem, / quam sanctus Numa mentulam vocabat*] (Martial, *Epigrams*, trans. Bailey, 11.15).

43. Peacham, *Garden* (1593), 148.

44. It is easy to read this passage at first as the actualization of the threatened rape; it is only when one reads on that one realizes that the clause "while hee tooke his full pleasure of her" is part of the husband's command rather than narration.

45. Wilson, *Art of Rhetoric*, 201.

46. Sherry (1550): "Garnyshing as the word it selfe declareth, is when the oracion is gaylye set oute and floryshed with diuerse goodly figures, causyng much pleasuntnes and delectacion to the hearer" (C₃v).

47. *Periphrasis* was in this sense closely related to *paraphrasis*, or the act of expounding upon a "thyng, word, or sentence" in order to make it "more evident and lightsom" (Peacham [1593], X₂v). For *periphrasis* and *paraphrasis*, see also Wilson, 201; Hoskins, 47.

48. See Peacham's *Garden* (1593), where he places *periphrasis* in the "third order" of figures dedicated to "amplification" rather than among the "tropes of sentences."

49. "When a maker," Puttenham explains, "will seem to use circumlocution to set forth any thing pleasantly and figuratively, yet no less plain to a ripe reader than if it were named expressly," that is a good use of the figure, but if "no man can perceive it to be the thing intended, this is a foul oversight in any writer" (279).

50. Hoskins, 46.

51. Hoskins, 46–47.

52. Hoskins, 47. For a similar moment, see Quintilian's discussion of the epithet, 8.6.41.

53. Quintilian, 8.6.59. See also Susenbrotus, C₅r.

54. Quintilian, 8.6.61. [*Quicquid enim significari brevius potest et cum ornatu latius ostenditur.*]

55. Peacham writes of *periphrasis* that "this exornation serueth only to garnish the Oration with varietie of wordes, and neuer encreaseth matter" ([1593], O₂r). For Melanchthon, "endless periphrases and monstrous metaphors" mark the middle style at its worst: "There are faulty places in this category, swollen and puffed up, which try to appear grandiose, which produce nothing effective, but have endless periphrases and monstrous metaphors. These were once called Asiatic, for in Asia where they had a corrupt and improper kind of discourse, they still affected praise of eloquence by a display of immoderate ornament" [*Viciosi sunt in hoc genere, tumidi et inflati, qui nimis grandes videri cupiunt, qui nihil proprie efferunt, sed perpetuas habent periphrases, et prodigiosas metaphoras. Hi vocabantur olim Asiatici. Nam in Asia cum sermonis genus haberent corruptum et improprium, tamen affectabant eloquentiae laudem ostentatione immodici ornatus.*] (trans. La Fontaine, 347). See also Nashe: "I am not ignorant how eloquent our gowned age is growen of late, so that euerie mœchanicall mate abhorres the english he was borne too, and plucks with a solemn periphrasis his *vt vales* from the inkhorne" (1:307–308). Robert Ernst Curtius understands *periphrasis* as an attribute of the mannerist style of the late middle ages, in which "the *ornatus* is piled on indiscriminately and meaninglessly" (274). Scott praises neologisms as an important alternative to *periphrasis*: "If we should make no new words we should not be able to express our meaning in divers new inventions without much circumstance and ambage of speech, which all languages labour to avoid, because the conceit, being so quick itself, it is much pleased with the soon delivery and quick receiving of the message sent by the tongue and pen (the ambassadors and agents of the mind) and, contrary, is much perplexed and offended with the tediousness and difficulty of long circumlocutions, unready and ambiguous speech" (49).

56. Quintilian, 8.6.61. [*cui nomen Latine datum est non sane aptum orationis virtuti circumlocutio. Verum hoc ut, cum decorem habet, periphrasis, ita, cum in vitium incidit, περισσολογία dicitur.*] Puttenham, 343.

57. Sprat, 113.

58. Ramus, *Arguments in Rhetoric*, 139. [*At periphrasis omnibus propriis verbis effici potest: nec idcirco tropus ullus est omnino, sed argumenti genus ex dialectico definitionis loco*] (212).

59. Fraunce, *Lawiers Logike*, Q$_4$r.
60. Fraunce, *Lawiers Logike*, R$_2$v, R$_3$v.
61. Fraunce, *Lawiers Logike*, R$_3$v.
62. Fraunce, *Lawiers Logike*, S$_1$r.
63. As Teskey writes of Edmund Spenser's *Faerie Queene*: "Acts of grasping and penetrating leave us ... empty-handed or in an empty place." "Philosophy," he continues, "in the broad, Renaissance sense of the term as *scientia*—is the open project of explaining the *things* of this world. . . . Philosophy reduces the flux of existence, and the flux of our consciousness inside existence, to a gigantic array of hard-surfaced things. . . . As the flux of existence is reduced to an array of things, so is the flux of consciousness reduced to the solitary, contemplating subject. This subject grasps the phenomena as if they were things" ("'And Therefore as a Stranger Give It Welcome,'" 346).
64. Wilson, *Art of Rhetoric*, 241.
65. Pamphilia is not wrong to be suspicious of Echo's uncanny ability to reveal what a speaker might wish to hide. In the poem by Edward de Vere, for example, each word with which the lover concludes the first four lines of her lament compels Echo to call out the name of her beloved (who happens to be hiding nearby):

"O heavens," quoth she, "who was the first that bred in me this fever?"
  Echo: Vere.
"Who was the first that gave the wound, whose scar I wear forever?"
  Echo: Vere.
"What tyrant Cupid to my harms usurps the golden quiver?" *Echo*: Vere.
"What wight first caught this heart, and can from bondage it deliver?"
  Echo: Vere.

Echo's naming is something that this lover pathologically courts. She stages a series of *periphrases* as questions so that she might hear the very name that she withholds (*The New Oxford Book of Sixteenth-Century Verse*, 159).
66. Alexander writes of this moment: "The interrupted text here straddles life and death, mimetically crossing a threshold with much the same ambiguity of conclusion or continuation that we see in the 'And' with which Part 1 of the *Urania* ends" (*Writing after Sidney*, 321).
67. Interestingly, when Alarinus tells the story of Myra's downfall, it turns on a slander that he withholds. A jealous suitor "raysed a most detestable slander on her, and how? or by whom? but alas, by me saying she had: Rather (I beseech you) imagine, if you can let any ill imagination enter into your thoughts of so excellent a creature, then put mee to rehearse it, or boldly thinke any ill with this consideration, that it was the root of it selfe, that the Devill invented it, and then pitty her and mee, who unjustly suffered, or indeed onely her, since shee alone deserves pitty, being injur'd, and for one

so unworthy, yet to her just: This was none of my least afflictions, since it was the course whereby her fate was govern'd, leading her to her end, and making me part of the mischiefe" (*Part 1*, 593). At the center of Alarinus's story is a slander that he refuses to repeat. Yet this central act of withholding distracts from the curious slip in Alarinus's syntax: "but alas, by me saying she had: rather (I beseech you) imagine." Was Alarinus the instrument or the object of this slander? By withholding the slander itself, Alarinus's "by me" comes to modify "saying" rather than what "she had" (e.g., "a child"). In spite of the subsequent insistence that he is to blame only insofar as she was "injur'd" on his behalf, his use of *periphrasis* paradoxically implicates him as an agent in the original act of "saying" that he now withholds, and Alarinus therefore looks like a collaborator in Myra's end.

68. E.g., "False," Liana says of Alanius, and then she turns to the word itself: "false, murdering word, which with itself carries death, and millions of tortures joynd with it" (*Part 1*, 247). When at the opening of *The Second Part*, Selarinus laments the loss of his beloved, he is surprised to find that he can speak of her death without dying from the speaking of it: "Lost, O she is lost, dead, ay mee, dead, and shall Selarinus live to say Philastella is dead, and nott dy with that word?" (*Part 2*, 1). While we might expect that the ability to speak a phrase like "Philastella is dead" is the very sign of life (that the difference between being alive and being dead is that the former permits you to speak of the latter), Selarinus seems to think that the act of calling Philastella "dead" ought to end his existence. See also Amphilanthus on his separation from Pamphilia: "Though to mee (now, alas, to late) the word 'depart' bee death. To her, I pray itt may prove butt deaths elder brother, sleepe" (*Part 2*, 295).

69. Montaigne, D_4v. On biblical *periphrases* for death, see Strode, *The anatomie of mortalitie* (1618), "a most sweete *Periphrasis* of death" (P_3v); Lemnius, *An Herbal for the Bible* (1587), "And by a most elegant *Periphrasis* or circumlocution he sheweth, how man, being in his best flourishing time, doth by little and little decay" (Q_6r).

70. "Let vs remove her strangenesse from her, let vs converse, frequent, and acquaint our selves with her, let vs have nothing so much in minde as death, let vs at all times and seasons, and in the vgliest manner that may be, yea with all faces shapen and represent the same vnto our imagination" (Montaigne, D_5r).

71. Sidney, *Countess of Pembroke's Arcadia*, 61.

72. Sidney, *Countess of Pembroke's Arcadia* (1598), 1 (Newberry Case Y 1565-.S556).

73. See also *Part 1*, 23.

74. See also *Part 1*, 11, 20, 28.

75. See also *Part 1*, 21.
76. See also *Part 1*, 11.
77. After Urania roused the delinquent Perissus to action, Perissus asks: "Is Perissus the second time conquer'd?" (*Part 1*, 15).
78. See Urania "under the shade of a well-spread Beech" (*Part 1*, 1).
79. Regretting the fact that her cruelty has sent Floristello away, she declares her suitability for him: "Beesides I ame nott the shepheardes daughter, by his owne relation and some tokens hee hath given mee, Why may I not bee a princess? And such a princess is lost. And why nott I the same? And then why may I nott love the Albanian Prince? . . . why Urania, the beautie and wounder of the world for worthe, was butt a sheapherdes as I ame in show when Steriamus first loved her, when Parselius first loved her" (*Part 2*, 103–104). This shepherdess does not have the story quite right: Steriamus only falls in love with Urania after he too has been cured by the magical waters (of his love for Pamphilia); thus, Urania is already revealed to be a princess when Steriamus falls in love with her.
80. See Parker, *Inescapable Romance*, which describes romance as "a form which simultaneously projects the end it seeks and defers or wanders from a goal which would mean . . . the end of the quest itself" (173).
81. In *The First Part* of the *Urania*, it is the union of Pamphilia and Amphilanthus that holds out the promise of narrative closure. Each goes about inscribing ciphers of the other onto this and that surface (each also has the name of the other inscribed in their heart's flesh). Traveling as the Knight of the Cipher, Amphilanthus suggests that the union of cipher to key will demonstrate the excessive value of that cipher: "Although a Cipher were nothing in it selfe," he insists, "yet joyned to the figures of her worth, whose name was therein, it was made above the valew of her selfe and Country" (*Part 1*, 339). And while *The First Part* concludes with a version of this union—"Pamphilia is the Queene of all content; Amphilanthus joying worthily in her"—the subsequent "And" indicates a kind of remainder that *The Second Part* is quick to take up, separating the pair once again in its very first paragraph (*Part 1*, 661).
82. Lamb, 129–130.
83. Lamb, 130.
84. This is the conceptual limit of even the most sophisticated of topical readings. See also Roberts, who warns against "simple referential correspondence," describing instead "a process of mediation and progressive, experimental alteration of form": "The marital adventures of Pamphilia are autobiographical," she continues, "mainly in the sense that they permit the author consciously and unconsciously to reorder herself, and through this ongoing struggle to narrate herself in the conditional or the subjunctive mode, as

she could have, should have, or might have been" ("'The Knott never to be Untide,'" 125–126).

85. As Lamb writes: "Faire Designe is more than a character, and even more than a shadowing of her son Wil by William Herbert. By the conclusion of the manuscript continuation, he has become the moving principle or the 'design' of the *Urania*; the *Urania* has become merged with his interests; he has become inseparable from the text itself. In the text's emphasis on its beauty or fairness, the youth's design displayed on his clothing serves as a visual expression of the art of Wroth's romance, which with its winding plots and ornate language, is also a faire 'design' in the early modern sense of 'a piece of decorative work, an artistic device'" (125).

86. In "*The Shepheardes Calender*, Dialogue, and Periphrasis," Greene suggests that the *Calender* is a *periphrasis* for the dialogic lyric it can discuss but not realize: the *Calender* itself is a piece of criticism invested in thinking through a hypothesis—"gesturing toward a poem of now or later that it cannot, or will not, be" (10). The *Calender* is thus about a kind of discourse, "a discourse that lies just beyond the circumscription of the *Calender*, the fondly remembered and eagerly anticipated dialogic speech-that-they-do-not-now-have" (16).

CODA: *INDECOROUS* FORMS

1. Bacon, 139. For the broader object of Bacon's critique, see Vickers's helpful, if pointed, "The Myth of Francis Bacon's Anti-Humanism," 135–158; and Mueller, esp. 68–72.

2. E.g. Mann, 27; Nicholson, *Uncommon Tongues*, 164.

3. Jonson, *Discoveries*, 108–109. The full passage from Bacon reads: "Men began to hunt more after words than matter; and more after the choiceness of the phrase, and the round and clean composition of the sentence, and the sweet falling of the clauses, and the varying and illustration of their works with tropes and figures, than after the weight of matter, worth of subject, soundness of argument, life of invention, or depth of judgment" (139). For a reading of the "symmetry" of Bacon's sentence "as a matrix against which the oppositions between cause and effect, false and true, eloquence and plainness, become inescapably clear and convincing," see Vickers, *Francis Bacon and Renaissance Prose*, 124.

4. Bacon, 139.

5. As Barish writes, "Jonson has eliminated Bacon's dichotomy between rhetorical curiosity and solidity of thought, and lumped together the phrases from both sides of Bacon's antithesis in a single top-heavy series" (*Ben Jonson and the Language of Prose Comedy*, 59).

6. Barish, *Ben Jonson*, 41–89.

7. Barish, *Ben Jonson*, 56–57. On Jonson and "the exploded period" (83) as a worldview, see esp. Barish, *Ben Jonson*, 38–39, 56–57, 77, 79, 83–84.

8. Barish, *Ben Jonson*, 76. For "the plain style," see Trimpi.

9. For example, Barish writes that in *Every Man Out*, "Jonson is making comic capital out of the misapplication of devices sacred to classical oratory" (*Ben Jonson*, 110); more recently, Turner writes that "specialized or arcane formulations work in the service of a critique of character as it is revealed in language" (*English Renaissance Stage*, 224). The chorus discusses the genre of *Every Man Out* (*In.* 225–266). On "comical satire," see Kernan, *The Cankered Muse*, 157–162; Rhodes, 131–140; Barton, 58–73; Ostovich, "Introduction," in *Every Man Out of His Humour*, 11–13.

10. Barish, *Ben Jonson*, 3.

11. See Maus, 42–64. See esp. "the law of the conservation of matter" (44).

12. Spenser, *The Faerie Queene*, 2.9.50.3–4; Sidney, *Defence*, 216.

13. For Fastidius, 2.1.124–125; for Macilente, 3.3.73–74. On *Every Man Out* as "the first professional play to be printed with commonplace markers that pointed out vernacular 'sentences'" as well as the presence of those *sententiae* in early, vernacular commonplace books, see Lesser and Stallybrass, 395. Ostovich writes that "*EMO* was not only Jonson's biggest hit as a printed text but also the most popular play-text published by anyone in the period" ("Introduction," 31). On Jonson's relation to John Hoskins, the author of *Directions for Speech and Style*, see Ostovich, "Introduction," 28, 35.

14. Defending Mistress Saviolina against Carlo's charge that her speech is "Nothing but sound, sound, a mere echo!" Fastidius counters that "she has the most harmonious and musical strain of wit that ever tempted a true ear . . . she doth give it that sweet, quick grace and exornation in the composure that (by this good heaven) she does observe as pure a phrase and use as choice figures in her ordinary conferences as any be i' the *Arcadia*" (2.1.490–508). Carlo replies that she cribs from Robert Greene (2.1.509–510). Fungoso proposes to "lie a-bed and read the *Arcadia*" while his tailor makes him a new suit after the fashion of Fastidius (3.1.307). Watson describes *Every Man Out*'s characters as "enslaved" to their "literary self-conceptions" (*Ben Jonson's Parodic Strategy*, 61). He writes of Fungoso's declaration: "One fantasy—the same implausible romance from which Lady Saviolina draws—will do until the next is ready; reading the *Arcadia* will serve as a sort of temporary prosthesis to his uncomfortably ordinary self-hood, until the grand new costume can generate a grand new identity" (69). For the play's most Spenserian moments, see Sordido's hanging, 3.2.1–133; the vision of the Queen, 5.4.1–40; and Carlo on men and pigs, 5.3.160–166.

15. E.g., Carlo advises Sogliardo to write himself letters in the name of another and addressed to "their 'worshipful, right rare, and noble qualified friend or kinsman, *Signor Insulo Sogliardo*': give yourself style enough" (1.2.79–81); the "O sweet Fastidius Brisk! O fine courtier!" that thrice punctuates Fallace's extended *apostrophe* (4.1.28–29, 32–33, 39–40); Fastidius's praise of the life of the courtier (what Macielente calls his "*encomion*") as "O, the most celestial, and full of wonder and delight that can be imagined" with the conclusion that "what else, confined within the amplest verge of poesy, to be mere *umbrae* and imperfect figures conferred with the most essential felicity of your court" (4.5.16–34). The attention to *epithets* culminates in Macilente's conversion when faced with the Queen in the original ending to the play: "Blessèd, divine, unblemished, sacred, pure, / Glorious, immortal, and indeed immense— /O, that I had a world of attributes / to lend or add to this high majesty!" (5.4.1–5).

16. The "List of Characters" appeared in the Q1 printing of the play as well as subsequent editions (see ed. Ostovich, 101). Turner describes this kind of scene as "emblematic": "primarily rhetorical in its effect: it opens a discursive field rather than a space of 'action,' providing a frame for the linguistic exploration of an idea, intellectual problem, tone, or emotional development. It produces meaning in an associative way, since it depends on perceived similarity between some qualities of characters or aspects of ideas that are explicitly represented and others that are not" (*English Renaissance Stage*, 224).

17. Barish writes that "Jonson begins, in this play, to experiment with a wider range of traditional rhetorical figures. These tend to group themselves most heavily, or at least to become evident, at certain key moments, notably at the point in the stage life of each character when he abandons himself without restraint to his ruling passion" (107). See 104–113 more generally.

18. Ostovich, "'So Sudden and Strange a Cure,'" 318. Lawrence Danson writes that "the play is so hedged about and intertwined with elaborate self-commentary that it seems to disappear into another play that is about the difficult condition of being a play" (184).

19. As Danson describes it, "the strange difficulty of *Every Man Out* is comparable to the difficulty one has in breathing while thinking about breathing" (184).

20. I am grateful to Katherine Schaap Williams for this point.

21. As Blissett discusses, *Every Man Out* was likely the first play performed at the Globe in 1599, and Jonson references "this faire-fil'd Globe" in his revised conclusion of the Quarto edition (167). Thinking of the unusual structure of the play in relation to the theater of its original performance, Blissett writes that the interlocking sets of characters "within the sphere of

the theatre, produce some effect of radial symmetry or a dynamic of rotation": "The characters here spread or 'run' in stains, encroach or retract like tentacles, and the main scene of walking, in the aisles of St. Paul's, is round and round in a ring" (168).

22. Writing of Asper's determination to "prodigally spend myself," Maus describes "The Jonsonian Poet" as "a self-consuming artificer": "The achievement of 'fullness' not only guarantees the quality of the poetic product, but constitutes a kind of reinforcement for a 'selfe' or 'spirit' imagined as a limited quality, dissolved and depleted by the act of creation" (61–62).

23. Maus, 44. She distinguishes this problem from that of *copia* (thinking of Terrence Cave): "For the writers Cave considers . . . the problem is the management of plentitude, not (as with Jonson) the problem of making a little go a long way" (61).

24. Sidney, *Defence*, 246–247.

25. When Carlo delivers the prologue and announces the conceit of the play, he establishes the basic expectation that all humors will be undone before the conclusion: "S'blood, an he get me out of his humor he has put me in, I'll ne'er trust none of his tribe again, while I live" (*Ind.* 341–342). Danson writes: "The condition of the play has been the display of its humors; the condition of its ending is the displacement of those humors; the play is therefore oddly cannibalistic in aiming all along at the nullification of the characters that give it life" (186). Watson describes this as the "self-limiting nature of the parodic strategy": "At the end of the play the satiric manipulator stands, not gloating in the midst of his profits, but bewildered on the brink of the dramatic and moral void his victories threaten to generate" (*Ben Jonson's Parodic Strategy*, 48).

26. "To the perfection of compliment (which is the dial of the thought, and guided by the sun of your beauties) are required these three projects: the gnomon, the puntilios, and the superficies. The superficies is that we call 'place'; the puntilios, 'circumstance'; and the gnomon, 'ceremony'; in either of which, for a stranger to err, 'tis easy and facile, and such am I" (2.1.207–213). See Turner, *English Renaissance Stage*, 235–236.

27. Barish wrote that in *Every Man Out*, Jonson's characters travestied rhetoric and its figures in order to "burst the bonds of realism altogether and carry the whole play into the realm of the semifabulous": "Jonson's rhetorical innovations produce marvels of the grotesque, not the plausible" (*Ben Jonson*, 112–113).

28. See "adulterate" in *Oxford English Dictionary*. In contrast to my argument, Turner understands the Chorus's discussion of Carlo's *similes* to operate within the contained logic of "the emblematic scene" (224).

29. See "*confundo*" in *Lewis and Short*.

30. In this way, his *poesie* is similar to what Maus describes as Jonson's "most successful and exciting characters," who "tend to be masters of the inspired assemblage of haphazard materials" (47).

31. Barish, *Ben Jonson*, 83. Rhodes describes *Every Man Out* as a species of urban realism representing "the spaces between people which the city creates" (135). See also William N. West, who writes that "Jonson's early playwriting is a theatricalization of the encyclopedic combinatory method, in which individual elements are manipulated and arranged to produce every possible combination while they remain unchanged" (147).

32. Barish, *Ben Jonson*, 47, 50, 48. See 47–54 and 105–107 more generally.

33. For Puntarvolo's collaboration, see 4.3.136–142.

34. Spenser, *The Faerie Queene*, 2.3.5.6.

BIBLIOGRAPHY

Adamson, Sylvia, Gavin Alexander, and Katrin Ettenhuber, eds. *Renaissance Figures of Speech*. Cambridge: Cambridge University Press, 2007.
Addison, Catherine. "From Literal to Figurative: An Introduction to the Study of Simile." *College English* 55, no. 4 (1993): 402–419.
———. "'So Stretched Out Huge in Length': Reading the Extended Simile." *Style* 35, no. 3 (2001): 498–516.
Adelman, Janet. *The Common Liar*. New Haven, Conn.: Yale University Press, 1973.
Agricola, Rudolph. *Letters*. Translated by Adrie Van Der Laan and Fokke Akkerman. Tempe: Arizona Center for Medieval and Renaissance Studies, 2002.
Alexander, Gavin, "Prosopopoeia: The Speaking Figure." In *Renaissance Figures of Speech*, ed. Sylvia Adamson, Gavin Alexander, and Katrin Ettenhuber, 97–112. Cambridge: Cambridge University Press, 2007.
———, ed. *Sidney's 'The Defence of Poesy' and Selected Renaissance Literary Criticism*. London: Penguin, 2004.
———. "Sidney's Interruptions." *Studies in Philology* 98 (2001): 184–204.
———. *Writing after Sidney: The Literary Response to Sir Philip Sidney, 1596–1640*. Oxford: Oxford University Press, 2006.
Altman, Joel B. *The Tudor Play of Mind*. Berkeley: University of California Press, 1978.
Anderson, Judith H. "'Nat worth a boterflye': *Muiopotmos* and *The Nun's Priest's Tale*." *Journal of Medieval and Renaissance Studies* 1 (1971): 89–106.
———. *Translating Investments: Metaphor and the Dynamics of Cultural Change in Tudor-Stuart England*. New York: Fordham University Press, 2005.
———. *Words That Matter: Linguistic Perception in the English Renaissance*. Stanford, Calif.: Stanford University Press, 1996.
Anderson, Judith H., and Joan Pong Linton, eds. *Go Figure: Energies, Forms, and Institutions in the Early Modern World*. New York: Fordham University Press, 2011.
Aristotle. *Poetics*. Edited and translated by Stephen Halliwell. Loeb Classical Library. Cambridge, Mass.: Harvard University Press, 1995.

———. *The Rhetoric and Poetics of Aristotle.* Translated by Rhys Roberts and Ingram Bywater. New York: Modern Library, 1954.
———. *Topica.* Translated by E. S. Forster. Loeb Classical Library. Cambridge, Mass.: Harvard University Press, 1966.
Ascham, Roger. *The Schoolmaster* (1570). Ed. Lawrence V. Ryan. Charlottesville: University Press of Virginia for the Folger Shakespeare Library, 1967.
Attridge, Derek. *Peculiar Language: Literature as Difference from the Renaissance to James Joyce.* Ithaca, N.Y.: Cornell University Press, 1988.
Auerbach, Eric. "Figura." In *Scenes from the Drama of European Literature*, 11–76. New York: Median, 1959.
Augustine. *De Doctrina Christiana.* Translated by R. P. H. Greene. Oxford: Clarendon, 1995.
———. *Of the citie of God.* Translated by John Healey. London, 1610.
Bacon, Francis. *The Major Works.* Edited by Brian Vickers. Oxford: Oxford University Press, 1996.
Baines, Barbara J. "Antonio's Revenge: Marston's Play on Revenge Plays." *Studies in English Literature, 1500–1900* 23, no. 2 (1982): 277–294.
Baldwin, T. W. *Small Latine & Lesse Greeke.* 2 vols. Urbana: University of Illinois Press, 1947.
Barish, Jonas. *Ben Jonson and the Language of Prose Comedy.* Cambridge, Mass.: Harvard University Press, 1960.
———. "Prose Style of John Lyly." *ELH* 23 (1956): 14–35.
Barret, J. K. *Untold Futures: Time and Literary Culture in Renaissance England.* Ithaca, N.Y.: Cornell University Press, 2016.
Barthes, Roland. "The Old Rhetoric: An Aide-Mèmoire." In *The Semiotic Challenge*, trans. Richard Howard. New York: Hill and Wang, 1988.
———. *S/Z: An Essay.* Translated by Richard Miller. New York: Hill and Wang, 1970.
Barton, Anne. *Ben Jonson, Dramatist.* Cambridge: Cambridge University Press, 1984.
Berger Jr., Harry. *The Absence of Grace.* Stanford, Calif.: Stanford University Press, 2000.
———. *The Allegorical Temper.* New Haven, Conn.: Yale University Press, 1957.
———. *Imaginary Audition.* Berkeley: University of California Press, 1989.
———. "Narrative as Rhetoric in *The Faerie Queene*." In *Situated Utterances: Texts, Bodies, and Cultural Representation.* New York: Fordham University Press, 2005.
———. *Second World and Green World.* Berkeley: University of California Press, 1988.

Blank, Paula. *Broken English: Dialects and the Politics of Language in Renaissance Writings.* New York: Routledge, 1996.
———. *Shakespeare and the Mismeasure of Renaissance Man.* Ithaca, N.Y.: Cornell University Press, 2006.
Blissett, William. "The Oddness of Every Man Out of His Humor." In *The Elizabethan Theatre, XII,* ed. A. L. Magnusson and C. E. McGee, 157–179. Toronto: Meany, 1993.
Bloom, Gina. *Voice in Motion: Staging Gender, Shaping Sound in Early Modern England.* Philadelphia: University of Pennsylvania Press, 2007.
Blount, Thomas. *The Academie of Eloquence.* London, 1654.
Blundeville, Thomas. *The arte of logick.* London, 1617.
Boethius. *De topicis differentiis.* Translated by Eleonore Stump. Ithaca, N.Y.: Cornell University Press, 1978.
Brayman Hackel, Heidi. *Reading Material in Early Modern England.* Cambridge: Cambridge University Press, 2005.
Brinsley, John. *Ludus Literarius.* London, 1612.
Brown, Georgia. *Redefining Elizabethan Literature.* Cambridge: Cambridge University Press, 2004.
Brown, Marshall, and Susan Wolfson, eds. *Reading for Form.* Seattle: University of Washington Press, 2006.
Bruster, Douglas. "The Materiality of Shakespearean Form." In *Shakespeare and Historical Formalism,* ed. Stephen Cohen, 31–45. London: Ashgate, 2007.
Bryskett, Lodowick. *The discourse of ciuill life.* London, 1606.
Burckhardt, Sigurd. *Shakespearean Meanings.* Princeton, N.J.: Princeton University Press, 1968.
Burke, Kenneth. *A Grammar of Motives.* Berkeley: University of California Press, 1969.
———. *A Rhetoric of Motives.* Berkeley: University of California Press, 1950.
Burrow, Colin. *Epic Romance: Homer to Milton.* Oxford: Clarendon, 1993.
———. "Original Fictions: Metamorphoses in 'The Faerie Queene.'" In *Ovid Renewed: Ovidian Influences on Literature and Art from the Middle Ages to the Twentieth Century,* 99–119. Cambridge: Cambridge University Press, 1988.
Burton, Ben, and Elizabeth Scott-Baumann, eds. *The Work of Form: Poetics and Materiality on Early Modern Culture.* Oxford: Oxford University Press, 2014.
Bushnell, Rebecca. *A Culture of Teaching: Early Modern Humanism in Theory and Practice.* Ithaca, N.Y.: Cornell University Press, 1996.
Campbell, Mary Baine. *Wonder and Science: Imagining Worlds in Early Modern Europe.* Ithaca, N.Y.: Cornell University Press, 1999.

Campion, Thomas. *Observations in the Art of English Poesie* [1602]. In *Elizabethan Critical Essays*, ed. G. Gregory Smith, 2:327–355. Oxford: Oxford University Press, 1904.
Carey, John. "Structure and Rhetoric in Sidney's *Arcadia*." In *Sir Philip Sidney: An Anthology of Modern Criticism*, ed. Dennis Kay, 245–264. Oxford: Clarendon, 1987.
Carruthers, Mary. *The Book of Memory: A Study of Memory in Medieval Culture*. Cambridge: Cambridge University Press, 1990.
Carrell, Jennifer Lee. "A Pack of Lies in the Looking Glass: Lady Mary Wroth's *Urania* and the Magic Mirror of Romance." *Studies in English Literature, 1500–1900* 34 (1994): 79–107.
Carson, Anne. *If Not, Winter: Fragments of Sappho*. New York: Knopf, 2002.
Cavanagh, Sheila T. *Cherished Torment: The Emotional Geography of Lady Mary Wroth's Urania*. Pittsburgh, Penn.: Duquesne University Press, 2001.
Cave, Terrence. *The Cornucopian Text: Problems of Writing in the French Renaissance*. Oxford: Oxford University Press, 1979.
Chapman, Seymour. "On Defining 'Form.'" *New Literary History* 2 (1971): 217–228.
Chapman's Homer: The Iliad. Edited by Allardyce Nicoll. Princeton, N.J.: Princeton University Press, 1998.
Cicero. *De Officiis*. Translated by Walter Miller. Loeb Classic Library. Cambridge, Mass.: Harvard University Press, 1915.
———. *De Oratore*. Translated by E. W. Sutton and H. Rackam. 2 vols. Loeb Classic Library. 1942; repr., Cambridge, Mass.: Harvard University Press, 1976.
———. *M.T. Ciceronis Orationum volumen primum-tertium*. Pariis: Apud Simonem Colinaeum, 1532.
———. *Orations: Pro Sestio. In Vatinium*. Translated by R. Gardner. Loeb Classical Library. Cambridge, Mass.: Harvard University Press, 1958.
———. *Orator*. Translated by H. M. Hubbel. Loeb Classical Library. Cambridge, Mass.: Harvard University Press, 1939.
———. *Topica*. Translated by H. M. Hubbel. Loeb Classical Library. Cambridge, Mass.: Harvard University Press, 1949.
Cleveland, John. *Poems*. London, 1651.
Cohen, Ralph, ed. Special Issue: Form and Its Alternatives. *New Literary History* 2 (1971): 199–356.
Cohen, Stephen, ed. *Shakespeare and Historical Formalism*. London: Ashgate, 2007.
Conybeare, John. *Letters and Exercises of the Elizabethan Schoolmaster John Conybeare*. Edited by Frederick Cornwallis Conybear. London: Henry Frowde, 1905.

Cooney, Helen. "Guyon and His Palmer: Spenser's Emblem of Temperance." *Review of English Studies* 51, no. 202 (2000): 169–192.
Crane, Mary Thomas. *Framing Authority: Sayings, Self, and Society in Sixteenth-Century England*. Princeton, N.J.: Princeton University Press, 1993.
Crewe, Jonathan. *Unredeemed Rhetoric*. Baltimore, Md.: Johns Hopkins University Press, 1982.
Croll, Morris W. "The Sources of the Euphuistic Rhetoric." In *Style, Rhetoric, and Rhythm*, ed. J. Max Patrick et al., 241–295. Woodbridge, Ct.: Ox Bow, 1966.
Cummings, Brian. *The Literary Culture of the Reformation: Grammar and Grace*. Oxford: Oxford University Press, 2002.
Curtius, Robert Ernst. *European Literature and the Latin Middle Ages*. Translated by William R. Trask. London: Routledge, 1948.
Danby, John F. *Poets on Fortune's Hill*. London: Faber and Faber, 1952.
Daniel, Samuel. "A Defence of Rhyme" [1603]. In *Sidney's 'The Defence of Poesy' and Selected Renaissance Literary Criticism*, ed. Gavin Alexander, 207–233. London: Penguin, 2004.
Danson, Lawrence. "Jonsonian Comedy and the Discovery of the Social Self." *Publications of the Modern Language Association* 99, no. 2 (1984): 179–193.
Daston, Lorraine. "Historical Epistemology." In *Questions of Evidence: Proof, Practice, and Persuasion Across Disciplines*, ed. J. Chandler, A. I. Davidson, and H. Harootunian, 282–289. Chicago: University of Chicago Press, 1991.
Davis, Alex. "Revolution by Degrees: Philip Sidney and *Gradatio*." *Modern Philology* 108, no. 4 (2011): 488–506.
Davis, Joel. "Multiple *Arcadias* and the Literary Quarrel between Fulke Greville and the Countess of Pembroke." *Studies in Philology* 101, no. 4 (2004): 401–430.
Day, Angel. *The English Secretorie*. London, 1586.
De Grazia, Margreta. "Lost Potential in Grammar and Nature: Sidney's *Astrophil and Stella*." *Studies in English Literature, 1500–1900* 21 (1981): 21–35.
Della Casa, Giovanni. *Galateo, Of Manners and Behaviours in Familiar Conversation* [1576]. Translated by Robert Peterson. Edited by Herbert Reid. Privately printed, 1892.
Demetrius. *On Style*. Translated by Doreen C. Innes. Loeb Classical Library. Cambridge, Mass.: Harvard University Press, 1995.
Dickenson, R. J. "The Tristia: Poetry in Exile." In *Ovid*, ed. J. W. Binns, 154–190. London: Routledge, 1973.
Dimock, Wai Chee. "Subjunctive Time: Henry James's Possible Wars." *Narrative* 17 (2009): 242–254.

Dolven, Jeff. "The Method of Spenser's Stanza." *Spenser Studies* 19 (2004): 17–25.
———. *Scenes of Instruction in Renaissance Romance*. Chicago: University of Chicago Press, 2007.
Dubrow, Heather. *The Challenges of Orpheus: Lyric Poetry and Early Modern England*. Baltimore, Md.: Johns Hopkins University Press, 2008.
———. *Deixis in the Early Modern English Lyric: Unsettling Spatial Anchors Like "Here," "This," "Come."* New York: Palgrave Macmillan, 2015.
———. *Echoes of Desire: English Petrarchism and Its Counterdiscourses*. Ithaca, N.Y.: Cornell University Press, 1995.
———. "Guess Who's Coming to Dinner? Reinterpreting Formalism in the Country House Poem." *Modern Language Quarterly* 61, no. 1 (2000): 59–77.
———. *Shakespeare and Domestic Loss: Forms of Deprivation, Mourning, and Recuperation*. Cambridge: Cambridge University Press, 1999.
———. "'You may be wondering why I called you all here today': Patterns of Gathering in the Early Modern Lyric." In *The Work of Form: Poetics and Materiality on Early Modern Culture*, ed. Ben Burton and Elizabeth Scott-Baumann, 23–28. Oxford: Oxford University Press, 2014.
Dundas, Judith. "'Muiopotmos': A World of Art." *Yearbook of English Studies* 5 (1975): 30–38.
Eggert, Katherine. *Disknowledge: Literature, Alchemy, and the End of Humanism in Renaissance England*. Philadelphia: University of Pennsylvania Press, 2015.
Empson, William. *Some Versions of Pastoral*. New York: New Directions, 1974.
Enterline, Lynn. *The Rhetoric of the Body: From Ovid to Shakespeare*. Cambridge: Cambridge University Press, 2000.
———. *Shakespeare's Schoolroom: Rhetoric, Discipline, Emotion*. Philadelphia: University of Pennsylvania Press, 2012.
Erasmus. *Copia: Foundations of the Abundant Style*. Translated by Betty I. Knott. In *Collected Works of Erasmus*, vol. 24. Edited by Craig R. Thompson. Toronto: University of Toronto Press, 1978.
———. *The Correspondence of Erasmus: Letters 142–297 [1501–1514]*. Translated by R. A. B. Mynors and D. F. S. Thomson. In *Collected Works of Erasmus*, vol. 2. Toronto: University of Toronto Press, 1975.
———. *De Conscribendis Epsitolis*. Translated by Charles Fantazzi. In *Collected Works of Erasmus*, vol. 25. Toronto: University of Toronto Press, 1974.
———. *De Copia Verborum Ac Rervm*. Ed. Betty I. Knott. In *Opera Omnia Desiderii Erasmi Roterodami, Ordinis Primi Tomvs Sextvs*. Amsterdam: Huygens Institut/Brill, 1988.

———. *De Ratione Studii*. Translated by Brian McGregor. In *Collected Works of Erasmus*, vol. 24. Edited by Craig R. Thompson. Toronto: University of Toronto Press, 1978.

———. *De Ratione Studii*. Ed. Jean-Claude Margolin. In *Opera Omnia Desiderii Erasmi Roterodami, Ordinis Primi Tomvs Secvndus*. Amsterdam: Huygens Institut/Brill, 1971.

———. *Opus Epistolarvm Des. Erasmi Roterodami*. Vol. 1. Edited by P. S. Allen. Oxford: Oxford University Press, 1905.

———. *Parabolae sive Similia*. Edited by J. C. Margolin. In *Opera Omnia Desiderii Erasmi Roterodami, Ordinis Primi Tomvs Qvintvs*. Amsterdam: Huygens Institut/Brill, 1975.

———. *Parabolae sive Similia*. Translated by R. A. B. Mynors. In *Collected Works of Erasmus*, vol. 23. Edited by Craig R. Thompson. Toronto: University of Toronto Press, 1978.

Ettenhuber, Katrin. "Hyperbole: Exceeding Similitude." In *Renaissance Figures of Speech*, ed. Sylvia Adamson, Gavin Alexander, and Katrin Ettenhuber, 197–213. Cambridge: Cambridge University Press, 2007.

Fahnestock, Jeanne. *Rhetorical Figures in Science*. New York: Oxford University Press, 1999.

Fenner, Dudley. *The Artes of Logike and Rethorike*. London, 1584.

Ferguson, Margaret. *Dido's Daughters: Literacy, Gender, and Empire in Early Modern England and France*. Chicago: University of Chicago Press, 2003.

———. *Trials of Desire: Renaissance Defenses of Poetry*. New Haven, Conn.: Yale University Press, 1983.

Ferry, Anne. *Milton's Epic Voice: The Narrator in Paradise Lost*. Chicago: University of Chicago Press, 1983.

Fienberg, Nona. "Mary Wroth's Poetics of the Self." *Studies in English Literature, 1500–1900* 42, no. 1 (2002): 121–136.

Fletcher, Angus. *Allegory: The Theory of a Symbolic Mode*. Ithaca, N.Y.: Cornell University Press.

Florio, John. "Epistle to the Second Book, Dedicated to Elizabeth, Countess of Rutland." In *Sidney: The Critical Heritage*, ed. M. Garrett, 168. London: Routledge, 1996.

Forshall, Frederic H. *Westminster School*. London: Wyman & Sons, 1884.

Fowler, Alastair. "Oxford and London Marginalia to *The Faerie Queene*." *Notes & Queries* 206 (1961): 416–419.

Fowler, Alastair, and Michael Leslie. "Drummond's Copy of *The Faerie Queene*." *Times Literary Supplement* (July 17, 1981): 821–822.

Fox, Cora. "Spenser's Grieving Adicia and the Gender Politics of Renaissance Ovidianism," *ELH* 69 (2002): 385–412.

Fraunce, Abraham. *The Arcadian Rhetorike*. London, 1588.

———. *The Lawiers Logike*. London, 1588.
Fuchs, Barbara. *Romance*. New York: Routledge, 2004.
Fulbecke, William. *A direction or preparatiue to the study of the lawe*. London, 1600.
Fuller, Thomas. *The History of the Worthies of England*. London, 1662.
Fumerton, Patricia. *Cultural Aesthetics: Renaissance Literature and the Practice of Social Ornament*. Chicago: University of Chicago Press, 1991.
Gaonkar, Dilip Parmeschwar. "Contingency and Probability." In *A Companion to Rhetoric and Rhetorical Criticism*, ed. W. Jost and W. Olmsted, 5–21. Malden, Mass.: Blackwell, 2004.
Garrett, Martin, ed. *Sidney: The Critical Heritage*. London: Routledge, 1996.
Gascoigne, George. "Certayne Notes of Instruction" [1575]. In *Elizabethan Critical Essays*, ed. G. Gregory Smith, 1:46–57. Oxford: Oxford University Press, 1904.
Genette, Gérard. *Figures of Literary Discourse*. Translated by Alan Sheridan. New York: Columbia University Press, 1982.
Goeglein, Tamara. "'Wherein hath Ramus been so offensious?': Poetic Examples in the English Ramist Logic Manuals." *Rhetorica* 14, no. 1 (1996): 73–101.
Grafton, Anthony, and Lisa Jardine. *From Humanism to the Humanities: Education and the Liberal Arts in Fifteenth-and Sixteenth-Century Europe*. Cambridge, Mass.: Harvard University Press, 1986.
———. "'Studied for Action': How Gabriel Harvey Read His Livy." *Past & Present* 129 (1990): 30–78.
Granger, Thomas. *Divine Logike*. London, 1620.
Green, Lawrence D. "Grammatica Movet: Renaissance Grammar Books and *Elocutio*." In *Rhetorica Movet*, ed. P. L. Oesterreich and T. O. Sloane, 73–115. Leiden: Brill, 1999.
Greenblatt, Stephen. *Renaissance Self-Fashioning: From More to Shakespeare*. Chicago: University of Chicago Press, 1980.
Greene, Roland. *Five Words: Critical Semantics in the Age of Shakespeare and Cervantes*. Chicago: University of Chicago Press, 2013.
———. "A Primer of Spenser's Worldmaking: Alterity in the Bower of Bliss." In *Worldmaking Spenser: Explorations in the Early Modern Age*, ed. P. Cheney and L. Silberman, 9–31. Lexington: University Press of Kentucky, 2000.
———. "*The Shepheardes Calender*, Dialogue, and Periphrasis." *Spenser Studies* 8 (1987): 1–33.
Gregerson, Linda. "The Limbs of Truth: Milton's Use of Simile in *Paradise Lost*." *Milton Studies* 14 (1980): 135–152.
Hackett, Helen. "'Yet tell me some such fiction': Lady Mary Wroth's *Urania* and the 'Femininity' of Romance." In *Women, Texts, and Histories, 1575–*

1760, ed. Clare Brant and Diane Purkiss, 39–68. London: Routledge, 1992.
Hacking, Ian. "Styles of Scientific Reasoning." In *Post-Analytic Philosophy*, ed. John Rajchman and Cornel West, 145–164. New York: Columbia University Press, 1985.
Halpern, Richard. *The Poetics of Primitive Accumulation: English Renaissance Culture and the Genealogy of Capital*. Ithaca, N.Y.: Cornell University, 1991.
Hannay, Margaret. *Mary Sidney, Lady Wroth*. Surrey: Ashgate, 2010.
Hartman, Geoffrey. "'The Voice of the Shuttle': Language from the Point of View of Literature." In *Beyond Formalism: Literary Essays 1958–1970*, 337–355. New Haven, Conn.: Yale University Press, 1970.
Harvey, Gabriel. *Ciceronianus*. Translated by Clarence A. Forbes. Lincoln: University of Nebraska Press, 1945.
———. *A New Letter of Notable Contents*. London, 1593.
———. *Pierces Supererogation*. London, 1593.
———. *Rhetor*. Translated by Mark Reynolds. 2001. http://comp.uark.edu/~mreynold/engtran.pdf.
Hazard, Mary E. "An Essay to Amplify 'Ornament': Some Renaissance Theory and Practice." *Studies in English Literature, 1500–1900* 16, no. 1 (1976): 15–32.
Hazlitt, William. "From Lectures Chiefly on the Dramatic Literature of the Age of Elizabeth." In *Sidney: The Critical Heritage*, ed. M. Garrett, 318–322. London: Routledge, 1996.
Heller-Roazen, Daniel. *Fortune's Faces: The Roman de la Rose and the Poetics of Contingency*. Baltimore, Md.: Johns Hopkins University Press, 2003.
Herrick, Marvin Theodore. *Comic Theory in the Sixteenth Century*. Urbana: University of Illinois Press, 1950.
Heylyn, Peter. *Microcosmus, or A little description of the great world*. Oxford, 1621.
Hillman, David. "Puttenham, Shakespeare, and the Abuse of Rhetoric." *Studies in English Literature, 1500–1900* 36, no. 1 (Winter 1996): 73–90.
Hobbes, Thomas. "A Briefe of the Art of Rhetorique" [1637]. In *The Rhetorics of Thomas Hobbes and Bernard Lamy*, ed. John T. Harwood. Carbondale: Southern Illinois University Press, 1986.
Hollander, John. "Spenser and the Mingled Measure." *English Literary Renaissance* 1, no. 3 (1971): 226–238.
———. *The Untuning of the Sky*. Princeton, N.J.: Princeton University Press, 1961.
Holleran, James V. "Spenser's Braggadochio." In *Studies in English Renaissance Literature*, ed. Waldo F. McNeir, 20–39. Baton Rouge: Louisiana State University, 1962.

Hoole, Charles. *Examinatio Grammaticae Latine in usum scholarum adornatae.* London, 1661.
———. *The Latine Grammar Fitted for the Use of Schools.* London, 1651.
———. *A new discovery of the old art of teaching.* London, 1661.
Horace. *Satires, Epistles, and Ars Poetica.* Translated by H. Rushton Fairclough. Loeb Classical Library. Cambridge, Mass.: Harvard University Press, 1926.
Hoskins, John. *Directions for Speech and Style* [c. 1601]. Edited by Hoyt E. Hudson. Princeton, N.J.: Princeton University Press, 1935.
Howard, Jean. "The New Historicism in Renaissance Studies." *English Literary Renaissance* 16, no. 1 (1986): 13–43.
Howell, James. *Epistolae Ho-elianae.* London, 1650.
Howell, Wilbur Samuel. *Logic and Rhetoric in England, 1500–1700.* Princeton, N.J.: Princeton University Press, 1956.
Huston, Dennis J. "The Function of the Mock Hero in Spenser's 'Faerie Queene.'" *Modern Philology* 66, no. 3 (1969): 212–217.
Hutson, Lorna. "Fortunate Travelers: Reading for the Plot in Sixteenth-Century England." *Representations* 41 (1993): 83–103.
———. *The Invention of Suspicion: Law and Mimesis in Shakespeare and Renaissance Drama.* Oxford: Oxford University Press, 2007.
James, Heather. "Ben Jonson's Light Reading." In *A Handbook to the Reception of Ovid*, ed. John F. Miller and Carole Newlands, 246–261. Sussex: John Wiley and Sons, 2014.
———. "Flower Power." *Spenser Review* 44.2, no. 30 (Fall 2014).
———. "Ovid and the Question of Politics in Early Modern England." *ELH* 70, no. 2 (2003): 343–373.
———. "The Poet's Toys: Christopher Marlowe and the Liberties of Erotic Elegy." *Modern Language Quarterly* 67, no. 1 (2006): 103–127.
Jardine, Lisa. *Francis Bacon, Discovery, and the Art of Discourse.* Cambridge: Cambridge University Press, 1974.
Jarvis, Simon. "For a Poetics of Verse." *PMLA* 125, no. 4 (2010): 931–935.
Javitch, Daniel. *Poetry and Courtliness in Renaissance England.* Princeton, N.J.: Princeton University Press, 1978.
Johnson, John. *Academy of Love.* London, 1641.
Jonson, Ben. *Ben Jonson.* 11 vols. Edited by C. H. Herford and P. Simpson. Oxford: Oxford University Press, 1925.
———. *Discoveries.* Edited by Maurice Castelain. Paris: Hachette, 1906.
———. *Every Man Out of His Humour* [1600]. Edited by Helen Ostovich. Manchester: Manchester University Press, 2001.
Joseph, Sister Miriam. *Shakespeare's Use of the Arts of Language* [1947]. Philadelphia: Paul Dry Books, 2005.

Kahn, Victoria. *Rhetoric, Prudence, and Skepticism in the Renaissance*. Ithaca, N.Y.: Cornell University Press, 1985.
Kalas, Rayna. *Frame, Glass, Verse: The Technology of Poetic Invention*. Ithaca, N.Y.: Cornell University Press, 2007.
Kastan, David. *Shakespeare after Theory*. New York: Routledge, 1999.
Kearns, Terrance Brophy. "Rhetorical Devices and the Mock-Heroic in Spenser's *Muiopotmos*." *Publications of the Arkansas Philological Association* 9, no. 2 (1983): 58–66.
Keilin, Sean. *Vulgar Eloquence: On the Renaissance Invention of English Literature*. New Haven, Conn.: Yale University Press, 2006.
Kernan, Alvin. *The Cankered Muse*. New Haven, Conn.: Yale University Press.
King, John. *Lectures upon Jonas*. London, 1593.
Kinney, Arthur. *Humanist Poetics: Thought, Rhetoric, and Fiction in Sixteenth-Century England*. Amherst: University of Massachusetts Press, 1988.
Kinney, Clare R. "'Beleeve this butt a fiction': Female Authorship, Narrative Undoing, and the Limits of Romance in *The Second Part of the Countess of Montgomery's Urania*." *Spenser Studies* 17 (2003): 239–250.
———. "The Gentlewoman Reader Writes Back: Mrs. Stanley's *Sir Philip Sidney's Arcadia Moderniz'd*." *Sidney Journal* 27, no. 2 (2009): 39–52.
Kintgen, Eugene R. *Reading in Tudor England*. Pittsburgh, Penn.: University of Pittsburgh Press, 1996.
Knell, Thomas. *An answer at large, to a most hereticall, trayterous, and papisticall byll in English verse*. London, 1570.
La Drière, Craig. "Form." In *The Dictionary of World Literature*, ed. Joseph T. Shipley, 167–171. New York: Philosophical Library, 1953.
Lamb, Mary Ellen. "The Biopolitics of Romance in Mary Wroth's *The Countess of Montgomery's Urania*." *English Literary Renaissance* 31 (2001): 165–188.
Lamy, Bernard. *The Art of Speaking* [1676]. In *The Rhetorics of Thomas Hobbes and Bernard Lamy*, ed. John T. Harwood. Carbondale: Southern Illinois University Press, 1986.
Lanham, Richard. *The Old Arcadia*. New Haven, Conn.: Yale University Press, 1965.
Latour, Bruno. *Pandora's Hope: Essays on the Reality of Science Studies*. Cambridge, Mass.: Harvard University Press, 1999.
Leff, Michael. "The Habitation of Rhetoric." In *Contemporary Rhetorical Theory: A Reader*, ed. John Louis Lucaites, Celeste Michelle Condit, and Sally Caudhill, 52–64. New York: Guildford, 1999.
Leighton, Angela. *On Form: Poetry, Aestheticism, and the Legacy of a Word*. Oxford: Oxford University Press, 2007.

Lemnius, Levinus. *An Herbal for the Bible*. London, 1587.
Lesser, Zachary, and Peter Stallybrass. "The First Literary Hamlet and the Commonplacing of Professional Plays." *Shakespeare Quarterly* 59, no. 4 (2008): 371–420.
Levao, Ronald. *Renaissance Minds and Their Fictions*. Berkeley: University of California Press, 1985.
Levine, Caroline. *Forms: Whole, Rhythm, Hierarchy, Network*. Princeton, N.J.: Princeton University Press, 2015.
Levinson, Marjorie. "What Is New Formalism." *Publications of the Modern Language Association* 122 (2007): 558–569.
Lily, William. [*A short introduction of grammar*]. London, 1567.
Lindheim, Nancy. *The Structures of Sidney's Arcadia*. Toronto: University of Toronto Press, 1982.
Lochman, Daniel T. "Friendship's Passion: Love-Fellowship in Sidney's New Arcadia." In *Discourse and Representations of Friendship in Early Modern Europe, 1500–1700*, ed. D. T. Lochman, M. López, and L. Hutson, 65–79. Surrey: Ashgate, 2010.
Longinus. *On the Sublime*. Translated by W. H. Fyfe. Revised by Donald Russell. 2nd ed. Loeb Classical Library. Cambridge, Mass.: Harvard University Press, 1995.
Luckyj, Christina. "The Politics of Genre in Early Women's Writing: The Case of Lady Mary Wroth." *English Studies in Canada* 27, no. 3 (2001): 253–282.
MacCaffrey, Isabel. *Spenser's Allegory: The Anatomy of Imagination*. Princeton, N.J.: Princeton University Press, 1976.
Mack, Peter. *Elizabethan Rhetoric: Theory and Practice*. Cambridge: Cambridge University Press, 2002.
———. *A History of Renaissance Rhetoric*. Oxford: Oxford University Press, 2011.
———. "Ramus and Ramism: Rhetoric and Dialectic." In *Ramus, Pedagogy, and the Liberal Arts*, ed. S. J. Reid and E. A. Wilson, 7–23. Surrey: Ashgate, 2011.
———. "Synoiceosis and Antithesis in *The Winter's Tale*." In *Rhetorica Movet*, ed. P. L. Oesterreich and T. O. Sloane, 187–97. Leiden: Brill, 1999.
Mackay, Ellen. "Indecorum." In *Early Modern Theatricality*, ed. Henry S. Turner, 306–326. Oxford: Oxford University Press, 2013.
Magnusson, Lynne. "A Play of Modals: Grammar and Potential Action in Early Shakespeare." *Shakespeare Survey* 62 (2009): 69–80.
Mancinus. *Here begynneth a right frutefull treatyse*. Translated by Alexander Bercley. London, 1518.

Mann, Jenny C. *Outlaw Rhetoric: Figuring Vernacular Eloquence in Shakespeare's England.* Ithaca, N.Y.: Cornell University Press, 2012.
Mantuan, Battista. *The eglogs of the poet B. Mantuan.* Translated by George Turbeville. London, 1567.
Markham, Garvis. *The English Arcadia.* London, 1607.
Marston, John. *Antonio's Revenge.* Edited by W. Reavley Gaír. Manchester: Manchester University Press, 1978.
Martial. *Epigrams.* Translated by D. R. Shackleton Bailey. 3 Vols. Loeb Classical Library. Cambridge, Mass.: Harvard University Press, 1993.
———. *Ex otio negotium. Or, Martial his epigrams translated.* Translated by R. Fletcher. London, 1656.
Maus, Katherine Eisman. "Satiric and Ideal Economies in the Jonsonian Imagination." *English Literary Renaissance* 19, no. 1 (1989): 42–64.
Mazzio, Carla. *The Inarticulate Renaissance: Language Trouble in an Age of Eloquence.* Philadelphia: University of Pennsylvania Press, 2009.
———. "Sins of the Tongue." *Modern Language Studies* 28, no. 3/4 (1998): 95–124.
McAlindon, T. *Shakespeare and Decorum.* London: Macmillan, 1973.
McCall, Marsh H. *Ancient Rhetorical Theories of Simile and Comparison.* Cambridge, Mass.: Harvard University Press, 1969.
McCanles, Michael. *The Text of Sidney's Arcadian World.* Durham, N.C.: Duke University Press, 1989.
McCoy, Richard C. *Sir Philip Sidney: Rebellion in Arcadia.* New Brunswick, N.J.: Rutgers University Press, 1979.
McFaul, Tom. "Friendship in Sidney's Arcadias." *Studies in English Literature, 1500–1900* 49 (2009): 20–21.
Melanchthon, Philip. *A Critical Translation of Philip Melancthon's Elementorum Rhetorices Libri Duo.* Translated by Sister Mary Joan La Fontaine. PhD diss., University of Michigan, 1968.
———. *Elementorum Rhetorices Libri Duo.* Basil, 1567.
Menon, Mahadvi. *Wanton Words: Rhetoric and Sexuality in English Renaissance Drama.* Toronto: University of Toronto Press, 2004.
Miller, Jacqueline T. "Ladies of the Oddest Passion." *Modern Philology* 103, no. 4 (2006): 452–473.
Miller, Naomi. *Changing the Subject: Mary Wroth and Figurations of Gender in Early Modern England.* Lexington: University Press of Kentucky, 1996.
Mitchell, Marea. "Dorothy Stanley's Enterprise: *Sir Philip Sidney's Arcadia Moderniz'd* (1725)." *Sidney Journal* 28, no. 2 (2010): 63–76.
Monfassani, John. "Humanism and Rhetoric." In *Renaissance Humanism: Foundations, Form, and Legacy*, 3rd ed., ed. Albert Rabil Jr., 171–235. Philadelphia: University of Pennsylvania Press, 1988.
Montaigne. *Essays.* Translated by John Florio. London, 1613.

Montefusco, Lucia Calboli. "The *Rhetoric to Alexander*: How to Win Our Case by Playing with Contraries." *Rhetorica* 29, no. 3 (2011): 280–292.
Morton, Timothy. "An Object-Oriented Defense of Poetry." *New Literary History* 43 (2012): 205–224.
Moss, Ann. "Horace in the Sixteenth Century: Commentators into Critics." In *The Cambridge History of Literary Criticism*, vol. 3: *The Renaissance*, ed. G. P. Norton, 66–76. Cambridge: Cambridge University Press, 1999.
———. *Printed Commonplace-Books and the Structuring of Renaissance Thought*. Oxford: Clarendon, 1996.
Mueller, Janel. "Periodos." In *Renaissance Figures of Speech*, ed. Sylvia Adamson, Gavin Alexander, and Katrin Ettenhuber, 61–80. Cambridge: Cambridge University Press, 2007.
Murphy, James J., ed. *Renaissance Eloquence*. Berkeley: University of California Press, 1983.
Nashe, Thomas. "To The Gentlemen Students of both Vniversities" [1589]. In *Elizabethan Critical Essays*, ed. Gregory G. Smith, 1:307–320. Oxford: Oxford University Press, 1904.
Nelson, Norman E. *Peter Ramus and the Confusion of Logic, Rhetoric, and Poetry*. Ann Arbor: University of Michigan Press, 1947.
The New Oxford Book of Sixteenth-Century Verse. Edited by Emrys Jones. Oxford: Oxford University Press, 1991.
Nicholson, Catherine. "Othello and the Geography of Persuasion." *English Literary Renaissance* 40, no. 1 (2010): 56–87.
———. *Uncommon Tongues: Eloquence and Eccentricity in the English Renaissance*. Philadelphia: University of Pennsylvania Press, 2014.
Nimis, Stephen A. *Narrative Semiotics in the Epic Tradition: The Simile*. Bloomington: Indiana University Press, 1987.
Nohrnberg, James. *The Analogy of* The Faerie Queene. Princeton, N.J.: Princeton University Press, 1976.
Nuttall, A. D. *The Alternative Trinity: Gnostic Heresy in Marlowe, Milton, and Blake*. Oxford: Clarendon, 1998.
Oesterreuch, Peter L., and Thomas O. Sloane, eds. *Rhetorica Movet: Studies in Historical and Modern Rhetoric in Honour of Heinrich F. Plett*. Leiden: Brill, 1999.
Ong, Walter J. *Ramus, Method, and the Decay of Dialogue: From the Art of Discourse to the Art of Reason*. Chicago: University of Chicago Press, 1958.
Ortiz, Joseph M. *Broken Harmony*. Ithaca, N.Y.: Cornell University Press, 2011.
Ostovich, Helen M., ed. *Every Man Out of His Humour*. Manchester: Manchester University Press, 2001.

———. "'So Sudden and Strange a Cure': A Rudimentary Masque in *Every Man Out of His Humour*." *English Literary Renaissance* 22, no. 3 (1992): 315–332.

Parker, Patricia. "Hysteron Proteron: Or the Preposterous." In *Renaissance Figures of Speech*, ed. S. Adamson, G. Alexander, and K. Ettenhuber. Cambridge: Cambridge University Press, 2007.

———. *Inescapable Romance: Studies in the Poetics of a Mode*. Princeton, N.J.: Princeton University Press, 1979.

———. *Literary Fat Ladies: Rhetoric, Gender, Property*. London: Methuen, 1987.

———. "*Othello* and *Hamlet*: Dilation, Spying, and the 'Secret Place' of Woman." *Representations* 44 (1993): 60–95.

———. "Preposterous Events." *Shakespeare Quarterly* 43, no. 2 (1992): 186–213.

———. "Rude Mechanicals." In *Subject and Object in Renaissance Culture*, ed. M. De Grazia, M. Quilligan and P. Stallybrass. Cambridge: Cambridge University Press, 1996.

Passannante, Gerard. "The Art of Reading Earthquakes: On Harvey's Wit, Ramus's Method, and the Renaissance of Lucretius." *Renaissance Quarterly* 61, no. 3 (2008): 821.

Patey, Douglas Lane. *Probability and Literary Form: Philosophic Theory and Literary Practice in the Augustan Age*. Cambridge: Cambridge University Press, 1984.

Peacham, Henry. *The Compleat Gentleman*. London, 1622.

———. *The Garden of Eloquence*. London, 1577.

———. *The Garden of Eloquence*. London, 1593.

Plato. *Gorgias and Phaedrus*. Translated by James H. Nichols. Ithaca, N.Y.: Cornell University Press, 1998.

Plett, Heinrich F. "The Place and Function of Style in Renaissance Poetics." In *Renaissance Eloquence*, ed. James J. Murphy, 356–375. Berkeley: University of California Press, 1983.

———. *Rhetoric and Renaissance Culture*. Berlin: Walter de Gruyter, 2004.

Pomeroy, Ralph S. "The Ramist as Fallacy-Hunter: Abraham Fraunce and *The Lawiers Logik*." *Renaissance Quarterly* 40, no. 2 (1987): 224–246.

Pugh, Syrithe. *Spenser and Ovid*. Burlington: Ashgate, 2005.

Purchas, Samuel. *Purchas his Pilgrimage*. London, 1613.

Puttenham, George. *The Art of English Poesy* [1589]. Edited by F. Whigham and W. A. Rebhorn. Ithaca, N.Y.: Cornell University Press, 2007.

Quilligan, Maureen. "The Comedy of Female Authority in *The Faerie Queene*." *English Literary Renaissance* 17, no. 2 (1987): 156–171.

Quint, David. "Bragging Rights: Honor and Courtesy in Shakespeare and Spenser." In *Creative Imitation: New Essays in Renaissance Literature in*

Honor of Thomas M. Greene, ed. David Quint et al., 391–430. Binghamton: Medieval & Renaissance Texts & Studies, 1992.

Quintilian. *Institutio Oratoria*. Translated by Harold Edgeworth Butler. Loeb Classical Library. Cambridge, Mass.: Harvard University Press, 1922.

Rainolde, Richard. *A boke called the Foundacion of rhetorike*. London, 1563.

Ramachandran, Ayesha. "Clarion in the Bower of Bliss: Poetry and Politics in Spenser's 'Muiopotmos.'" *Spenser Studies* 20 (2005): 77–106.

———. *The Worldmakers: Global Imagining in Early Modern Europe*. Chicago: University of Chicago Press, 2015.

Ramus, Peter. *Arguments in Rhetoric against Quintilian* [1549]. Translated by Carole Newlands. Carbondale: Southern Illinois University Press, 2010.

———. *A Compendium of the Art of Logick and Rhetorick*. Translated by R. F. London, 1651.

———. *The Logike of Peter Ramus*. Translated by Roland Macilmaine [1574]. Edited by Catherine M. Dunn. Northridge, Calif.: San Fernando Valley State College, 1969.

———. *P. Rami Dialecticae Libri Dvo*. Cambridge, 1584.

———. *Peter Ramus . . . his Dialectica*. Translated by R. F. London, 1632.

———. *Peter Ramus His Logic*. Translated by R. F. London, 1636.

———. *Peter Ramus's Attack on Cicero: Text and Translation of Ramus's* Brutinae Questiones [1548]. Translated by Carole Newlands. Davis, Calif.: Hemagoras, 1992.

———. *Ramus, of Vermandois, the King's Professor, his Dialectica in two books*. Trans. R. F. London, 1632.

Rasmussen, Mark David. *Renaissance Literature and Its Formal Engagements*. New York: Palgrave, 2002.

Rebhorn, Wayne. *The Emperor of Men's Minds*. Ithaca, N.Y.: Cornell University Press, 1995.

———. "Outlandish Fears: Defining Decorum in Renaissance Rhetoric." *Intertexts* 4, no. 1 (2000): 3–24.

Reiss, Timothy J. "From Trivium to Quadrivium: Ramus, Method, and Mathematical Technology." In *The Renaissance Computer: Knowledge Technology in the First Age of Print*, ed. N. Rhodes and J. Sawday, 45–58. London: Routledge, 2000.

———. *Knowledge, Discovery, and Imagination in Early Modern Europe*. Cambridge: Cambridge University Press, 1997.

Reynolds, Henry. *Mythomystes*. London, 1632.

Rhetoric to Alexander. Translated by David C. Mirhady. Loeb Classical Library. Cambridge, Mass.: Harvard University Press, 2011.

Rhetorica Ad Herennium. Translated by Harry Caplan. Loeb Classical Library. Cambridge, Mass.: Harvard University Press, 1954.

Rhodes, Neil. *The Elizabethan Grotesque*. London: Routledge, 1980.
Richards, I. A. "The Places and the Figures." *Kenyon Review* 11, no. 1 (1949): 17–30.
Riddell, James A., and Stanley Stewart. *Jonson's Spenser: Evidence and Historical Criticism*. Pittsburgh, Penn.: Duquesne University Press, 1995.
Rix, Herbert David. *Rhetoric in Spenser's Poetry*. State College: Pennsylvania State Press, 1940.
Roberts, Josephine A. "'The Knott Never to Bee Untide': The Controversy Regarding Marriage in Mary Wroth's *Urania*." In *Reading Mary Wroth: Representing Alternatives in Early Modern England*, ed. Naomi J. Miller and Gary Waller, 109–132. Knoxville: University of Tennessee Press, 1991.
———. "An Unpublished Literary Quarrel Concerning the Suppression of Mary Wroth's *Urania*." *Notes and Queries* 24 (1977): 532–535.
Roche, Robert. *Eustathia*. London, 1599.
Roche, Thomas P. "Ending the New Arcadia: Virgil and Ariosto." *Sidney Newsletter* 10, no. 1 (1989): 3–12.
Roth, Michael S. "'All You've Got Is History.'" Foreword to *Metahistory: The Historical Imagination in Nineteenth-Century Europe*. 40th anniversary ed. Baltimore, Md.: Johns Hopkins University Press, 2014.
Salzman, Paul. "Contemporary References in Mary Wroth's *Urania*." *Review of English Studies* 29, no. 114 (1978): 179–181.
———. "The Strang[e] Constructions of Mary Wroth's *Urania*." In *English Renaissance Prose: History, Language, and Politics*, ed. Neil Rhodes, 109–124. Tempe: Arizona State University Press, 1997.
Sanchez, Melissa. *Erotic Subjects: The Sexuality of Politics in Early Modern English Literature*. Oxford: Oxford University Press, 2011.
Scaliger, Julius Caesar. *Poetices Libri Septem* [1561]. Stuttgart: Freidrich Frommann Verlag, 1964.
———. *Select Translations from Scaliger's Poetics*. Translated by Frederick Morgan Padelford. New York: Henry Holt, 1905.
Schanze, Hemult. "Problems and Trends in German Rhetoric to 1500." In *Renaissance Eloquence*, ed. James J. Murphy, 105–125. Berkeley: University of California Press, 1983.
Scoloker, Anthony. *Daiphantus*. London, 1604.
Scott, William. *The Model of Poesy* [1599]. Edited by Gavin Alexander. Cambridge: Cambridge University Press, 2013.
Seneca. *Epistles 1–65*. Translated by Richard Gummere. Loeb Classical Library. Cambridge, Mass.: Harvard University Press, 1967.
———. *Epistles 93–124*. Translated by Richard M. Gummere. Loeb Classical Library. Cambridge, Mass.: Harvard University Press, 1925.

Shakespeare, William. *As You Like It.* 3rd ed. Edited by Juliet Dusinberre. London: Arden, 2006.
Sharon-Zisser, Shirley. *The Risks of Simile in Renaissance Rhetoric.* New York: Peter Lang, 2000.
Shaw, Samuel. *Words Made Visible.* London, 1679.
Shelby, L. R. "Medieval Masons' Tools. II. Compass and Square." *Technology and Culture* 6, no. 2 (1965): 236–248.
Sherman, William H. *John Dee: The Politics of Reading and Writing in the English Renaissance.* Amherst: University of Massachusetts Press, 1995.
———. *Used Books: Marking Readers in Renaissance England.* Philadelphia: University of Pennsylvania Press, 2008.
Sherry, Richard. *A Treatise of Schemes and Tropes.* London, 1550.
———. *A Treatise of the Figures of Grammer and Rhetorike.* London, 1555.
Sidney, Philip. *Astrophil and Stella.* In *The Major Works*, ed. Katherine Duncan-Jones, 153–211. Oxford: Oxford University Press, 1989.
———. *The Countess of Pembroke's Arcadia.* London, 1598.
———. *The Countess of Pembroke's Arcadia.* Edited by Maurice Evans. London: Penguin, 1977.
———. *The Defence of Poesy.* In *The Major Works*, ed. Katherine Duncan-Jones, 212–250. Oxford: Oxford University Press, 1989.
———. *Old Arcadia.* Edited by Katherine Duncan-Jones. Oxford: Oxford University Press, 1985.
Slaughter, M. M. *Universal Languages and Scientific Taxonomy in the Seventeenth Century.* Cambridge: Cambridge University Press, 1982.
Slights, William M. "The Edifying Margins of Renaissance English Books." *Renaissance Quarterly* 42, no. 4 (1989): 682–716.
Smith, G. Gregory. *Elizabethan Critical Essays.* 2 vols. Oxford: Oxford University Press, 1904.
Smith, Jessica Nash. "(Dis)membering Quintilian's Corpus: Ramus Reads the Body Rhetoric." *Exemplaria* 11, no. 2 (1999): 399–429.
Smith, John. *The Mysterie of Rhetorique Unveil'd.* London, 1656.
Sontag, Susan. *Against Interpretation.* New York: Octagon, 1961.
Spencer, Thomas. *Art of Logick.* London, 1628.
Spenser, Edmund. *The faerie queen: The shepheards calendar: together with the other works.* London, 1617.
———. *The Faerie Queene.* 2nd rev. ed. Edited by A. C. Hamilton. Harlow: Longman, 2001.
———. *The Yale Edition of the Shorter Poems of Edmund Spenser.* Edited by W. Oram et al. New Haven, Conn.: Yale University Press, 1989.
Spiller, Elizabeth. *Science, Reading, and Renaissance Literature: The Art of Making Knowledge, 1580–1670.* Cambridge: Cambridge University Press, 2004.
Sprat, Thomas. *The History of the Royal Society of London.* London, 1667.

Stallybrass, Peter, and Ann Rosalind Jones. "Fetishizing the Glove in Renaissance Europe." *Critical Inquiry* 28, no. 1 (2001): 114–132.
Stanley, Dorothy. *Sir Philip Sidney's Arcadia Moderniz'd*. London, 1725.
Stapleton, M. L. *Spenser's Ovidian Poetics*. Newark: University of Delaware Press, 2002.
Stephanson, Raymond. "The Epistemological Challenge of Nashe's *The Unfortunate Traveller*." *Studies in English Literature, 1500–1900* 23, no. 1 (1983): 21–36.
Stewart, Alan. *Close Readers: Humanism and Sodomy in Early Modern England*. Princeton, N.J.: Princeton University Press, 1997.
Stewart, Susan. "Rhyme and Freedom." In *The Sound of Poetry/The Poetry of Sound*, ed. Marjorie Perloff and Craig Dworkin, 29–48. Chicago: University of Chicago Press, 2009.
Stillman, Robert. "The Perils of Fancy: Poetry and Self-Love in *The Old Arcadia*." *Texas Studies in Literature and Language* 26, no. 1 (1984): 14.
Strode, George. *The anatomie of mortalitie*. London, 1618.
Struever, Nancy S. *The Language of History in the Renaissance*. Princeton, N.J.: Princeton University Press, 1970.
Susenbrotus, Johannes. *Epitome Troporum Ac Schematum of Joannes Susenbrotus: Text, Translation, and Commentary*. Translated by Xavier Brennan. PhD diss., University of Illinois, 1953.
Taylor, Barry. *Vagrant Writing: Social and Semiotic Disorders in the English Renaissance*. Toronto: University of Toronto Press, 1991.
Temple, William. *Analysis of Sidney's Apology for Poetry*. Translated by John Webster. Binghamton, N.Y.: Medieval & Renaissance Texts & Studies, 1984.
Terence. *The Woman of Andros; The Self Tormentor; The Eunuch*. Translated by John Barsby. Loeb Classical Library. Cambridge, Mass.: Harvard University Press, 2001.
Teskey, Gordon. *Allegory and Violence*. Ithaca, N.Y.: Cornell University Press, 1996.
———. "'And Therefore as a Stranger Give It Welcome': Courtesy and Thinking." *Spenser Studies* 18 (2003): 343–359.
Trimpi, Wesley. *Ben Jonson's Poems: A Study of the Plain Style*. Stanford, Calif.: Stanford University Press, 1962.
Turner, Henry S. *The English Renaissance Stage: Geometry, Poetics, and the Practical Spatial Arts, 1580–1630*. Oxford: Oxford University Press, 2006.
———. "Lessons from Literature for the Historian of Science (and Vice Versa): Reflections on 'Form.'" *Isis* (2010): 578–589.
Tuve, Rosemond. *Elizabethan and Metaphysical Imagery*. Chicago: University of Chicago Press, 1947.
Udall, Nicholas. *Floures for Latine*. London, 1533.

Vickers, Brian. *Classical Rhetoric in English Poetry*. Carbondale: Southern Illinois University Press, 1970.
———. *Francis Bacon and Renaissance Prose*. Cambridge: Cambridge University Press, 1968.
———. *In Defence of Rhetoric*. Oxford: Clarendon, 1989.
———. "The Myth of Francis Bacon's Anti-Humanism." In *Humanism and Early Modern Philosophy*, ed. Jill Kraye and M. W. F. Stone, 135–158. London: Routledge, 2000.
———. "Rhetorical and Anti-Rhetorical Tropes." *Comparative Criticism* 3 (1981): 105–132.
Vinsauf, Geoffrey of. *Poetria Nova*. Translated by Margaret F. Nims. Toronto: Pontifical Institute of Medieval Studies, 1967.
Vives, Juan Luis. *De Ratione Dicendi: A Treatise on Rhetoric*. Translated by James Francis Cooney. PhD diss., Ohio State University, 1966.
———. *On Education*. Translated by Foster Watson. Totowa, N.J.: Rowman and Littlefield, 1971.
Walker, Jeffrey. *Rhetoric and Poetics in Antiquity*. Oxford: Oxford University Press, 2000.
Wallace, Andrew. "'Noursled up in life and manners wilde': Spenser's Georgic Educations." *Spenser Studies* 19 (2007): 65–92.
Warley, Christopher. *Reading Class through Shakespeare, Donne, and Milton*. Cambridge: Cambridge University Press, 2014.
Watson, Robert N. *Back to Nature: The Green and the Real in the Late Renaissance*. Philadelphia: University of Pennsylvania Press, 2006.
———. *Ben Jonson's Parodic Strategy*. Cambridge: Cambridge University Press, 1987.
Weaver, William P. "*Triplex Est Copia*: Philip Melanchthon's Invention of Rhetorical Figures." *Rhetorica* 29, no. 4 (Autumn 2011): 367–402.
Webbe, William. *A Discourse of English Poetry*. London, 1586.
Webster, John, trans. *William Temples' Analysis of Sidney's Apology for Poetry*. Binghamton, N.Y.: Medieval & Renaissance Texts & Studies, 1984.
West, William N. *Theaters and Encyclopedias in Early Modern Europe*. Cambridge: Cambridge University Press, 2002.
Westney, Lizette Islyn. *Parabolae Sive Similia: Its Relationship to Sixteenth-Century English Literature*. Translated by Lizette Islyn Westney. Salzburg: Institut für Anglistik and Amerikanistik, Universität Salzburg, 1981.
Whaler, James. "Grammatical Nexus of the Miltonic Simile." *Journal of English and Germanic Philology* 30, no. 3 (1931): 327–335.
———. "The Miltonic Simile." *Publication of the Modern Language Association* 46, no. 4 (1931): 1034–1074.
———. "Similes in *Paradise Lost*." *Modern Philology* 28, no. 3 (1931): 313–327.

Whigham, Frank. *Ambition and Privilege: The Social Tropes of Elizabethan Courtesy Theory.* Berkeley: University of California Press, 1984.
White, Hayden. *Metahistory: The Historical Imagination in Nineteenth-Century Europe.* 40th anniversary ed. Baltimore, Md.: Johns Hopkins University Press, 2014.
Whiting, Nathaneel. *Le hore di recreatione.* London, 1637.
Whittaker, C. R. *Rome and Its Frontiers: The Dynamics of Empire.* London: Routledge, 2004.
Williams, Gareth. "Ovid's Exilic Poetry: Worlds Apart." In *Brill's Companion to Ovid*, ed. Barbara Weiden Boyd, 337–381. Leiden: Brill, 2002.
Williams, Grant. "Resisting the Psychotic Library: Periphrasis and Paranoia in Burton's *Anatomy of Melancholy.*" *Exemplaria* 15, no. 1 (2003): 199–221.
Willis, Richard. *De Re Poetica* [1573]. Translated by A. D. S. Fowler. Oxford: Basil Blackwell, 1958.
Wilson, H. S. "Gabriel Harvey's Orations on Rhetoric." *ELH* 12 (1945): 167–182.
Wilson, Thomas. *The Art of Rhetoric* [1560]. Edited by Peter Medine. University Park: Pennsylvania State University Press, 1993.
———. *Rule of Reason* [1551]. Edited by Richard S. Sprague. Northridge, Calif.: San Fernando Valley State College, 1972.
Wofford, Susan. *The Choice of Achilles: The Ideology of Figure in the Epic.* Stanford, Calif.: Stanford University Press, 1992.
Wolfe, Jessica. *Homer and the Question of Strife from Erasmus to Hobbes.* Toronto: University of Toronto Press, 2015.
Wolfson, Susan. *Formal Charges: The Shaping of Poetry in British Romanticism.* Stanford, Calif.: Stanford University Press, 1997.
———. "Reading for Form." *Modern Language Quarterly* 61 (2000): 1–16.
Wotton, Anthony. *The Art of Logick.* London, 1626.
Wroth, Mary. *The First Part of The Countess of Montgomery's Urania.* Edited by Josephine Roberts. Tempe: Arizona Center for Medieval and Renaissance Studies, 1995.
———. *The Second Part of The Countess of Montgomery's Urania.* Edited by Josephine A. Roberts. Completed by Suzanne Gossett and Janel Mueller. Tempe: Arizona Center for Medieval and Renaissance Studies, 1999.
Wynne-Davies, Marion. "'So Much Worth': Autobiographical Narratives in the Work of Lady Mary Wroth." In *Betraying Our Selves: Forms of Self-Representation in Early Modern English Texts*, ed. H. Dragsta, S. Ottoway, and H. Wilcox, 76–93. New York: St. Martin Press, 2000.

INDEX

Academy of Eloquence, The. See Blount, Thomas
Academy of Love, The. See Johnson, John
Addison, Catherine, 244n12
Adelman, Janet, 227n96, 228n100
Advancement of Learning, The. See Bacon, Francis
affectation, 7, 9, 50, 54–55, 65, 67, 72, 91–92, 126–127, 140, 191n66, 212n7, 217n33, 224n69
Agricola, Rudolph (*De Inventione Dialectica*), 27–28, 197n28
Alarinus, 156, 265–266n67
Alexander, Gavin, 8, 122, 184n15, 223n66, 250n8, 253n36, 255n51, 261n28, 265n66
Alexander, William, 121–122, 130, 136
allegory, 82, 91, 101–104, 143, 151–152, 259n13, 259–260n14
alliteration, 46, 79, 114, 140, 234n44, 257n67. See also *paroemion*; *tautologia*
Altman, Joel B., 127, 253n36
Amphilanthus, 71, 82, 89, 90–91, 93, 146, 154–155, 157, 162–163, 267n81
amplification, 36, 41, 84–85, 131–132, 142–144, 151–152, 197n32, 227n99, 244n20, 256n55. *See also* copia
anadiplosis, 62, 65, 225–226n87. See also *anadiplosis*; *climax*; *gradatio*
analysis, 4, 56–58
Analysis of Sidney's Apology for Poetry. See Temple, William
anaphora. See repetitio
Anaxius, 120–123, 128–134, 138, 139, 257n75
Anderson, Judith H., 183n7, 186n27, 193n84, 211n2, 246n35, 257n66; and Joan Pong Linton, 184n15, 188

antimetabole, 62, 64, 123, 136–138, 223–224n66, 257n73. See also *chiasmus*; repetition
antithesis, 14, 36, 39, 71, 120–140, 141–142, 165–166, 205n88, 218n38, 220–221n51, 234n42, 251nn16–17,19, 252nn23,26,28, 252–253n32, 253n36, 254nn38,43, 255n50, 256nn56,60, 257nn67,73, 258nn80,84, 259n86, 268n5. See also *contentio*; contraries
Antissia, 76, 81–91, 93, 167, 232n23
Antissius, 76, 82
Antonio's Revenge. See Marston, John
aposiopesis, 16, 25, 122
apostrophe, 93
appropriateness. See *decorum*; *propon*
Arcadia, The (Old). *See* Sidney, Philip; *and names of individual characters*
Arcadia, The (revised). *See* Sidney, Philip; *and names of individual characters*
Arcadian Rhetorike, The. See Fraunce, Abraham
Archimago, 115–119, 249n104
Arguments in Rhetoric Against Quintilian. See Ramus, Peter
Aristotle, 8, 32, 202n61, 213n12; *Poetics*, 14, 32–33, 77–78, 80, 87–88, 93, 187n32; *Rhetoric*, 3–4, 45, 93, 97, 100, 113, 124, 126–127, 130–131, 184n13, 223n61, 234n42, 236n52, 251nn17,18,19; *Topica*, 68–69, 227n94
Arte of logick, The (1617). *See* Blundeville, Thomas
Artes of Logike and Rhethorike, The. See Fenner, Dudley
Art of English Poesy, The. See Puttenham, George
Art of Logick, The (1626). *See* Wotton, Anthony

295

Art of Logick, The (1628). *See* Spencer, Thomas
Art of Speaking, The. *See* Lamy, Benrard
articulus, 58–59, 221n54. *See also asyndeton*
As You Like It. *See* Shakespeare, William
Ascham, Roger (*The Schoolmaster*), 5, 58
Asper, 168–169, 175–177. *See also* Maciliente
Astrophil, 54–55
Astrophil and Stella. *See* Sidney, Philip; and names of individual characters
asyndeton, 56. *See also articulus*
Attack on Cicero (*Questions of Brutus*). *See* Ramus, Peter, and Ramism
Attridge, Derek, 92, 242n104
Auerbach, Erich, 8, 188n39
Augustine: *The City of God*, 138, 235–236n47, 259n77; *On Christian Doctrine*, 231n16
axes of relation, 7, 25, 45, 54, 68–69, 123, 173, 209n130

Bacon, Francis, 192n76; *The Advancement of Learning*, 165–166, 234n29, 268nn1,3,5
Baines, Barbara J., 247n57
Baldwin, T. W., 217nn35–36, 218–219n34, 219n47
Barish, Jonas, 166, 174, 228n101, 255n50, 268n5, 269nn7,9, 270n17, 271n27, 272n31
Barret, J. K., 191n64
Barthes, Roland, 190n61, 258n80
Battista, Mantuan (*Eclogues*), 74
Belphoebe, 99–100, 107, 117–118
Berger, Harry Jr., 43, 183n6, 194nn7,9,10, 213n12, 224n72, 245–255n28
Blank, Paula, 5
Blissett, William, 270–271n21
Blount, Thomas (*The Academy of Eloquence*), 191–192n73
Blundeville, Thomas (*The arte of logick*), 207n101, 210n131, 216–217n31
body, 7, 29, 51–55, 65–99, 73–75, 80, 140, 214–215n21, 215n22, 228n104, 236n49, 254n44, 258n80
Boethius (*De topicis differentiis*), 246n29
Braggadochio, 99–101, 106–107, 113–119, 175

Brayman Hackel, Heidi. *See* Brayman, Heidi
Brayman, Heidi, 64, 223n62
breath, 85–86, 123, 130–131, 140, 159, 168, 255n53
Brinsley, John (*Ludus Literarius*), 4–5, 56–57, 93, 108–109, 148–149, 217n36, 218n43, 220n51, 262n35, 267n37
Briske, Fastidius, 167, 171–175, 269n14, 270n15
Brown, Georgia, 223n29
Buffone, Carlo, 167, 170–177, 269n14, 270n15, 271n25
Burckhardt, Sigurd, 183n7, 211n2, 246n35, 257n66
Burke, Kenneth, 13, 55, 190n62, 217n32
Burton, Ben, 8, 189n46

cacozelia, 91–92. *See also* affectation
Candiana, 160–162, 267n79
Campbell, Mary Baine, 185n16
Campion, Thomas (*Observations in the Art of English Poesie*), 9–10, 189n53
Carey, John, 250–251n11, 251n15
Carrell, Jennifer Lee, 260n21, 261n26
Carson, Anne, 77
Cavanagh, Sheila T., 232–233n23
cause, causation, 8, 24, 33, 36–40, 45, 46, 54–55 68, 122–123, 139–140, 149–150, 153, 169, 189n51, 209n96, 216n30, 226–227n91, 228n101, 235–236n47, 250n10, 268n3
Cave, Terrence, 247n45, 271n23
celare artem, 2, 10, 76
certain knowledge, 27, 157. *See also* necessary knowledge
Certayne Notes of Instruction. *See* Gascoigne, George
Chapman, George, 245–246n28
character, 9, 74, 78, 89, 91, 123, 129, 139, 145, 167–168, 170, 174, 211–212n6, 230n8, 238n61, 250–251n11
chiasmus, 64. *See also antimetabole*; repetition
chimera, 29, 67, 73–75, 80, 135, 173
Cicero, 4, 27, 29, 30, 57, 62, 217n36, 219n46, 220n50, 259n86; *De Officiis*, 230–231n10, 235n47; *De Senectute*, 56; *On the Orator [De Oratore]*, 75, 78–79, 81, 131, 229n3, 231n15, 232n17,

255n53; *Orations*, 58, 59, 62, 221–222n54; *Orator*, 25, 31, 54, 92–93, 216n28, 236–237n52, 242n99
Ciceronianus. See Harvey, Gabriel
circumlocutio, 142, 147, 152, 262nn35,37, 263nn39,49, 264n55, 266n69. *See also* definition; *periphrasis*
City of God, The. See Augustine
Clarion, 1–2, 18–19
Cleophila 50–53, 65–72, 224n69. *See also* Pyrocles
Cleveland, John (*Poems*), 262n37
climax, 40, 52–55, 62, 64–65, 213n16. See also *anadiplosis*; *gradatio*; *sorites*
clothing, 34, 52–53, 55, 58, 83–84, 215n22, 238n61
Cohen, Ralph, 188–189n45
Coleridge, Samuel Taylor, 75, 244n15
commonplace books, 4, 16, 103–106, 111, 214n19, 269n13
commoratio, 36
comparison, 14, 33, 36, 91, 98, 125, 128, 226n89, 243n7, 253n35
Compleat Gentleman, The. See Peacham, Henry [1576–1643]
composition: *decorum* within, 6, 74–76, 78, 236n48; history of, 2–3, 10–12, 18–19, 103–108, 113, 117, 123, 144, 184–185n15; origin of (figures or places), 7, 24, 26, 34–35, 67, 217n35; preposterous model of, 50, 55–57, 62, 67; traditional paradigms of, 5, 25, 39–40, 55–57, 62, 213n12; *simile* in, 103–108. See also *formulas*
conjugation, 37–38, 227n93. See also *polyptoton*
conspicuousness, 2–4, 9, 11–12, 16, 18–19, 25, 41, 44–45, 50, 58, 65–68, 72, 76, 81, 86, 91–93, 103, 107, 118–119, 123–127, 138, 146, 147, 150–152, 163, 166, 167, 169, 175, 183n6
contentio, 122, 124–125, 128, 133. See also *antithesis*; contraries
contingent knowledge, 12, 24, 28, 185n17, 253n36. *See also* modality; necessary knowledge; persuasive knowledge
contraries, 14, 33, 36, 120–140, 240n78. See also *antithesis*; *contentio*
Cooney, Helen, 102, 245n27

copia, 53, 99, 106, 123, 129–132, 147, 151, 271n23. *See also* amplification
Cordatus, 168, 169–170, 172, 173
correctio, 76, 85. See also *epanorthosis*
Crane, Mary Thomas, 197n28, 217n35, 221n53, 243n7, 245n23
Crewe, Jonathan, 70, 228n101
Croll, Morris W., 238–239n64
Cummings, Brian, 249n95
cumulatio, 230–231n10
Curtius, Robert Ernst, 264n55

Danby, John F., 139–140
Daniel, Samuel (*Defence of Rhyme*), 9–10, 258n79
Danson, Lawrence, 270nn18–19, 271n25
Daston, Lorraine, 17
Davis, Alex, 213–214n16, 216n30, 228n101
Davis, Joel, 250n2
Day, Angel (*The English Secretorie*), 229n2, 233n33
De Conscribendis Epistolis. See Erasmus, Desiderius
decorum, 6–7; and class, 81, 111–112, 236n51; and conspicuousness, 113, 127, 169–170, 177; definitions of, 6–7, 40, 73–75, 187nn30,32, 230n6; Horace and, 73–74, 229n2; qualitative dimension of, 40, 67, 74, 78–79, 86–87, 230nn5,6; quantitative dimension of, 40, 67, 74–76, 86–87, 111–112, 140, 169–170, 177, 212n8, 230nn5,9, 236n49; and Ramus, 6–7; and value, 85, 87–89; and world making, 7, 92–93, 169–170, 177, 235–236n47, 259n86. See also *indecorous*
Defence of Rhyme, A. See Daniel, Samuel
definition, 14, 36, 144, 153, 205n89, 228n11. See also *circumlocutio*; *periphrasis*
deformity (and disformity), 7, 29, 75–76, 80, 107, 149, 152, 167, 173, 175–177, 189n50, 191n66, 199n42, 231n15, 236n49, 263n39. *See also* body; *decorum*: quantitative dimension of; transformation
delight. See pleasure
Della Casa, Giovanni (*Galateo*), 75
Demetrius (*On Style*), 7, 77, 112, 213n16, 234n41, 241n84

De Re Poetica. *See* Willis, Richard
De Senectute. *See* Cicero
design, 7, 15, 40, 74, 80, 88, 112, 139–140, 162–163, 268n85. *See also decorum*: quantitative dimension of
De topicis differentiis. *See* Boethius
Dialecticae Libri Duo. *See* Fraunce, Abraham: *The Lawiers Logike*; Ramus, Peter
Dimock, Wai Chee, 190–191n63
dispositio, 5, 27–31, 55, 128, 197n32, 200n45, 217–218n36, 254n40. *See also* judgment
Directions for Speech and Style. *See* Hoskins, John
Divine Logike. *See* Granger, Thomas
dog (Puntarvolo's), 17–18, 167, 175–177
"doing, the, and the thing done," 2–3, 4, 7, 16, 58, 101–104, 107, 113, 123, 124, 144, 146. *See also* composition: history of; *formulas*; maker's knowledge; *poesie*
Dolorindus, 86–87
Dolven, Jeff, 58, 127, 185n18, 201n60, 217n35, 243n9, 245n26, 253n36
Donatus, 50, 66, 226n77
Dorus, 50–55, 65–72, 76, 215n27, 216n29, 253n25. *See also* Musidorus
Drummond, William, 104
Dubrow, Heather, 8
Duessa, 135–136

echo, 65, 269n14
Echo, 154–155, 265n65
Eclogues of the poet B. Mantuan, The. *See* Mantuan, Battista
Eggert, Katherine, 46, 210nn132,135, 246n42, 261n31
Elementorum Rhetorices Libri Duo. *See* Fraunce, Abraham: *The Arcadian Rhetorike*; Melanchthon, Philip
ellipsis, 77, 147, 218n38
Eloquentia, 29–31, 33
emotion, 3, 9, 24–25, 42–43, 49–53, 74, 78, 82–83, 85, 130, 196n24, 211n5, 217n33, 220–221n51, 229n4, 251n15, 254n538
Empson, William, 245n28
emptiness, 7, 8, 50–54, 56, 62, 65–67, 70, 79, 85–86, 115, 176–177, 225n84, 234n39, 239n73. *See also vanus*; vaunt
enallage, 84, 87, 218n38
English Arcadia, The. *See* Markham, Garvis

English Secretorie, The. *See* Day, Angel
Enterline, Lynn, 188n42, 211n5, 230n8
epanalepsis, 3, 15, 40, 41. *See also* repetition
epanodos, 41–46, 49, 60, 62, 208nn114,119, 209n130. *See also* repetition
epanorthosis, 76, 85, 113, 122. *See also correctio*
epithet, 57, 76, 78, 80–81, 87–91, 93, 159, 167, 223n61, 240nn78,81, 241nn83,84,88, 247n59, 262n37, 270n15
Epitome of Tropes and Schemes. *See* Susenbrotus, Johannes
epizeuxis, 40, 191n66, 220n50
Erasmus, Desiderius, 84, 106, 110; *De Conscribendis Epistolis*, 109–110; *The Correspondence of Erasmus*, 238–239n64; *On Copia of Words and Ideas* (*De Copia Verborum Ac Rerum*), 17, 35, 61–62, 84, 106, 215n22, 222n55, 239n66, 241nn83,84, 247n50; *On the Method of Study* (*De Ratione Studii*), 106, 248nn73,75; *Parallels* (*Parabolae sive Similia*), 104, 110, 246n39
ethos, 74, 78, 85, 213n12, 230n8. *See also* character
Ettenhuber, Katrin, 191n69, 227n96, 228n100
Eunuchus. *See* Terence
Every Man Out of His Humour. *See* Jonson, Ben
example: of figures, 12, 16, 41, 43, 48–49, 57, 64, 71–72, 121–122, 128, 149, 191–192n73, 196n24, 203–204n73, 205n91, 208n119, 218n43, 218–219n44, 219n46; the figure, 98
extenuatio, 36. *See also litotes*

Faerie Queene, The. *See* Spenser, Edmund; *and names of individual characters*
Fahnestock, Jeanne, 17, 192n78, 251n19
Faire Design, 162–163, 268n85
fallacy, 12, 34, 38, 207nn101,102. *See also* form: homology; sophistry
falsum, 66, 225n77. *See* truth-value
fetish, 53–54, 66–67
Fenner, Dudley (*The Artes of Logike and Rhethorike*), 5, 27, 37–39, 126, 128, 205n92, 218n43
Ferguson, Margaret, 5, 186n29

Ferry, Anne, 245–246n28
fiction, 2–3, 7, 12–13, 17–18, , 32–35, 39–40, 44–47, 49–50, 66, 70–71, 110–111, 113, 119, 123, 127, 138–140, 145–147, 162–163, 172, 190–191n63. *See also* plausibility; possibility; probability
fictum, 66, 225n77. *See also* fiction; plausibility; possibility; probability
Fienberg, Nona, 260n19
figure pointing, 3, 16, 17, 18, 48–50, 52, 57, 62, 64, 71, 93, 103–104, 122, 165, 166, 167, 169, 170, 174, 214n18, 219nn46,47. See also *formulas*
Fletcher, Angus, 77
Florio, John, 122, 157
Floristello, 160–162
Floures for Latine. *See* Udall, Nicholas
flowers, 1, 18–19, 146, 154, 193nn84,85,86,87
form: criticism of, 8, 19, 74–75, 140, 167, 168, 170, 175–177, 188n43, 188–189n45, 189nn51–52, 231n12; definition of, 7–13; and dog, 17–18, 167, 169, 175–177; and "the doing," 2–4, 17, 58, 103–104, 123–124, 144–146; and empty, 8, 14–15, 17–18, 50–55, 62, 65–67, 70–71, 81, 85–86, 113–115, 145–146, 153, 175–177, 224n69; and fiction, 2–3, 12–13, 17, 32–34, 39–40, 44–46, 66, 70–71, 110–111, 123, 127, 138–140, 145–147, 163, 190–191n63; and *figura*, 7–8; and generative constraint, 4–5, 9, 14, 39–40, 44–45, 57–58, 65–67, 77, 85, 117–118, 134, 192n78, 251n12 (*see also* form: and reproducibility); and history of composition, 2–3, 10–12, 62, 67, 103–108, 118, 123, 144, 189n51 (see also *formulas*); and homology, 12, 14, 34–38, 44–45, 49, 54–55, 110–111, 123–127, 131–132, 144, 153, 184n12, 186n27, 192n78, 197n32, 205nn87–89, 210n131, 226–227n91, 243nn7–8; and labor, 2–3, 9–12, 39–40, 57–58, 75–76, 97, 107, 109–110, 114, 118, 123, 176–177; and "law of the conservation of forms," 166–170, 177; and making, 2–5, 10–12, 17–18, 39–40, 48–49, 57–58, 70–71, 103–108, 113–114, 117–118, 124, 134, 145–146, 168–169, 173–177, 189nn46,52; and plausibility, 15, 40, 45–46, 50, 54–55, 67–68, 107–108, 125; and *poesie*, 2–3, 9–12, 48–50, 54–55, 65–71, 74–76, 103, 106–108, 126–127, 123, 144, 167, 175–177, 184n8; and possibility, 2–3, 17, 19, 34–35, 38. 44–46, 49, 70–71, 76, 138–140, 168, 177, 187n37; and probability, 2–3, 9, 50, 70–71, 125–126, 127; and Proteus, 17–18, 84, 193n80, 239n66; and reproducibility, 3, 48–49, 56–58, 64–65, 70–72, 175–177 (*see also* form: generative constraint); and style, 10–11, 134; and time, 15, 97–103, 107, 109–112, 114, 123, 177; and transformation, 2–3, 8, 11–12, 15, 17–18, 49, 58, 84, 87, 103–105, 114–115, 124, 168, 170, 173–177, 190n58, 193n80; and world making, 2–4, 7, 12–14, 17, 38–40, 44–46, 59–50, 55, 67, 70–71, 76–77, 106, 134, 138–140, 142–143, 166–169, 175–177, 187n37, 258n79
formulas, 4–5, 14, 39–40, 49, 50, 57–58, 64–65, 84, 103, 111, 134, 186n21, 211–212n6, 217n36
Foundacion of Rhetorike, The. *See* Rainolde, Richard
Fraunce, Abraham, 26–28, 33, 195n15; *The Arcadian Rhetorike*,16, 27, 36, 40–42, 71–72, 124, 126, 191–192n73, 218n43, 220–221n51; *The Lawiers Logike*, 26–28, 31–32, 35, 37–39, 110, 152, 191–192n73, 198n37, 205n92, 206n96, 207nn101,102, 227n93
Fuchs, Barbara, 191n72
Fulbecke, William (*A direction or preparatiue to the study of the law*), 234n38
Fuller, Thomas (*The History of the Worthies of England*), 222–223n57
Fumerton, Patricia, 82, 233n27, 237n54

Galateo. *See* Della Casa, Giovanni
Gaonkar, Dilip Parmeschwar, 185n17
Garden of Eloquence, The. *See* Peacham, Henry [1546-1634]
Gascoigne, George: *Certayne Notes of Instruction*, 46, 184–185n15, 189–190n54; and *epanodos*, 208–209n119
Genette, Gérard, 224n72
Goeglein, Tamara, 203–204n73
Gorgias. *See* Plato

300   Index

gradatio, 52–55, 58, 62, 65, 65–70,
  72, 152, 213–214n16, 215–216n27,
  216nn30,31, 217n32, 220n50,
  225–226n87, 226n89, 227–227n91,
  227nn92,99, 228n101. See also *anadiplosis*; *climax*; repetition; *sorites*
Grafton, Anthony and Lisa Jardine, 3, 58,
  105–106, 195n17, 221n52
Grammar. See Lily, William
Granger, Thomas (*Divine Logike*), 37,
  206n93, 206–207n101
Green, Lawrence D., 218n38
Greenblatt, Stephen, 209n129
Greene, Roland, 46, 194n11, 209n130,
  268n86
Gregerson, Linda, 244n12
Guyon, 42–43, 45, 100, 106, 113, 116,
  244n20, 249n104

Hackett, Helen, 261nn24,27
Hacking, Ian, 34–35
Halpern, Richard, 184n10, 245n23
Hartman, Geoffrey, 224n71
Harvey, Gabriel, 196n17; *Ciceronianus*,
  27; *Pierces Supererogation*, 127, 253n35;
  Rhetor, 29–30, 33, 58, 197n31, 199n42,
  200n49, 212n7, 219n46, 220n50
Hazlitt, William, 134
Heller-Roazen, Daniel, 185n17, 194n7
Herrick, Marvin Theodore, 229n3
heterocosm, 7, 24–26, 40, 44–45
Heylyn, Peter (*Microcosmus*), 124
Hillman, David, 187n30, 230n6
history, 3, 10–12, 23–24, 39, 99, 119,
  122, 139, 145, 147, 163, 190–191n63,
  192–193n79, 233n27. See also composition: history of; indicative
History of the Royal Society, The. See Sprat,
  Thomas
Hobbes, Thomas, 252–253n32
Hollander, John, 45, 234–235n45
Holleran, James V., 244n21
Hoole, Charles, 218n38; *A new discovery
  of the old art of teaching*, 109
Horace (*Art of Poetry*), 14, 29, 66–67,
  73–76, 229n2, 230n10, 231n11
Hoskins, John (*Directions for Speech and
  Style*), 16, 33–34, 38–39, 67, 68, 70,
  80, 85, 121–122, 128, 151–152, 207–
  208n105, 213n16, 216n31, 254n47,
  256n55, 269n13
Howard, Jean, 261n29

Howell, James (*Epistolae Ho-elianae*), 129,
  255n49
Howell, Wilbur Samuel, 186n22,
  196n23, 197n29, 205n92, 206n93
Hutson, Lorna, 184n15, 195n14
hyperbole, 70, 84, 149, 227nn98,99,
  228n100, 259n13

icon, 98
implausibility. See plausibility
impossibility. See possibility
improbability. See probability
indecorous: and aesthetic design, 14–15,
  40, 44–45, 67, 74–76, 80, 88–89,
  111–112, 138–140, 145–147, 152,
  162–163; and affectation, 7, 50, 54–55,
  65, 67, 72, 91–92, 126–127, 140,
  191n66, 224n69, 234n39; and axes of
  relation, 7, 25, 44–45, 54–55, 68–69,
  93, 123, 173, 209n130; definition of, 2,
  7, 25–26, 184n11; and deformity (disformity), 7, 29, 75–76, 80, 107, 152,
  167, 173, 175–177, 189n50, 191n66,
  199n42, 231n15, 236n49, 263n39; and
  "the doing," 7, 16–18, 58, 103–104,
  107, 113, 115–117, 123, 144; and emptiness, 7, 15, 18, 50, 54, 65–67, 70–71,
  78–79, 81, 85–86, 115, 176–177,
  224nn69,72, 225n84, 234n39, 239n73;
  and fiction, 7, 18, 33–35, 44–47,
  49–50, 66, 70–71, 113, 119, 145–147,
  162–163, 172; and *heterocosm*, 7, 24–
  26, 40, 44–45; and labor, 1–2, 9–10,
  39–40, 76–77, 101, 107, 111–112,
  114–115, 119, 176–177, 189n50; and
  nothing, 26, 37–38, 50, 65–67, 70–71,
  148 170, 175–177; and plausibility,15,
  18, 24–25, 40, 45–47, 50, 54–55, 66–
  68, 73–74, 79–81, 92–93, 101, 107,
  112–113, 115, 123, 127; and pleasure,
  14, 18–19, 46, 50–55, 66–67, 72, 76,
  80–81, 107, 113, 119, 167, 170–172,
  215–216n27; and *poesie*, 4–7, 9–10,
  17–18, 41–42, 50, 54–55, 65–69,
  75–76, 81, 86–87, 91, 93, 101, 113,
  107, 119, 123, 126–127, 144, 152, 169,
  173–177, 209n129; and possibility, 7,
  25, 34–35, 44–47, 66–67, 70–71, 76,
  90–93, 119, 123, 126–127, 163, 172,
  177; and probability, 24–25, 50, 66,
  70–71, 112–113, 126–127; and rhyme,
  9–10, 44, 114, 189n53, 189–190n54,

238–239n64; and romance, 15–16, 71, 132, 160–163, 166–167, 171–172; and transformation, 15, 17, 84, 87, 91, 104, 114, 173–174, 176–177; and value, 7, 10, 67–69, 70–71, 76–81, 85, 89–91, 93, 131–132, 154–155, 162–163, 171–172, 189n51, 226n90; and *vanus*, 7, 50, 65–66, 76, 91, 113–115; and verisimilitude, 18, 46–47, 66, 73–74; and vices, 7, 79–80, 91–92, 152, 189n50, 230–231n10; and "what may be," 4, 13, 24–25, 34–35, 45–46, 119, 123, 127; and world-making, 4, 7, 25–26, 32–35, 44–46, 50, 67–71, 76–78, 86–87, 90–93, 112–113, 115–117, 119, 123–124, 126–127, 138–140, 144, 162–163, 166–167, 170–177, 228n100
indicative, 3, 23–24, 43, 71, 99, 101, 112
illusio, 36
in utramque partem, 105, 127–128, 253n36. See also *antithesis*
Institutes of Oratory. See Quintilian
inventio/invention, 3–4, 24, 27, 29–30, 128, 170, 268n3; and beauty, 36; and capture, 4, 13, 46–47, 49; definition of, 4, 31–32, 194n11, 198n36; and origin of composition, 7, 9, 34–35, 39–40, 45, 49, 50, 55–56, 67, 165–166, 168–169, 217n35, 217–218n36; and possibility/plausibility/probability, 7, 24–25, 32–35, 46–47, 69, 81, 105, 110, 112, 123, 126–127, 194–195n12, 195n14, 204n75; and Ramism, 5, 13, 14, 27–38, 98, 110–111, 125–126, 153, 197n32, 198n36, 200n45, 203–204n73, 204n75, 205n92; role in thinking, 9, 13, 26, 32–35, 45, 46–47, 49, 81, 98–99, 110, 126–127, 168–169, 186n27, 195n21, 198n36, 200n45, 243n9; and Samuel Shaw (*Words Made Visible*), 142. See also form: homology
Inventione Dialectica, De. See Agricola, Rudolph
ironia, 36, 58, 190n62, 211–212n6, 220–221n52, 259n13. See also *illusio*
isocolon, 41, 84, 122, 123, 135–136, 138, 238n64

James, Heather, 18, 193nn85,86
Jardine, Lisa, 31, 196n23, 197n28, 198nn34–35. See also Grafton, Anthony and Lisa Jardine

Jarvis, Simon, 10
Johnson, John (*The Academy of Love*), 215–216n27
Jonson, Ben, 2, 101–104, 117–119, 193n86, 269n7; *Every Man Out of His Humour*, 17–18, 166–177, 269nn9,13, 269n14, 270nn17,21, 271nn22,23,25,27, 272nn30,31 (*see also names of individual characters*); reading *The Faerie Queene*, 101–105, 117–118, 167, 175, 245n24; *Timber: Or, Discoveries*, 2–3, 4, 16, 58, 103–104, 107, 113, 119, 124, 139, 165–166, 268n5
Joseph, Sister Miriam, 183n4, 184n12
judgment, 5, 19, 27, 29, 43, 82, 92–93, 111, 113, 165, 193n87, 234n39, 255n51, 268n3 See also *disposition*; reason

Kahn, Victoria, 247n49, 253n36
Kalas, Rayna, 183n7, 211n2, 231n13, 246n35, 257n66
Kastan, David, 190–191n63
Kearns, Terrance Brophy, 183n4
Keilin, Sean, 5, 186n24
King, John (*Lectures upon Jonas*), 222–223n57
Kinney, Claire, 256n62, 261n28
Kintgen, Eugene R., 105, 221n52
Knell, Thomas (*An answer at large*), 240n79
kosmos, 77–78, 82, 91, 233n30. See also *heterocosm*; ornament; world-making
labor, 1–2, 9–12, 16, 40, 50, 58, 76, 97, 99–112, 114, 116, 118–119, 123, 168, 176–177, 189n50, 248nn69,73, 258n81

La Drière, Craig, 10–11
Lamb, Mary Ellen, 162–163, 260n23, 268n85
Lamy, Bernard (*The Art of Speaking*), 254n39
Landino, 66
Lanham, Richard, 253n36
Latour, Bruno, 189n51, 210–211n1
"law of the conservation of forms, the" 166, 167–170, 177
Lawiers Logike, The. See Fraunce, Abraham
Leff, Michael, 6, 187n32
Leighton, Angela, 188–189n45, 231n12

Lemnius, Levinus (*An Herbal for the Bible*), 266n69
Lesser, Zachary and Peter Stallybrass, 269n13
Levao, Ronald, 194n11
Levine, Caroline, 187–188n38, 209n125, 231n12
Levinson, Marjorie, 188n43
Lily, William (*A Shorte introduction to grammar*), 56–57, 108
Limena, 159–160
Lindheim, Nancy, 140, 258n84
litotes, 36
Lochman, Daniel T., 223n59
Logike of the Most Excellent Philosopher P. Ramus Martyr, The (trans. Macilmaine). See Ramus, Peter
Longinus (*On the Sublime*), 242n1
Ludus Literarius. See Brinsley, John

MacCaffrey, Isabel, 182n6
Maciliente, 167–168, 170, 174–176, 270n15. See also Asper
Mack, Peter, 127, 196n23, 197n32, 210n1, 254n38
MacKay, Ellen, 6
maker's knowledge, 2–3, 4–5, 11, 12, 24, 48–49, 58, 103–104, 106, 108, 124, 134, 174, 176, 183n7, 183–184n8, 184n9, 202n70, 211n2, 246n35, 257n66, 258n81. See also fiction; pleasure; *poesie*; poet-maker; world-making
Mancinus (*Here begynneth a right frutefull treatyse*), 263n39
Mann, Jenny C., 5, 8, 122, 186n27, 190n59, 191nn68,73, 192n76, 223n58, 230–231n10, 250n10, 259n3
Mantuan, Battista (*Eclogues*), 74
manicule, 16, 210–211n1. See also figure pointing
marginalia, 4, 16, 18, 57–65, 80, 101–104, 117–119, 149, 158, 193n86, 212n7, 219n46, 245n24, 246n30, 262n37, 269n13
Markham, Garvis (*The English Arcadia*), 64–65, 223–224n66, 224n67
Marston, John (*Antonio's Revenge*), 104, 108
Martial, 193n86; *Epigrams*, 149
materiality, 8, 33, 48–49, 53, 66–67, 71, 86, 100, 102, 107–108, 114,
169, 183n7, 187–188n38, 188n45, 202–203n71, 211n2, 256n35, 257n66, 259–260n14, 269n11, 272n30 See also fetish; maker's knowledge; mechanical arts
Maus, Katherine Eisman, 166, 169, 269n11, 271nn22–23, 272n30
Mazzio, Carla, 5–6, 186n28, 200n45
McCall, Marsh H., 243n7
McCanles, Michael, 250–251n11
McFaul, Tom, 212n10
mechanical arts, 12, 43–44, 48, 58, 107, 134, 176, 183n7, 209n128, 211n2, 235n47, 246n35, 257n66, 269n14. See also maker's knowledge
Melanchthon, Philip, 197n28, 211n6, 247n50; *Elementorum Rhetorices Libri Duo*, 68, 131, 197n32, 216n28, 225n84, 226n89, 226–227n91, 231n11, 256nn55,56,58,60, 264n55
Menon, Mahadvi, 215n22
metaplasm, 56, 218n38
metonymy, 42, 53, 190n62, 210n31, 219n46
Miller, Jacqueline T., 187n30, 230n6
Miller, Naomi, 232–233n23
Mitis, 168, 172
modality, 4, 12, 13, 24, 71, 119, 145, 147, 163, 190–191n63, 261n28. See also fiction; history; *indecorous*: and "what may be"; philosophy
Model of Poesy, The. See Scott, William
Montaigne, 157–158, 258n78, 266n70
Morton, Timothy, 189n51
Mosellanus (*Table of Schemes and Tropes*), 57
Moss, Ann, 106, 247n50, 247n51
Muiptomos. See Spenser, Edmund; *and names of individual characters*
Musidorus, 50, 136–137, 253n35. See also Dorus
Myra, 156–157, 265–266n67
Mysterie of Rhetorique Unveil'd, The. See Smith, John

Narcissus, 154–155
Nashe, Thomas, 70; "To the Gentleman Students of both Universities" 106, 247n52, 264n55
necessary knowledge, 28. See also contingent knowledge; persuasive knowledge

Index   303

New Criticism, 8, 74–75, 140
new discovery of the old art of teaching, A.
  See Hoole, Charles
Nicholson, Catherine, 5, 207–208n105,
  214n20
Nimis, Stephen A., 245n28
Nohrnberg, James, 244n20
notation: manuscript marginalia (*see*
  marginalia); place of invention; 37–38,
  57, 205nn91,92, 206nn93,95,96,
  206–207n100, 207n102 (see also
  paronomasia)
nothing, 26, 37–38, 50, 65–67, 71, 148,
  170, 176–177, 225n84, 269n14. *See also*
  emptiness; *vanus*; vaunt
Nuttall, A. D., 244n12

obscurity, 145–147, 152, 163, 184n11
Observations in the Art of English Poesie.
  See Campion, Thomas
occupatio, 58, 221–222n54
Old Arcadia. See Sidney, Philip; *and names
  of individual characters*
On Christian Doctrine. See Augustine
On Copia of Words and Ideas. See Erasmus,
  Desiderius
On Education. See Vives, Juan Luis
On the Method of Study. See Erasmus,
  Desiderius
On the Orator. See Cicero
On Style. See Demetrius
On the Sublime. See Longinus
Ong, Walter J., 28, 32, 186n22, 196n23,
  197nn27,30, 198nn33,35, 201nn52,60,
  202nn61,63, 202–203n71, 208n106,
  243n10, 249n90
Orations. See Cicero
Orator. See Cicero
Orilena, 89, 148–149
ornament, 2, 6, 18, 40, 48, 55, 76,
  80–81, 85, 88, 100, 138, 152, 169,
  176, 183nn5,6, 184n11, 193n86,
  210–211n1, 215n22, 219n46, 220n50,
  233nn27,29, 245n28, 261n32; in Aristotle, 77–79, 87, 93, 223n30; children
  as, 82, 237n54; and excess, 65, 76,
  79–80, 83, 88–89, 127, 151, 191n66,
  214–215n21, 224n69, 232n18,
  234n39, 264n55; and Ramism, 28–30,
  34, 196n24, 205n87, 249n87; and
  thinking, 5–6, 12, 26, 65, 69, 125, 126,
  131–132, 147, 195n21, 216–217n31,
  226–227n91, 228n101; as weapon,
  100, 106–107, 113, 115–117, 118, 123,
  128, 131, 254n39
Ortiz, Joseph M., 234–235n45
Ostovich, Helen M., 168, 269n13
Ovid, 4, 8, 18, 33, 76, 82, 86, 91, 188n42,
  220n51, 237–238n58

Palmer, 42–45, 249n104
Pamela, 50–55, 65–67, 69, 120, 138–139
Pamphilia, 76, 82, 90, 145–146,
  154–155, 237n56, 241n91, 242n97,
  261nn28,30, 262n38, 265n65, 266n68,
  267nn79,81,84
parable, 98
Parallels. See Erasmus, Desiderius
parenthesis, 53, 122, 167, 190n59, 191n68,
  250n10
Parker, Patricia, 8, 54, 183n7, 186n27,
  188n44, 191n71, 199n41, 209n128,
  211n8, 237n56, 240n76, 246n35,
  247nn45,57, 257n66, 267n80
paroemion, 46, 79–80, 81, 114, 238n64,
  249n100. *See also* alliteration; *tautologia*
paronomasia, 37–39, 40, 49, 113, 115,
  206n104, 207–208 n105. *See also*
  notation
Parselius, 158–160, 267n79
Passannante, Gerard, 243n11
Patey, Douglas Lane, 192n77, 198n36
Peacham, Henry [1546–1634]: *The Garden of Eloquence* (1593), 15, 38–39, 45,
  68, 70, 85, 140, 144, 149, 152, 191n66,
  211n5, 213n16, 214n19, 217n33,
  221n53, 226nn89,90, 227n99, 240n81,
  254n39, 263nn47,48, 264n55; *The
  Garden of Eloquence* (1577), 213n16,
  218n41, 227n99
Peacham, Henry [1576–1643] (*The Compleat Gentleman*), 222–223n57
periergia, 189n50
period, 122, 130–131, 212n7, 220n50,
  230–231n10, 252–253n32, 255n53,
  269n7
periphrasis, 14, 36, 39, 84, 89, 141–163,
  167, 170–172, 175, 205n89, 239n66,
  259nn11,13, 259–260n14, 261n32,
  262nn35,37, 263nn47,48, 264n55,
  265–266n67, 266n69, 268n86. *See also
  circumlocutio*; definition

perissology, 152
Perissus, 145,159–160, 267n77
persuasive knowledge, 3–4, 8–9, 10, 27–28, 53, 79, 105, 106, 111, 184n13, 221n52, 233n35, 236n52. *See also* contingent knowledge; necessary knowledge; plausible; possible; probable
Philoclea, 16, 71, 120, 129–130
philosophy, 8–9, 12–13, 23, 26, 30, 39, 40, 65, 70, 79, 81, 86, 92–93, 99, 101, 112, 119, 127, 128, 147, 153, 157, 194n7, 195n21, 210n135, 228n100, 265n63. *See also* fiction; history; Plato; Ramus, Peter, and Ramism
Pierces Supererogation. *See* Harvey, Gabriel
Plato, 26, 112; *Gorgias*, 8, 26, 233n25
plausibility (and implausibility), 3–4, 7, 15, 18, 24–25, 40, 45–47, 50, 54–55, 66–68, 69, 73–74, 79–81, 92–93, 101, 107, 110, 112–113, 115, 123, 125–127, 192nn77,79, 212n8, 236n52, 271n27
pleasure, 14–15, 18–19, 46, 50–55, 66–67, 71–72, 76, 79–81, 107, 113, 119, 151, 167, 170–172, 175, 191n64, 193n87, 215–216n27, 217n33, 231n15, 235n48, 236n52, 238–239n64, 249n100
pleonasm, 88, 218n38
Plett, Heinrich F., 183n4, 203n72
poein, 39, 139–140, 258n80. *See also* poet-maker
poesie (also *poesy*): and criticism, 168; definition of, 2–3, 103, 124; and emptiness, 91; and form, 2–3, 9–12, 48–50, 54–55, 65–71, 74–76, 103, 106–108, 123, 126–127, 144, 167, 175–177, 184n8; and *indecorous*, 4–7, 9–10, 17–18, 41–42, 50, 54–55, 65–69, 75–76, 81, 86–87, 91, 93, 101, 107, 113, 119, 123, 126–127, 144, 152, 169, 173–177, 209n129; instruments of, 41, 49, 67–69, 103, 113, 174, 175, 209nn128,129; and labor, 10, 11, 101, 103, 119, 123; and methodology, 16–17, 144; and pleasure, 50, 53–55, 67, 81; and thinking, 5, 7, 12, 209n129; and world-making, 4, 66–67, 82, 87, 91, 93, 101, 113, 123, 127
poesy. See *poesie*
poet-maker, 2, 4, 10, 23–24, 32–34, 39, 40, 50–55, 72, 76, 80, 88, 107, 111, 113, 116, 123–124, 139–140, 166, 175–177, 193–194n2, 211n2, 224n69, 241n83, 242n104, 258 n81, 271n22. *See also poein*
Poetices Libri Septem. *See* Scaliger, Julius Caesar
Polarchos, 148
polyptoton, 3, 37–38, 49, 68–70, 77, 227nn92,93, 238–239n64. *See also* conjugation
Pomeroy, Ralph S., 207n102
possibility (and impossibility), 2–4, 7, 13, 17, 19, 23–25, 34–35, 38, 44–47,49, 66–67, 70–71, 76, 90–93, 119, 122, 123, 126–127, 138–139, 163, 168, 172–173, 177, 185n17, 192n77, 195n21, 197n37, 252–253n32, 254n38
probability (and improbability), 3–4, 24–25, 27, 50, 66, 70–71, 112–113, 125–127, 184n15, 185n17, 192n77, 195n14, 198n36, 218n43
prolepsis, 56, 208n114, 218n38
propon (approptiateness), 6, 78. See also *decorum*
proportion, 33–34, 40, 71, 74–74, 80–81, 111–112, 140, 220–221n51, 227n99, 228n104, 229n2, 231n52, 234–235n44, 236nn49,51, 236–237n52, 255n50, 259n86. See also *decorum*: quantitative; design
prosopopoeia, 29, 60, 62, 230n8
Proteus, 17–18, 84
Puntarvolo, 167, 170–172, 175–176, 272n33
Purchas, Samuel (*Purchas his Pilgrimage*), 215n22
Puttenham, George (*The Art of English Poesy*), 15, 43,52, 55, 69, 75, 79–80, 88, 98, 107, 114, 126, 128–129, 139–140, 143–144, 189n50, 208nn114,119, 211n2, 224n69, 234–235n45, 236nn49,52, 258n81
Pyrocles, 16, 50–51, 120, 129, 136–137, 253n35, 257n67. *See also* Cleophila; Zelmane

Questions of Brutus (*Attack on Cicero*). *See* Ramus, Peter and Ramism
Quilligan, Maureen, 244n21
Quint, David, 245n23, 247n52, 249n99
Quintilian (*Institutes of Oratory* [*Institutio Oratoria*]), 25, 35–36, 52–53, 65, 67,

Index 305

75, 79, 88–89, 91–92, 126, 128, 146, 149, 152, 204n80, 207n104, 226n90, 230–231n10, 232n18, 234n40, 239–240n73, 255n53, 257n73, 261n32, 263n39

Rainolde, Richard (*The Foundacion of Rhetorike*), 54, 216n29
Ramachandran, Ayesha, 185n16
Ramus, of Vermandois, the King's Professor, his Dialectica in two Books. See Ramus, Peter
Ramus, Peter, and Ramism, 5, 6–7, 14, 25–46, 98, 110, 125–126, 127, 144, 153, 190n62, 195n18, 196n23, 197nn28,32, 198nn33,34,35,36, 201nn52,60, 202n62, 202–203n71, 203–204n74, 205n92, 208n106, 243n11 (*see also* Fenner, Dudley; Fraunce, Abraham; Granger, Thomas; Harvey, Gabriel; Temple, William); *Arguments in Rhetoric Against Quintilian (Rhetorica distinctiones in Quintilianum)*, 6–7, 14, 31–2, 35–36, 126, 144, 153, 197n32, 198n33, 205nn88,89, 226n90, 252n27; *Dialecticae Libri Duo*, 27 (*see also* Fraunce, Abraham: *The Lawiers Logike*); *The Logike of the Most Excellent Philosopher P. Ramus Martyr*, 205n91, 207n102; *Questions of Brutus (Attack on Cicero [Brutinae Questiones])*, 14, 28–31, 35–36, 197n32, 200n45, 203–204n73, 252n28; *Ramus, of Vermandois, the King's Professor, his Dialectica in two Books* (trans. R.F.), 201n57; *Rhetoricae Libri Duo*, 27 (*see also* Fraunce, Abraham: *The Arcadian Rhetorike*)
reason 2, 5, 6, 12, 17, 25–38, 42–43, 53–55, 66, 68, 70, 80, 82, 92–93, 97, 124–126, 153, 189–190n54, 198nn33,34,35,36,37, 201nn54,57, 202n62, 205n91, 206nn93,94,96, 226n89, 236nn48,52, 240n78, 254n38, 255n51, 259n86. *See also* judgment; Palmer
Rebhorn, Wayne, 211n5, 214n19
Red Cross Knight, 103, 134–136
Reiss, Timothy J., 196n23, 197n30, 202n61–62
Renaissance Figures of Speech, 8, 191n69, 223n58
repetitio, 58, 221–222n54

repetition, 15, 41–42, 44, 54, 62, 64, 67–69, 85–86, 130, 135, 189n53, 191n66, 197n32, 220n50, 220–221n51. *See also antimetabole*; *chiasmus*; *epanalepsis*; *epanodos*; *gradation*; *repetition*; *rhyme*; *similiter cadens*; *similiter desinens*; *symploce*
Reynold, Henry (*Mythomystes*), 222–223n57
Rhetor. *See* Harvey, Gabriel
Rhetoric to Alexander, 251n19
Rhetorica Ad Herennium, 85, 124–125, 213n16, 218n43, 218–219n44, 239n69, 251n19, 252n23, 258n77
Rhetoricae Libri Duo. See Fraunce, Abraham: *The Arcadian Rhetorike*; Ramus, Peter
Rhodes, Neil, 272n31
rhyme, 9–10, 44, 46, 62, 91, 114, 189n53, 189–190n54, 238–239n64. *See also* repetition; *similiter cadens*; *similiter desinens*
Rix, Herbert David, 183n4
Roberts, Josephine A., 260–261n23, 267–268n84
Roche, Robert (*Eustathia*), 230n9
Roche, Thomas, 257n75
romance, 15–16, 17, 62–64, 71, 82, 99, 100, 124, 127, 132, 161–163, 169, 171–172, 191nn71,72, 237n56, 267n80, 268n85, 269n14
Rosindy, 82–87, 91, 238n64, 262n36
Roth, Michael S., 192n79

Sanchez, Melissa, 232–233n23, 260n19
Sansjoy, 134–136
Scaliger, Julius Caesar, 241n83; *Poetices Libri Septem*, 183–184n8
school, schoolroom, 3–5, 6, 13–14, 18–19, 39–40, 42, 48–62, 66, 84, 93, 97–98, 100–101, 104–106, 108–110, 113, 114, 123, 127, 128–129, 141–143, 148–149, 165, 167, 185n19, 215nn27–28, 217n35, 217–218n36, 218n43, 218–219n44, 219n47, 230n8, 248n75
Schoolmaster, The. See Ascham, Roger
Scoloker, Anthony (*Daiphantus*), 222–223n57
Scott, William (*The Model of Poesy*), 65, 74, 132, 193n2, 224n69, 231n14, 241nn83,88, 247n59, 255n51, 264n55
Scott-Baumann, Elizabeth, 8, 189n46

Seneca (*Epistles*), 110, 238n61
sentence. *See* period; syntax
Shakespeare, William (*As You Like It*), 105, 214n18
Sharon-Zisser, Shirley, 246n39
Shaw, Samuel (*Words Made Visible*), 141–143, 259n2
Sherman, William, 192n75, 193n86, 210–211n1, 262n37
Sherry, Richard: *A Treatise of Schemes and Tropes*, 3, 19, 103–104, 125, 150, 193n87, 213n16, 218n41, 243n8, 252n26, 263nn39,46; *A Treatise of the Figures of Grammer and Rhetorike*, 149, 213n16
Shorte introduction to grammar, A. *See* Lily, William
Sidney, Philip, 3–4; *The Arcadia* (Old), 50–55, 66–72, 76 (*see also names of individual characters*); *The Arcadia* (Revised), 16, 62–65, 120–140, 144–145, 158–160, 167 (*see also names of individual characters*); *Astrophil and Stella*, 54–55, 71–72, 110, 213–214n16 (*see also names of individual characters*); *The Defence of Poesy*, 3–4, 23–27, 32–34, 40, 46, 67, 92–93, 99, 101, 111–112, 116, 119, 124, 127, 166–167, 169, 177, 184nn9,15, 195n21, 210n135, 231n15, 242n104
simile 14–15, 17, 36, 39, 83, 89, 97–119, 123, 130, 135, 153, 167, 172–175, 177, 205n87, 233n27, 242n1, 243nn3,7, 244nn12,15, 245nn24,26, 245–246n28, 246nn30,39,44, 247n57, 248n73, 249n87, 258n81, 271n28. *See also* comparison; similitude
similiter cadens (*homoioptoton*), 9, 114, 238–239n64. *See also* repetition; rhyme
similiter desinens (*homoioteleuton*), 9, 58, 62, 87, 189n53, 238–239n64. *See also* repetition; rhyme
similitude, 98–102, 104–105, 109–115, 227n99, 243n7, 244n20, 245–246n28, 246n29, 248n69, 249n82. See also comparison; *simile*
Sir Philip Sidney's Arcadia Moderniz'd. *See* Stanley, Dorothy
Slaughter, M. M., 202n61
Smith, John (*The Mysterie of Rhetorique Unveil'd*), 191–193n73, 213–214n16, 227n92, 239n70, 249n82

Sogliardo, 167, 170, 172, 270n15
Solon's Law, 28–31, 38
Sontag, Susan, 144
sophistry, 12, 38, 43, 153, 207n102, 212n7, 234n39, 267–268n84. *See also* fallacy; form: homology
soraismus. *See cumulatio*
sorites, 54, 216–217n31, 226n89. *See also anadiplosis; climax; gradatio*
Spencer, Thomas (*The Art of Logick*), 206n96
Spenser, Edmund: *The Faerie Queene*, 4, 7, 13, 14, 16, 39, 40–46, 62, 95–119, 123, 128, 134–136, 138, 166–167, 175, 191–192n73, 194n6, 205n91, 209nn129,130, 249n104, 260–261n23, 265n63; 269n14 (*see also names of individual characters*); *The faerie queen: The shepheards calendar: together with the other works of Englands arch-poët, Edm. Spenser*, 101; *Muiopotmos*, 1–2, 18–19, 183nn4,5, 193nn84,85 (*see also names of individual characters*); *The Shepheardes Calender*, 104, 230n6, 268n6
Spiller, Elizabeth, 24, 185n16, 194n6
Sprat, Thomas (*The History of the Royal Society*), 153
sprezzatura, 1, 10, 76, 113, 232n20. *See also celare artem*
Stallybrass, Peter and Ann Rosalind Jones, 215n25
Stanley, Dorothy (*Sir Philip Sidney's Arcadia Moderniz'd*), 132–134, 256n62, 257n65
Stewart, Susan, 190n58
Stillman, Robert, 214n20
Strode, George (*The anatomie of mortalitie*), 266n69
Struever, Nancy, 259n86
Sturm, John, 55
subjunctive, 4, 12, 13, 23–25, 33, 34, 46, 49, 111, 116, 119, 123, 127, 190–191n63, 249n95, 267–268n84. *See also* contingent knowledge; fiction; modality
superlative, 46, 64, 69, 70, 72, 89–91, 133, 149, 159, 224n67
Susenbrotus, Johannes (*Epitome of Tropes and Schemes*), 48, 49, 62, 125, 147, 159, 186n21, 211n6, 218nn41,43, 223n60, 227n98, 241n83, 257n73, 263n39

Index 307

sweetness, 15, 40, 51, 64, 65, 68, 74, 86, 89, 157, 171, 215–216n27, 220–221n51, 224n67
symploce, 40, 191n6. *See also* repetition
synecdoche, 53, 84, 190n62, 218n38, 220n50
syntax, 54, 68–69, 87, 97–101, 104, 108–109, 111, 113, 114, 118, 119, 143, 166, 174, 184n11, 218n41, 228n101, 242n1, 251n15, 265–266n67

Table of Schemes and Tropes. *See* Mosellanus
tautologia, 79–80, 249n100. *See also* alliteration; *paroemion*
Taylor, Barry, 236n51
Temple, William (*Analysis of Sidney's Apology for Poetry*), 32–35, 40, 46, 195n17, 202nn68,70, 203–204n73, 204n75, 205n87, 249n87
Terence, 169–170, 219n46; *Eunuchus*, 66, 225n77
Teskey, Gordon, 185n18, 188–189n45, 265n63
Timber: Or, Discoveries. *See* Jonson, Ben
time (and temporality), 2, 9, 11–12, 15, 97–103, 106–110, 114, 143, 161, 163, 177, 242n104, 243n9, 248nn69,73. *See also* contingent knowledge; fiction; history; modality
topical readers, 144–147, 162–163, 260nn19,20, 260–261n23, 267–268n84
transformation, 2, 8, 11–12, 15, 17, 18–19, 26, 46, 84, 87, 91, 104, 114, 119, 170, 172–174, 176–177
Treatise of Schemes and Tropes, A. *See* Sherry, Richard
Treatise of the Figures of Grammer and Rhetorike, A. *See* Sherry, Richard
Trompart, 106, 113–117, 244n20
"tropological fantasia" (*figural fantasia, periphrastical fantasia*), 26, 67, 170–172, 195–196n21
truth-value, 3, 8–9, 15, 24–26, 32–35, 46, 49–50, 65–66, 68–70, 90–93, 125, 207n102, 209n129, 210n135, 225n77, 227nn98,99. *See also* contingent knowledge; fiction; history; necessary knowledge; persuasive knowledge; philosophy; plausibility; possibility; probability

Turbeville, George, 74
Turner, Henry S., 183n7, 184–185n15, 189n52, 211n2, 246n35, 255n51, 257n66, 269n9, 270n16, 271n28
Tuve, Rosemond, 184n11

Urania, The Countess of Montgomery's. *See* Wroth, Mary; *and names of individual characters*
Urania (in Sidney's revised *Arcadia*), 62, 64, 223n59
Urania (in Wroth's *Urania*), 82, 85–87, 158–160, 267nn77,78,79
Udall, Nicholas (*Floures for Latine*), 66

value, 2, 7, 10, 14, 27, 38, 66–71, 76–81, 85, 89–91, 93, 110, 131–132, 154–155, 162–163, 171–172, 176–177, 189n51, 226n90, 233n29, 256n58. *See also* axes of relation; world-making
vanity, 7, 65–66, 76, 91, 113, 142, 168, 175. *See also vanus*; vaunt
vanus, 7, 50, 65–66, 225n77. *See also* vanity; vaunt
vaunt, 51–52, 65–66, 71, 100, 106–107, 113–115. *See also* vanity; *vanus*
verisimilitude, 18, 47, 66, 73. *See also* plausibility
vices of style, 7, 79–80, 88, 92, 152, 189n50, 230n10, 234n40, 249n100. *See also* affectation, *cacozelia, cumulatio, periergia, perissology*
Vickers, Brian, 9, 184n10, 185n19, 190n62, 192n76, 195n15, 196nn23,24, 211n5, 213n12, 217–218n36, 230nn5,8, 268nn1,3
Vinsauf, Geoffrey of (*Poetria Nova*), 262n33
Virgil, 35–36, 57, 220–221n51, 245–246n28
Vives, Juan Luis, 106, 197n28, 247n50, 258n77; *On Education*, 57, 230n6; *On the Right Way of Speaking (De Ratione Dicendi)*, 128, 254n44, 255n50

Wallace, Andrew, 248n67
Walker, Jeffrey, 26, 67, 195–196n21, 239n67. *See also* "tropological fantasia"
Warley, Christopher, 71, 186–187n29, 187n37, 188n43
Watson, Robert N., 246n44, 269n14, 271n25

Weaver, William P., 256n55
Webbe, William (*A Discourse of English Poetry*), 230n6
West, William, 272n31
Whaler, James, 245–246n28
Whigham, Frank, 254n39
White, Hayden, 17, 192–193n79
Whiting, Nathaneel (*Le hore di recreatione*), 222n57
widow of Polidorus, the, 156–157
Williams, Gareth, 237–238n58
Williams, Grant, 259–260n14
Willis, Richard (*De Re Poetica*), 193–194n2, 234–235n45
Wilson, Thomas (*The Art of Rhetoric*), 24, 55, 75, 86, 150, 153, 195n14, 233n34, 236n48, 238–239n64, 248n69
wind, 9, 65, 78–79, 85–86, 212n7, 224n69, 234n39
Wofford, Suzanne, 99, 244n15
Wolfe, Jessica, 251n12, 254n39
Wolfson, Susan, 8, 188n43, 231n12, 244n15
Words Made Visible. *See* Shaw, Samuel
world-making, 2–4, 7, 12, 13–14, 17, 19, 23–26, 32–35, 38, 39, 44–47, 49, 50, 55, 67–71, 72, 76–78, 86–87, 89–93, 111–113, 115–117, 119, 121–123, 126–127, 134, 138–140, 141–144, 162–163, 166–167, 170–177, 185n16, 194nn9,10, 209nn129,130, 210n135, 214n20, 228nn100,101, 244n12, 250–251n11, 258n81, 261n28
Work of Form, The, 8
Wotton, Anthony (*The Art of Logick*), 201n57, 205n91
Wroth, Mary (*The Urania*), 13, 14, 16, 39, 76–77, 81–93, 141–163, 167, 260n19, 261n28, 262n38, 265n66, 267n81, 268n85. *See also names of individual characters*
Wynne-Davies, Marion, 144, 260n20, 261n24

Xenophon, 112–113, 194n6

Zelmane, 16, 71, 120–123, 128–134, 138, 139–140, 253n35, 257n75. *See also* Pyrocles
Zeno, 54, 216n28
zeugma, 3, 41, 56, 135–136, 218n38

www.ingramcontent.com/pod-product-compliance
Lightning Source LLC
Chambersburg PA
CBHW030434300426
44112CB00009B/1002